Springer Undergraduate Mathematics Series

## Other books in this series

Marek Capiński and Tomasz Zastawniak

# Mathematics for Finance

## An Introduction to Financial Engineering

Marek Capiński
Graduate School of Business, National Louis University, 33-300 Nowy Sącz, ul. Zielona 27, Poland

Tomasz Zastawniak
Department of Mathematics, University of Hull, Cottingham Road, Kingston upon Hull, HU6 7RX, UK

British Library Cataloguing in Publication Data
Capiński, Marek, 1951-
Mathematics for finance : an introduction to financial engineering. - (Springer undergraduate mathematics series)
1. Business mathematics 2. Finance - Mathematical models
I. Title II. Zastawniak, Tomasz, 1959-
332'.0151
ISBN 978-1-85233-330-0

Library of Congress Cataloging-in-Publication Data
Capiński, Marek, 1951-
Mathematics for finance : an introduction to financial engineering / Marek Capiński and Tomasz Zastawniak.
p. cm. — (Springer undergraduate mathematics series)
Includes bibliographical references and index.
ISBN 1-85233-330-8 (alk. paper)
1. Finance - Mathematical models. 2. Investments - Mathematics. 3. Business mathematics. I. Zastawniak, Tomasz, 1959- II. Title. III. Series.
HG106.C36 2003
332.6'01'51—dc21 2003045431



9 8 7

Springer Science+Business Media
springer.com

# Preface

True to its title, this book itself is an excellent financial investment. For the price of one volume it teaches two Nobel Prize winning theories, with plenty more included for good measure. How many undergraduate mathematics textbooks can boast such a claim?

Building on mathematical models of bond and stock prices, these two theories lead in different directions: Black–Scholes arbitrage pricing of options and other derivative securities on the one hand, and Markowitz portfolio optimisation and the Capital Asset Pricing Model on the other hand. Models based on the principle of no arbitrage can also be developed to study interest rates and their term structure. These are three major areas of mathematical finance, all having an enormous impact on the way modern financial markets operate. This textbook presents them at a level aimed at second or third year undergraduate students, not only of mathematics but also, for example, business management, finance or economics.

The contents can be covered in a one-year course of about 100 class hours. Smaller courses on selected topics can readily be designed by choosing the appropriate chapters. The text is interspersed with a multitude of worked examples and exercises, complete with solutions, providing ample material for tutorials as well as making the book ideal for self-study.

Prerequisites include elementary calculus, probability and some linear algebra. In calculus we assume experience with derivatives and partial derivatives, finding maxima or minima of differentiable functions of one or more variables, Lagrange multipliers, the Taylor formula and integrals. Topics in probability include random variables and probability distributions, in particular the binomial and normal distributions, expectation, variance and covariance, conditional probability and independence. Familiarity with the Central Limit Theorem would be a bonus. In linear algebra the reader should be able to solve systems of linear equations, add, multiply, transpose and invert matrices, and compute determinants. In particular, as a reference in probability theory we recommend our book: M. Capiński and T. Zastawniak, *Probability Through Problems*, Springer-Verlag, New York, 2001.

In many numerical examples and exercises it may be helpful to use a computer with a spreadsheet application, though this is not absolutely essential. Microsoft Excel files with solutions to selected examples and exercises are available on our web page at the addresses below.

We are indebted to Nigel Cutland for prompting us to steer clear of an inaccuracy frequently encountered in other texts, of which more will be said in Remark 4.1. It is also a great pleasure to thank our students and colleagues for their feedback on preliminary versions of various chapters. We are also grateful to the readers of the first and second printings of this book, and particularly to Andrzej Palczewski, for indicating some mistakes, corrected in this printing, and suggesting various improvements.

Readers of this book are cordially invited to visit the web page below and click on the accompanying website to check for the latest downloads and corrections, or to contact the authors. Your comments will be greatly appreciated.

Marek Capiński and Tomasz Zastawniak
July 2004

www.springeronline.com/1-85233-330-8

# Contents

# 1
# Introduction: A Simple Market Model

## 1.1 Basic Notions and Assumptions

Suppose that two assets are traded: one risk-free and one risky security. The former can be thought of as a bank deposit or a bond issued by a government, a financial institution, or a company. The risky security will typically be some stock. It may also be a foreign currency, gold, a commodity or virtually any asset whose future price is unknown today.

Throughout the introduction we restrict the time scale to two instants only: today, $t = 0$, and some future time, say one year from now, $t = 1$. More refined and realistic situations will be studied in later chapters.

The position in risky securities can be specified as the number of shares of stock held by an investor. The price of one share at time $t$ will be denoted by $S(t)$. The current stock price $S(0)$ is known to all investors, but the future price $S(1)$ remains uncertain: it may go up as well as down. The difference $S(1) - S(0)$ as a fraction of the initial value represents the so-called *rate of return*, or briefly *return*:

$$K_S = \frac{S(1) - S(0)}{S(0)},$$

which is also uncertain. The dynamics of stock prices will be discussed in Chapter 3.

The risk-free position can be described as the amount held in a bank account. As an alternative to keeping money in a bank, investors may choose to invest in bonds. The price of one bond at time $t$ will be denoted by $A(t)$. The current bond price $A(0)$ is known to all investors, just like the current stock price. However, in contrast to stock, the price $A(1)$ the bond will fetch at time 1 is also known with certainty. For example, $A(1)$ may be a payment guaranteed by the institution issuing bonds, in which case the bond is said to mature at time 1 with face value $A(1)$. The return on bonds is defined in a similar way as that on stock,

$$K_A = \frac{A(1) - A(0)}{A(0)}.$$

Chapters 2, 10 and 11 give a detailed exposition of risk-free assets.

Our task is to build a mathematical model of a market of financial securities. A crucial first stage is concerned with the properties of the mathematical objects involved. This is done below by specifying a number of assumptions, the purpose of which is to find a compromise between the complexity of the real world and the limitations and simplifications of a mathematical model, imposed in order to make it tractable. The assumptions reflect our current position on this compromise and will be modified in the future.

## Assumption 1.1 (Randomness)

The future stock price $S(1)$ is a *random variable* with at least two different values. The future price $A(1)$ of the risk-free security is a known number.

## Assumption 1.2 (Positivity of Prices)

All stock and bond prices are strictly positive,

$$A(t) > 0 \quad \text{and} \quad S(t) > 0 \quad \text{for } t = 0, 1.$$

The total wealth of an investor holding $x$ stock shares and $y$ bonds at a time instant $t = 0, 1$ is

$$V(t) = xS(t) + yA(t).$$

The pair $(x, y)$ is called a *portfolio*, $V(t)$ being the *value* of this portfolio or, in other words, the *wealth* of the investor at time $t$.

The jumps of asset prices between times 0 and 1 give rise to a change of the portfolio value:

$$V(1) - V(0) = x(S(1) - S(0)) + y(A(1) - A(0)).$$

This difference (which may be positive, zero, or negative) as a fraction of the initial value represents the return on the portfolio,

$$K_V = \frac{V(1) - V(0)}{V(0)}.$$

The returns on bonds or stock are particular cases of the return on a portfolio (with $x = 0$ or $y = 0$, respectively). Note that because $S(1)$ is a random variable, so is $V(1)$ as well as the corresponding returns $K_S$ and $K_V$. The return $K_A$ on a risk-free investment is deterministic.

## Example 1.1

Let $A(0) = 100$ and $A(1) = 110$ dollars. Then the return on an investment in bonds will be

$$K_A = 0.10,$$

that is, 10%. Also, let $S(0) = 50$ dollars and suppose that the random variable $S(1)$ can take two values,

$$S(1) = \begin{cases} 52 & \text{with probability } p, \\ 48 & \text{with probability } 1 - p, \end{cases}$$

for a certain $0 < p < 1$. The return on stock will then be

$$K_S = \begin{cases} 0.04 & \text{if stock goes up,} \\ -0.04 & \text{if stock goes down,} \end{cases}$$

that is, 4% or −4%.

## Example 1.2

Given the bond and stock prices in Example 1.1, the value at time 0 of a portfolio with $x = 20$ stock shares and $y = 10$ bonds is

$$V(0) = 2,000$$

dollars. The time 1 value of this portfolio will be

$$V(1) = \begin{cases} 2,140 & \text{if stock goes up,} \\ 2,060 & \text{if stock goes down,} \end{cases}$$

so the return on the portfolio will be

$$K_V = \begin{cases} 0.07 & \text{if stock goes up,} \\ 0.03 & \text{if stock goes down,} \end{cases}$$

that is, 7% or 3%.

### Exercise 1.1

Let $A(0) = 90$, $A(1) = 100$, $S(0) = 25$ dollars and let

$$S(1) = \begin{cases} 30 & \text{with probability } p, \\ 20 & \text{with probability } 1-p, \end{cases}$$

where $0 < p < 1$. For a portfolio with $x = 10$ shares and $y = 15$ bonds calculate $V(0)$, $V(1)$ and $K_V$.

### Exercise 1.2

Given the same bond and stock prices as in Exercise 1.1, find a portfolio whose value at time 1 is

$$V(1) = \begin{cases} 1,160 & \text{if stock goes up,} \\ 1,040 & \text{if stock goes down.} \end{cases}$$

What is the value of this portfolio at time 0?

It is mathematically convenient and not too far from reality to allow arbitrary real numbers, including negative ones and fractions, to represent the risky and risk-free positions $x$ and $y$ in a portfolio. This is reflected in the following assumption, which imposes no restrictions as far as the trading positions are concerned.

## Assumption 1.3 (Divisibility, Liquidity and Short Selling)

An investor may hold any number $x$ and $y$ of stock shares and bonds, whether integer or fractional, negative, positive or zero. In general,

$$x, y \in \mathbb{R}.$$

The fact that one can hold a fraction of a share or bond is referred to as *divisibility*. Almost perfect divisibility is achieved in real world dealings whenever the volume of transactions is large as compared to the unit prices.

The fact that no bounds are imposed on $x$ or $y$ is related to another market attribute known as *liquidity*. It means that any asset can be bought or sold on demand at the market price in arbitrary quantities. This is clearly a mathematical idealisation because in practice there exist restrictions on the volume of trading.

If the number of securities of a particular kind held in a portfolio is positive, we say that the investor has a *long position*. Otherwise, we say that a *short position* is taken or that the asset is *shorted*. A short position in risk-free securities may involve issuing and selling bonds, but in practice the same financial effect is more easily achieved by borrowing cash, the interest rate being determined by the bond prices. Repaying the loan with interest is referred to as *closing* the short position. A short position in stock can be realised by *short selling*. This means that the investor borrows the stock, sells it, and uses the proceeds to make some other investment. The owner of the stock keeps all the rights to it. In particular, she is entitled to receive any dividends due and may wish to sell the stock at any time. Because of this, the investor must always have sufficient resources to fulfil the resulting obligations and, in particular, to *close* the short position in risky assets, that is, to repurchase the stock and return it to the owner. Similarly, the investor must always be able to close a short position in risk-free securities, by repaying the cash loan with interest. In view of this, we impose the following restriction.

### Assumption 1.4 (Solvency)

The wealth of an investor must be non-negative at all times,

$$V(t) \geq 0 \quad \text{for } t = 0, 1.$$

A portfolio satisfying this condition is called *admissible*.

In the real world the number of possible different prices is finite because they are quoted to within a specified number of decimal places and because there is only a certain final amount of money in the whole world, supplying an upper bound for all prices.

### Assumption 1.5 (Discrete Unit Prices)

The future price $S(1)$ of a share of stock is a random variable taking only finitely many values.

## 1.2 No-Arbitrage Principle

In this section we are going to state the most fundamental assumption about the market. In brief, we shall assume that the market does not allow for risk-free profits with no initial investment.

For example, a possibility of risk-free profits with no initial investment can emerge when market participants make a mistake. Suppose that dealer $A$ in New York offers to buy British pounds at a rate $d_A = 1.62$ dollars to a pound, while dealer $B$ in London sells them at a rate $d_B = 1.60$ dollars to a pound. If this were the case, the dealers would, in effect, be handing out free money. An investor with no initial capital could realise a profit of $d_A - d_B = 0.02$ dollars per each pound traded by taking simultaneously a short position with dealer $B$ and a long position with dealer $A$. The demand for their generous services would quickly compel the dealers to adjust the exchange rates so that this profitable opportunity would disappear.

### Exercise 1.3

On 19 July 2002 dealer $A$ in New York and dealer $B$ in London used the following rates to change currency, namely euros (EUR), British pounds (GBP) and US dollars (USD):

| dealer $A$ | buy | sell |
|---|---|---|
| 1.0000 EUR | 1.0202 USD | 1.0284 USD |
| 1.0000 GBP | 1.5718 USD | 1.5844 USD |

| dealer $B$ | buy | sell |
|---|---|---|
| 1.0000 EUR | 0.6324 GBP | 0.6401 GBP |
| 1.0000 USD | 0.6299 GBP | 0.6375 GBP |

Spot a chance of a risk-free profit without initial investment.

The next example illustrates a situation when a risk-free profit could be realised without initial investment in our simplified framework of a single time step.

## Example 1.3

Suppose that dealer $A$ in New York offers to buy British pounds a year from now at a rate $d_A = 1.58$ dollars to a pound, while dealer $B$ in London would sell British pounds immediately at a rate $d_B = 1.60$ dollars to a pound. Suppose further that dollars can be borrowed at an annual rate of 4%, and British pounds can be invested in a bank account at 6%. This would also create an opportunity for a risk-free profit without initial investment, though perhaps not as obvious as before.

For instance, an investor could borrow 10,000 dollars and convert them into 6,250 pounds, which could then be deposited in a bank account. After one year interest of 375 pounds would be added to the deposit, and the whole amount could be converted back into 10,467.50 dollars. (A suitable agreement would have to be signed with dealer $A$ at the beginning of the year.) After paying back the dollar loan with interest of 400 dollars, the investor would be left with a profit of 67.50 dollars.

Apparently, one or both dealers have made a mistake in quoting their exchange rates, which can be exploited by investors. Once again, increased demand for their services will prompt the dealers to adjust the rates, reducing $d_A$ and/or increasing $d_B$ to a point when the profit opportunity disappears.

We shall make an assumption forbidding situations similar to the above example.

### Assumption 1.6 (No-Arbitrage Principle)

There is no admissible portfolio with initial value $V(0) = 0$ such that $V(1) > 0$ with non-zero probability.

In other words, if the initial value of an admissible portfolio is zero, $V(0) = 0$, then $V(1) = 0$ with probability 1. This means that no investor can lock in a profit without risk and with no initial endowment. If a portfolio violating this principle did exist, we would say that an *arbitrage* opportunity was available.

Arbitrage opportunities rarely exist in practice. If and when they do, the gains are typically extremely small as compared to the volume of transactions, making them beyond the reach of small investors. In addition, they can be more subtle than the examples above. Situations when the No-Arbitrage Principle is violated are typically short-lived and difficult to spot. The activities of investors (called arbitrageurs) pursuing arbitrage profits effectively make the market free of arbitrage opportunities.

The exclusion of arbitrage in the mathematical model is close enough to reality and turns out to be the most important and fruitful assumption. Arguments based on the No-arbitrage Principle are the main tools of financial mathematics.

## 1.3 One-Step Binomial Model

In this section we restrict ourselves to a very simple example, in which the stock price $S(1)$ takes only two values. Despite its simplicity, this situation is sufficiently interesting to convey the flavour of the theory to be developed later on.

## Example 1.4

Suppose that $S(0) = 100$ dollars and $S(1)$ can take two values,

$$S(1) = \begin{cases} 125 & \text{with probability } p, \\ 105 & \text{with probability } 1 - p, \end{cases}$$

where $0 < p < 1$, while the bond prices are $A(0) = 100$ and $A(1) = 110$ dollars. Thus, the return $K_S$ on stock will be 25% if stock goes up, or 5% if stock goes down. (Observe that both stock prices at time 1 happen to be higher than that at time 0; 'going up' or 'down' is relative to the other price at time 1.) The

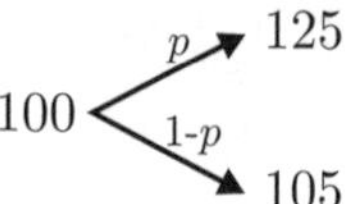


**Figure 1.1** One-step binomial tree of stock prices

risk-free return will be $K_A = 10\%$. The stock prices are represented as a tree in Figure 1.1.

In general, the choice of stock and bond prices in a binomial model is constrained by the No-Arbitrage Principle. Suppose that the possible up and down stock prices at time 1 are

$$S(1) = \begin{cases} S^{\mathrm{u}} & \text{with probability } p, \\ S^{\mathrm{d}} & \text{with probability } 1 - p, \end{cases}$$

where $S^{\mathrm{d}} < S^{\mathrm{u}}$ and $0 < p < 1$.

## Proposition 1.1

If $S(0) = A(0)$, then

$$S^{\mathrm{d}} < A(1) < S^{\mathrm{u}},$$

or else an arbitrage opportunity would arise.

## Proof

We shall assume for simplicity that $S(0) = A(0) = 100$ dollars. Suppose that $A(1) \leq S^{\mathrm{d}}$. In this case, at time 0:

- Borrow \$100 risk-free.
- Buy one share of stock for \$100.

This way, you will be holding a portfolio $(x, y)$ with $x = 1$ shares of stock and $y = -1$ bonds. The time 0 value of this portfolio is

$$V(0) = 0.$$

At time 1 the value will become

$$V(1) = \begin{cases} S^{\mathrm{u}} - A(1) & \text{if stock goes up,} \\ S^{\mathrm{d}} - A(1) & \text{if stock goes down.} \end{cases}$$

If $A(1) \leq S^{\mathrm{d}}$, then the first of these two possible values is strictly positive, while the other one is non-negative, that is, $V(1)$ is a non-negative random variable such that $V(1) > 0$ with probability $p > 0$. The portfolio provides an arbitrage opportunity, violating the No-Arbitrage Principle.

Now suppose that $A(1) \geq S^{\mathrm{u}}$. If this is the case, then at time 0:

- Sell short one share for \$100.
- Invest \$100 risk-free.

As a result, you will be holding a portfolio $(x, y)$ with $x = -1$ and $y = 1$, again of zero initial value,

$$V(0) = 0.$$

The final value of this portfolio will be

$$V(1) = \begin{cases} -S^{\mathrm{u}} + A(1) & \text{if stock goes up,} \\ -S^{\mathrm{d}} + A(1) & \text{if stock goes down,} \end{cases}$$

which is non-negative, with the second value being strictly positive, since $A(1) \geq S^{\mathrm{u}}$. Thus, $V(1)$ is a non-negative random variable such that $V(1) > 0$ with probability $1 - p > 0$. Once again, this indicates an arbitrage opportunity, violating the No-Arbitrage Principle. □

The common sense reasoning behind the above argument is straightforward: Buy cheap assets and sell (or sell short) expensive ones, pocketing the difference.

## 1.4 Risk and Return

Let $A(0) = 100$ and $A(1) = 110$ dollars, as before, but $S(0) = 80$ dollars and

$$S(1) = \begin{cases} 100 & \text{with probability } 0.8, \\ 60 & \text{with probability } 0.2. \end{cases}$$

Suppose that you have \$10,000 to invest in a portfolio. You decide to buy $x = 50$ shares, which fixes the risk-free investment at $y = 60$. Then

$$V(1) = \begin{cases} 11,600 & \text{if stock goes up,} \\ 9,600 & \text{if stock goes down,} \end{cases}$$

$$K_V = \begin{cases} 0.16 & \text{if stock goes up,} \\ -0.04 & \text{if stock goes down.} \end{cases}$$

The *expected return*, that is, the mathematical expectation of the return on the portfolio is

$$E(K_V) = 0.16 \times 0.8 - 0.04 \times 0.2 = 0.12,$$

that is, 12%. The *risk* of this investment is defined to be the standard deviation of the random variable $K_V$:

$$\sigma_V = \sqrt{(0.16 - 0.12)^2 \times 0.8 + (-0.04 - 0.12)^2 \times 0.2} = 0.08,$$

that is 8%. Let us compare this with investments in just one type of security.

If $x = 0$, then $y = 100$, that is, the whole amount is invested risk-free. In this case the return is known with certainty to be $K_A = 0.1$, that is, 10% and the risk as measured by the standard deviation is zero, $\sigma_A = 0$.

On the other hand, if $x = 125$ and $y = 0$, the entire amount being invested in stock, then

$$V(1) = \begin{cases} 12,500 & \text{if stock goes up,} \\ 7,500 & \text{if stock goes down,} \end{cases}$$

and $E(K_S) = 0.15$ with $\sigma_S = 0.20$, that is, 15% and 20%, respectively.

Given the choice between two portfolios with the same expected return, any investor would obviously prefer that involving lower risk. Similarly, if the risk levels were the same, any investor would opt for higher return. However, in the case in hand higher return is associated with higher risk. In such circumstances the choice depends on individual preferences. These issues will be discussed in Chapter 5, where we shall also consider portfolios consisting of several risky securities. The emerging picture will show the power of portfolio selection and portfolio diversification as tools for reducing risk while maintaining the expected return.

### Exercise 1.4

For the above stock and bond prices, design a portfolio with initial wealth of \$10,000 split fifty-fifty between stock and bonds. Compute the expected return and risk as measured by standard deviation.

## 1.5 Forward Contracts

A *forward contract* is an agreement to buy or sell a risky asset at a specified future time, known as the *delivery date*, for a price $F$ fixed at the present moment, called the *forward price*. An investor who agrees to buy the asset is said to *enter into a long forward contract* or to *take a long forward position*. If an investor agrees to sell the asset, we speak of a *short forward contract* or a *short forward position*. No money is paid at the time when a forward contract is exchanged.

### Example 1.5

Suppose that the forward price is \$80. If the market price of the asset turns out to be \$84 on the delivery date, then the holder of a long forward contract will buy the asset for \$80 and can sell it immediately for \$84, cashing the difference of \$4. On the other hand, the party holding a short forward position will have to sell the asset for \$80, suffering a loss of \$4. However, if the market price of the asset turns out to be \$75 on the delivery date, then the party holding a long forward position will have to buy the asset for \$80, suffering a loss of \$5. Meanwhile, the party holding a short position will gain \$5 by selling the asset above its market price. In either case the loss of one party is the gain of the other.

In general, the party holding a long forward contract with delivery date 1 will benefit if the future asset price $S(1)$ rises above the forward price $F$. If the asset price $S(1)$ falls below the forward price $F$, then the holder of a long forward contract will suffer a loss. In general, the payoff for a long forward position is $S(1) - F$ (which can be positive, negative or zero). For a short forward position the payoff is $F - S(1)$.

Apart from stock and bonds, a portfolio held by an investor may contain forward contracts, in which case it will be described by a triple $(x, y, z)$. Here $x$ and $y$ are the numbers of stock shares and bonds, as before, and $z$ is the number of forward contracts (positive for a long forward position and negative for a short position). Because no payment is due when a forward contract is exchanged, the initial value of such a portfolio is simply

$$V(0) = xS(0) + yA(0).$$

At the delivery date the value of the portfolio will become

$$V(1) = xS(1) + yA(1) + z(S(1) - F).$$

Assumptions 1.1 to 1.5 as well as the No-Arbitrage Principle extend readily to this case.

The forward price $F$ is determined by the No-Arbitrage Principle. In particular, it can easily be found for an asset with no carrying costs. A typical example of such an asset is a stock paying no dividend. (By contrast, a commodity will usually involve storage costs, while a foreign currency will earn interest, which can be regarded as a negative carrying cost.)

A forward position guarantees that the asset will be bought for the forward price $F$ at delivery. Alternatively, the asset can be bought now and held until delivery. However, if the initial cash outlay is to be zero, the purchase must be financed by a loan. The loan with interest, which will need to be repaid at the delivery date, is a candidate for the forward price. The following proposition shows that this is indeed the case.

## Proposition 1.2

Suppose that $A(0) = 100$, $A(1) = 110$, and $S(0) = 50$ dollars, where the risky security involves no carrying costs. Then the forward price must be $F = 55$ dollars, or an arbitrage opportunity would exist otherwise.

## Proof

Suppose that $F > 55$. Then, at time 0:

- Borrow \$50.
- Buy the asset for $S(0) = 50$ dollars.
- Enter into a short forward contract with forward price $F$ dollars and delivery date 1.

The resulting portfolio $(1, -\frac{1}{2}, -1)$ consisting of stock, a risk-free position, and a short forward contract has initial value $V(0) = 0$. Then, at time 1:

- Close the short forward position by selling the asset for $F$ dollars.
- Close the risk-free position by paying $\frac{1}{2} \times 110 = 55$ dollars.

The final value of the portfolio, $V(1) = F - 55 > 0$, will be your arbitrage profit, violating the No-Arbitrage Principle.

On the other hand, if $F < 55$, then at time 0:

- Sell short the asset for \$50.
- Invest this amount risk-free.
- Take a long forward position in stock with forward price $F$ dollars and delivery date 1.

The initial value of this portfolio $(-1, \frac{1}{2}, 1)$ is also $V(0) = 0$. Subsequently, at time 1:

- Cash \$55 from the risk-free investment.
- Buy the asset for $F$ dollars, closing the long forward position, and return the asset to the owner.

Your arbitrage profit will be $V(1) = 55 - F > 0$, which once again violates the No-Arbitrage Principle. It follows that the forward price must be $F = 55$ dollars. □

### *Exercise 1.5*

Let $A(0) = 100$, $A(1) = 112$ and $S(0) = 34$ dollars. Is it possible to find an arbitrage opportunity if the forward price of stock is $F = 38.60$ dollars with delivery date 1?

### *Exercise 1.6*

Suppose that $A(0) = 100$ and $A(1) = 105$ dollars, the present price of pound sterling is $S(0) = 1.6$ dollars, and the forward price is $F = 1.50$ dollars to a pound with delivery date 1. How much should a sterling bond cost today if it promises to pay £100 at time 1? *Hint:* The forward contract is based on an asset involving negative carrying costs (the interest earned by investing in sterling bonds).

## 1.6 Call and Put Options

Let $A(0) = 100$, $A(1) = 110$, $S(0) = 100$ dollars and

$$S(1) = \begin{cases} 120 & \text{with probability } p, \\ 80 & \text{with probability } 1 - p, \end{cases}$$

where $0 < p < 1$.

A *call option* with *strike price* or *exercise price* \$100 and *exercise time* 1 is a contract giving the holder the right (but no obligation) to purchase a share of stock for \$100 at time 1.

If the stock price falls below the strike price, the option will be worthless. There would be little point in buying a share for \$100 if its market price is \$80, and no-one would want to exercise the right. Otherwise, if the share price rises to \$120, which is above the strike price, the option will bring a profit of \$20 to the holder, who is entitled to buy a share for \$100 at time 1 and may sell it immediately at the market price of \$120. This is known as *exercising* the option. The option may just as well be exercised simply by collecting the difference of \$20 between the market price of stock and the strike price. In practice, the latter is often the preferred method because no stock needs to change hands.

As a result, the payoff of the call option, that is, its value at time 1 is a random variable

$$C(1) = \begin{cases} 20 & \text{if stock goes up,} \\ 0 & \text{if stock goes down.} \end{cases}$$

Meanwhile, $C(0)$ will denote the value of the option at time 0, that is, the price for which the option can be bought or sold today.

## Remark 1.1

At first sight a call option may resemble a long forward position. Both involve buying an asset at a future date for a price fixed in advance. An essential difference is that the holder of a long forward contract is committed to buying the asset for the fixed price, whereas the owner of a call option has the right but no obligation to do so. Another difference is that an investor will need to pay to purchase a call option, whereas no payment is due when exchanging a forward contract.

In a market in which options are available, it is possible to invest in a portfolio $(x, y, z)$ consisting of $x$ shares of stock, $y$ bonds and $z$ options. The time 0 value of such a portfolio is

$$V(0) = xS(0) + yA(0) + zC(0).$$

At time 1 it will be worth

$$V(1) = xS(1) + yA(1) + zC(1).$$

Just like in the case of portfolios containing forward contracts, Assumptions 1.1 to 1.5 and the No-Arbitrage Principle can be extended to portfolios consisting of stock, bonds and options.

Our task will be to find the time 0 price $C(0)$ of the call option consistent with the assumptions about the market and, in particular, with the absence of arbitrage opportunities. Because the holder of a call option has a certain right, but never an obligation, it is reasonable to expect that $C(0)$ will be positive: one needs to pay a premium to acquire this right. We shall see that the option price $C(0)$ can be found in two steps:

**Step 1**

Construct an investment in $x$ stocks and $y$ bonds such that the value of the investment at time 1 is the same as that of the option,

$$xS(1) + yA(1) = C(1),$$

no matter whether the stock price $S(1)$ goes up to \$120 or down to \$80. This is known as *replicating* the option.

**Step 2**
Compute the time 0 value of the investment in stock and bonds. It will be shown that it must be equal to the option price,

$$xS(0) + yA(0) = C(0),$$

because an arbitrage opportunity would exist otherwise. This step will be referred to as *pricing* or *valuing* the option.

**Step 1 (Replicating the Option)**
The time 1 value of the investment in stock and bonds will be

$$xS(1) + yA(1) = \begin{cases} x120 + y110 & \text{if stock goes up,} \\ x80 + y110 & \text{if stock goes down.} \end{cases}$$

Thus, the equality $xS(1) + yA(1) = C(1)$ between two random variables can be written as

$$\begin{cases} x120 + y110 = 20, \\ x80 + y110 = \ \ 0. \end{cases}$$

The first of these equations covers the case when the stock price goes up to \$120, whereas the second equation corresponds to the case when it drops to \$80. Because we want the value of the investment in stock and bonds at time 1 to match exactly that of the option *no matter whether the stock price goes up or down*, these two equations are to be satisfied simultaneously. Solving for $x$ and $y$, we find that

$$x = \frac{1}{2}, \quad y = -\frac{4}{11}.$$

To replicate the option we need to buy $\frac{1}{2}$ a share of stock and take a short position of $-\frac{4}{11}$ in bonds (or borrow $\frac{4}{11} \times 100 = \frac{400}{11}$ dollars in cash).

**Step 2 (Pricing the Option)**
We can compute the value of the investment in stock and bonds at time 0:

$$xS(0) + yA(0) = \frac{1}{2} \times 100 - \frac{4}{11} \times 100 \cong 13.6364$$

dollars. The following proposition shows that this must be equal to the price of the option.

## Proposition 1.3

If the option can be replicated by investing in the above portfolio of stock and bonds, then $C(0) = \frac{1}{2}S(0) - \frac{4}{11}A(0)$, or else an arbitrage opportunity would exist.

## Proof

Suppose that $C(0) + \frac{4}{11}A(0) > \frac{1}{2}S(0)$. If this is the case, then at time 0:

- Issue and sell 1 option for $C(0)$ dollars.
- Borrow $\frac{4}{11} \times 100 = \frac{400}{11}$ dollars in cash (or take a short position $y = -\frac{4}{11}$ in bonds by selling them).
- Purchase $x = \frac{1}{2}$ shares of stock for $xS(0) = \frac{1}{2} \times 100 = 50$ dollars.

The cash balance of these transactions is positive, $C(0) + \frac{4}{11}A(0) - \frac{1}{2}S(0) > 0$. Invest this amount risk-free. The resulting portfolio consisting of shares, risk-free investments and a call option has initial value $V(0) = 0$. Subsequently, at time 1:

- If stock goes up, then settle the option by paying the difference of \$20 between the market price of one share and the strike price. You will pay nothing if stock goes down. The cost to you will be $C(1)$, which covers both possibilities.
- Repay the loan with interest (or close your short position $y = -\frac{4}{11}$ in bonds). This will cost you $\frac{4}{11} \times 110 = 40$ dollars.
- Sell the stock for $\frac{1}{2}S(1)$ obtaining either $\frac{1}{2} \times 120 = 60$ dollars if the price goes up, or $\frac{1}{2} \times 80 = 40$ dollars if it goes down.

The cash balance of these transactions will be zero, $-C(1)+\frac{1}{2}S(1)-\frac{4}{11}A(1) = 0$, regardless of whether stock goes up or down. But you will be left with the initial risk-free investment of $C(0) + \frac{4}{11}A(0) - \frac{1}{2}S(0)$ plus interest, thus realising an arbitrage opportunity.

On the other hand, if $C(0) + \frac{4}{11}A(0) < \frac{1}{2}S(0)$, then, at time 0:

- Buy 1 option for $C(0)$ dollars.
- Buy $\frac{4}{11}$ bonds for $\frac{4}{11} \times 100 = \frac{400}{11}$ dollars.
- Sell short $x = \frac{1}{2}$ shares of stock for $\frac{1}{2} \times 100 = 50$ dollars.

The cash balance of these transactions is positive, $-C(0)-\frac{4}{11}A(0)+\frac{1}{2}S(0) > 0$, and can be invested risk-free. In this way you will have constructed a portfolio with initial value $V(0) = 0$. Subsequently, at time 1:

- If stock goes up, then exercise the option, receiving the difference of \$20 between the market price of one share and the strike price. You will receive nothing if stock goes down. Your income will be $C(1)$, which covers both possibilities.
- Sell the bonds for $\frac{4}{11}A(1) = \frac{4}{11} \times 110 = 40$ dollars.
- Close the short position in stock, paying $\frac{1}{2}S(1)$, that is, $\frac{1}{2} \times 120 = 60$ dollars if the price goes up, or $\frac{1}{2} \times 80 = 40$ dollars if it goes down.

The cash balance of these transactions will be zero, $C(1)+\frac{4}{11}A(1)-\frac{1}{2}S(1) = 0$, regardless of whether stock goes up or down. But you will be left with an arbitrage profit resulting from the risk-free investment of $-C(0) - \frac{4}{11}A(0) + \frac{1}{2}S(0)$ plus interest, again a contradiction with the No-Arbitrage Principle. □

Here we see once more that the arbitrage strategy follows a common sense pattern: Sell (or sell short if necessary) expensive securities and buy cheap ones, as long as all your financial obligations arising in the process can be discharged, regardless of what happens in the future.

Proposition 1.3 implies that today's price of the option must be

$$C(0) = \frac{1}{2}S(0) - \frac{4}{11}A(0) \cong 13.6364$$

dollars. Anyone who would sell the option for less or buy it for more than this price would be creating an arbitrage opportunity, which amounts to handing out free money. This completes the second step of our solution.

### Remark 1.2

Note that the probabilities $p$ and $1-p$ of stock going up or down are irrelevant in pricing and replicating the option. This is a remarkable feature of the theory and by no means a coincidence.

### Remark 1.3

Options may appear to be superfluous in a market in which they can be replicated by stock and bonds. In the simplified one-step model this is in fact a valid objection. However, in a situation involving multiple time steps (or continuous time) replication becomes a much more onerous task. It requires adjustments to the positions in stock and bonds at every time instant at which there is a change in prices, resulting in considerable management and transaction costs. In some cases it may not even be possible to replicate an option precisely. This is why the majority of investors prefer to buy or sell options, replication being normally undertaken only by specialised dealers and institutions.

#### *Exercise 1.7*

Let the bond and stock prices $A(0)$, $A(1)$, $S(0)$, $S(1)$ be as above. Compute the price $C(0)$ of a call option with exercise time 1 and a) strike price \$90, b) strike price \$110.

#### *Exercise 1.8*

Let the prices $A(0)$, $S(0)$, $S(1)$ be as above. Compute the price $C(0)$ of a call option with strike price \$100 and exercise time 1 if a) $A(1) = 105$ dollars, b) $A(1) = 115$ dollars.

A *put* option with strike price \$100 and exercise time 1 gives the right to *sell* one share of stock for \$100 at time 1. This kind of option is worthless if the stock goes up, but it brings a profit otherwise, the payoff being

$$P(1) = \begin{cases} 0 & \text{if stock goes up,} \\ 20 & \text{if stock goes down,} \end{cases}$$

given that the prices $A(0)$, $A(1)$, $S(0)$, $S(1)$ are the same as above. The notion of a portfolio may be extended to allow positions in put options, denoted by $z$, as before.

The replicating and pricing procedure for puts follows the same pattern as for call options. In particular, the price $P(0)$ of the put option is equal to the time 0 value of a replicating investment in stock and bonds.

## Remark 1.4

There is some similarity between a put option and a short forward position: both involve selling an asset for a fixed price at a certain time in the future. However, an essential difference is that the holder of a short forward contract is committed to selling the asset for the fixed price, whereas the owner of a put option has the right but no obligation to sell. Moreover, an investor who wants to buy a put option will have to pay for it, whereas no payment is involved when a forward contract is exchanged.

### *Exercise 1.9*

Once again, let the bond and stock prices $A(0)$, $A(1)$, $S(0)$, $S(1)$ be as above. Compute the price $P(0)$ of a put option with strike price \$100.

An investor may wish to trade simultaneously in both kinds of options and, in addition, to take a forward position. In such cases new symbols $z_1, z_2, z_3, \ldots$ will need to be reserved for all additional securities to describe the positions in a portfolio. A common feature of these new securities is that their payoffs depend on the stock prices. Because of this they are called *derivative securities* or *contingent claims*. The general properties of derivative securities will be discussed in Chapter 7. In Chapter 8 the pricing and replicating schemes will be extended to more complicated (and more realistic) market models, as well as to other financial instruments.

## 1.7 Managing Risk with Options

The availability of options and other derivative securities extends the possible investment scenarios. Suppose that your initial wealth is \$1,000 and compare the following two investments in the setup of the previous section:

- buy 10 shares; at time 1 they will be worth

$$10 \times S(1) = \begin{cases} 1,200 & \text{if stock goes up,} \\ 800 & \text{if stock goes down;} \end{cases}$$

or

- buy $1,000/13.6364 \cong 73.3333$ options; in this case your final wealth will be

$$73.3333 \times C(1) \cong \begin{cases} 1,466.67 & \text{if stock goes up,} \\ 0.00 & \text{if stock goes down.} \end{cases}$$

If stock goes up, the investment in options will produce a much higher return than shares, namely about 46.67%. However, it will be disastrous otherwise: you will lose all your money. Meanwhile, when investing in shares, you would gain just 20% or lose 20%. Without specifying the probabilities we cannot compute the expected returns or standard deviations. Nevertheless, one would readily agree that investing in options is more risky than in stock. This can be exploited by adventurous investors.

*Exercise 1.10*

In the above setting, find the final wealth of an investor whose initial capital of \$1,000 is split fifty-fifty between stock and options.

Options can also be employed to reduce risk. Consider an investor planning to purchase stock in the future. The share price today is $S(0) = 100$ dollars, but the investor will only have funds available at a future time $t = 1$, when the share price will become

$$S(1) = \begin{cases} 160 & \text{with probability } p, \\ 40 & \text{with probability } 1-p, \end{cases}$$

for some $0 < p < 1$. Assume, as before, that $A(0) = 100$ and $A(1) = 110$ dollars, and compare the following two strategies:

- wait until time 1, when the funds become available, and purchase the stock for $S(1)$;

or

- at time 0 borrow money to buy a call option with strike price \$100; then, at time 1 repay the loan with interest and purchase the stock, exercising the option if the stock price goes up.

The investor will be open to considerable risk if she chooses to follow the first strategy. On the other hand, following the second strategy, she will need to borrow $C(0) \cong 31.8182$ dollars to pay for the option. At time 1 she will have to repay \$35 to clear the loan and may use the option to purchase the stock, hence the cost of purchasing one share will be

$$S(1) - C(1) + 35 = \begin{cases} 135 & \text{if stock goes up,} \\ 75 & \text{if stock goes down.} \end{cases}$$

Clearly, the risk is reduced, the spread between these two figures being narrower than before.

### Exercise 1.11

Compute the risk as measured by the standard deviation of the cost of buying one share with and without the option if a) $p = 0.25$, b) $p = 0.5$, c) $p = 0.75$.

### Exercise 1.12

Show that the risk (as measured by the standard deviation of the cost of buying one share) of the above strategy involving an option is a half of that when no option is purchased, no matter what the probability $0 < p < 1$ is.

If two options are bought, then the risk will be reduced to nil:

$$S(1) - 2 \times C(1) + 70 = 110 \text{ with probability } 1.$$

This strategy turns out to be equivalent to a long forward contract, since the forward price of the stock is exactly \$110 (see Section 1.5). It is also equivalent to borrowing money to purchase a share for \$100 today and repaying \$110 to clear the loan at time 1.

Chapter 9 on financial engineering will discuss various ways of managing risk with options: magnifying or reducing risk, dealing with complicated risk exposure, and constructing payoff profiles tailor made to meet the specific needs of an investor.

# 2
# Risk-Free Assets

## 2.1 Time Value of Money

It is a fact of life that \$100 to be received after one year is worth less than the same amount today. The main reason is that money due in the future or locked in a fixed term account cannot be spent right away. One would therefore expect to be compensated for postponed consumption. In addition, prices may rise in the meantime and the amount will not have the same purchasing power as it would have at present. Finally, there is always a risk, even if a negligible one, that the money will never be received. Whenever a future payment is uncertain to some degree, its value today will be reduced to compensate for the risk. (However, in the present chapter we shall consider situations free from such risk.) As generic examples of risk-free assets we shall consider a bank deposit or a bond.

The way in which money changes its value in time is a complex issue of fundamental importance in finance. We shall be concerned mainly with two questions:

> What is the future value of an amount invested or borrowed today?
>
> What is the present value of an amount to be paid or received at a certain time in the future?

The answers depend on various factors, which will be discussed in the present chapter. This topic is often referred to as the *time value of money*.

### 2.1.1 Simple Interest

Suppose that an amount is paid into a bank account, where it is to earn *interest*. The *future value* of this investment consists of the initial deposit, called the *principal* and denoted by $P$, plus all the interest earned since the money was deposited in the account.

To begin with, we shall consider the case when interest is attracted only by the principal, which remains unchanged during the period of investment. For example, the interest earned may be paid out in cash, credited to another account attracting no interest, or credited to the original account after some longer period.

After one year the interest earned will be $rP$, where $r > 0$ is the *interest rate*. The value of the investment will thus become $V(1) = P + rP = (1+r)P$. After two years the investment will grow to $V(2) = (1 + 2r)P$. Consider a fraction of a year. Interest is typically calculated on a daily basis: the interest earned in one day will be $\frac{1}{365}rP$. After $n$ days the interest will be $\frac{n}{365}rP$ and the total value of the investment will become $V(\frac{n}{365}) = (1 + \frac{n}{365}r)P$. This motivates the following rule of *simple interest*: The value of the investment at time $t$, denoted by $V(t)$, is given by

$$V(t) = (1 + tr)P, \tag{2.1}$$

where time $t$, expressed in years, can be an arbitrary non-negative real number; see Figure 2.1. In particular, we have the obvious equality $V(0) = P$. The number $1+rt$ is called the *growth factor*. Here we assume that the interest rate $r$ is constant. If the principal $P$ is invested at time $s$, rather than at time 0, then the value at time $t \geq s$ will be

$$V(t) = (1 + (t-s)r)P. \tag{2.2}$$

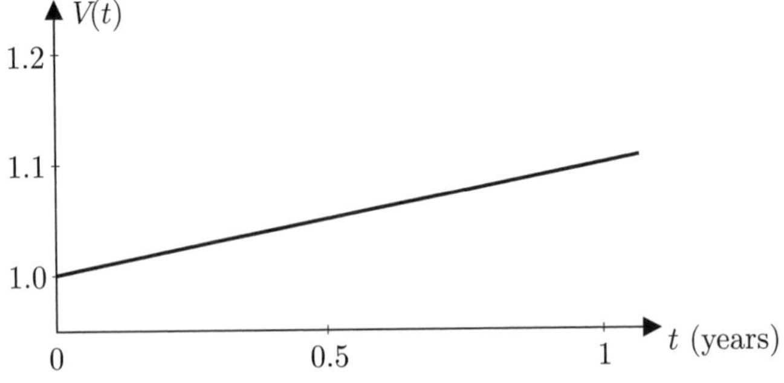


**Figure 2.1** Principal attracting simple interest at 10% ($r = 0.1$, $P = 1$)

Throughout this book the unit of time will be one year. We shall transform any period expressed in other units (days, weeks, months) into a fraction of a year.

## Example 2.1

Consider a deposit of \$150 held for 20 days and attracting simple interest at a rate of 8%. This gives $t = \frac{20}{365}$ and $r = 0.08$. After 20 days the deposit will grow to $V(\frac{20}{365}) = (1 + \frac{20}{365} \times 0.08) \times 150 \cong 150.66$.

The *return* on an investment commencing at time $s$ and terminating at time $t$ will be denoted by $K(s,t)$. It is given by

$$K(s,t) = \frac{V(t) - V(s)}{V(s)}. \tag{2.3}$$

In the case of simple interest

$$K(s,t) = (t-s)r,$$

which clearly follows from (2.2). In particular, the interest rate is equal to the return over one year,

$$K(0,1) = r.$$

As a general rule, interest rates will always refer to a period of one year, facilitating the comparison between different investments, independently of their actual duration. By contrast, the return reflects both the interest rate *and* the length of time the investment is held.

### *Exercise 2.1*

A sum of \$9,000 paid into a bank account for two months (61 days) to attract simple interest will produce \$9,020 at the and of the term. Find the interest rate $r$ and the return on this investment.

### *Exercise 2.2*

How much would you pay today to receive \$1,000 at a certain future date if you require a return of 2%?

### *Exercise 2.3*

How long will it take for a sum of \$800 attracting simple interest to become \$830 if the rate is 9%? Compute the return on this investment.

*Exercise 2.4*

Find the principal to be deposited initially in an account attracting simple interest at a rate of 8% if \$1,000 is needed after three months (91 days).

The last exercise is concerned with an important general problem: Find the initial sum whose value at time $t$ is given. In the case of simple interest the answer is easily found by solving (2.1) for the principal, obtaining

$$V(0) = V(t)(1 + rt)^{-1}. \tag{2.4}$$

This number is called the *present* or *discounted value* of $V(t)$ and $(1 + rt)^{-1}$ is the *discount factor*.

Example 2.2

A *perpetuity* is a sequence of payments of a fixed amount to be made at equal time intervals and continuing indefinitely into the future. For example, suppose that payments of an amount $C$ are to be made once a year, the first payment due a year hence. This can be achieved by depositing

$$P = \frac{C}{r}$$

in a bank account to earn simple interest at a constant rate $r$. Such a deposit will indeed produce a sequence of interest payments amounting to $C = rP$ payable every year.

In practice simple interest is used only for short-term investments and for certain types of loans and deposits. It is not a realistic description of the value of money in the longer term. In the majority of cases the interest already earned can be reinvested to attract even more interest, producing a higher return than that implied by (2.1). This will be analysed in detail in what follows.

### 2.1.2 Periodic Compounding

Once again, suppose that an amount $P$ is deposited in a bank account, attracting interest at a constant rate $r > 0$. However, in contrast to the case of simple interest, we assume that the interest earned will now be added to the principal periodically, for example, annually, semi-annually, quarterly, monthly, or perhaps even on a daily basis. Subsequently, interest will be attracted not just by the original deposit, but also by all the interest earned so far. In these circumstances we shall talk of *discrete* or *periodic compounding*.

## Example 2.3

In the case of monthly compounding the first interest payment of $\frac{r}{12}P$ will be due after one month, increasing the principal to $(1+\frac{r}{12})P$, all of which will attract interest in the future. The next interest payment, due after two months, will thus be $\frac{r}{12}(1+\frac{r}{12})P$, and the capital will become $(1+\frac{r}{12})^2P$. After one year it will become $(1+\frac{r}{12})^{12}P$, after $n$ months it will be $(1+\frac{r}{12})^nP$, and after $t$ years $(1+\frac{r}{12})^{12t}P$. The last formula admits $t$ equal to a whole number of months, that is, a multiple of $\frac{1}{12}$.

In general, if $m$ interest payments are made per annum, the time between two consecutive payments measured in years will be $\frac{1}{m}$, the first interest payment being due at time $\frac{1}{m}$. Each interest payment will increase the principal by a factor of $1+\frac{r}{m}$. Given that the interest rate $r$ remains unchanged, after $t$ years the *future value* of an initial principal $P$ will become

$$V(t)=\left(1+\frac{r}{m}\right)^{tm}P, \tag{2.5}$$

because there will be $tm$ interest payments during this period. In this formula $t$ must be a whole multiple of the period $\frac{1}{m}$. The number $\left(1+\frac{r}{m}\right)^{tm}$ is the *growth factor*.

The exact value of the investment may sometimes need to be known at time instants between interest payments. In particular, this may be so if the account is closed on a day when no interest payment is due. For example, what is the value after 10 days of a deposit of \$100 subject to monthly compounding at 12%? One possible answer is \$100, since the first interest payment would be due only after one whole month. This suggests that (2.5) should be extended to arbitrary values of $t$ by means of a step function with steps of duration $\frac{1}{m}$, as shown in Figure 2.2. Later on, in Remark 2.6 we shall see that the extension consistent with the No-Arbitrage Principle should use the right-hand side of (2.5) for all $t \geq 0$.

### *Exercise 2.5*

How long will it take to double a capital attracting interest at 6% compounded daily?

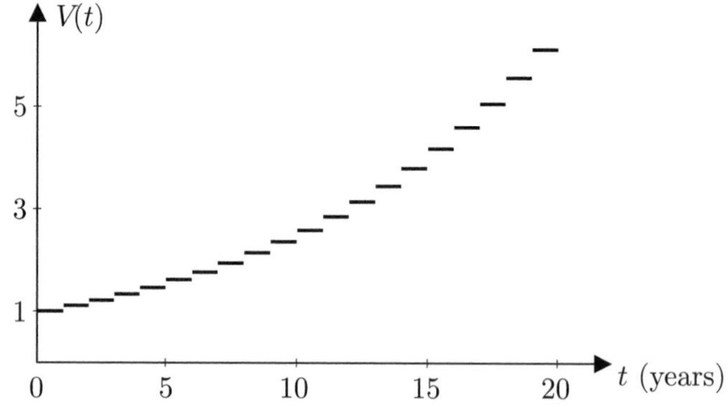


**Figure 2.2** Annual compounding at 10% ($m = 1$, $r = 0.1$, $P = 1$)

### *Exercise 2.6*

What is the interest rate if a deposit subject to annual compounding is doubled after 10 years?

### *Exercise 2.7*

Find and compare the future value after two years of a deposit of \$100 attracting interest at a rate of 10% compounded a) annually and b) semi-annually.

## Proposition 2.1

The future value $V(t)$ increases if any one of the parameters $m$, $t$, $r$ or $P$ increases, the others remaining unchanged.

## Proof

It is immediately obvious from (2.5) that $V(t)$ increases if $t$, $r$ or $P$ increases. To show that $V(t)$ increases as the compounding frequency $m$ increases, we need to verify that if $m < k$, then

$$\left(1 + \frac{r}{m}\right)^{tm} < \left(1 + \frac{r}{k}\right)^{tk}.$$

The latter clearly reduces to

$$\left(1 + \frac{r}{m}\right)^{m} < \left(1 + \frac{r}{k}\right)^{k},$$

which can be verified directly using the binomial formula:

$$\begin{aligned}\left(1+\frac{r}{m}\right)^m &= 1+r+\frac{1-\frac{1}{m}}{2!}r^2+\cdots+\frac{\left(1-\frac{1}{m}\right)\times\cdots\times\left(1-\frac{m-1}{m}\right)}{m!}r^m \\ &\leq 1+r+\frac{1-\frac{1}{k}}{2!}r^2+\cdots+\frac{\left(1-\frac{1}{k}\right)\times\cdots\times\left(1-\frac{m-1}{k}\right)}{m!}r^m \\ &< 1+r+\frac{1-\frac{1}{k}}{2!}r^2+\cdots+\frac{\left(1-\frac{1}{k}\right)\times\cdots\times\left(1-\frac{k-1}{k}\right)}{k!}r^k \\ &= \left(1+\frac{r}{k}\right)^k.\end{aligned}$$

The first inequality holds because each term of the sum on the left-hand side is no greater than the corresponding term on the right-hand side. The second inequality is true because the sum on the right-hand side contains $m-k$ additional non-zero terms as compared to the sum on the left-hand side. This completes the proof. □

### *Exercise 2.8*

Which will deliver a higher future value after one year, a deposit of $\$1,000$ attracting interest at 15% compounded daily, or at 15.5% compounded semi-annually?

### *Exercise 2.9*

What initial investment subject to annual compounding at 12% is needed to produce $\$1,000$ after two years?

The last exercise touches upon the problem of finding the present value of an amount payable at some future time instant in the case when periodic compounding applies. Here the formula for the *present* or *discounted value* of $V(t)$ is

$$V(0) = V(t)(1+\frac{r}{m})^{-tm},$$

the number $(1+\frac{r}{m})^{-tm}$ being the *discount factor*.

### Remark 2.1

Fix the terminal value $V(t)$ of an investment. It is an immediate consequence of Proposition 2.1 that the present value increases if any one of the factors $r$, $t$, $m$ decreases, the other ones remaining unchanged.

### *Exercise 2.10*

Find the present value of \$100,000 to be received after 100 years if the interest rate is assumed to be 5% throughout the whole period and a) daily or b) annual compounding applies.

One often requires the value $V(t)$ of an investment at an intermediate time $0 < t < T$, given the value $V(T)$ at some fixed future time $T$. This can be achieved by computing the present value of $V(T)$, taking it as the principal, and running the investment forward up to time $t$. Under periodic compounding with frequency $m$ and interest rate $r$, this obviously gives

$$V(t) = \left(1 + \frac{r}{m}\right)^{-(T-t)m} V(T). \tag{2.6}$$

To find the return on a deposit attracting interest compounded periodically we use the general formula (2.3) and readily arrive at

$$K(s,t) = \frac{V(t) - V(s)}{V(s)} = (1 + \frac{r}{m})^{(t-s)m} - 1.$$

In particular,

$$K(0, \frac{1}{m}) = \frac{r}{m},$$

which provides a simple way of computing the interest rate given the return.

### *Exercise 2.11*

Find the return over one year under monthly compounding with $r = 10\%$.

### *Exercise 2.12*

Which is greater, the interest rate $r$ or the return $K(0,1)$ if the compounding frequency $m$ is greater than 1?

### Remark 2.2

The return on a deposit subject to periodic compounding is *not* additive. Take, for simplicity, $m = 1$. Then

$$K(0,1) = K(1,2) = r,$$
$$K(0,2) = (1+r)^2 - 1 = 2r + r^2,$$

and clearly $K(0,1) + K(1,2) \neq K(0,2)$.

### 2.1.3 Streams of Payments

An *annuity* is a sequence of finitely many payments of a fixed amount due at equal time intervals. Suppose that payments of an amount $C$ are to be made once a year for $n$ years, the first one due a year hence. Assuming that annual compounding applies, we shall find the present value of such a stream of payments. We compute the present values of all payments and add them up to get

$$\frac{C}{1+r}+\frac{C}{(1+r)^2}+\frac{C}{(1+r)^3}+\cdots+\frac{C}{(1+r)^n}.$$

It is sometimes convenient to introduce the following seemingly cumbersome piece of notation:

$$\mathrm{PA}(r,n)=\frac{1}{1+r}+\frac{1}{(1+r)^2}+\cdots+\frac{1}{(1+r)^n}. \tag{2.7}$$

This number is called the *present value factor for an annuity.* It allows us to express the present value of an annuity in a concise form:

$$\mathrm{PA}(r,n)\times C.$$

The expression for $\mathrm{PA}(r,n)$ can be simplified by using the formula

$$a+qa+q^2a+\cdots+q^{n-1}a=a\frac{1-q^n}{1-q}.$$

In our case $a=\frac{1}{1+r}$ and $q=\frac{1}{1+r}$, hence

$$\mathrm{PA}(r,n)=\frac{1-(1+r)^{-n}}{r}. \tag{2.8}$$

#### Remark 2.3

Note that an initial bank deposit of

$$P=\mathrm{PA}(r,n)\times C=\frac{C}{1+r}+\frac{C}{(1+r)^2}+\cdots+\frac{C}{(1+r)^n}$$

attracting interest at a rate $r$ compounded annually would produce a stream of $n$ annual payments of $C$ each. A deposit of $C(1+r)^{-1}$ would grow to $C$ after one year, which is just what is needed to cover the first annuity payment. A deposit of $C(1+r)^{-2}$ would become $C$ after two years to cover the second payment, and so on. Finally, a deposit of $C(1+r)^{-n}$ would deliver the last payment of $C$ due after $n$ years.

## Example 2.4

Consider a loan of $\$1,000$ to be paid back in 5 equal instalments due at yearly intervals. The instalments include both the interest payable each year calculated at 15% of the current outstanding balance and the repayment of a fraction of the loan. A loan of this type is called an *amortised loan.* The amount of each instalment can be computed as

$$\frac{1,000}{\mathrm{PA}(15\%,5)} \cong 298.32.$$

This is because the loan is equivalent to an annuity from the point of view of the lender.

### *Exercise 2.13*

What is the amount of interest included in each instalment? How much of the loan is repaid as part of each instalment? What is the outstanding balance of the loan after each instalment is paid?

### *Exercise 2.14*

How much can you borrow if the interest rate is 18%, you can afford to pay $\$10,000$ at the end of each year, and you want to clear the loan in 10 years?

### *Exercise 2.15*

Suppose that you deposit $\$1,200$ at the end of each year for 40 years, subject to annual compounding at a constant rate of 5%. Find the balance after 40 years.

### *Exercise 2.16*

Suppose that you took a mortgage of $\$100,000$ on a house to be paid back in full by 10 equal annual instalments, each consisting of the interest due on the outstanding balance plus a repayment of a part of the amount borrowed. If you decided to clear the mortgage after eight years, how much money would you need to pay on top of the 8th instalment, assuming that a constant annual compounding rate of 6% applies throughout the period of the mortgage?

Recall that a *perpetuity* is an infinite sequence of payments of a fixed amount $C$ occurring at the end of each year. The formula for the present value of a perpetuity can be obtained from (2.7) in the limit as $n \to \infty$:

$$\lim_{n\to\infty} \mathrm{PA}(r,n) \times C = \frac{C}{1+r} + \frac{C}{(1+r)^2} + \frac{C}{(1+r)^3} + \cdots = \frac{C}{r}. \tag{2.9}$$

The limit amounts to taking the sum of a geometric series.

## Remark 2.4

The present value of a perpetuity is given by the same formula as in Example 2.2, even though periodic compounding has been used in place of simple interest. In both cases the annual payment $C$ is exactly equal to the interest earned throughout the year, and the amount remaining to earn interest in the following year is always $\frac{C}{r}$. Nevertheless, periodic compounding allows us to view the same sequence of payments in a different way: The present value $\frac{C}{r}$ of the perpetuity is decomposed into infinitely many parts, as in (2.9), each responsible for producing one future payment of $C$.

## Remark 2.5

Formula (2.8) for the annuity factor is easier to memorise in the following way, using the formula for a perpetuity: The sequence of $n$ payments of $C = 1$ can be represented as the difference between two perpetuities, one starting now and the other after $n$ years. (Cutting off the tail of a perpetuity, we obtain an annuity.) In doing so we need to compute the present value of the latter perpetuity. This can be achieved by means of the discount factor $(1+r)^{-n}$. Hence,

$$\mathrm{PA}(r,n) = \frac{1}{r} - \frac{1}{r} \times \frac{1}{(1+r)^n} = \frac{1-(1+r)^{-n}}{r}.$$

### *Exercise 2.17*

Find a formula for the present value of an infinite stream of payments of the form $C$, $C(1+g)$, $C(1+g)^2, \ldots$, growing at a constant rate $g$. By the tail-cutting procedure find a formula for the present value of $n$ such payments.

### 2.1.4 Continuous Compounding

Formula (2.5) for the future value at time $t$ of a principal $P$ attracting interest at a rate $r > 0$ compounded $m$ times a year can be written as

$$V(t) = \left[\left(1 + \frac{r}{m}\right)^{\frac{m}{r}}\right]^{tr} P.$$

In the limit as $m \to \infty$, we obtain

$$V(t) = \mathrm{e}^{tr} P, \tag{2.10}$$

where

$$\mathrm{e} = \lim_{x \to \infty} \left(1 + \frac{1}{x}\right)^x$$

is the base of natural logarithms. This is known as *continuous compounding*. The corresponding *growth factor* is $\mathrm{e}^{tr}$. A typical graph of $V(t)$ is shown in Figure 2.3.

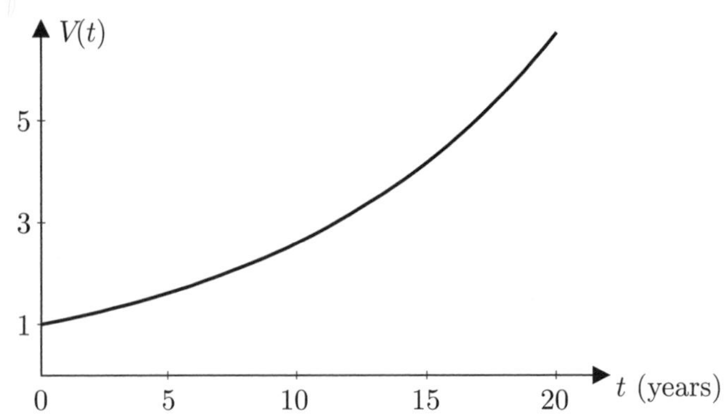


**Figure 2.3** Continuous compounding at 10% ($r = 0.1$, $P = 1$)

The derivative of $V(t) = \mathrm{e}^{tr} P$ is

$$V'(t) = r\mathrm{e}^{tr} P = rV(t).$$

In the case of continuous compounding the rate of the growth is proportional to the current wealth.

Formula (2.10) is a good approximation of the case of periodic compounding when the frequency $m$ is large. It is simpler and lends itself more readily to transformations than the formula for periodic compounding.

### *Exercise 2.18*

How long will it take to earn \$1 in interest if \$1,000,000 is deposited at 10% compounded continuously?

### *Exercise 2.19*

In 1626 Peter Minuit, governor of the colony of New Netherland, bought the island of Manhattan from Indians paying with beads, cloth, and trinkets worth \$24. Find the value of this sum in year 2000 at 5% compounded a) continuously and b) annually.

## Proposition 2.2

Continuous compounding produces higher future value than periodic compounding with any frequency $m$, given the same initial principal $P$ and interest rate $r$.

## Proof

It suffices to verify that

$$\mathrm{e}^{tr} > (1 + \frac{r}{m})^{tm} = \left[(1 + \frac{r}{m})^{\frac{m}{r}}\right]^{rt}.$$

The inequality holds because the sequence $(1+\frac{r}{m})^{\frac{m}{r}}$ is increasing and converges to e as $m \nearrow \infty$. □

### *Exercise 2.20*

What will be the difference between the value after one year of \$100 deposited at 10% compounded monthly and compounded continuously? How frequent should the periodic compounding be for the difference to be less than \$0.01?

The present value under continuous compounding is obviously given by

$$V(0) = V(t)\mathrm{e}^{-tr}.$$

In this case the *discount factor* is $\mathrm{e}^{-tr}$. Given the terminal value $V(T)$, we clearly have

$$V(t) = \mathrm{e}^{-r(T-t)}V(T). \tag{2.11}$$

### *Exercise 2.21*

Find the present value of $\$1,000,000$ to be received after 20 years assuming continuous compounding at 6%.

### *Exercise 2.22*

Given that the future value of $\$950$ subject to continuous compounding will be $\$1,000$ after half a year, find the interest rate.

The return $K(s,t)$ defined by (2.3) on an investment subject to continuous compounding fails to be additive, just like in the case of periodic compounding. It proves convenient to introduce the *logarithmic return*

$$k(s,t) = \ln \frac{V(t)}{V(s)}. \tag{2.12}$$

## Proposition 2.3

The logarithmic return is additive,

$$k(s,t) + k(t,u) = k(s,u).$$

## Proof

This is an easy consequence of (2.12):

$$\begin{aligned} k(s,t) + k(t,u) &= \ln \frac{V(t)}{V(s)} + \ln \frac{V(u)}{V(t)} \\ &= \ln \frac{V(t)}{V(s)} \frac{V(u)}{V(t)} = \ln \frac{V(u)}{V(s)} = k(s,u). \end{aligned}$$

□

If $V(t)$ is given by (2.10), then $k(s,t) = r(t-s)$, which enables us to recover the interest rate

$$r = \frac{k(s,t)}{t-s}.$$

### *Exercise 2.23*

Suppose that the logarithmic return over 2 months on an investment subject to continuous compounding is 3%. Find the interest rate.

### 2.1.5 How to Compare Compounding Methods

As we have already noticed, frequent compounding will produce a higher future value than less frequent compounding if the interest rates and the initial principal are the same. We shall consider the general circumstances in which one compounding method will produce either the same or higher future value than another method, given the same initial principal.

#### Example 2.5

Suppose that certificates promising to pay \$120 after one year can be purchased or sold now, or at any time during this year, for \$100. This is consistent with a constant interest rate of 20% under annual compounding. If an investor decided to sell such a certificate half a year after the purchase, what price would it fetch? Suppose it is \$110, a frequent first guess based on halving the annual profit of \$20. However, this turns out to be too high a price, leading to the following arbitrage strategy:

- Borrow \$1,000 to buy 10 certificates for \$100 each.
- After six months sell the 10 certificates for \$110 each and buy 11 new certificates for \$100 each. The balance of these transactions is nil.
- After another six months sell the 11 certificates for \$110 each, cashing \$1,210 in total, and pay \$1,200 to clear the loan with interest. The balance of \$10 would be the arbitrage profit.

A similar argument shows that the certificate price after six months cannot be too low, say, \$109.

The price of a certificate after six months is related to the interest rate under semi-annual compounding: If this rate is $r$, then the price is $100\left(1+\frac{r}{2}\right)$ dollars and vice versa. Arbitrage will disappear if the corresponding growth factor $\left(1+\frac{r}{2}\right)^2$ over one year is equal to the growth factor 1.2 under annual compounding,

$$\left(1+\frac{r}{2}\right)^2 = 1.2,$$

which gives $r \cong 0.1909$, or 19.09%. If so, then the certificate price after six months should be $100\left(1+\frac{0.1909}{2}\right) \cong 109.54$ dollars.

The idea based on considering the growth factors over a fixed period, typically one year, can be used to compare any two compounding methods.

## Definition 2.1

We say that two compounding methods are *equivalent* if the corresponding growth factors over a period of one year are the same. If one of the growth factors exceeds the other, then the corresponding compounding method is said to be *preferable*.

## Example 2.6

Semi-annual compounding at 10% is equivalent to annual compounding at 10.25%. Indeed, in the former case the growth factor over a period of one year is

$$\left(1+\frac{0.1}{2}\right)^2 = 1.1025,$$

which is the same as the growth factor in the latter case. Both are preferable to monthly compounding at 9%, for which the growth factor over one year is only

$$\left(1+\frac{0.09}{12}\right)^{12} \cong 1.0938.$$

We can freely switch from one compounding method to another equivalent method by recalculating the interest rate. In the chapters to follow we shall normally use either annual or continuous compounding.

### *Exercise 2.24*

Find the rate for continuous compounding equivalent to monthly compounding at 12%.

### *Exercise 2.25*

Find the frequency of periodic compounding at 20% to be equivalent to annual compounding at 21%.

Instead of comparing the growth factors, it is often convenient to compare the so-called effective rates as defined below.

## Definition 2.2

For a given compounding method with interest rate $r$ the *effective rate* $r_{\mathrm{e}}$ is one that gives the same growth factor over a one year period under annual compounding.

In particular, in the case of periodic compounding with frequency $m$ and rate $r$ the effective rate $r_{\mathrm{e}}$ satisfies

$$\left(1+\frac{r}{m}\right)^{m}=1+r_{\mathrm{e}}.$$

In the case of continuous compounding with rate $r$

$$\mathrm{e}^{r}=1+r_{\mathrm{e}}.$$

## Example 2.7

In the case of semi-annual compounding at 10% the effective rate is 10.25%, see Example 2.6.

## Proposition 2.4

Two compounding methods are equivalent if and only if the corresponding effective rates $r_{\mathrm{e}}$ and $r'_{\mathrm{e}}$ are equal, $r_{\mathrm{e}}=r'_{\mathrm{e}}$. The compounding method with effective rate $r_{\mathrm{e}}$ is preferable to the other method if and only if $r_{\mathrm{e}}>r'_{\mathrm{e}}$.

## Proof

This is because the growth factors over one year are $1+r_{\mathrm{e}}$ and $1+r'_{\mathrm{e}}$, respectively. □

## Example 2.8

In Exercise 2.8 we have seen that daily compounding at 15% is preferable to semi-annual compounding at 15.5%. The corresponding effective rates $r_{\mathrm{e}}$ and $r'_{\mathrm{e}}$ can be found from

$$1+r_{\mathrm{e}}=\left(1+\frac{0.15}{365}\right)^{365}\cong 1.1618,$$

$$1+r'_{\mathrm{e}}=\left(1+\frac{0.155}{2}\right)^{2}\cong 1.1610.$$

This means that $r_{\mathrm{e}}$ is about 16.18% and $r'_{\mathrm{e}}$ about 16.10%.

## Remark 2.6

Recall that formula (2.5) for periodic compounding, that is,

$$V(t)=\left(1+\frac{r}{m}\right)^{tm}P,$$

admits only time instants $t$ being whole multiples of the compounding period $\frac{1}{m}$. An argument similar to that in Example 2.5 shows that the appropriate no-arbitrage value of an initial sum $P$ at any time $t \geq 0$ should be $\left(1+\frac{r}{m}\right)^{tm} P$. A reasonable extension of (2.5) is therefore to use the right-hand side for all $t \geq 0$ rather than just for whole multiples of $\frac{1}{m}$. From now on we shall always use this extension.

In terms of the effective rate $r_{\mathrm{e}}$ the future value can be written as

$$V(t) = (1 + r_{\mathrm{e}})^t P.$$

for all $t \geq 0$. This applies both to continuous compounding and to periodic compounding extended to arbitrary times as in Remark 2.6. Proposition 2.4 implies that, given the same initial principal, equivalent compounding methods will produce the same future value for all times $t \geq 0$. Similarly, a compounding method preferable to another one will produce a higher future value for all $t > 0$.

## Remark 2.7

Simple interest does not fit into the scheme for comparing compounding methods. In this case the future value $V(t)$ is a linear function of time $t$, whereas it is an exponential function if either continuous or periodic compounding applies. The graphs of such functions have at most two intersection points, so they can never be equal to one another for all times $t \geq 0$ (except for the trivial case of zero principal).

### *Exercise 2.26*

What is the present value of an annuity consisting of monthly payments of an amount $C$ continuing for $n$ years? Express the answer in terms of the effective rate $r_{\mathrm{e}}$.

### *Exercise 2.27*

What is the present value of a perpetuity consisting of bimonthly payments of an amount $C$? Express the answer in terms of the effective rate $r_{\mathrm{e}}$.

## 2.2 Money Market

The money market consists of risk-free (more precisely, default-free) securities. An example is a *bond*, which is a financial security promising the holder a sequence of guaranteed future payments. Risk-free means here that these payments will be delivered with certainty. (Nevertheless, even in this case risk cannot be completely avoided, since the market prices of such securities may fluctuate unpredictably; see Chapters 10 and 11.) There are many kinds of bonds like treasury bills and notes, treasury, mortgage and debenture bonds, commercial papers, and others with various particular arrangements concerning the issuing institution, duration, number of payments, embedded rights and guarantees.

### 2.2.1 Zero-Coupon Bonds

The simplest case of a bond is a *zero-coupon bond*, which involves just a single payment. The issuing institution (for example, a government, a bank or a company) promises to exchange the bond for a certain amount of money $F$, called the *face value*, on a given day $T$, called the *maturity date*. Typically, the life span of a zero-coupon bond is up to one year, the face value being some round figure, for example 100. In effect, the person or institution who buys the bond is lending money to the bond writer.

Given the interest rate, the present value of such a bond can easily be computed. Suppose that a bond with face value $F = 100$ dollars is maturing in one year, and the annual compounding rate $r$ is 12%. Then the present value of the bond should be

$$V(0) = F(1+r)^{-1} \cong 89.29$$

dollars.

In reality, the opposite happens: Bonds are freely traded and their prices are determined by market forces, whereas the interest rate is implied by the bond prices,

$$r = \frac{F}{V(0)} - 1. \tag{2.13}$$

This formula gives the implied annual compounding rate. For instance, if a one-year bond with face value \$100 is being traded at \$91, then the implied rate is 9.89%.

For simplicity, we shall consider *unit bonds* with face value equal to one unit of the home currency, $F = 1$.

Typically, a bond can be sold at any time prior to maturity at the market price. This price at time $t$ is denoted $B(t,T)$. In particular, $B(0,T)$ is the current, time 0 price of the bond, and $B(T,T) = 1$ is equal to the face value. Again, these prices determine the interest rates by applying formulae (2.6) and (2.11) with $V(t) = B(t,T)$, $V(T) = 1$. For example, the implied annual compounding rate satisfies the equation

$$B(t,T) = (1+r)^{-(T-t)}.$$

The last formula has to be suitably modified if a different compounding method is used. Using periodic compounding with frequency $m$, we need to solve the equation

$$B(t,T) = \left(1 + \frac{r}{m}\right)^{-m(T-t)}.$$

In the case of continuous compounding the equation for the implied rate satisfies

$$B(t,T) = \mathrm{e}^{-r(T-t)}.$$

Of course all these different implied rates are equivalent to one another, since the bond price does not depend on the compounding method used.

## Remark 2.8

In general, the implied interest rate may depend on the trading time $t$ as well as on the maturity time $T$. This is an important issue, which will be discussed in Chapters 10 and 11. For the time being, we adopt the simplifying assumption that the interest rate remains constant throughout the period up to maturity.

### *Exercise 2.28*

An investor paid \$95 for a bond with face value \$100 maturing in six months. When will the bond value reach \$99 if the interest rate remains constant?

### *Exercise 2.29*

Find the interest rates for annual, semi-annual and continuous compounding implied by a unit bond with $B(0.5, 1) = 0.9455$.

Note that $B(0,T)$ is the discount factor and $B(0,T)^{-1}$ is the growth factor for each compounding method. These universal factors are all that is needed to compute the time value of money, without resorting to the corresponding interest rates. However, interest rates are useful because they are more intuitive.

For an average bank customer the information that a one-year \$100 bond can be purchased for \$92.59 may not be as clear as the equivalent statement that a deposit will earn 8% interest if kept for one year.

### 2.2.2 Coupon Bonds

Bonds promising a sequence of payments are called *coupon bonds*. These payments consist of the face value due at maturity, and *coupons* paid regularly, typically annually, semi-annually, or quarterly, the last coupon due at maturity. The assumption of constant interest rates allows us to compute the price of a coupon bond by discounting all the future payments.

#### Example 2.9

Consider a bond with face value $F = 100$ dollars maturing in five years, $T = 5$, with coupons of $C = 10$ dollars paid annually, the last one at maturity. This means a stream of payments of $10, 10, 10, 10, 110$ dollars at the end of each consecutive year. Given the continuous compounding rate $r$, say 12%, we can find the price of the bond:

$$V(0) = 10\mathrm{e}^{-r} + 10\mathrm{e}^{-2r} + 10\mathrm{e}^{-3r} + 10\mathrm{e}^{-4r} + 110\mathrm{e}^{-5r} \cong 90.27$$

dollars.

#### *Exercise 2.30*

Find the price of a bond with face value \$100 and \$5 annual coupons that matures in four years, given that the continuous compounding rate is a) 8% or b) 5%.

#### *Exercise 2.31*

Sketch the graph of the price of the bond in Exercise 2.30 as a function of the continuous compounding rate $r$. What is the value of this function for $r = 0$? What is the limit as $r \to \infty$?

#### Example 2.10

We continue Example 2.9. After one year, once the first coupon is cashed, the bond becomes a four-year bond worth

$$V(1) = 10\mathrm{e}^{-r} + 10\mathrm{e}^{-2r} + 10\mathrm{e}^{-3r} + 110\mathrm{e}^{-4r} \cong 91.78$$

dollars. Observe that the total wealth at time 1 is

$$V(1)+C=V(0)\mathrm{e}^{r}.$$

Six months later the bond will be worth

$$V(1.5)=10\mathrm{e}^{-0.5r}+10\mathrm{e}^{-1.5r}+10\mathrm{e}^{-2.5r}+110\mathrm{e}^{-3.5r}\cong 97.45$$

dollars. After four years the bond will become a zero-coupon bond with face value \$110 and price

$$V(4)=110\mathrm{e}^{-r}\cong 97.56$$

dollars.

An investor may choose to sell the bond at any time prior to maturity. The price at that time can once again be found by discounting all the payments due at later times.

### *Exercise 2.32*

Sketch the graph of the price of the coupon bond in Examples 2.9 and 2.10 as a function of time.

### *Exercise 2.33*

How long will it take for the price of the coupon bond in Examples 2.9 and 2.10 to reach \$95 for the first time?

The coupon can be expressed as a fraction of the face value. Assuming that coupons are paid annually, we shall write $C=iF$, where $i$ is called the *coupon rate*.

## Proposition 2.5

Whenever coupons are paid annually, the coupon rate is equal to the interest rate for annual compounding if and only if the price of the bond is equal to its face value. In this case we say that the bond sells *at par*.

## Proof

To avoid cumbersome notation we restrict ourselves to an example. Suppose that annual compounding with $r=i$ applies, and consider a bond with face value $F=100$ maturing in three years, $T=3$. Then the price of the bond is

$$\frac{C}{1+r}+\frac{C}{(1+r)^2}+\frac{F+C}{(1+r)^3}=\frac{rF}{1+r}+\frac{rF}{(1+r)^2}+\frac{F(1+r)}{(1+r)^3}$$

$$= \frac{rF}{1+r} + \frac{rF}{(1+r)^2} + \frac{F}{(1+r)^2} = \frac{rF}{1+r} + \frac{F(1+r)}{(1+r)^2} = F.$$

Conversely, note that

$$\frac{C}{1+r} + \frac{C}{(1+r)^2} + \frac{F+C}{(1+r)^3}$$

is one-to-one as a function of $r$ (in fact, a strictly decreasing function), so it assumes the value $F$ exactly once, and we know this happens for $r = i$. □

### Remark 2.9

If a bond sells below the face value, it means that the implied interest rate is higher than the coupon rate (since the price of a bond decreases when the interest rate goes up). If the bond price is higher than the face value, it means that the interest rate is lower than the coupon rate. This may be important information in real circumstances, where the bond price is determined by the market and gives an indication of the level of interest rates.

### *Exercise 2.34*

A bond with face value $F = 100$ and annual coupons $C = 8$ maturing after three years, at $T = 3$, is trading at par. Find the implied continuous compounding rate.

## 2.2.3 Money Market Account

An investment in the money market can be realised by means of a financial intermediary, typically an investment bank, who buys and sells bonds on behalf of its customers (thus reducing transaction costs). The risk-free position of an investor is given by the level of his or her account with the bank. It is convenient to think of this account as a tradable asset, which is indeed the case, since the bonds themselves are tradable. A long position in the money market involves buying the asset, that is, investing money. A short position amounts to borrowing money.

First, consider an investment in a zero-coupon bond closed prior to maturity. An initial amount $A(0)$ invested in the money market makes it possible to purchase $A(0)/B(0,T)$ bonds. The value of each bond will fetch

$$B(t,T) = \mathrm{e}^{-(T-t)r} = \mathrm{e}^{rt}\mathrm{e}^{-rT} = \mathrm{e}^{rt}B(0,T)$$

at time $t$. As a result, the investment will reach

$$A(t) = \frac{A(0)}{B(0,T)} B(t,T) = A(0)e^{rt}$$

at time $t \leq T$.

### Exercise 2.35

Find the return on a 75-day investment in zero-coupon bonds if $B(0,1) = 0.89$.

### Exercise 2.36

The return on a bond over six months is 7%. Find the implied continuous compounding rate.

### Exercise 2.37

After how many days will a bond purchased for $B(0,1) = 0.92$ produce a 5% return?

The investment in a bond has a finite time horizon. It will be terminated with $A(T) = A(0)e^{rT}$ at the time $T$ of maturity of the bond. To extend the position in the money market beyond $T$ one can reinvest the amount $A(T)$ into a bond newly issued at time $T$, maturing at $T' > T$. Taking $A(T)$ as the initial investment with $T$ playing the role of the starting time, we have

$$A(t') = A(T)e^{r(t'-T)} = A(0)e^{rt'}$$

for $T \leq t' \leq T'$. By repeating this argument, we readily arrive at the conclusion that an investment in the money market can be prolonged for as long as required, the formula

$$A(t) = A(0)e^{rt} \tag{2.14}$$

being valid for all $t \geq 0$.

### Exercise 2.38

Suppose that one dollar is invested in zero-coupon bonds maturing after one year. At the end of each year the proceeds are reinvested in new bonds of the same kind. How many bonds will be purchased at the end of year 9? Express the answer in terms of the implied continuous compounding rate.

An alternative way to prolong an investment in the money market for as long as required is to reinvest the face value of any bonds maturing at time $T$ in other bonds issued at time 0, but maturing at a later time $t > T$. Having invested $A(0)$ initially to buy unit bonds maturing at time $T$, we will have the sum of $A(0)/B(0,T)$ at our disposal at time $T$. At this time we chose a bond maturing at time $t$, its price at $T$ being $B(T,t)$. At time $t$ this investment will be worth

$$\frac{A(0)}{B(0,T)B(T,t)} = \frac{A(0)}{B(0,t)} = A(0)\mathrm{e}^{rt},$$

the same as in (2.14).

Finally, consider coupon bonds as a tool to manufacture an investment in the money market. Suppose for simplicity that the first coupon $C$ is due after one year. At time 0 we buy $A(0)/V(0)$ coupon bonds. After one year we cash the coupon and sell the bond for $V(1)$, receiving the total sum $C + V(1) = V(0)\mathrm{e}^{r}$ (see Example 2.10). Because the interest rate is constant, this sum of money is certain. In this way we have effectively created a zero-coupon bond with face value $V(0)\mathrm{e}^{r}$ maturing at time 1. It means that the scheme worked out above for zero-coupon bonds applies to coupon bonds as well, resulting in the same formula (2.14) for $A(t)$.

### *Exercise 2.39*

The sum of $1,000 is invested in five-year bonds with face value $100 and $8 coupons paid annually. All coupons are reinvested in bonds of the same kind. Assuming that the bonds are trading at par and the interest rate remains constant throughout the period to maturity, compute the number of bonds held during each consecutive year of the investment.

As we have seen, under the assumption that the interest rate is constant, the function $A(t)$ does not depend on the way the money market account is run, that is, it neither depends on the types of bonds selected for investment nor on the method of extending the investment beyond the maturity of the bonds.

Throughout most of this book we shall assume $A(t)$ to be deterministic and known. Indeed, we assume that $A(t) = \mathrm{e}^{rt}$, where $r$ is a constant interest rate. Variable interest rates will be considered in Chapter 10 and a random money market account will be studied in Chapter 11.

# 3
# Risky Assets

The future prices of any asset are unpredictable to a certain extent. In this chapter we shall typically be concerned with common stock, though any security such as foreign currency, a commodity, or even a partially unpredictable future cash flow can be considered. Market prices depend on the choices and decisions made by a great number of agents acting under conditions of uncertainty. It is therefore reasonable to treat the prices of assets as random. However, little more can be said in a fully general situation. We shall therefore impose specific conditions on asset prices, motivated by a need for the mathematical model to be realistic and relevant on the one hand, and tractable on the other hand.

## 3.1 Dynamics of Stock Prices

The price of stock at time $t$ will be denoted by $S(t)$. It is assumed to be strictly positive for all $t$. We take $t = 0$ to be the present time, $S(0)$ being the current stock price, known to all investors. The future prices $S(t)$ for $t > 0$ remain unknown, in general. Mathematically, $S(t)$ can be represented as a positive random variable on a probability space $\Omega$, that is,

$$S(t) : \Omega \to (0, \infty).$$

The probability space $\Omega$ consists of all feasible price movement 'scenarios' $\omega \in \Omega$. We shall write $S(t, \omega)$ to denote the price at time $t$ if the market follows scenario $\omega \in \Omega$.

The current stock price $S(0)$ known to all investors is simply a positive number, but it can be thought of as a constant random variable. The unknown future prices $S(t)$ for $t > 0$ are non-constant random variables. This means that for each $t > 0$ there are at least two scenarios $\omega, \widetilde{\omega} \in \Omega$ such that $S(t,\omega) \neq S(t,\widetilde{\omega})$.

We assume that time runs in a discrete manner, $t = n\tau$, where $n = 0, 1, 2, 3, \ldots$ and $\tau$ is a fixed time step, typically a year, a month, a week, a day, or even a minute or a second to describe some hectic trading. Because we take one year as the unit measure of time, a month corresponds to $\tau = 1/12$, a week corresponds to $\tau = 1/52$, a day to $\tau = 1/365$, and so on.

To simplify our notation we shall write $S(0), S(1), S(2), \ldots, S(n), \ldots$ instead of $S(0), S(\tau), S(2\tau), \ldots, S(n\tau), \ldots$, identifying $n$ with $n\tau$. This convention will in fact be adopted for many other time-dependent quantities.

## Example 3.1

Consider a market that can follow just two scenarios, boom or recession, denoted by $\omega_1$ and $\omega_2$, respectively. The current share price of a certain stock is \$10, which may rise to \$12 after one year if there is a boom or come down to \$7 in the case of recession. In these circumstances $\Omega = \{\omega_1, \omega_2\}$ and, putting $\tau = 1$, we have

| Scenario | $S(0)$ | $S(1)$ |
|---|---|---|
| $\omega_1$ (boom) | 10 | 12 |
| $\omega_2$ (recession) | 10 | 7 |

## Example 3.2

Suppose that there are three possible market scenarios, $\Omega = \{\omega_1, \omega_2, \omega_3\}$, the stock prices taking the following values over two time steps:

| Scenario | $S(0)$ | $S(1)$ | $S(2)$ |
|---|---|---|---|
| $\omega_1$ | 55 | 58 | 60 |
| $\omega_2$ | 55 | 58 | 52 |
| $\omega_3$ | 55 | 52 | 53 |

These price movements can be represented as a tree, see Figure 3.1. It is convenient to identify the scenarios with paths through the tree leading from the single node on the left (the 'root' of the tree) to the rightmost branch tips.

Such a tree structure of price movements, if found realistic and desirable, can readily be implemented in a mathematical model.

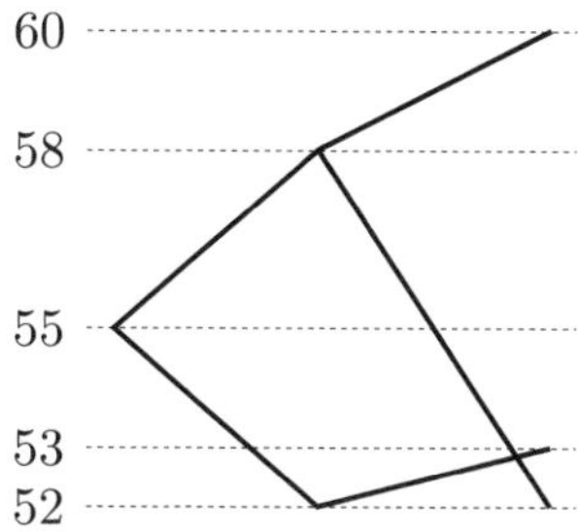


**Figure 3.1** Tree of price movements in Example 3.2

*Exercise 3.1*

Sketch a tree representing the scenarios and price movements in Example 3.1.

*Exercise 3.2*

Suppose that the stock price on any given day can either be 5% higher or 4% lower than on the previous day. Sketch a tree representing possible stock price movements over the next three days, given that the price today is \$20. How many different scenarios can be distinguished?

### 3.1.1 Return

It proves convenient to describe the dynamics of stock prices $S(n)$ in terms of returns. We assume that the stock pays no dividends.

#### Definition 3.1

The *rate of return*, or briefly the *return* $K(n,m)$ over a time interval $[n,m]$ (in fact $[m\tau, n\tau]$), is defined to be the random variable

$$K(n,m) = \frac{S(m) - S(n)}{S(n)}.$$

The return over a single time step $[n-1,n]$ will be denoted by $K(n)$, that is

$$K(n) = K(n-1,n) = \frac{S(n) - S(n-1)}{S(n-1)},$$

which implies that

$$S(n) = S(n-1)(1 + K(n)). \tag{3.1}$$

## Example 3.3

In the situation considered in Example 3.2 the returns are random variables taking the following values:

| Scenario | $K(1)$ | $K(2)$ |
|---|---|---|
| $\omega_1$ | 5.45% | 3.45% |
| $\omega_2$ | 5.45% | −10.34% |
| $\omega_3$ | −5.45% | 1.92% |

### *Exercise 3.3*

Given the following returns and assuming that $S(0) = 45$ dollars, find the possible stock prices in a three-step economy and sketch a tree of price movements:

| Scenario | $K(1)$ | $K(2)$ | $K(3)$ |
|---|---|---|---|
| $\omega_1$ | 10% | 5% | −10% |
| $\omega_2$ | 5% | 10% | 10% |
| $\omega_3$ | 5% | −10% | 10% |

## Remark 3.1

If the stock pays a dividend of $\text{div}(n)$ at time $n$, then the definition of return has to be modified. Typically, when a dividend is paid, the stock price drops by that amount. Since the right to a dividend is decided prior to the payment day, the drop of stock price is already reflected in $S(n)$. As a result, an investor who buys stock at time $n-1$ paying $S(n-1)$ and wishes to sell the stock at time $n$ will receive $S(n) + \text{div}(n)$ and the return must reflect this:

$$K(n) = \frac{S(n) - S(n-1) + \text{div}(n)}{S(n-1)}.$$

### *Exercise 3.4*

Introduce the necessary modifications in Exercise 3.3 if a dividend of \$1 is paid at the end of each time step.

It is important to understand the relationship between one-step returns and the return over a longer time interval.

## Example 3.4

Suppose that $S(0) = 100$ dollars.

1. Consider a scenario in which $S(1) = 110$ and $S(2) = 100$ dollars. In this case $K(0,2) = 0\%$, while $K(1) = 10\%$ and $K(2) \cong -9.09\%$, the sum of the one-step returns $K(1)$ and $K(2)$ being positive and greater than $K(0,2)$.
2. Consider another scenario with lower price $S(1) = 90$ dollars and with $S(2) = 100$ dollars as before. Then $K(1) = -10\%$ and $K(2) \cong 11.11\%$, their sum being once again greater than $K(0,2) = 0\%$.
3. In a scenario such that $S(1) = 110$ and $S(2) = 121$ dollars we have $K(0,2) = 21\%$, which is greater than $K(1) + K(2) = 10\% + 10\% = 20\%$.

### *Exercise 3.5*

Find $K(0,2)$ and $K(0,3)$ for the data in Exercise 3.3 and compare the results with the sums of one-step returns $K(1)+K(2)$ and $K(1)+K(2)+K(3)$, respectively.

## Remark 3.2

The non-additivity of returns, already observed in Chapter 2 for deterministic returns, is worth pointing out, since it is common practice to compute the average of recorded past returns as a prediction for the future. This may result in misrepresenting the information, for example, overestimating the future return if the historical prices tend to fluctuate, or underestimating if they do not.

## Proposition 3.1

The precise relationship between consecutive one-step returns and the return over the aggregate period is

$$1 + K(n,m) = (1 + K(n+1))(1 + K(n+2)) \cdots (1 + K(m)).$$

## Proof

Compare the following two formulae for $S(m)$:

$$S(m) = S(n)(1 + K(n,m))$$

and

$$S(m) = S(n)(1 + K(n+1))(1 + K(n+2)) \cdots (1 + K(m)).$$

Both of them follow from Definition 3.1. □

### Exercise 3.6

In each of the following three scenarios find the one-step returns, assuming that $K(1) = K(2)$:

| Scenario | $S(0)$ | $S(2)$ |
|---|---|---|
| $\omega_1$ | 35 | 41 |
| $\omega_2$ | 35 | 32 |
| $\omega_3$ | 35 | 28 |

### Exercise 3.7

Given that $K(1) = 10\%$ or $-10\%$, and $K(0,2) = 21\%$, $10\%$ or $-1\%$, find a possible structure of scenarios such that $K(2)$ takes at most two different values.

The lack of additivity is often an inconvenience. This can be rectified by introducing the logarithmic return on a risky security, motivated by similar considerations for risk-free assets in Chapter 2.

### Definition 3.2

The *logarithmic return* over a time interval $[n, m]$ (more precisely, $[\tau n, \tau m]$) is a random variable $k(n, m)$ defined by

$$k(n, m) = \ln \frac{S(m)}{S(n)}.$$

The one-step logarithmic return will be denoted simply by $k(n)$, that is,

$$k(n) = k(n-1, n) = \ln \frac{S(n)}{S(n-1)},$$

so that

$$S(n) = S(n-1)\mathrm{e}^{k(n)}. \tag{3.2}$$

The relationship between the return $K(m, n)$ and the logarithmic return $k(m, n)$ is obvious by comparing their definitions, namely

$$1 + K(m, n) = \mathrm{e}^{k(m,n)}.$$

Because of this we can readily switch from one return to the other.

### Remark 3.3

If the stock pays a dividend of $\mathrm{div}(n)$ at time $n$ and this is reflected in the price $S(n)$, then the following version of the logarithmic return should be used:

$$k(n) = \ln \frac{S(n) + \mathrm{div}(n)}{S(n-1)}.$$

Consecutive one-step logarithmic returns can be combined in an additive manner to find the return during the overall time period.

#### *Exercise 3.8*

For the data in Example 3.2 find the random variables $k(1)$, $k(2)$ and $k(0,2)$. Compare $k(0,2)$ with $k(1) + k(2)$.

### Proposition 3.2

If no dividends are paid, then

$$k(n,m) = k(n+1) + k(n+2) + \cdots + k(m).$$

### Proof

On the one hand,

$$S(m) = S(n)\mathrm{e}^{k(n,m)}$$

by the definition of the logarithmic return. On the other hand, using one-step logarithmic returns repeatedly, we obtain,

$$S(m) = S(n)\mathrm{e}^{k(n+1)}\mathrm{e}^{k(n+2)} \cdots \mathrm{e}^{k(m)} = S(n)\mathrm{e}^{k(n+1)+k(n+2)+\cdots+k(m)}.$$

The result follows by comparing these two expressions. □

## 3.1.2 Expected Return

Suppose that the probability distribution of the return $K$ over a certain time period is known. Then we can compute the mathematical expectation $E(K)$, called the *expected return*.

### Example 3.5

We estimate the probabilities of recession, stagnation and boom to be 1/4, 1/2, 1/4, respectively. If the predicted annual returns on some stock in these scenarios are $-6\%$, $4\%$, $30\%$, respectively, then the expected annual return is

$$-6\% \times \frac{1}{4} + 4\% \times \frac{1}{2} + 30\% \times \frac{1}{4} = 8\%.$$

### *Exercise 3.9*

With the probabilities of recession, stagnation and boom equal to $1/2$, $1/4$, $1/4$ and the predicted annual returns in the first two of these scenarios at $-5\%$ and $6\%$, respectively, find the annual return in the remaining scenario if the expected annual return is known to be $6\%$.

### *Exercise 3.10*

Suppose that the stock prices in the following three scenarios are

| Scenario | $S(0)$ | $S(1)$ | $S(2)$ |
|---|---|---|---|
| $\omega_1$ | 100 | 110 | 120 |
| $\omega_2$ | 100 | 105 | 100 |
| $\omega_3$ | 100 | 90 | 100 |

with probabilities $1/4$, $1/4$, $1/2$, respectively. Find the expected returns $E(K(1))$, $E(K(2))$ and $E(K(0,2))$. Compare $1+E(K(0,2))$ with $(1+E(K(1)))(1+E(K(2)))$.

The last exercise shows that the relation established in Proposition 3.1 does not extend to expected returns. For that we need an additional assumption.

### Proposition 3.3

If the one-step returns $K(n+1),\ldots,K(m)$ are independent, then

$$1+E(K(n,m)) = (1+E(K(n+1)))(1+E(K(n+2)))\cdots(1+E(K(m))).$$

### Proof

This is an immediate consequence of Proposition 3.1 and the fact that the expectation of a product of independent random variables is the product of expectations. (Note that if the $K(i)$ are independent, then so are the random variables $1+K(i)$ for $i=n+1,\ldots,m$.) □

*Exercise 3.11*

Suppose that the time step is taken to be three months, $\tau = 1/4$, and the quarterly returns $K(1), K(2), K(3), K(4)$ are independent and identically distributed. Find the expected quarterly return $E(K(1))$ and the expected annual return $E(K(0,4))$ if the expected return $E(K(0,3))$ over three quarters is 12%.

Remark 3.4

In the case of logarithmic returns additivity extends to expected returns, even if the one-step returns are not independent. Namely

$$E(k(n,m)) = E(k(n+1)) + E(k(n+2)) + \cdots + E(k(m)).$$

This is because the expectation of a sum of random variables is the sum of expectations.

Remark 3.5

In practice it is difficult to estimate the probabilities and returns in each scenario, needed to compute the expected return. What can readily be computed is the average return over a past period. The result can be used as an estimate for the expected future return. For example, if the stock prices on the last 10 consecutive days were \$98, \$100, \$99, \$95, \$88, \$82, \$89, \$98, \$101, \$105, then the average of the resulting nine daily returns would be about 0.77%. However, the average of the last four daily returns would be about 6.18%. (We use logarithmic returns because of their additivity.) This shows that the result may depend heavily on the choice of data. Using historical prices for prediction is a complex statistical issue belonging to *Econometrics*, which is beyond the scope of this book.

## 3.2 Binomial Tree Model

We shall discuss an extremely important model of stock prices. On the one hand, the model is easily tractable mathematically because it involves a small number of parameters and assumes an identical simple structure at each node of the tree of stock prices. On the other hand, it captures surprisingly many features of real-world markets.

The model is defined by the following conditions.

## Condition 3.1

The one-step returns $K(n)$ on stock are identically distributed independent random variables such that

$$K(n) = \begin{cases} u & \text{with probability } p, \\ d & \text{with probability } 1-p, \end{cases}$$

at each time step $n$, where $-1 < d < u$ and $0 < p < 1$.

This condition implies that the stock price $S(n)$ can move up or down by a factor $1+u$ or $1+d$ at each time step. The inequalities $-1 < d < u$ guarantee that all prices $S(n)$ will be positive if $S(0)$ is.

Let $r$ be the return on a risk-free investment over a single time step of length $\tau$.

## Condition 3.2

The one-step return $r$ on a risk-free investment is the same at each time step and

$$d < r < u.$$

The last condition describes the movements of stock prices in relation to risk-free assets such as bonds or cash held in a bank account. The inequalities $d < r < u$ are justified because of Proposition 1.1 in Chapter 1 (which will be generalised in Proposition 4.2).

Since $S(1)/S(0) = 1+K(1)$, Condition 3.1 implies that the random variable $S(1)$ can take two different values,

$$S(1) = \begin{cases} S(0)(1+u) & \text{with probability } p, \\ S(0)(1+d) & \text{with probability } 1-p. \end{cases}$$

### *Exercise 3.12*

How many different values do the random variables $S(2)$ and $S(3)$ take? What are these values and the corresponding probabilities?

The values of $S(n)$ along with the corresponding probabilities can be found for any $n$ by extending the solution to Exercise 3.12. In an $n$-step tree of stock prices each scenario (or path through the tree) with exactly $i$ upward and $n-i$ downward price movements produces the same stock price $S(0)(1+u)^i(1+$

$d)^{n-i}$ at time $n$. There are $\binom{n}{i}$ such scenarios, the probability of each equal to $p^i(1-p)^{n-i}$. As a result,

$$S(n) = S(0)(1+u)^i(1+d)^{n-i} \text{ with probability } \binom{n}{i} p^i(1-p)^{n-i} \tag{3.3}$$

for $i = 0, 1, \ldots, n$. The stock price $S(n)$ at time $n$ is a discrete random variable with $n+1$ different values. The distribution of $S(n)$ as given by (3.3) is shown in Figure 3.2 for $n = 10$, $p = 0.5$, $S(0) = 1$, $u = 0.1$ and $d = -0.1$.

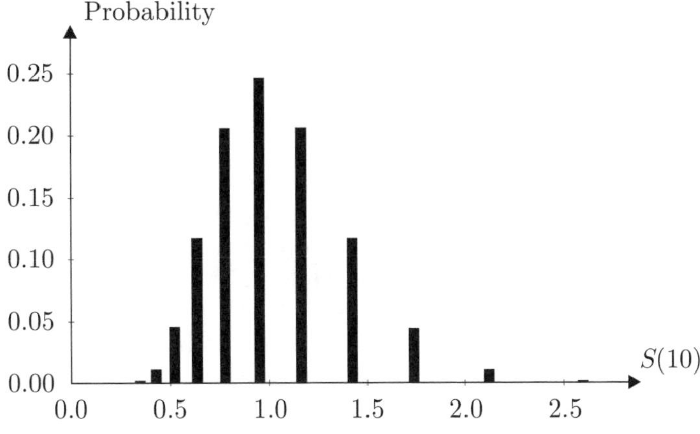


**Figure 3.2** Distribution of $S(10)$

The number $i$ of upward price movements is a random variable with a *binomial distribution*. The same is true for the number $n - i$ of downward movements. We therefore say that the price process follows a *binomial tree*. In an $n$-step binomial tree the set $\Omega$ of all scenarios, that is, $n$-step paths moving up or down at each step has $2^n$ elements. An example of a two-step binomial tree of stock prices is shown in Figure 3.3 and a three-step tree in Figure 3.4.

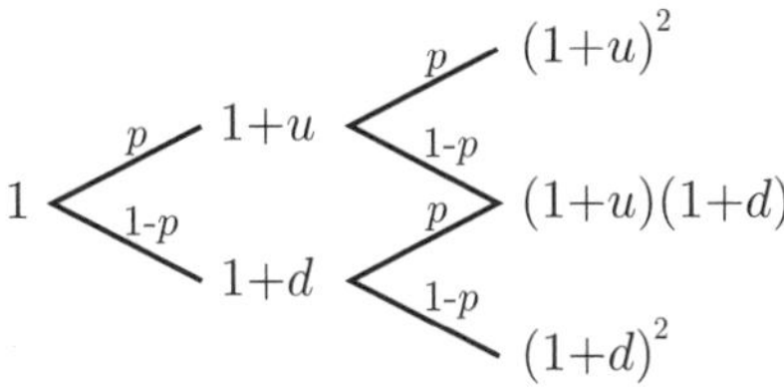


**Figure 3.3** Two-step binomial tree of stock prices

In both figures $S(0) = 1$ for simplicity.

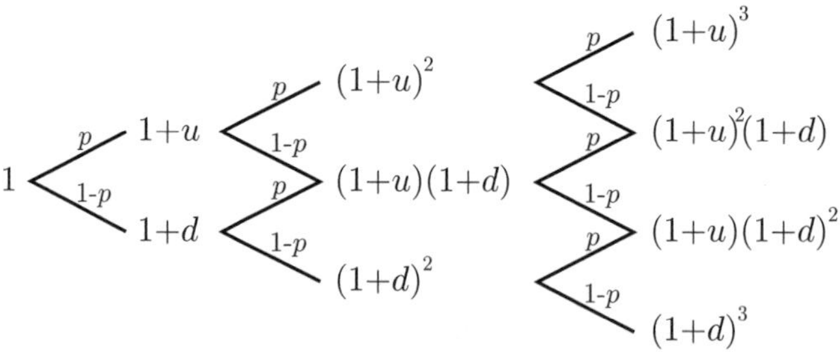


**Figure 3.4** Three-step binomial tree of stock prices

*Exercise 3.13*

Find $d$ and $u$ if $S(1)$ can take two values, \$87 or \$76, and the top possible value of $S(2)$ is \$92.

*Exercise 3.14*

Suppose that the risk-free rate under continuous compounding is 14%, the time step $\tau$ is one month, $S(0) = 22$ dollars and $d = -0.01$. Find the bounds on the middle value of $S(2)$ consistent with Condition 3.2.

*Exercise 3.15*

Suppose that \$32, \$28 and $x$ are the possible values of $S(2)$. Find $x$, assuming that stock prices follow a binomial tree. Can you complete the tree? Can this be done uniquely?

*Exercise 3.16*

Suppose that stock prices follow a binomial tree, the possible values of $S(2)$ being \$121, \$110 and \$100. Find $u$ and $d$ when $S(0) = 100$ dollars. Do the same when $S(0) = 104$ dollars.

### 3.2.1 Risk-Neutral Probability

While the future value of stock can never be known with certainty, it is possible to work out expected stock prices within the binomial tree model. It is then natural to compare these expected prices and risk-free investments. This simple idea will lead us towards powerful and surprising applications in the theory of derivative securities (for example, options, forwards, futures), to be studied in later chapters.

To begin with, we shall work out the dynamics of expected stock prices $E(S(n))$. For $n = 1$

$$E(S(1)) = pS(0)(1+u) + (1-p)S(0)(1+d) = S(0)(1+E(K(1))),$$

where

$$E(K(1)) = pu + (1-p)d$$

is the expected one-step return. This extends to any $n$ as follows.

## Proposition 3.4

The expected stock prices for $n = 0, 1, 2, \ldots$ are given by

$$E(S(n)) = S(0)(1+E(K(1)))^n.$$

## Proof

Since the one-step returns $K(1), K(2), \ldots$ are independent, so are the random variables $1+K(1), 1+K(2), \ldots$. It follows that

$$\begin{aligned} E(S(n)) &= E(S(0)(1+K(1))(1+K(2))\cdots(1+K(n))) \\ &= S(0)E(1+K(1))E(1+K(2))\cdots E(1+K(n)) \\ &= S(0)(1+E(K(1)))(1+E(K(2)))\cdots(1+E(K(n))). \end{aligned}$$

Because the $K(n)$ are identically distributed, they all have the same expectation,

$$E(K(1)) = E(K(2)) = \cdots = E(K(n)),$$

which proves the formula for $E(S(n))$. □

If the amount $S(0)$ were to be invested risk-free at time 0, it would grow to $S(0)(1+r)^n$ after $n$ steps. Clearly, to compare $E(S(n))$ and $S(0)(1+r)^n$ we only need to compare $E(K(1))$ and $r$.

An investment in stock always involves an element of risk, simply because the price $S(n)$ is unknown in advance. A typical risk-averse investor will require that $E(K(1)) > r$, arguing that he or she should be rewarded with a higher expected return as a compensation for risk. The reverse situation when $E(K(1)) < r$ may nevertheless be attractive to some investors if the risky return is high with small non-zero probability and low with large probability. (A typical example is a lottery, where the expected return is negative.) An investor of this kind can be called a risk-seeker. We shall return to this topic in Chapter 5, where a precise definition of risk will be developed. The border case of a market in which $E(K(1)) = r$ is referred to as risk-neutral.

It proves convenient to introduce a special symbol $p_*$ for the probability as well as $E_*$ for the corresponding expectation satisfying the condition

$$E_*(K(1)) = p_* u + (1 - p_*)d = r \tag{3.4}$$

for risk-neutrality, which implies that

$$p_* = \frac{r-d}{u-d}.$$

We shall call $p_*$ the *risk-neutral probability* and $E_*$ the *risk-neutral expectation.* It is important to understand that $p_*$ is an abstract mathematical object, which may or may not be equal to the actual market probability $p$. Only in a risk-neutral market do we have $p = p_*$. Even though the risk-neutral probability $p_*$ may have no relation to the actual probability $p$, it turns out that for the purpose of valuation of derivative securities the relevant probability is $p_*$, rather than $p$. This application of the risk-neutral probability, which is of great practical importance, will be discussed in detail in Chapter 8.

### *Exercise 3.17*

Let $u = 2/10$ and $r = 1/10$. Investigate the properties of $p_*$ as a function of $d$.

### *Exercise 3.18*

Show that $d < r < u$ if and only if $0 < p_* < 1$.

Condition (3.4) implies that

$$p_*(u - r) + (1 - p_*)(d - r) = 0.$$

Geometrically, this means that the pair $(p_*, 1 - p_*)$ regarded as a vector on the plane $\mathbb{R}^2$ is orthogonal to the vector with coordinates $(u - r, d - r)$, which represents the possible one-step gains (or losses) of an investor holding a single share of stock, the purchase of which was financed by a cash loan attracting interest at a rate $r$, see Figure 3.5. The line joining the points $(1, 0)$ and $(0, 1)$ consists of all points with coordinates $(p, 1 - p)$, where $0 < p < 1$. One of these points corresponds to the actual market probability and one to the risk-neutral probability.

Another interpretation of condition (3.4) for the risk-neutral probability is illustrated in Figure 3.6. If masses $p_*$ and $1 - p_*$ are attached at the points with coordinates $u$ and $d$ on the real axis, then the centre of mass will be at $r$.

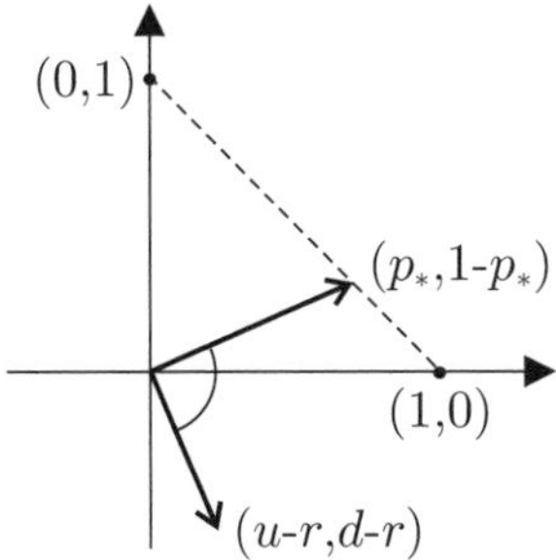


**Figure 3.5** Geometric interpretation of risk-neutral probability $p_*$

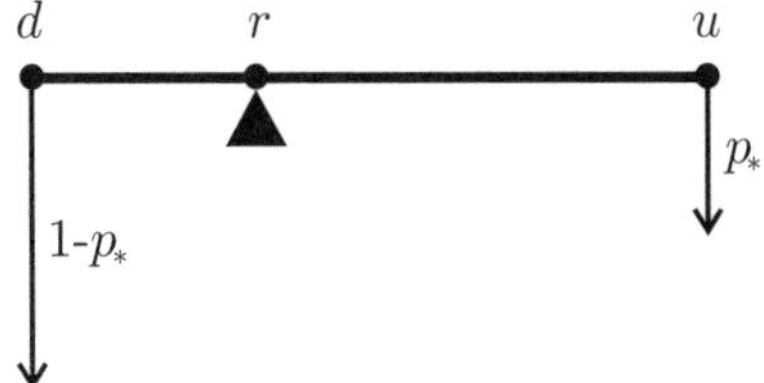


**Figure 3.6** Barycentric interpretation of risk-neutral probability $p_*$

### 3.2.2 Martingale Property

By Proposition 3.4 the expectation of $S(n)$ with respect to the risk-neutral probability $p_*$ is

$$E_*(S(n)) = S(0)(1+r)^n, \tag{3.5}$$

since $r = E_*(K(1))$.

#### Example 3.6

Consider a two-step binomial tree model such that $S(0) = 100$ dollars, $u = 0.2$, $d = -0.1$ and $r = 0.1$. Then $p_* = 2/3$ is the risk-neutral probability, and the expected stock price after two steps is

$$E_*(S(2)) = S(0)(1+r)^2 = 121$$

dollars. After one time step, once it becomes known whether the stock price has gone up or down, we shall need to recompute the expectation of $S(2)$. Suppose that the stock price has gone up to \$120 after the first step. In these circumstances the set of possible scenarios reduces to those for which $S(1) = 120$ dollars, and the tree of stock prices reduces to the subtree in Figure 3.7. Given that $S(1) = 120$ dollars, the risk-neutral expectation of $S(2)$ will therefore be

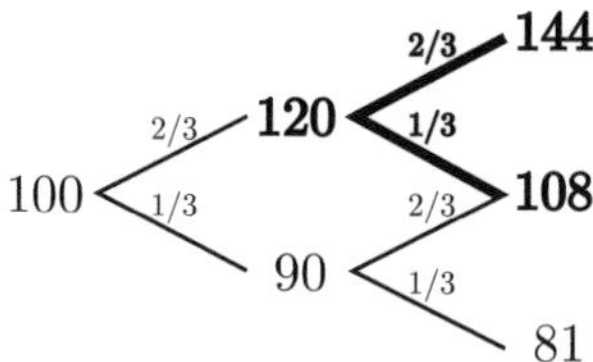


**Figure 3.7** Subtree such that $S(1) = 120$ dollars

$\frac{2}{3} \times 144 + \frac{1}{3} \times 108 = 132$ dollars, which is equal to $120(1+r)$. Formally, this can be written using the conditional expectation[1] of $S(2)$ given that $S(1) = 120$,

$$E_*(S(2)|S(1) = 120) = 120(1 + r).$$

Similarly, if the stock price drops to \$90 after one time step, the set of possible scenarios will reduce to those for which $S(1) = 90$ dollars, and the tree of stock prices will reduce to the subtree in Figure 3.8. Given that $S(1) = 90$ dollars,

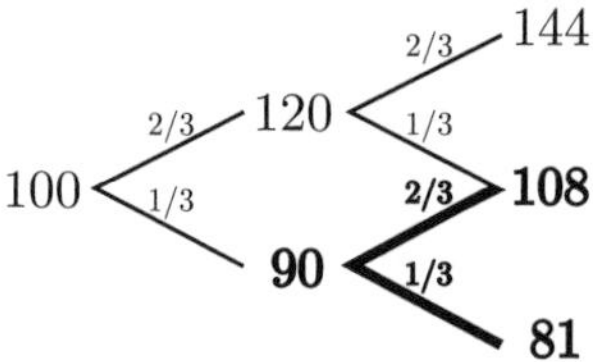


**Figure 3.8** Subtree such that $S(1) = 90$ dollars

the risk-neutral expectation of $S(2)$ will be $\frac{2}{3} \times 108 + \frac{1}{3} \times 81 = 99$ dollars, which is equal to $90(1 + r)$. This can be written as

$$E_*(S(2)|S(1) = 90) = 90(1 + r).$$

The last two formulae involving conditional expectation can be written as a single equality, properly understood:

$$E_*(S(2)|S(1)) = S(1)(1 + r).$$

This analysis can be extended to any time step in the binomial tree model. Suppose that $n$ time steps have passed and the stock price has become $S(n)$. What is the risk-neutral expectation of the price $S(n+1)$ after one more step?

[1] The conditional expectation of a random variable $\xi$ given an event $A$ such that $P(A) \neq 0$ is defined by $E(\xi|A) = E(\xi 1_A)/P(A)$, where $1_A$ is the indicator random variable, equal to 1 on $A$ and 0 on the complement of $A$.

### Proposition 3.5

Given that the stock price $S(n)$ has become known at time $n$, the risk-neutral conditional expectation of $S(n+1)$ will be

$$E_*(S(n+1)|S(n)) = S(n)(1+r).$$

### Proof

Suppose that $S(n) = x$ after $n$ time steps. Then

$$E_*(S(n+1)|S(n) = x) = p_* x(1+u) + (1-p_*)x(1+d)$$

because $S(n+1)$ takes the value $x(1+u)$ with probability $p_*$ and $x(1+d)$ with probability $1-p_*$. But $p_*(1+u)+(1-p_*)(1+d) = 1+r$ by (3.4), which implies that

$$E_*(S(n+1)|S(n) = x) = x(1+r)$$

for any possible value $x$ of $S(n)$, completing the proof. □

Dividing both sides of the equality in Proposition 3.5 by $(1+r)^{n+1}$, we obtain the following important result for the *discounted stock prices* $\widetilde{S}(n) = S(n)\,(1+r)^{-n}$.

### Corollary 3.6 (Martingale Property)

For any $n = 0, 1, 2, \ldots$

$$E_*(\widetilde{S}(n+1)|S(n)) = \widetilde{S}(n).$$

We say that the discounted stock prices $\widetilde{S}(n)$ form a *martingale* under the risk-neutral probability $p_*$. The probability $p_*$ itself is also referred to as the *martingale probability*.

#### *Exercise 3.19*

Let $r = 0.2$. Find the risk-neutral conditional expectation of $S(3)$ given that $S(2) = 110$ dollars.

## 3.3 Other Models

This section may be skipped at first reading because the main ideas to follow later do not depend on the models presented here.

### 3.3.1 Trinomial Tree Model

A natural generalisation of the binomial tree model extends the range of possible values of the one-step returns $K(n)$ to three. The idea is to allow the price not only to move up or down, but also to take an intermediate value at any given step.

#### Condition 3.3

The one-step returns $K(n)$ are independent random variables of the form

$$K(n) = \begin{cases} u & \text{with probability } p, \\ n & \text{with probability } q, \\ d & \text{with probability } 1-p-q, \end{cases}$$

where $d < n < u$ and $0 < p, q, p+q < 1$.

This means that $u$ and $d$ represent upward and downward price movements, as before, whereas $n$ stands for the middle price movement, typically a neutral one, $n = 0$.

#### Condition 3.4

The one-step return $r$ on a risk-free investment is the same at each time step and

$$d < r < u.$$

Since $S(1)/S(0) = 1 + K(1)$, Condition 3.3 implies that $S(1)$ takes three different values,

$$S(1) = \begin{cases} S(0)(1+u) & \text{with probability } p, \\ S(0)(1+n) & \text{with probability } q, \\ S(0)(1+d) & \text{with probability } 1-p-q. \end{cases}$$

*Exercise 3.20*

How many different values does the random variable $S(2)$ take? What are these values and the corresponding probabilities?

The condition $E_*(K(n)) = r$ for risk-neutral probabilities $p_*, q_*$ can be written as

$$p_*(u-r) + q_*(n-r) + (1-p_*-q_*)(d-r) = 0. \tag{3.6}$$

The triple $(p_*, q_*, 1 - p_* - q_*)$ regarded as a vector in $\mathbb{R}^3$ is orthogonal to the vector with coordinates $(u - r, n - r, d - r)$ representing the possible one-step gains (or losses) of an investor holding a singe share of stock, the purchase of which was financed by a cash loan. This means that $(p_*, q_*, 1 - p_* - q_*)$ lies on the intersection of the triangle $\{(a, b, c) : a, b, c \geq 0, a+b+c = 1\}$ and the plane orthogonal to the gains vector $(u-r, n-r, d-r)$, as in Figure 3.9. Condition 3.4

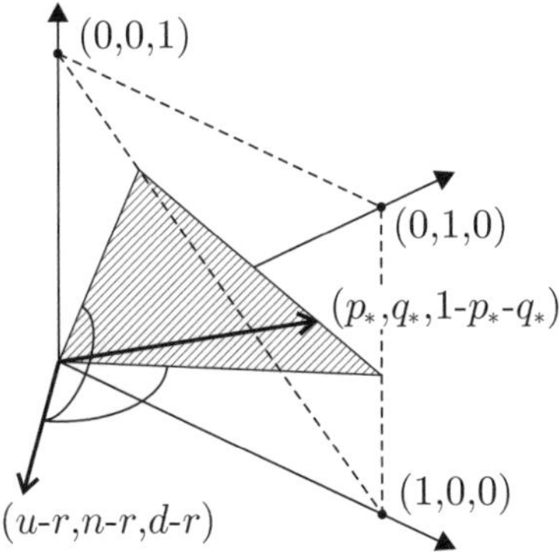


**Figure 3.9** Geometric interpretation of risk-neutral probabilities $p_*, q_*$

guarantees that the intersection is non-empty, since the line containing the vector $(u - r, n - r, d - r)$ does not pass through the positive octant. In this case there are infinitely many risk-neutral probabilities, the intersection being a line segment.

Another interpretation of condition (3.6) for the risk-neutral probability is illustrated in Figure 3.10. If masses $p_*$, $q_*$ and $1 - p_* - q_*$ are attached at the points with coordinates $u$, $n$ and $d$ on the real axis, then the centre of mass will be at $r$.

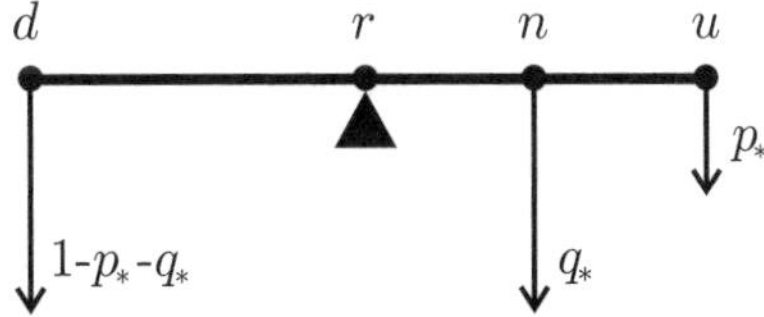


**Figure 3.10** Barycentric interpretation of risk-neutral probabilities $p_*, q_*$

### *Exercise 3.21*

Let $u = 0.2$, $n = 0$, $d = -0.1$, and $r = 0$. Find all risk-neutral probabilities.

## 3.3.2 Continuous-Time Limit

Discrete-time and discrete-price models have apparent disadvantages. They clearly restrict the range of asset price movements as well as the set of time instants at which these movements may occur. In this section we shall outline an approach free from such restrictions. It will be obtained by passing to the continuous-time limit from the binomial tree model.

We shall consider a sequence of binomial tree models with time step $\tau = \frac{1}{N}$, letting $N \to \infty$. For all binomial tree models in the approximating sequence it will be assumed that the probability of upward and downward price movements is $\frac{1}{2}$ in each step.

In this context it proves convenient to use the logarithmic return

$$k(n) = \ln(1 + K(n)) = \begin{cases} \ln(1+u) & \text{with probability } 1/2, \\ \ln(1+d) & \text{with probability } 1/2. \end{cases}$$

In place of the risk-free rate of return over one time step, we shall use the equivalent continuous compounding rate $r$, so that the return over a time step of length $\tau$ will be $e^{\tau r}$.

We denote by $m$ the expectation and by $\sigma$ the standard deviation of the logarithmic return $k(1)+k(2)+\cdots+k(N)$ over the unit time interval from 0 to 1, consisting of $N$ steps of lengt $\tau$. The logarithmic returns $k(1), k(2), \ldots, k(N)$ are identically distributed and independent, just as $K(1), K(2), \ldots, K(N)$ are. It follows that

$$\begin{aligned} m &= E\left(k(1) + k(2) + \cdots + k(N)\right) \\ &= E(k(1)) + E(k(2)) + \cdots + E(k(N)) = NE(k(n)), \\ \sigma^2 &= \operatorname{Var}\left(k(1) + k(2) + \cdots + k(N)\right) \\ &= \operatorname{Var}\left(k(1)\right) + \operatorname{Var}\left(k(2)\right) + \cdots + \operatorname{Var}\left(k(N)\right) = N\operatorname{Var}\left(k(n)\right) \end{aligned}$$

for each $n = 1, 2, \ldots, N$. This means that each $k(n)$ has expectation $\frac{m}{N} = m\tau$ and standard deviation $\sqrt{\frac{\sigma^2}{N}} = \sigma\sqrt{\tau}$, so the two possible values of each $k(n)$ must be

$$\begin{aligned} \ln(1+u) &= m\tau + \sigma\sqrt{\tau}, \\ \ln(1+d) &= m\tau - \sigma\sqrt{\tau}. \end{aligned} \tag{3.7}$$

*Exercise 3.22*

Find $m$ and $\sigma$ for $u = 0.02$, $d = -0.01$ and $\tau = 1/12$.

Introducing a sequence of independent random variables $\xi(n)$, each with two values

$$\xi(n) = \begin{cases} +\sqrt{\tau} & \text{with probability } 1/2, \\ -\sqrt{\tau} & \text{with probability } 1/2, \end{cases}$$

we can write the logarithmic return as

$$k(n) = m\tau + \sigma\xi(n).$$

*Exercise 3.23*

Find the expectation and variance of $\xi(n)$ and $k(n)$.

*Exercise 3.24*

Write $S(1)$ and $S(2)$ in terms of $m$, $\sigma$, $\tau$, $\xi(1)$ and $\xi(2)$.

Next, we introduce an important sequence of random variables $w(n)$, called a *symmetric random walk*, such that

$$w(n) = \xi(1) + \xi(2) + \cdots + \xi(n),$$

and $w(0) = 0$. Clearly, $\xi(n) = w(n) - w(n-1)$. Because of the last equality, the $\xi(n)$ are referred to as the increments of $w(n)$.

From now on we shall often write $S(t)$ and $w(t)$ instead of $S(n)$ and $w(n)$ for $t = \tau n$, where $n = 1, 2, \ldots$ .

## Proposition 3.7

The stock price at time $t = \tau n$ is given by

$$S(t) = S(0)\exp(mt + \sigma w(t)).$$

## Proof

By (3.2)

$$\begin{aligned} S(t) &= S(n\tau) = S(n\tau - \tau)\mathrm{e}^{k(n)} \\ &= S(n\tau - 2\tau)\mathrm{e}^{k(n-1)+k(n)} \\ &= \cdots = S(0)\mathrm{e}^{k(1)+\cdots+k(n)} \\ &= S(0)\mathrm{e}^{mn\tau+\sigma(\xi(1)+\cdots+\xi(n))} \\ &= S(0)\mathrm{e}^{mt+\sigma w(t)}, \end{aligned}$$

as required. □

In order to pass to the continuous-time limit we use the approximation

$$e^x \approx 1 + x + \frac{1}{2}x^2,$$

accurate for small values of $x$, to obtain

$$\frac{S(n\tau+\tau)}{S(n\tau)} = e^{k(n+1)} \approx 1 + k(n+1) + \frac{1}{2}k(n+1)^2.$$

Then, we compute

$$k(n+1)^2 = (m\tau + \sigma\xi(n+1))^2 = \sigma^2\tau + \cdots ,$$

where the dots represent all terms with powers of $\tau$ higher than 1, which will be omitted because they are much smaller than the leading term whenever $\tau$ is small. Next,

$$\begin{aligned}\frac{S(n\tau+\tau)}{S(n\tau)} &\approx 1 + m\tau + \sigma\xi(n+1) + \frac{1}{2}\sigma^2\tau \\ &= 1 + \left(m + \frac{1}{2}\sigma^2\right)\tau + \sigma\xi(n+1),\end{aligned}$$

and so

$$S(n\tau+\tau) - S(n\tau) \approx \left(m + \frac{1}{2}\sigma^2\right) S(n\tau)\tau + \sigma S(n\tau)\xi(n+1).$$

Since $\xi(n+1) = w(n\tau+\tau) - w(n\tau)$, we obtain an approximate equation describing the dynamics of stock prices:

$$S(t+\tau) - S(t) \approx \left(m + \frac{1}{2}\sigma^2\right) S(t)\tau + \sigma S(t)(w(t+\tau) - w(t)), \tag{3.8}$$

where $t = n\tau$. The solution $S(t)$ of this approximate equation is given by the same formula as in Proposition 3.7.

For any $N = 1, 2, \ldots$ we consider a binomial tree model with time step of length $\tau = \frac{1}{N}$. Let $S_N(t)$ be the corresponding stock prices and let $w_N(t)$ be the corresponding symmetric random walk with increments $\xi_N(t) = w_N(t) - w_N(t - \frac{1}{N})$, where $t = \frac{n}{N}$ is the time after $n$ steps.

### *Exercise 3.25*

Compute the expectation and variance of $w_N(t)$, where $t = \frac{n}{N}$.

We shall use the Central Limit Theorem[2] to obtain the limit as $N \to \infty$ of the random walk $w_N(t)$. To this end we put

$$x(n) = \frac{k(n) - m\tau}{\sigma\sqrt{\tau}}$$

for each $n = 1, 2, \ldots$, which is a sequence of independent identically distributed random variables, each with expectation 0 and variance 1. The Central Limit Theorem implies that

$$\frac{x(1) + x(2) + \cdots + x(n)}{\sqrt{n}} \to X$$

in distribution as $n \to \infty$, where $X$ is a random variable with standard normal distribution (mean 0 and variance 1).

Let us fix any $t > 0$. Because the random walk $w_N$ is only defined at discrete times being whole multiples of the step $\tau = \frac{1}{N}$, we consider $w_N(t_N)$, where $t_N$ is the whole multiple of $\frac{1}{N}$ nearest to $t$. Then, clearly, $Nt_N$ is a whole number for each $N$, and we can write

$$w_N(t_N) = \sqrt{t_N}\,\frac{x(1) + x(2) + \cdots + x(Nt_N)}{\sqrt{Nt_N}}.$$

As $N \to \infty$, we have $t_N \to t$ and $Nt_N \to \infty$, so that

$$w_N(t_N) \to W(t)$$

in distribution, where $W(t) = \sqrt{t}X$. The last equality means that $W(t)$ is normally distributed with mean 0 and variance $t$.

This argument, based on the Central Limit Theorem, works for any single fixed time $t > 0$. It is possible to extend the result to obtain a limit for all times $t \geq 0$ *simultaneously*, but this is beyond the scope of this book. The limit $W(t)$ is called the *Wiener process* (or *Brownian motion*). It inherits many of the properties of the random walk, for example:

1. $W(0) = 0$, which corresponds to $w_N(0) = 0$.
2. $E(W(t)) = 0$, corresponding to $E(w_N(t)) = 0$ (see the solution of Exercise 3.25).
3. $\operatorname{Var}(W(t)) = t$, with the discrete counterpart $\operatorname{Var}(w_N(t)) = t$ (see the solution of Exercise 3.25).
4. The increments $W(t_3) - W(t_2)$ and $W(t_2) - W(t_1)$ are independent for $0 \leq t_1 \leq t_2 \leq t_3$; so are the increments $w_N(t_3) - w_N(t_2)$ and $w_N(t_2) - w_N(t_1)$.

[2] See, for example, Capiński and Zastawniak (2001).

5. $W(t)$ has a normal distribution with mean 0 and variance $t$, that is, with density $\frac{1}{\sqrt{2\pi t}}\mathrm{e}^{-\frac{x^2}{2t}}$. This is related to the distribution of $w_N(t)$. The latter is not normal, but approaches the normal distribution in the limit according to the Central Limit Theorem.

An important difference between $W(t)$ and $w_N(t)$ is that $W(t)$ is defined for all $t \geq 0$, whereas the time in $w_N(t)$ is discrete, $t = n/N$ for $n = 0, 1, 2, \ldots$ .

The price process obtained in the limit from $S_N(t)$ as $N \to \infty$ will be denoted by $S(t)$. While $S_N(t)$ satisfies the approximate equation (3.8) with the appropriate substitutions, namely

$$S_N(t+\frac{1}{N}) - S_N(t) \approx \left(m + \frac{1}{2}\sigma^2\right) S_N(t)\frac{1}{N} + \sigma S_N(t)(w_N(t+\frac{1}{N}) - w_N(t)),$$

the continuous-time stock prices $S(t)$ satisfy an equation of the form

$$\mathrm{d}S(t) = \left(m + \frac{1}{2}\sigma^2\right) S(t)\mathrm{d}t + \sigma S(t)\mathrm{d}W(t). \tag{3.9}$$

Here $\mathrm{d}S(t) = S(t+\mathrm{d}t) - S(t)$ and $\mathrm{d}W(t) = W(t+\mathrm{d}t) - W(t)$ are the increments of $S(t)$ and $W(t)$ over an infinitesimal time interval $\mathrm{d}t$. The explicit formulae for the solutions are also similar,

$$S_N(t) = S_N(0)\exp(mt + \sigma w_N(t))$$

in the discrete case, whereas

$$S(t) = S(0)\exp(mt + \sigma W(t))$$

in the continuous case.

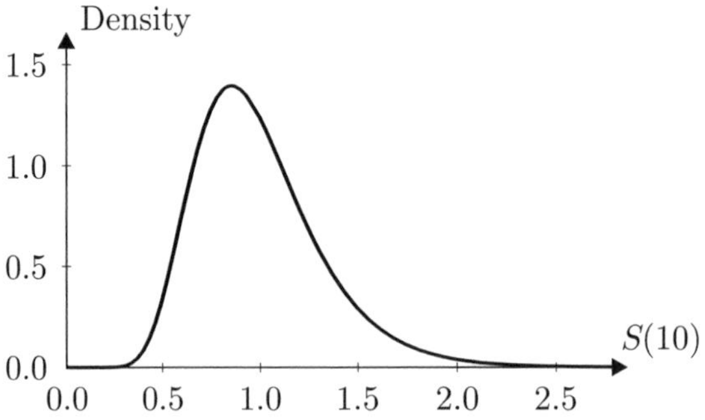


**Figure 3.11** Density of the distribution of $S(10)$

Since $W(t)$ has a normal distribution with mean 0 and variance $t$, it follows that $\ln S(t)$ has a normal distribution with mean $\ln S(0) + mt$ and variance $\sigma^2 t$. Because of this it is said that the continuous-time price process $S(t)$ has the *log normal distribution*. The number $\sigma$ is called the *volatility* of the price $S(t)$. The density of the distribution of $S(t)$ is shown in Figure 3.11 for $t = 10$, $S(0) = 1$, $m = 0$ and $\sigma = 0.1$. This can be compared with the discrete distribution in Figure 3.2.

## Remark 3.6

Equation (3.9) and the increments $\mathrm{d}S(t)$, $\mathrm{d}W(t)$ and $\mathrm{d}t$ are introduced above only informally by analogy with the discrete case. They can be given a precise status in *Stochastic Calculus*, a theory with fundamental applications in advanced mathematical finance. In particular, (3.9) is an example of what is known as a *stochastic differential equation*.

# 4 Discrete Time Market Models

Having discussed a number of different models of stock price dynamics, we shall now generalise and pursue a little further some of the ideas introduced in Chapter 1. In particular, we shall reformulate and extend the general notions and assumptions underlying mathematical finance already mentioned in that chapter.

As in Chapter 3, we assume that time runs in steps of fixed length $\tau$. For many time-dependent quantities we shall simplify the notation by writing $n$ in place of the time $t = n\tau$ of the $n$th step.

## 4.1 Stock and Money Market Models

Suppose that $m$ risky assets are traded. These will be referred to as stocks. Their prices at time $n = 0, 1, 2, \ldots$ are denoted by $S_1(n), \ldots, S_m(n)$. In addition, investors have at their disposal a risk-free asset, that is, an investment in the money market. Unless stated otherwise, we take the initial level of the risk-free investment to be one unit of the home currency, $A(0) = 1$. However, in some numerical examples and exercises we shall often take $A(0) = 100$ for convenience. Because the money market account can be manufactured using bonds (see Chapter 2), we shall frequently refer to a risk-free investment as a position in bonds, finding it convenient to think of $A(n)$ as the bond price at time $n$.

The risky positions in assets number $1, \ldots, m$ will be denoted by $x_1, \ldots, x_m$, respectively, and the risk-free position by $y$. The wealth of an investor holding such positions at time $n$ will be

$$V(n) = \sum_{j=1}^{m} x_j S_j(n) + yA(n). \tag{4.1}$$

Assumptions 1.1 to 1.5 of Chapter 1 can readily be adapted to this general setting. The motivation and interpretation of these assumptions are the same as in Chapter 1, with the natural changes from one to several time steps and from one to several risky assets.

### Assumption 4.1 (Randomness)

The future stock prices $S_1(n), \ldots, S_m(n)$ are random variables for any $n = 1, 2, \ldots$. The future prices $A(n)$ of the risk-free security for any $n = 1, 2, \ldots$ are known numbers.

### Assumption 4.2 (Positivity of Prices)

All stock and bond prices are strictly positive,

$$S(n) > 0 \quad \text{and} \quad A(n) > 0 \quad \text{for } n = 0, 1, 2, \ldots .$$

### Assumption 4.3 (Divisibility, Liquidity and Short Selling)

An investor may buy, sell and hold any number $x_k$ of stock shares of each kind $k = 1, \ldots, m$ and take any risk-free position $y$, whether integer or fractional, negative, positive or zero. In general,

$$x_1, \ldots, x_m, y \in \mathbb{R}.$$

### Assumption 4.4 (Solvency)

The wealth of an investor must be non-negative at all times,

$$V(n) \geq 0 \quad \text{for } n = 0, 1, 2, \ldots .$$

### Assumption 4.5 (Discrete Unit Prices)

For each $n = 0, 1, 2, \ldots$ the share prices $S_1(n), \ldots, S_m(n)$ are random variables taking only finitely many values.

### 4.1.1 Investment Strategies

The positions held by an investor in the risky and risk-free assets can be altered at any time step by selling some assets and investing the proceeds in other assets. In real life cash can be taken out of the portfolio for consumption or injected from other sources. Nevertheless, we shall assume that no consumption or injection of funds takes place in our models to keep things as simple as possible.

Decisions made by any investor of when to alter his or her portfolio and how many assets to buy or sell are based on the information currently available. We are going to exclude the unlikely possibility that investors could foresee the future, as well as the somewhat more likely (but illegal) one that they will act on insider information. However, all the historical information about the market up to and including the time instant when a particular trading decision is executed will be freely available.

#### Example 4.1

Let $m = 2$ and suppose that

$$\begin{array}{lll} S_1(0) = \ 60, & S_1(1) = \ 65, & S_1(2) = \ 75, \\ S_2(0) = \ 20, & S_2(1) = \ 15, & S_2(2) = \ 25, \\ A(0) = 100, & A(1) = 110, & A(2) = 121, \end{array}$$

in a certain market scenario. At time 0 initial wealth $V(0) = 3,000$ dollars is invested in a portfolio consisting of $x_1(1) = 20$ shares of stock number one, $x_2(1) = 65$ shares of stock number two, and $y(1) = 5$ bonds. Our notational convention is to use 1 rather than 0 as the argument in $x_1(1)$, $x_2(1)$ and $y(1)$ to reflect the fact that this portfolio will be held over the first time step. At time 1 this portfolio will be worth $V(1) = 20 \times 65 + 65 \times 15 + 5 \times 110 = 2,825$ dollars. At that time the number of assets can be altered by buying or selling some of them, as long as the total value remains $\$2,825$. For example, we could form a new portfolio consisting of $x_1(2) = 15$ shares of stock one, $x_2(2) = 94$ shares of stock two, and $y(2) = 4$ bonds, which will be held during the second time step. The value of this portfolio will be $V(2) = 15 \times 75 + 94 \times 25 + 4 \times 121 = 3,959$ dollars at time 2, when the positions in stocks and bonds can be adjusted once again, as long as the total value remains $\$3,959$, and so on. However, if no adjustments are made to the original portfolio, then it will be worth $\$2,825$ at time 1 and $\$3,730$ at time 2.

## Definition 4.1

A *portfolio* is a vector $(x_1(n), \ldots, x_m(n), y(n))$ indicating the number of shares and bonds held by an investor between times $n-1$ and $n$. A sequence of portfolios indexed by $n = 1, 2, \ldots$ is called an *investment strategy*. The *wealth* of an investor or the *value of the strategy* at time $n \geq 1$ is

$$V(n) = \sum_{j=1}^{m} x_j(n)S_j(n) + y(n)A(n).$$

At time $n = 0$ the *initial wealth* is given by

$$V(0) = \sum_{j=1}^{m} x_j(1)S_j(0) + y(1)A(0).$$

We have seen in Example 4.1 that the contents of a portfolio can be adjusted by buying or selling some assets at any time step, as long as the current value of the portfolio remains unaltered.

## Definition 4.2

An investment strategy is called *self-financing* if the portfolio constructed at time $n \geq 1$ to be held over the next time step $n+1$ is financed entirely by the current wealth $V(n)$, that is,

$$\sum_{j=1}^{m} x_j(n+1)S_j(n) + y(n+1)A(n) = V(n). \tag{4.2}$$

## Example 4.2

Let the stock and bond prices be as in Example 4.1. Suppose that an initial wealth of $V(0) = 3,000$ dollars is invested by purchasing $x_1(1) = 18.22$ shares of the first stock, short selling $x_2(1) = -16.81$ shares of the second stock, and buying $y(1) = 22.43$ bonds. The time 1 value of this portfolio will be $V(1) = 18.22 \times 65 - 16.81 \times 15 + 22.43 \times 110 = 3,399.45$ dollars. The investor will benefit from the drop of the price of the shorted stock. This example illustrates the fact that portfolios containing fractional or negative numbers of assets are allowed.

We do not impose any restrictions on the numbers $x_1(n), \ldots, x_m(n), y(n)$. The fact that they can take non-integer values is referred to as *divisibility*. Negative $x_j(n)$ means that stock number $j$ is *sold short* (in other words, a short position is taken in stock $j$), negative $y(n)$ corresponds to borrowing cash (taking a short position in the money market, for example, by issuing and selling a bond). The absence of any bounds on the size of these numbers means that the market is *liquid*, that is, any number of assets of each type can be purchased or sold at any time.

In practice some security measures to control short selling may be implemented by stock exchanges. Typically, investors are required to pay a certain percentage of the short sale as a security deposit to cover possible losses. If their losses exceed the deposit, the position must be closed. The deposit creates a burden on the portfolio, particularly if it earns no interest for the investor. However, restrictions of this kind may not concern dealers who work for major financial institutions holding large numbers of shares deposited by smaller investors. These shares may be borrowed internally in lieu of short selling.

## Example 4.3

We continue assuming that stock prices follow the scenario in Example 4.1. Suppose that 20 shares of the first stock are sold short, $x_1(1) = -20$. The investor will receive $20 \times 60 = 1,200$ dollars in cash, but has to pay a security deposit of, say 50%, that is, \$600. One time step later she will suffer a loss of $20 \times 65 - 1,200 = 100$ dollars. This is subtracted from the deposit and the position can be closed by withdrawing the balance of $600 - 100 = 400$ dollars. On the other hand, if 60 shares of the second stock are shorted, that is, $x_2(1) = -60$, then the investor will make a profit of $1,200 - 60 \times 15 = 300$ dollars after one time step. The position can be closed with final wealth $600 + 300 = 900$ dollars. In both cases the final balance should be reduced by $600 \times 0.1 = 60$ dollars, the interest that would have been earned on the amount deposited, had it been invested in the money market.

An investor constructing a portfolio at time $n$ has no knowledge of future stock prices. In particular, no insider dealing is allowed. Investment decisions can be based only on the performance of the market to date. This is reflected in the following definition.

## Definition 4.3

An investment strategy is called *predictable* if for each $n = 0, 1, 2, \ldots$ the portfolio $(x_1(n+1), \ldots, x_m(n+1), y(n+1))$ constructed at time $n$ depends only on the nodes of the tree of market scenarios reached up to and including time $n$.

The next proposition shows that the position taken in the risk-free asset is always determined by the current wealth and the positions in risky assets.

## Proposition 4.1

Given the initial wealth $V(0)$ and a predictable sequence $(x_1(n),\ldots,x_m(n))$, $n=1,2,\ldots$ of positions in risky assets, it is always possible to find a sequence $y(n)$ of risk-free positions such that $(x_1(n),\ldots,x_m(n),y(n))$ is a predictable self-financing investment strategy.

## Proof

Put

$$y(1)=\frac{V(0)-x_1(1)S_1(0)-\cdots-x_m(1)S_m(0)}{A(0)}$$

and then compute

$$V(1)=x_1(1)S_1(1)+\cdots+x_m(1)S_m(1)+y(1)A(1).$$

Next,

$$\begin{aligned}y(2)&=\frac{V(1)-x_1(2)S_1(1)-\cdots-x_m(2)S_m(1)}{A(1)},\\ V(2)&=x_1(2)S_1(2)+\cdots+x_m(2)S_m(2)+y(2)A(2),\end{aligned}$$

and so on. This clearly defines a self-financing strategy. The strategy is predictable because $y(n+1)$ can be expressed in terms of stock and bond prices up to time $n$. □

### *Exercise 4.1*

Find the number of bonds $y(1)$ and $y(2)$ held by an investor during the first and second steps of a predictable self-financing investment strategy with initial value $V(0)=200$ dollars and risky asset positions

$$\begin{aligned}x_1(1)&=35.24, & x_1(2)&=-40.50,\\ x_2(1)&=24.18, & x_2(2)&=\phantom{-}10.13,\end{aligned}$$

if the prices of assets follow the scenario in Example 4.1. Also find the time 1 value $V(1)$ and time 2 value $V(2)$ of this strategy.

## Example 4.4

Once again, suppose that the stock and bond prices follow the scenario in Example 4.1. If an amount $V(0)=100$ dollars were invested in a portfolio with

$x_1(1) = -12$, $x_2(1) = 31$ and $y(1) = 2$, then it would lead to insolvency, since the time 1 value of this portfolio is negative, $V(1) = -12\times 65+31\times 15+2\times 110 = -95$ dollars .

Such a portfolio, which is excluded by Assumption 4.4, would be impossible to construct in practice. No short position will be allowed unless it can be closed at any time and in any scenario (if necessary, by selling other assets in the portfolio to raise cash). This means that the wealth of an investor must be non-negative at all times.

### Definition 4.4

A strategy is called *admissible* if it is self-financing, predictable, and for each $n = 0, 1, 2, \ldots$

$$V(n) \geq 0$$

with probability 1.

#### *Exercise 4.2*

Consider a market consisting of one risk-free asset with $A(0) = 10$ and $A(1) = 11$ dollars, and one risky asset such that $S(0) = 10$ and $S(1) = 13$ or 9 dollars. On the $x, y$ plane draw the set of all portfolios $(x, y)$ such that the one-step strategy involving risky position $x$ and risk-free position $y$ is admissible.

## 4.1.2 The Principle of No Arbitrage

We are ready to formulate the fundamental principle underlying all mathematical models in finance. It generalises the simplified one-step version of the No-Arbitrage Principle in Chapter 1 to models with several time steps and several risky assets. Whereas the notion of a portfolio is sufficient to state the one-step version, in the general setting we need to use a sequence of portfolios forming an admissible investment strategy. This is because investors can adjust their positions at each time step.

### Assumption 4.6 (No-Arbitrage Principle)

There is no admissible strategy such that $V(0) = 0$ and $V(n) > 0$ with positive probability for some $n = 1, 2, \ldots$ .

### *Exercise 4.3*

Show that the No-Arbitrage Principle would be violated if there was a self-financing predictable strategy with initial value $V(0) = 0$ and final value $0 \neq V(2) \geq 0$, such that $V(1) < 0$ with positive probability.

The strategy in Exercise 4.3 clearly violates the solvency assumption (Assumption 4.4), since $V(1)$ may be negative. In fact, this assumption is not essential for the formulation of the No-Arbitrage Principle. An admissible strategy realising an arbitrage opportunity can be found whenever there is a predictable self-financing strategy (possibly violating Assumption 4.4) such that $V(0) = 0$ and $0 \neq V(n) \geq 0$ for some $n > 0$.

### *Exercise 4.4*

Consider a market with one risk-free asset and one risky asset that follows the binomial tree model. Suppose that whenever stock goes up, you can predict that it will go down at the next step. Find a self-financing (but not necessarily predictable) strategy with $V(0) = 0$, $V(1) \geq 0$ and $0 \neq V(2) \geq 0$.

This exercise indicates that predictability is an essential assumption in the No-Arbitrage Principle. An investor who could foresee the future behaviour of stock prices (here, if stock goes down at one step, you can predict what it will do at the next step) would always be able to find a suitable investment strategy to ensure a risk-free profit.

### *Exercise 4.5*

Consider a market with a risk-free asset such that $A(0) = 100$, $A(1) = 110$, $A(2) = 121$ dollars and a risky asset, the price of which can follow three possible scenarios,

| Scenario | $S(0)$ | $S(1)$ | $S(2)$ |
|---|---|---|---|
| $\omega_1$ | 100 | 120 | 144 |
| $\omega_2$ | 100 | 120 | 96 |
| $\omega_3$ | 100 | 90 | 96 |

Is there an arbitrage opportunity if a) there are no restrictions on short selling, and b) no short selling of the risky asset is allowed?

### *Exercise 4.6*

Given the bond and stock prices in Exercise 4.5, is there an arbitrage strategy if short selling of stock is allowed, but the number of units of each asset in a portfolio must be an integer?

### *Exercise 4.7*

Given the bond and stock prices in Exercise 4.5, is there an arbitrage strategy if short selling of stock is allowed, but transaction costs of 5% of the transaction volume apply whenever stock is traded.

## 4.1.3 Application to the Binomial Tree Model

We shall see that in the binomial tree model with several time steps Condition 3.2 is equivalent to the lack of arbitrage.

### Proposition 4.2

The binomial tree model admits no arbitrage if and only if $d < r < u$.

### Proof

We shall begin with a one-step binomial tree. This will then be used as a building block in the case of several time steps.

*One step.* Suppose that $r \leq d$. If so, then:

- Borrow 1 dollar at the risk-free rate.
- Buy $1/S(0)$ shares.

That is to say, construct a portfolio with $x = 1/S(0)$ and $y = -1$, the value of which is $V(0) = 0$. After one step, either $S(1) = S(0)(1 + d)$ and $V(1) = -r + d \geq 0$, or $S(1) = S(0)(1 + u)$ and $V(1) = -r + u > 0$, leading to arbitrage.

Suppose that $u \leq r$. In this case:

- Buy one bond.
- Sell short $1/S(0)$ shares.

The resulting portfolio with $x = -1/S(0)$ and $y = 1$ will once again have initial value $V(0) = 0$. After one step this portfolio will be worth $V(1) = r - u \geq 0$ if the stock price goes up, or $V(1) = r - d > 0$ if it goes down, also realising an arbitrage opportunity.

Finally, suppose that $d < r < u$. Every portfolio with $V(0) = 0$ must be of the form $x = a/S(0)$ and $y = -a$ for some real number $a$. Consider the following three cases:

1) $a = 0$ (a trivial portfolio consisting of no cash and no stock). Then $V(1) = 0$ identically.

2) $a > 0$ (a cash loan invested in stock). Then $V(1) = a(d - r) < 0$ if the price of stock goes down.

3) $a < 0$ (a long position in bonds financed by shorting stock). In this case $V(1) = a(u - r) < 0$ if stock goes up.

Arbitrage is clearly impossible when $d < r < u$.

The above argument shows that $d < r < u$ if and only if there is no arbitrage in the one-step case.

*Several steps.* Let $d < r < u$ and suppose there is an arbitrage strategy. The tree of stock prices can be considered as a collection of one-step subtrees, as in Figure 4.1. By taking the smallest $n$ for which $V(n) \neq 0$, we can find a one-step subtree with $V(n-1) = 0$ at its root and $V(n) \geq 0$ at each node growing out of this root, with $V(n) > 0$ at one or more of these nodes. By the one-step case this is impossible if $d < r < u$, leading to a contradiction.

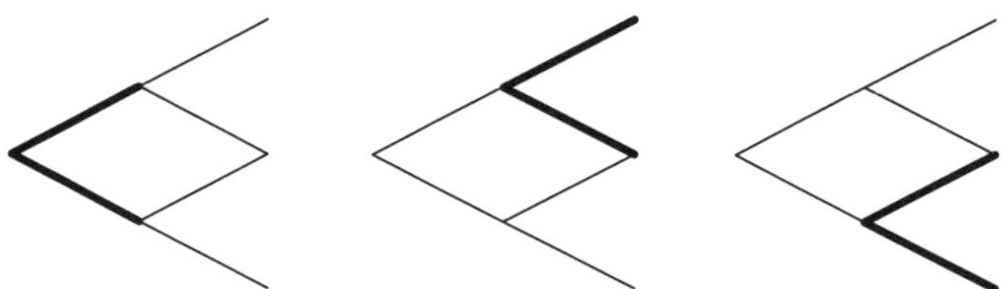

**Figure 4.1** One-step subtrees in a two-step binomial model

Conversely, suppose that there is no arbitrage in the binomial tree model with several steps. Then for any strategy such that $V(0) = 0$ it follows that $V(n) = 0$ for any $n$ and, in particular, $V(1) = 0$. This implies that $d < r < u$ by the above argument in the one-step case. □

We shall conclude this chapter with a brief discussion of a fundamental relationship between the risk-neutral probability and the No-Arbitrage Principle. First, we observe that the lack of arbitrage is equivalent to the existence of a risk-neutral probability in the binomial tree model.

## Proposition 4.3

The binomial tree model admits no arbitrage if and only if there exists a risk-neutral probability $p_*$ such that $0 < p_* < 1$.

## Proof

This is an immediate consequence of Exercise 3.18 and Proposition 4.2. □

### 4.1.4 Fundamental Theorem of Asset Pricing

In this section, which can be omitted on first reading, we return to the general setting under Assumptions 4.1 to 4.5.

We already know that the discounted stock prices in the binomial tree model form a martingale under the risk-neutral probability, see Proposition 3.5 and Corollary 3.6. The following result extends these observations to any discrete model.

## Theorem 4.4 (Fundamental Theorem of Asset Pricing)

The No-Arbitrage Principle is equivalent to the existence of a probability $P_*$ on the set of scenarios $\Omega$ such that $P_*(\omega) > 0$ for each scenario $\omega \in \Omega$ and the discounted stock prices $\widetilde{S}_j(n) = S_j(n)/A(n)$ satisfy

$$E_*(\widetilde{S}_j(n+1)|S(n)) = \widetilde{S}_j(n) \tag{4.3}$$

for any $j = 1, \ldots, m$ and $n = 0, 1, 2, \ldots$ , where $E_*(\,\cdot\,|S(n))$ denotes the conditional expectation with respect to probability $P_*$ computed once the stock price $S(n)$ becomes known at time $n$.

The proof of the Fundamental Theorem of Asset Pricing is quite technical and will be omitted.

## Definition 4.5

A sequence of random variables $X(0), X(1), X(2), \ldots$ such that

$$E_*(X(n+1)|S(n)) = X(n)$$

for each $n = 0, 1, 2, \ldots$ is said to be a *martingale* with respect to $P_*$.

Condition (4.3) can be expressed by saying that the discounted stock prices $\widetilde{S}_j(0), \widetilde{S}_j(1), \widetilde{S}_j(2), \ldots$ form a martingale with respect to $P_*$. The latter is called a *risk-neutral* or *martingale probability* on the set of scenarios $\Omega$. Moreover, $E_*$ is called a *risk-neutral* or *martingale expectation.*

## Example 4.5

Let $A(0) = 100$, $A(1) = 110$, $A(2) = 121$ and suppose that stock prices can follow four possible scenarios:

| Scenario | $S(0)$ | $S(1)$ | $S(2)$ |
|---|---|---|---|
| $\omega_1$ | 90 | 100 | 112 |
| $\omega_2$ | 90 | 100 | 106 |
| $\omega_3$ | 90 | 80 | 90 |
| $\omega_4$ | 90 | 80 | 80 |

The tree of stock prices is shown in Figure 4.2. The risk-neutral probability $P_*$ is represented by the branching probabilities $p_*, q_*, r_*$ at each node. Condition

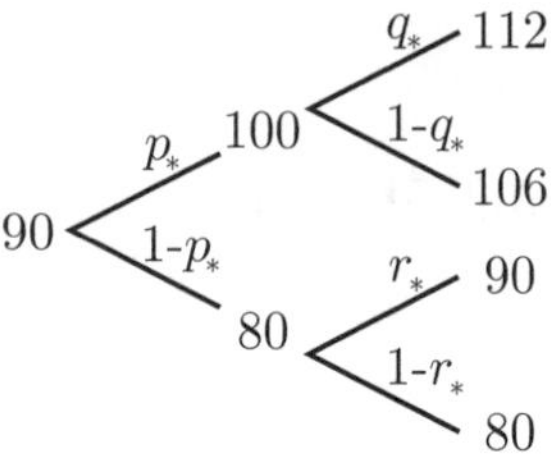


**Figure 4.2** Tree of stock prices in Example 4.5

(4.3) for $\widetilde{S}(n) = S(n)/A(n)$ can be written in the form of three equations, one for each node of the tree,

$$\frac{100}{110}p_* + \frac{80}{110}(1 - p_*) = \frac{90}{100},$$
$$\frac{112}{121}q_* + \frac{106}{121}(1 - q_*) = \frac{100}{110},$$
$$\frac{90}{121}r_* + \frac{80}{121}(1 - r_*) = \frac{80}{110}.$$

These can be solved to find

$$p_* = \frac{19}{20}, \quad q_* = \frac{2}{3}, \quad r_* = \frac{4}{5}.$$

For each scenario (each path through the tree) the corresponding risk-neutral probability can be computed as follows:

$$P_*(\omega_1) = p_* q_* = \frac{19}{20} \times \frac{2}{3} = \frac{19}{30},$$
$$P_*(\omega_2) = p_*(1 - q_*) = \frac{19}{20} \times \left(1 - \frac{2}{3}\right) = \frac{19}{60},$$
$$P_*(\omega_3) = (1 - p_*)r_* = \left(1 - \frac{19}{20}\right) \times \frac{4}{5} = \frac{1}{25},$$
$$P_*(\omega_4) = (1 - p_*)(1 - r_*) = \left(1 - \frac{19}{20}\right) \times \left(1 - \frac{4}{5}\right) = \frac{1}{100}.$$

By Theorem 4.4 the existence of a risk-neutral probability implies that there is no arbitrage.

## 4.2 Extended Models

Securities such as stock, which are traded independently of other assets, are called *primary securities*. By contrast, *derivative securities* such as, for example, options or forwards (in Chapter 1 we have seen some simple examples of these) are legal contracts conferring certain financial rights or obligations upon the holder, contingent on the prices of other securities, referred to as the *underlying securities*. An underlying security may be a primary security, as for a forward contract on stock, but it may also be a derivative security, as in the case of an option on futures. A derivative security cannot exist in its own right, unless the underlying security or securities are traded. Derivative securities are also referred to as *contingent claims* because their value is contingent on the underlying securities.

For example, the holder of a long forward contract on a stock is committed to buying the stock for the forward price at a specified time of delivery, no matter how much the actual stock price turns out to be at that time. The value of the forward position is contingent on the stock. It will become positive if the market price of stock turns out to be higher than the forward price on delivery. If the stock price turns out to be lower than the forward price, then the value of the forward position will be negative.

### Remark 4.1

The assumptions in Section 4.1, including the No-Arbitrage Principle, are stated for strategies consisting of primary securities only, such as stocks and bonds (or the money market account). Nevertheless, in many texts they are invoked in arbitrage proofs involving strategies constructed out of derivative securities in addition to stocks and bonds. To avoid this inaccuracy the assumptions need to be extended to strategies consisting of both primary and derivative securities.

The setting of Section 4.1, involving portfolios of risky stocks and the money market account, will be extended to include risky securities of various other kinds in addition to (and sometimes in place of) stock. In particular, to cover real-life situations we need to include derivative securities such as forwards or options, but also primary securities such as bonds of various maturities, the future prices of which may be random (except, of course, at maturity). We shall also relax the assumption that an investment in a money market account should be risk-free, with a view towards modelling random interest rates. In this way we prepare the stage for a detailed study of derivative securities in Chapters 6, 7 and 8, and random bond prices and the term structure of interest rates in Chapters 10 and 11.

Securities of various kinds will be treated on a similar footing as stock in Section 4.1. We shall denote by $S_1(n), \ldots, S_m(n)$ the time $n$ prices of $m$ different primary securities, typically $m$ different stocks, though they may also include other assets such as foreign currency, commodities or bonds of various maturities. Moreover, the price of one distinguished primary security, the money market account, will be denoted by $A(n)$. In addition, we introduce $k$ different derivative securities such as forwards, call and put options, or indeed any other contingent claims, whose time $n$ market prices will be denoted by $D_1(n), \ldots, D_k(n)$.

As opposed to stocks and bonds, we can no longer insist that the prices of all derivative securities should be positive. For example, at the time of exchanging a forward contract its value is zero, which may and often does become negative later on because the holder of a long forward position may have to buy the stock above its market price at delivery. The future prices $S_1(n), \ldots, S_m(n)$ and $A(n)$ of primary securities and the future prices $D_1(n), \ldots, D_k(n)$ of derivative securities may be random for $n = 1, 2, \ldots$, but we do not rule out the possibility that some of them, such as the prices of bonds at maturity, may in fact be known in advance, being represented by constant random variables or simply real numbers. All the current prices $S_1(0), \ldots, S_m(0), A(0), D_1(0), \ldots, D_k(0)$ are of course known at time 0, that is, are also just real numbers.

The positions in primary securities, including the money market account, will be denoted by $x_1, \ldots, x_m$ and $y$, and those in derivative securities by $z_1, \ldots, z_k$, respectively. The wealth of an investor holding such positions at time $n$ will be

$$V(n) = \sum_{j=1}^{m} x_j S_j(n) + yA(n) + \sum_{i=1}^{k} z_i D_i(n),$$

which extends formula (4.1).

The assumptions in Section 4.1 need to be replaced by the following.

## Assumption 4.1a (Randomness)

The asset prices $S_1(n), \ldots, S_m(n), A(n), D_1(n), \ldots, D_k(n)$ are random variables for any $n = 1, 2, \ldots$.

## Assumption 4.2a (Positivity of Prices)

The prices of primary securities, including the money market account, are positive,

$$S_1(n), \ldots, S_m(n), A(n) > 0 \quad \text{for } n = 0, 1, 2, \ldots \,.$$

## Assumption 4.3a (Divisibility, Liquidity and Short Selling)

An investor may buy, sell and hold any number of assets, whether integer or fractional, negative, positive or zero. In general,

$$x_1, \ldots, x_m, y, z_1, \ldots, z_k \in \mathbb{R}.$$

## Assumption 4.4a (Solvency)

The wealth of an investor must be non-negative at all times,

$$V(n) \geq 0 \quad \text{for } n = 0, 1, 2, \ldots \,.$$

## Assumption 4.5a (Discrete Unit Prices)

For each $n = 0, 1, 2, \ldots$ the prices $S_1(n), \ldots, S_m(n), A(n), D_1(n), \ldots, D_k(n)$ are random variables taking only finitely many values.

Definitions 4.1 to 4.4 also extend immediately to the case in hand.

## Definition 4.1a

A *portfolio* is a vector

$$(x_1(n), \ldots, x_m(n), y(n), z_1(n), \ldots, z_k(n))$$

indicating the number of primary and derivative securities held by an investor between times $n-1$ and $n$. A sequence of portfolios indexed by $n = 1, 2, \ldots$ is called an *investment strategy*. The *wealth* of an investor or the *value of the strategy* at time $n \geq 1$ is

$$V(n) = \sum_{j=1}^{m} x_j(n)S_j(n) + y(n)A(n) + \sum_{i=1}^{k} z_i(n)D_i(n).$$

At time $n = 0$ the *initial wealth* is given by

$$V(0) = \sum_{j=1}^{m} x_j(1)S_j(0) + y(1)A(0) + \sum_{i=1}^{k} z_i(1)D_i(0).$$

### Definition 4.2a

An investment strategy is called *self-financing* if the portfolio constructed at time $n \geq 1$ to be held over the next time step $n+1$ is financed entirely by the current wealth $V(n)$, that is,

$$\sum_{j=1}^{m} x_j(n+1)S_j(n) + y(n+1)A(n) + \sum_{i=1}^{k} z_i(n+1)D_i(n) = V(n).$$

### Definition 4.3a

An investment strategy is called *predictable* if for each $n = 0, 1, 2, \ldots$ the portfolio

$$(x_1(n+1), \ldots, x_m(n+1), y(n+1), z_1(n+1), \ldots, z_k(n+1))$$

constructed at time $n$ depends only on the nodes of the tree of market scenarios reached up to and including time $n$.

### Definition 4.4a

A strategy is called *admissible* if it is self-financing, predictable, and for each $n = 0, 1, 2, \ldots$

$$V(n) \geq 0$$

with probability 1.

The No-Arbitrage Principle extends without any modifications.

### Assumption 4.6a (No-Arbitrage Principle)

There is no admissible strategy such that $V(0) = 0$ and $V(n) > 0$ with positive probability for some $n = 1, 2, \ldots$ .

Finally, the Fundamental Theorem of Asset Pricing takes the following form.

### Theorem 4.4a (Fundamental Theorem of Asset Pricing)

The No-Arbitrage Principle is equivalent to the existence of a probability $P_*$ on the set of scenarios $\Omega$ such that $P_*(\omega) > 0$ for each scenario $\omega \in \Omega$ and the discounted prices of primary and derivative securities $\widetilde{S}_j(n) = S_j(n)/A(n)$ and $\widetilde{D}_i(n) = D_i(n)/A(n)$ form martingales with respect to $P_*$, that is, satisfy

$$E_*(\widetilde{S}_j(n+1)|S(n)) = \widetilde{S}_j(n), \quad E_*(\widetilde{D}_i(n+1)|S(n)) = \widetilde{D}_i(n)$$

for any $j = 1, \ldots, m$, any $i = 1, \ldots, k$ and any $n = 0, 1, 2, \ldots$, where $E_*(\,\cdot\,|S(n))$ denotes the conditional expectation with respect to probability $P_*$ computed once the stock price $S(n)$ becomes known at time $n$.

## Example 4.6

We shall use the same scenarios $\omega_1, \omega_2, \omega_3, \omega_4$, stock prices $S(0), S(1), S(2)$ and money market prices $A(0), A(1), A(2)$ as in Example 4.5. In addition, we consider a European call option giving the holder the right (but no obligation) to buy the stock for the strike price of $X = 85$ dollars at time 2.

In this situation we need to consider an extended model with three assets, the stock, the money market, and the option, with unit prices $S(n), A(n), C^{\mathrm{E}}(n)$, respectively, where $C^{\mathrm{E}}(n)$ is the market price of the option at time $n = 0, 1, 2$.

The time 2 option price is determined by the strike price and the stock price,

$$C^{\mathrm{E}}(2) = \max\{S(2) - X, 0\}.$$

The prices $C^{\mathrm{E}}(0)$ and $C^{\mathrm{E}}(1)$ can be found using the Fundamental Theorem of Asset Pricing. (Which explains the name of the theorem!) According to the theorem, there is a probability $P_*$ such that the discounted stock and option prices $\widetilde{S}(n) = S(n)/A(n)$ and $\widetilde{C}^{\mathrm{E}}(n) = C^{\mathrm{E}}(n)/A(n)$ are martingales, or else an arbitrage opportunity would exist. However, there is only one probability $P_*$ turning $\widetilde{S}(n)$ into a martingale, namely that found in Example 4.5. As a result, $\widetilde{C}^{\mathrm{E}}(n)$ must be a martingale with respect to the same probability $P_*$. This gives

$$C^{\mathrm{E}}(1) = \frac{A(1)}{A(2)} E_*(C^{\mathrm{E}}(2)|S(1)) \quad \text{and} \quad C^{\mathrm{E}}(0) = \frac{A(0)}{A(1)} E_*(C^{\mathrm{E}}(1)).$$

The values of $P_*$ for each scenario found in Example 4.5 can now be used to compute $C^{\mathrm{E}}(1)$ and then $C^{\mathrm{E}}(0)$. For example,

$$\begin{aligned} C^{\mathrm{E}}(1,\omega_1) = C^{\mathrm{E}}(1,\omega_2) &= \frac{A(1)}{A(2)} \frac{P_*(\omega_1)C^{\mathrm{E}}(2,\omega_1) + P_*(\omega_2)C^{\mathrm{E}}(2,\omega_2)}{P_*(\omega_1) + P_*(\omega_2)} \\ &= \frac{110}{121} \frac{\frac{19}{30} \times 27 + \frac{19}{60} \times 21}{\frac{19}{30} + \frac{19}{60}} \cong 22.73 \end{aligned}$$

dollars. Proceeding in a similar way, we obtain

| Scenario | $C^{\mathrm{E}}(0)$ | $C^{\mathrm{E}}(1)$ | $C^{\mathrm{E}}(2)$ |
|---|---|---|---|
| $\omega_1$ | 19.79 | 22.73 | 27.00 |
| $\omega_2$ | 19.79 | 22.73 | 21.00 |
| $\omega_3$ | 19.79 | 3.64 | 5.00 |
| $\omega_4$ | 19.79 | 3.64 | 0.00 |

### *Exercise 4.8*

Apply the Fundamental Theorem of Asset Pricing to find the time 0 and 1 prices of a put option with strike price \$110 maturing after two steps, given the same scenarios $\omega_1, \omega_2, \omega_3, \omega_4$, stock prices $S(0), S(1), S(2)$ and money market prices $A(0), A(1), A(2)$ as in Example 4.5.

# 5
# Portfolio Management

An investment in a risky security always carries the burden of possible losses or poor performance. In this chapter we analyse the advantages of spreading the investment among several securities. Even though the mathematical tools involved are quite simple, they lead to formidable results.

## 5.1 Risk

First of all, we need to identify a suitable quantity to measure risk. An investment in bonds returning, for example, 8% at maturity is free of risk, in which case the measure of risk should be equal to zero. If the return on an investment is, say 11% or 13%, depending on the market scenario, then the risk is clearly smaller as compared with an investment returning 2% or 22%, respectively. However, the spread of return values can hardly be used to measure risk because it ignores the probabilities. If the return rate is 22% with probability 0.99 and 2% with probability 0.01, the risk can be considered quite small, whereas the same rates of return occurring with probability 0.5 each would indicate a rather more risky investment. The desired quantity needs to capture the following two aspects of risk: 1) the distances between a certain reference value and the rates of return in each market scenario and 2) the probabilities of different scenarios.

The return $K$ on a risky investment is a random variable. It is natural to take the expectation $E(K)$ as the reference value. The *variance* $\mathrm{Var}(K)$ turns out to be a convenient measure of risk.

### *Exercise 5.1*

Compute the risk $\mathrm{Var}(K_1)$, $\mathrm{Var}(K_2)$ and $\mathrm{Var}(K_3)$ in each of the following three investment projects, where the returns $K_1$, $K_2$ and $K_3$ depend on the market scenario:

| Scenario | Probability | Return $K_1$ | Return $K_2$ | Return $K_3$ |
|---|---|---|---|---|
| $\omega_1$ | 0.25 | 12% | 11% | 2% |
| $\omega_2$ | 0.75 | 12% | 13% | 22% |

Which of these is the most risky and the least risky project?

### *Exercise 5.2*

Consider two scenarios, $\omega_1$ with probability $\frac{1}{4}$ and $\omega_2$ with probability $\frac{3}{4}$. Suppose that the return on a certain security is $K_1(\omega_1) = -2\%$ in the first scenario and $K_1(\omega_2) = 8\%$ in the second scenario. If the return on another security is $K_2(\omega_1) = -4\%$ in the first scenario, find the return $K_2(\omega_2)$ in the other scenario such that the two securities have the same risk.

In some circumstances the *standard deviation* $\sigma_K = \sqrt{\mathrm{Var}(K)}$ of the return is a more convenient measure of risk. If a quantity is measured in certain units, then the standard deviation will be expressed in the same units, so it can be related directly to the original quantity, in contrast to variance, which will be expressed in squared units.

## Example 5.1

Let the return on an investment be $K = 3\%$ or $-1\%$, both with probability 0.5. Then the risk is

$$\mathrm{Var}(K) = 0.0004 \quad \text{or} \quad \sigma_K = 0.02,$$

depending on whether we choose the variance or standard deviation. Now suppose that the return on another investment is double that on the first investment, being equal to $2K = 6\%$ or $-2\%$, also with probability 0.5 each. Then the risk of the second investment will be

$$\mathrm{Var}(2K) = 0.0016 \quad \text{or} \quad \sigma_{2K} = 0.04.$$

The risk as measured by the variance is quadrupled, while the standard deviation is simply doubled.

This illustrates the following general rule:

$$\text{Var}(aK) = a^2\text{Var}(K),$$
$$\sigma_{aK} = |a|\,\sigma_K$$

for any real number $a$.

## Remark 5.1

Another natural way to quantify risk would be to use the variance $\text{Var}(k)$ (or the standard deviation $\sigma_k$) of the logarithmic return $k$. The choice between $K$ and $k$ is dictated to a large extent by the properties needed to handle the task in hand. For example, if one is interested in a sequence of investments following one another in time, then the variance of the logarithmic return may be more useful as a measure of risk. This is because of the additivity of risks based on logarithmic returns:

$$\text{Var}(k(0,n)) = \text{Var}(k(1)) + \cdots + \text{Var}(k(n)),$$

where $k(i)$ is the logarithmic return in time step $i = 1, \ldots, n$ and $k(0,n)$ is the logarithmic return over the whole time interval from 0 to $n$, provided that the $k(i)$ are independent. The above formula holds because $k(0,n) = k(1) + \cdots + k(n)$ by Proposition 3.2, and the variance of a sum of independent random variables is the sum of their variances. (This is not necessarily so without independence.)

However, in the present chapter we shall be concerned with a portfolio of several securities held simultaneously over a single time step. The properties of $E(K)$ and $\text{Var}(K)$, where $K$ is the ordinary return on the portfolio (see formulae (5.4) and (5.5) below), are much more convenient for this purpose than those for the logarithmic return.

### *Exercise 5.3*

Consider two risky securities with returns $K_1$ and $K_2$ given by

| Scenario | Probability | Return $K_1$ | Return $K_2$ |
|---|---|---|---|
| $\omega_1$ | 0.5 | 10.53% | 7.23% |
| $\omega_2$ | 0.5 | 13.89% | 10.57% |

Compute the corresponding logarithmic returns $k_1$ and $k_2$ and compare $\text{Var}(k_1)$ with $\text{Var}(k_2)$ and $\text{Var}(K_1)$ with $\text{Var}(K_2)$.

## 5.2 Two Securities

We begin a detailed discussion of the relationship between risk and expected return in the simple situation of a portfolio with just two risky securities.

### Example 5.2

Suppose that the prices of two stocks behave as follows:

| Scenario | Probability | Return $K_1$ | Return $K_2$ |
|---|---|---|---|
| $\omega_1$ | 0.5 | 10% | −5% |
| $\omega_2$ | 0.5 | −5% | 10% |

If we split our money equally between these two stocks, then we shall earn 5% in each scenario (losing 5% on one stock, but gaining 10% on the other). Even though an investment in either stock separately involves risk, we have reduced the overall risk to nil by splitting the investment between the two stocks. This is a simple example of diversification, which is particularly effective here because the returns are negatively correlated.

In addition to the description of a portfolio in terms of the number of shares of each security held (developed in Section 4.1), we shall introduce another very convenient notation to describe the allocation of funds between the securities.

### Example 5.3

Suppose that the prices of two kinds of stock are $S_1(0) = 30$ and $S_2(0) = 40$ dollars. We prepare a portfolio worth $V(0) = 1,000$ dollars by purchasing $x_1 = 20$ shares of stock number 1 and $x_2 = 10$ shares of stock number 2. The allocation of funds between the two securities is

$$w_1 = \frac{30 \times 20}{1,000} = 60\%, \quad w_2 = \frac{10 \times 40}{1,000} = 40\%.$$

The numbers $w_1$ and $w_2$ are called the *weights*. If the stock prices change to $S_1(1) = 35$ and $S_2(1) = 39$ dollars, then the portfolio will be worth $V(1) = 20 \times 35 + 10 \times 39 = 1,090$ dollars. Observe that this amount is no longer split between the two securities as 60% to 40%, but as follows:

$$\frac{20 \times 35}{1,090} \cong 64.22\%, \quad \frac{10 \times 39}{1,090} \cong 35.78\%,$$

even though the actual number of shares of each stock in the portfolio remains unchanged.

The weights are defined by

$$w_1 = \frac{x_1 S_1(0)}{V(0)}, \quad w_2 = \frac{x_2 S_2(0)}{V(0)},$$

where $x_1$ and $x_2$ are share numbers of stock 1 and 2 in the portfolio. This means that $w_k$ is the percentage of the initial value of the portfolio invested in security number $k$. Observe that the weights always add up to 100%,

$$w_1 + w_2 = \frac{x_1 S_1(0) + x_2 S_2(0)}{V(0)} = \frac{V(0)}{V(0)} = 1. \tag{5.1}$$

If short selling is allowed, then one of the weights may be negative and the other one greater than 100%.

## Example 5.4

Suppose that a portfolio worth $V(0) = 1,000$ dollars is constructed by taking a long position in stock number 1 and a short position in stock number 2 in Example 5.3 with weights $w_1 = 120\%$ and $w_2 = -20\%$. The portfolio will consist of

$$x_1 = w_1 \frac{V(0)}{S_1(0)} = 120\% \times \frac{1,000}{30} = 40,$$
$$x_2 = w_2 \frac{V(0)}{S_2(0)} = -20\% \times \frac{1,000}{40} = -5$$

shares of type 1 and 2. If the stock prices change as in Example 5.3, then this portfolio will be worth

$$V(1) = x_1 S_1(1) + x_2 S_2(1) = V(0) \left( w_1 \frac{S_1(1)}{S_1(0)} + w_2 \frac{S_2(1)}{S_2(0)} \right)$$
$$= 1,000 \left( 120\% \times \frac{35}{30} - 20\% \times \frac{39}{40} \right) = 1,205$$

dollars, benefiting from both the rise of the price of stock 1 and the fall of stock 2. However, a small investor may have to face some restrictions on short selling. For example, it may be necessary to pay a security deposit equal to 50% of the sum raised by shorting stock number 2. The deposit, which would amount to $50\% \times 200 = 100$ dollars, can be borrowed at the risk-free rate and the interest paid on this loan will need to be subtracted from the final value $V(1)$ of the portfolio.

*Exercise 5.4*

Compute the value $V(1)$ of a portfolio worth initially $V(0) = 100$ dollars that consists of two securities with weights $w_1 = 25\%$ and $w_2 = 75\%$, given that the security prices are $S_1(0) = 45$ and $S_2(0) = 33$ dollars initially, changing to $S_1(1) = 48$ and $S_2(1) = 32$ dollars.

We can see in Example 5.4 and Exercise 5.4 that $V(1)/V(0)$ depends on the prices of securities only through the ratios $S_1(1)/S_1(0) = 1 + K_1$ and $S_2(1)/S_2(0) = 1 + K_2$. This indicates that the return on the portfolio should depend only on the weights $w_1, w_2$ and the returns $K_1, K_2$ on each of the two securities.

## Proposition 5.1

The return $K_V$ on a portfolio consisting of two securities is the weighted average

$$K_V = w_1 K_1 + w_2 K_2, \tag{5.2}$$

where $w_1$ and $w_2$ are the weights and $K_1$ and $K_2$ the returns on the two components.

## Proof

Suppose that the portfolio consists of $x_1$ shares of security 1 and $x_2$ shares of security 2. Then the initial and final values of the portfolio are

$$\begin{aligned} V(0) &= x_1 S_1(0) + x_2 S_2(0), \\ V(1) &= x_1 S_1(0)(1 + K_1) + x_2 S_2(0)(1 + K_2) \\ &= V(0)\left(w_1(1 + K_1) + w_2(1 + K_2)\right). \end{aligned}$$

As a result, the return on the portfolio is

$$K_V = \frac{V(1) - V(0)}{V(0)} = w_1 K_1 + w_2 K_2.$$

□

*Exercise 5.5*

Find the return on a portfolio consisting of two kinds of stock with weights $w_1 = 30\%$ and $w_2 = 70\%$ if the returns on the components are as follows:

| Scenario | Return $K_1$ | Return $K_2$ |
|---|---|---|
| $\omega_1$ | 12% | −4% |
| $\omega_2$ | 10% | 7% |

## Remark 5.2

A similar formula to (5.2) holds for logarithmic returns,

$$\mathrm{e}^{k_V} = w_1 \mathrm{e}^{k_1} + w_2 \mathrm{e}^{k_2}. \tag{5.3}$$

However, this is not particularly useful if the expectations and variances or standard deviations of returns need to be related to the weights. On the other hand, as will be seen below, formula (5.2) lends itself well to this task.

### *Exercise 5.6*

Verify formula (5.3).

## 5.2.1 Risk and Expected Return on a Portfolio

The expected return on a portfolio consisting of two securities can easily be expressed in terms of the weights and the expected returns on the components,

$$E(K_V) = w_1 E(K_1) + w_2 E(K_2). \tag{5.4}$$

This follows at once from (5.2) by the additivity of mathematical expectation.

## Example 5.5

Consider three scenarios with the probabilities given below (a trinomial model). Let the returns on two different stocks in these scenarios be as follows:

| Scenario | Probability | Return $K_1$ | Return $K_2$ |
|---|---|---|---|
| $\omega_1$ (recession) | 0.2 | −10% | −30% |
| $\omega_2$ (stagnation) | 0.5 | 0% | 20% |
| $\omega_3$ (boom) | 0.3 | 10% | 50% |

The expected returns on stock are

$$\begin{aligned} E(K_1) &= -0.2 \times 10\% + 0.5 \times \ \ 0\% + 0.3 \times 10\% = \ \ 1\%, \\ E(K_2) &= -0.2 \times 30\% + 0.5 \times 20\% + 0.3 \times 50\% = 19\%. \end{aligned}$$

Suppose that $w_1 = 60\%$ of available funds is invested in stock 1 and 40% in stock 2. The expected return on such a portfolio is

$$\begin{aligned} E(K_V) &= w_1 E(K_1) + w_2 E(K_2) \\ &= 0.6 \times 1\% + 0.4 \times 19\% = 8.2\%. \end{aligned}$$

### *Exercise 5.7*

Compute the weights in a portfolio consisting of two kinds of stock if the expected return on the portfolio is to be $E(K_V) = 20\%$, given the following information on the returns on stock 1 and 2:

| Scenario | Probability | Return $K_1$ | Return $K_2$ |
|---|---|---|---|
| $\omega_1$ (recession) | 0.1 | −10% | 10% |
| $\omega_2$ (stagnation) | 0.5 | 0% | 20% |
| $\omega_3$ (boom) | 0.4 | 20% | 30% |

To compute the variance of $K_V$ we need to know not only the variances of the returns $K_1$ and $K_2$ on the components in the portfolio, but also the covariance between the two returns.

### Theorem 5.2

The variance of the return on a portfolio is given by

$$\mathrm{Var}(K_V) = w_1^2 \mathrm{Var}(K_1) + w_2^2 \mathrm{Var}(K_2) + 2w_1 w_2 \mathrm{Cov}(K_1, K_2). \tag{5.5}$$

### Proof

Substituting $K_V = w_1 K_1 + w_2 K_2$ and collecting the terms with $w_1^2$, $w_2^2$ and $w_1 w_2$, we compute

$$\begin{aligned} \mathrm{Var}(K_V) &= E(K_V^2) - E(K_V)^2 \\ &= w_1^2[E(K_1^2) - E(K_1)^2] + w_2^2[E(K_2^2) - E(K_2)^2] \\ &\quad + 2w_1 w_2 [E(K_1 K_2) - E(K_1)E(K_2)] \\ &= w_1^2 \mathrm{Var}(K_1) + w_2^2 \mathrm{Var}(K_2) + 2w_1 w_2 \mathrm{Cov}(K_1, K_2). \end{aligned}$$

□

To avoid clutter, we introduce the following notation for the expectation and variance of a portfolio and its components:

$$\begin{aligned} \mu_V &= E(K_V), \quad & \sigma_V &= \sqrt{\operatorname{Var}(K_V)}, \\ \mu_1 &= E(K_1), \quad & \sigma_1 &= \sqrt{\operatorname{Var}(K_1)}, \\ \mu_2 &= E(K_2), \quad & \sigma_2 &= \sqrt{\operatorname{Var}(K_2)}. \end{aligned}$$

We shall also use the correlation coefficient

$$\rho_{12} = \frac{\operatorname{Cov}(K_1, K_2)}{\sigma_1 \sigma_2}. \tag{5.6}$$

Formulae (5.4) and (5.5) can be written as

$$\mu_V = w_1 \mu_1 + w_2 \mu_2, \tag{5.7}$$

$$\sigma_V^2 = w_1^2 \sigma_1^2 + w_2^2 \sigma_2^2 + 2 w_1 w_2 \rho_{12} \sigma_1 \sigma_2. \tag{5.8}$$

## Remark 5.3

For risky securities the returns $K_1$ and $K_2$ are always assumed to be non-constant random variables. Because of this $\sigma_1, \sigma_2 > 0$ and $\rho_{12}$ is well defined, since the denominator $\sigma_1 \sigma_2$ in (5.6) is non-zero.

## Example 5.6

We use the following data:

| Scenario | Probability | Return $K_1$ | Return $K_2$ |
|---|---|---|---|
| $\omega_1$ (recession) | 0.4 | $-10\%$ | 20% |
| $\omega_2$ (stagnation) | 0.2 | 0% | 20% |
| $\omega_3$ (boom) | 0.4 | 20% | 10% |

We want to compare the risk of a portfolio such that $w_1 = 40\%$ and $w_2 = 60\%$ with the risks of its components as measured by the variance. Direct computations give

$$\sigma_1^2 \cong 0.0184, \quad \sigma_2^2 \cong 0.0024, \quad \rho_{12} \cong -0.96309.$$

By (5.8)

$$\begin{aligned} \sigma_V^2 &\cong (0.4)^2 \times 0.0184 + (0.6)^2 \times 0.0024 \\ &\quad + 2 \times 0.4 \times 0.6 \times (-0.96309) \times \sqrt{0.0184} \times \sqrt{0.0024} \\ &\cong 0.000736. \end{aligned}$$

Observe that the variance $\sigma_V^2$ is smaller than $\sigma_1^2$ and $\sigma_2^2$.

## Example 5.7

Consider another portfolio with weights $w_1 = 80\%$ and $w_2 = 20\%$, all other things being the same as in Example 5.6. Then

$$\begin{aligned}\sigma_V^2 &\cong (0.8)^2 \times 0.0184 + (0.2)^2 \times 0.0024 \\ &\quad +2 \times 0.8 \times 0.2 \times (-0.96309) \times \sqrt{0.0184} \times \sqrt{0.0024} \\ &\cong 0.009824,\end{aligned}$$

which is between $\sigma_1^2$ and $\sigma_2^2$.

## Proposition 5.3

The variance $\sigma_V^2$ of a portfolio cannot exceed the greater of the variances $\sigma_1^2$ and $\sigma_2^2$ of the components,

$$\sigma_V^2 \leq \max\{\sigma_1^2, \sigma_2^2\},$$

if short sales are not allowed.

## Proof

Let us assume that $\sigma_1^2 \leq \sigma_2^2$. If short sales are not allowed, then $w_1, w_2 \geq 0$ and

$$w_1\sigma_1 + w_2\sigma_2 \leq (w_1 + w_2)\sigma_2 = \sigma_2.$$

Since the correlation coefficient satisfies $-1 \leq \rho_{12} \leq 1$, it follows that

$$\begin{aligned}\sigma_V^2 &= w_1^2\sigma_1^2 + w_2^2\sigma_2^2 + 2w_1w_2\rho_{12}\sigma_1\sigma_2 \\ &\leq w_1^2\sigma_1^2 + w_2^2\sigma_2^2 + 2w_1w_2\sigma_1\sigma_2 \\ &= (w_1\sigma_1 + w_2\sigma_2)^2 \leq \sigma_2^2.\end{aligned}$$

If $\sigma_1^2 \geq \sigma_2^2$, the proof is analogous. □

## Example 5.8

Now consider a portfolio with weights $w_1 = -50\%$ and $w_2 = 150\%$ (allowing short sales of security 1), all the other data being the same as in Example 5.6. The variance of this portfolio is

$$\begin{aligned}\sigma_V^2 &\cong (-0.5)^2 \times 0.0184 + (1.5)^2 \times 0.0024 \\ &\quad +2 \times (-0.5) \times 1.5 \times (-0.96309) \times \sqrt{0.0184} \times \sqrt{0.0024} \\ &\cong 0.0196,\end{aligned}$$

which is greater than both $\sigma_1^2$ and $\sigma_2^2$.

### *Exercise 5.8*

Using the data in Example 5.6, find the weights in a portfolio with expected return $\mu_V = 46\%$ and compute the risk $\sigma_V^2$ of this portfolio.

The correlation coefficient always satisfies $-1 \leq \rho_{12} \leq 1$. The next proposition is concerned with the two special cases when $\rho_{12}$ assumes one of the extreme values 1 or $-1$, which means perfect positive or negative correlation between the securities in the portfolio.

### Proposition 5.4

If $\rho_{12} = 1$, then $\sigma_V = 0$ when $\sigma_1 \neq \sigma_2$ and

$$w_1 = -\frac{\sigma_2}{\sigma_1 - \sigma_2}, \quad w_2 = \frac{\sigma_1}{\sigma_1 - \sigma_2}. \tag{5.9}$$

(Short sales are necessary, since either $w_1$ or $w_2$ is negative.)

If $\rho_{12} = -1$, then $\sigma_V = 0$ for

$$w_1 = \frac{\sigma_2}{\sigma_1 + \sigma_2}, \quad w_2 = \frac{\sigma_1}{\sigma_1 + \sigma_2}. \tag{5.10}$$

(No short sales are necessary, since both $w_1$ and $w_2$ are positive.)

### Proof

Let $\rho_{12} = 1$. Then (5.8) takes the form

$$\sigma_V^2 = w_1^2\sigma_1^2 + w_2^2\sigma_2^2 + 2w_1w_2\sigma_1\sigma_2 = (w_1\sigma_1 + w_2\sigma_2)^2$$

and $\sigma_V^2 = 0$ if and only if $w_1\sigma_1 + w_2\sigma_2 = 0$. This is equivalent to $\sigma_1 \neq \sigma_2$ and (5.9) because $w_1 + w_2 = 1$.

Now let $\rho_{12} = -1$. Then (5.8) becomes

$$\sigma_V^2 = w_1^2\sigma_1^2 + w_2^2\sigma_2^2 - 2w_1w_2\sigma_1\sigma_2 = (w_1\sigma_1 - w_2\sigma_2)^2$$

and $\sigma_V^2 = 0$ if and only if $w_1\sigma_1 - w_2\sigma_2 = 0$. The last equality is equivalent to (5.10) because $w_1 + w_2 = 1$. □

Each portfolio can be represented by a point with coordinates $\sigma_V$ and $\mu_V$ on the $\sigma, \mu$ plane. Figure 5.1 shows two typical lines representing portfolios with $\rho_{12} = -1$ (left) and $\rho_{12} = 1$ (right). The bold segments correspond to portfolios without short selling.

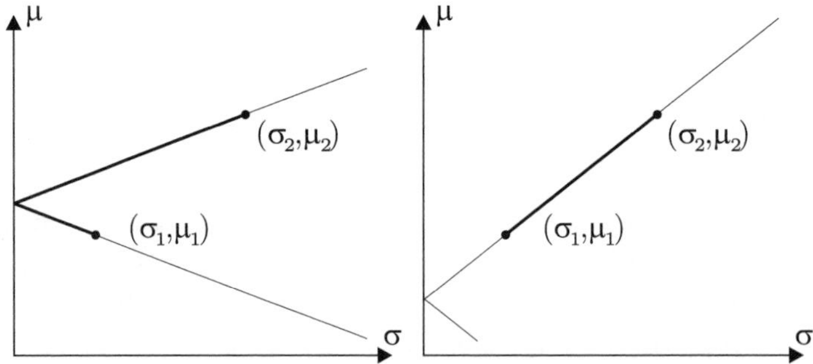


**Figure 5.1** Typical portfolio lines with $\rho_{12} = -1$ and 1

Suppose that $\rho_{12} = -1$. It follows from the proof of Proposition 5.4 that $\sigma_V = |w_1\sigma_1 - w_2\sigma_2|$. In addition, $\mu_V = w_1\mu_1 + w_2\mu_2$ by (5.7) and $w_1 + w_2 = 1$ by (5.1). We can choose $s = w_2$ as a parameter. Then $1 - s = w_1$ and

$$\sigma_V = |(1-s)\sigma_1 - s\sigma_2|,$$
$$\mu_V = (1-s)\mu_1 + s\mu_2.$$

These parametric equations describe the line in Figure 5.1 with a broken segment between $(\sigma_1, \mu_1)$ and $(\sigma_2, \mu_2)$. As $s$ increases, the point $(\sigma_V, \mu_V)$ moves along the line in the direction from $(\sigma_1, \mu_1)$ to $(\sigma_2, \mu_2)$.

If $\rho_{12} = 1$, then $\sigma_V = |w_1\sigma_1 + w_2\sigma_2|$. We choose $s = w_2$ as a parameter once again, and obtain the parametric equations

$$\sigma_V = |(1-s)\sigma_1 + s\sigma_2|,$$
$$\mu_V = (1-s)\mu_1 + s\mu_2$$

of the line in Figure 5.1 with a straight segment between $(\sigma_1, \mu_1)$ and $(\sigma_2, \mu_2)$.

If no short selling is allowed, then $0 \leq s \leq 1$ in both cases, which corresponds to the bold line segments.

### *Exercise 5.9*

Suppose that there are just two scenarios $\omega_1$ and $\omega_2$ and consider two risky securities with returns $K_1$ and $K_2$. Show that $K_1 = aK_2 + b$ for some numbers $a \neq 0$ and $b$, and deduce that $\rho_{12} = 1$ or $-1$.

Our next task is to find a portfolio with minimum risk for any given $\rho_{12}$ such that $-1 < \rho_{12} < 1$. Again, we take $s = w_2$ as a parameter. Then (5.7) and (5.8) take the form

$$\mu_V = (1-s)\mu_1 + s\mu_2, \tag{5.11}$$

$$\sigma_V^2 = (1-s)^2\sigma_1^2 + s^2\sigma_2^2 + 2s(1-s)\rho_{12}\sigma_1\sigma_2. \tag{5.12}$$

Obviously, $\mu_V$ as a function of $s$ is a straight line and $\sigma_V^2$ is a quadratic function of $s$ with a positive coefficient at $s^2$ (namely $\sigma_1^2 + \sigma_2^2 - 2\rho_{12}\sigma_1\sigma_2 > \sigma_1^2 + \sigma_2^2 - 2\sigma_1\sigma_2 = (\sigma_1 - \sigma_2)^2 \geq 0$). The problem of minimising the variance $\sigma_V^2$ (or, equivalently, the standard deviation $\sigma_V$) of a portfolio is solved in the next theorem. First we find the minimum without any restrictions on short sales. If short sales are not allowed, we shall have to take into account the bounds $0 \leq s \leq 1$ on the parameter.

## Theorem 5.5

For $-1 < \rho_{12} < 1$ the portfolio with minimum variance is attained at

$$s_0 = \frac{\sigma_1^2 - \rho_{12}\sigma_1\sigma_2}{\sigma_1^2 + \sigma_2^2 - 2\rho_{12}\sigma_1\sigma_2}. \tag{5.13}$$

If short sales are not allowed, then the smallest variance is attained at

$$s_{\min} = \begin{cases} 0 & \text{if } s_0 < 0, \\ s_0 & \text{if } 0 \leq s_0 \leq 1, \\ 1 & \text{if } 1 < s_0. \end{cases}$$

## Proof

We compute the derivative of $\sigma_V^2$ with respect to $s$ and equate it to 0:

$$-2\,(1-s)\,\sigma_1^2 + 2s\sigma_2^2 + 2(1-s)\rho_{12}\sigma_1\sigma_2 - 2s\rho_{12}\sigma_1\sigma_2 = 0.$$

Solving for $s$ gives the above $s_0$. The second derivative is positive,

$$2\sigma_1^2 + 2\sigma_2^2 - 4\rho_{12}\sigma_1\sigma_2 > 2\sigma_1^2 + 2\sigma_2^2 - 4\sigma_1\sigma_2 = 2\,(\sigma_1 - \sigma_2)^2 \geq 0,$$

which shows that there is a minimum at $s_0$. It is a global minimum because $\sigma_V^2$ is a quadratic function of $s$.

If short sales are not allowed, then we need to find the minimum for $0 \leq s \leq 1$. If $0 \leq s_0 \leq 1$, then the minimum is at $s_0$. If $s_0 < 0$, then the minimum is at 0, and if $s_0 > 1$, then it is at 1, since $\sigma_V^2$ is a quadratic function of $s$ with a positive coefficient at $s^2$. This is illustrated in Figure 5.2. The bold parts of the curve correspond to portfolios with no short selling. □

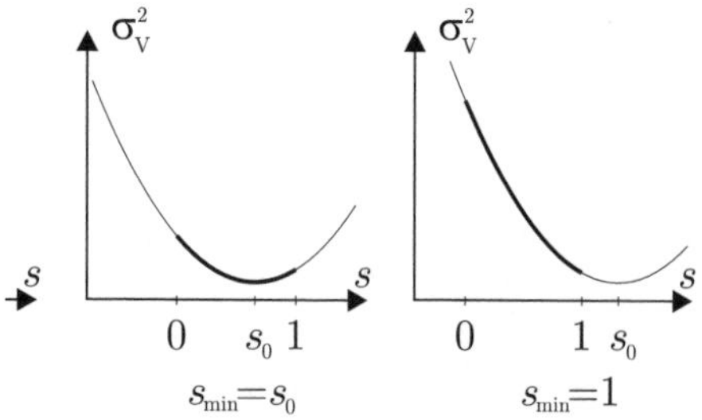


**Figure 5.2** The minimum of $\sigma_V^2$ as a function of $s$

The line on the $\sigma, \mu$ plane defined by the parametric equations (5.11) and (5.12) represents all possible portfolios with given $\sigma_1, \sigma_2 > 0$ and $-1 \leq \rho_{12} \leq 1$. The parameter $s$ can be any real number whenever there are no restrictions on short selling. If short selling is not allowed, then $0 \leq s \leq 1$ and we only obtain a segment of the line. As $s$ increases from 0 to 1, the corresponding point $(\sigma_V, \mu_V)$ travels along the line in the direction from $(\sigma_1, \mu_1)$ to $(\sigma_2, \mu_2)$. Figure 5.3 shows two typical examples of such lines, with $\rho_{12}$ close to but greater than $-1$ (left) and with $\rho_{12}$ close to but smaller than 1 (right). Portfolios without short selling are indicated by the bold line segments.

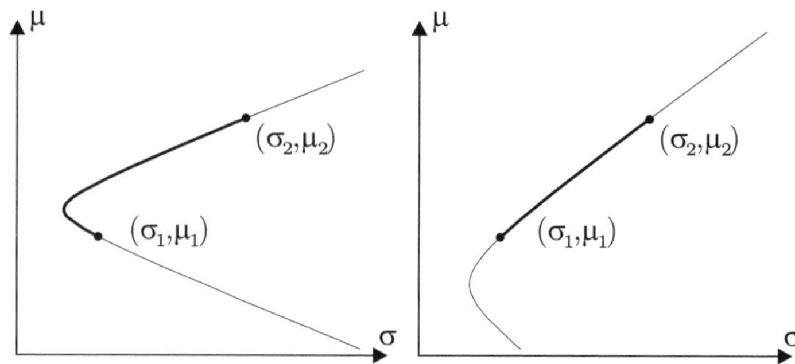


**Figure 5.3** Typical portfolio lines with $-1 < \rho_{12} < 1$

Figure 5.4 illustrates the following corollary.

## Corollary 5.6

Suppose that $\sigma_1 \leq \sigma_2$. The following three cases are possible:

1) If $-1 \leq \rho_{12} < \frac{\sigma_1}{\sigma_2}$, then there is a portfolio without short selling such that $\sigma_V < \sigma_1$ (lines 4 and 5 in Figure 5.4);

2) If $\rho_{12} = \frac{\sigma_1}{\sigma_2}$, then $\sigma_V \geq \sigma_1$ for each portfolio (line 3 in Figure 5.4);

3) If $\frac{\sigma_1}{\sigma_2} < \rho_{12} \leq 1$, then there is a portfolio with short selling such that $\sigma_V < \sigma_1$, but for each portfolio without short selling $\sigma_V \geq \sigma_1$ (lines 1 and 2 in Figure 5.4).

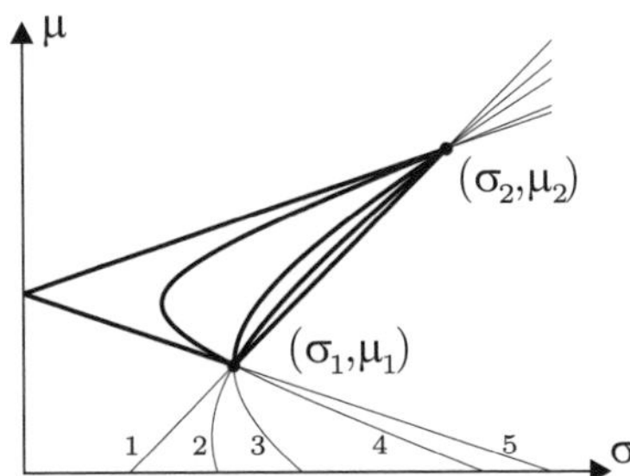


**Figure 5.4** Portfolio lines for various values of $\rho_{12}$

## Proof

1) If $-1 \leq \rho_{12} < \frac{\sigma_1}{\sigma_2}$, then $\frac{\sigma_1}{\sigma_1+\sigma_2} > s_0 > 0$. But $\frac{\sigma_1}{\sigma_1+\sigma_2} < 1$, so $0 < s_0 < 1$, which means that the portfolio with minimum variance, which corresponds to the parameter $s_0$, involves no short selling and satisfies $\sigma_V < \sigma_1$.

2) If $\rho_{12} = \frac{\sigma_1}{\sigma_2}$, then $s_0 = 0$. As a result, $\sigma_V \geq \sigma_1$ for every portfolio because $\sigma_1^2$ is the minimum variance.

3) Finally, if $\frac{\sigma_1}{\sigma_2} < \rho_{12} \leq 1$, then $s_0 < 0$. In this case the portfolio with minimum variance that corresponds to $s_0$ involves short selling of security 1 and satisfies $\sigma_V < \sigma_1$. For $s \geq s_0$ the variance $\sigma_V$ is an increasing function of $s$, which means that $\sigma_V > \sigma_1$ for every portfolio without short selling. □

The above corollary is important because it shows when it is possible to construct a portfolio with risk lower than that of any of its components. In case 1) this is possible without short selling. In case 3) this is also possible, but only if short selling is allowed. In case 2) it is impossible to construct such a portfolio.

## Example 5.9

Suppose that

$$\sigma_1^2 = 0.0041, \quad \sigma_2^2 = 0.0121, \quad \rho_{12} = 0.9796.$$

Clearly, $\sigma_1 < \sigma_2$ and $\frac{\sigma_1}{\sigma_2} < \rho_{12} < 1$, so this is case 3) in Corollary 5.6. Our task will be to find the portfolio with minimum risk with and without short selling.

Using Theorem 5.5, we compute

$$s_0 \cong -1.1663, \quad s_{\min} = 0.$$

It follows that in the portfolio with minimum risk the weights of securities should be $w_1 \cong 2.1663$ and $w_2 \cong -1.1663$ if short selling is allowed. Without short selling $w_1 = 1$ and $w_2 = 0$.

### *Exercise 5.10*

Compute the weights in the portfolio with minimum risk for the data in Example 5.6. Does this portfolio involve short selling?

We conclude this section with a brief discussion of portfolios in which one of the securities is risk-free. The variance of the risky security (a stock) is positive, whereas that of the risk-free component (a bond) is zero.

## Proposition 5.7

The standard deviation $\sigma_V$ of a portfolio consisting of a risky security with expected return $\mu_1$ and standard deviation $\sigma_1 > 0$, and a risk-free security with return $r_F$ and standard deviation zero depends on the weight $w_1$ of the risky security as follows:

$$\sigma_V = |w_1|\,\sigma_1.$$

## Proof

Let $\sigma_1 > 0$ and $\sigma_2 = 0$. Then (5.7) reduces to $\sigma_V^2 = w_1^2\sigma_1^2$, and the formula for $\sigma_V$ follows by taking the square root. □

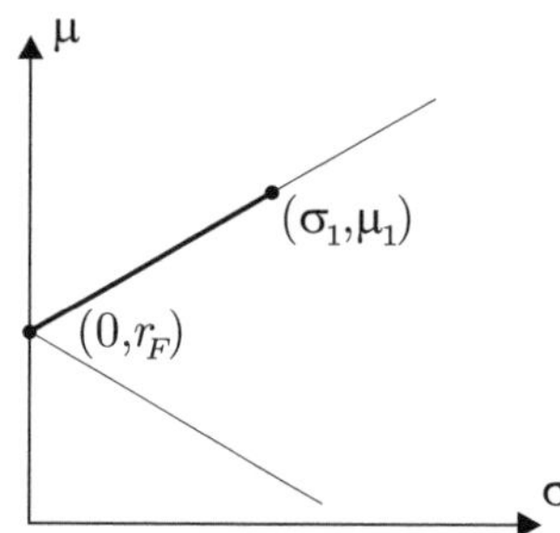


**Figure 5.5** Portfolio line for one risky and one risk-free security

The line on the $\sigma, \mu$ plane representing portfolios constructed from one risky and one risk-free security is shown in Figure 5.5. As usual, the bold line segment corresponds to portfolios without short selling.

# 5.3 Several Securities

## 5.3.1 Risk and Expected Return on a Portfolio

A portfolio constructed from $n$ different securities can be described in terms of their weights

$$w_i = \frac{x_i S_i(0)}{V(0)}, \quad i = 1, \dots, n,$$

where $x_i$ is the number of shares of type $i$ in the portfolio, $S_i(0)$ is the initial price of security $i$, and $V(0)$ is the amount initially invested in the portfolio. It will prove convenient to arrange the weights into a one-row matrix

$$\boldsymbol{w} = \begin{bmatrix} w_1 & w_2 & \cdots & w_n \end{bmatrix}.$$

Just like for two securities, the weights add up to one, which can be written in matrix form as

$$1 = \boldsymbol{u}\boldsymbol{w}^T, \tag{5.14}$$

where

$$\boldsymbol{u} = \begin{bmatrix} 1 & 1 & \cdots & 1 \end{bmatrix}$$

is a one-row matrix with all $n$ entries equal to 1, $\boldsymbol{w}^T$ is a one-column matrix, the transpose of $\boldsymbol{w}$, and the usual matrix multiplication rules apply. The *attainable set* consists of all portfolios with weights $\boldsymbol{w}$ satisfying (5.14), called the *attainable portfolios*.

Suppose that the returns on the securities are $K_1, \dots, K_n$. The expected returns $\mu_i = E(K_i)$ for $i = 1, \dots, n$ will also be arranged into a one-row matrix

$$\boldsymbol{m} = \begin{bmatrix} \mu_1 & \mu_2 & \cdots & \mu_n \end{bmatrix}.$$

The covariances between returns will be denoted by $c_{ij} = \mathrm{Cov}(K_i, K_j)$. They are the entries of the $n \times n$ *covariance matrix*

$$\boldsymbol{C} = \begin{bmatrix} c_{11} & c_{12} & \cdots & c_{1n} \\ c_{21} & c_{22} & \cdots & c_{2n} \\ \vdots & \vdots & \ddots & \vdots \\ c_{n1} & c_{n2} & \cdots & c_{nn} \end{bmatrix}.$$

It is well known that the covariance matrix is symmetric and positive definite. The diagonal elements are simply the variances of returns, $c_{ii} = \operatorname{Var}(K_i)$. In what follows we shall assume, in addition, that $\boldsymbol{C}$ has an inverse $\boldsymbol{C}^{-1}$.

## Proposition 5.8

The expected return $\mu_V = E(K_V)$ and variance $\sigma_V^2 = \operatorname{Var}(K_V)$ of the return $K_V = w_1K_1 + \cdots + w_nK_n$ on a portfolio with weights $\boldsymbol{w} = [w_1, \ldots, w_n]$ are given by

$$\mu_V = \boldsymbol{m}\boldsymbol{w}^T, \tag{5.15}$$

$$\sigma_V^2 = \boldsymbol{w}\boldsymbol{C}\boldsymbol{w}^T. \tag{5.16}$$

## Proof

The formula for $\mu_V$ follows by the linearity of expectation,

$$\mu_V = E(K_V) = E\left(\sum_{i=1}^n w_iK_i\right) = \sum_{i=1}^n w_i\mu_i = \boldsymbol{m}\boldsymbol{w}^T.$$

For $\sigma_V^2$ we use the linearity of covariance with respect to each of its arguments,

$$\begin{aligned}\sigma_V^2 &= \operatorname{Var}(K_V) = \operatorname{Var}\left(\sum_{i=1}^n w_iK_i\right)\\ &= \operatorname{Cov}\left(\sum_{i=1}^n w_iK_i, \sum_{j=1}^n w_jK_j\right) = \sum_{i,j=1}^n w_iw_jc_{ij}\\ &= \boldsymbol{w}\boldsymbol{C}\boldsymbol{w}^T.\end{aligned}$$

□

### *Exercise 5.11*

Compute the expected return $\mu_V$ and standard deviation $\sigma_V$ of a portfolio consisting of three securities with weights $w_1 = 40\%$, $w_2 = -20\%$, $w_3 = 80\%$, given that the securities have expected returns $\mu_1 = 8\%$, $\mu_2 = 10\%$, $\mu_3 = 6\%$, standard deviations $\sigma_1 = 1.5$, $\sigma_2 = 0.5$, $\sigma_3 = 1.2$ and correlations $\rho_{12} = 0.3$, $\rho_{23} = 0.0$, $\rho_{31} = -0.2$.

We shall solve the following two problems:

1. To find a portfolio with the smallest variance in the attainable set. It will be called the *minimum variance portfolio*.

2. To find a portfolio with the smallest variance among all portfolios in the attainable set whose expected return is equal to a given number $\mu_V$. The family of such portfolios, parametrised by $\mu_V$, is called the *minimum variance line*.

Since the variance is a continuous function of the weights, bounded below by 0, the minimum clearly exists in both cases.

## Proposition 5.9 (Minimum Variance Portfolio)

The portfolio with the smallest variance in the attainable set has weights

$$\boldsymbol{w} = \frac{\boldsymbol{u}\boldsymbol{C}^{-1}}{\boldsymbol{u}\boldsymbol{C}^{-1}\boldsymbol{u}^T}.$$

## Proof

We need to find the minimum of (5.16) subject to the constraint (5.14). To this end we can use the method of Lagrange multipliers. Let us put

$$F(\boldsymbol{w}, \lambda) = \boldsymbol{w}\boldsymbol{C}\boldsymbol{w}^T - \lambda\boldsymbol{u}\boldsymbol{w}^T,$$

where $\lambda$ is a Lagrange multiplier. Equating to zero the partial derivatives of $F$ with respect to the weights $w_i$ we obtain $2\boldsymbol{w}\boldsymbol{C} - \lambda\boldsymbol{u} = 0$, that is,

$$\boldsymbol{w} = \frac{\lambda}{2}\boldsymbol{u}\boldsymbol{C}^{-1},$$

which is a necessary condition for a minimum. Substituting this into constraint (5.14) we obtain

$$1 = \frac{\lambda}{2}\boldsymbol{u}\boldsymbol{C}^{-1}\boldsymbol{u}^T,$$

where we use the fact that $\boldsymbol{C}^{-1}$ is a symmetric matrix because $\boldsymbol{C}$ is. Solving this for $\lambda$ and substituting the result into the expression for $\boldsymbol{w}$ will give the asserted formula. □

## Proposition 5.10 (Minimum Variance Line)

The portfolio with the smallest variance among attainable portfolios with expected return $\mu_V$ has weights

$$\boldsymbol{w} = \frac{\begin{vmatrix} 1 & \boldsymbol{u}\boldsymbol{C}^{-1}\boldsymbol{m}^T \\ \mu_V & \boldsymbol{m}\boldsymbol{C}^{-1}\boldsymbol{m}^T \end{vmatrix} \boldsymbol{u}\boldsymbol{C}^{-1} + \begin{vmatrix} \boldsymbol{u}\boldsymbol{C}^{-1}\boldsymbol{u}^T & 1 \\ \boldsymbol{m}\boldsymbol{C}^{-1}\boldsymbol{u}^T & \mu_V \end{vmatrix} \boldsymbol{m}\boldsymbol{C}^{-1}}{\begin{vmatrix} \boldsymbol{u}\boldsymbol{C}^{-1}\boldsymbol{u}^T & \boldsymbol{u}\boldsymbol{C}^{-1}\boldsymbol{m}^T \\ \boldsymbol{m}\boldsymbol{C}^{-1}\boldsymbol{u}^T & \boldsymbol{m}\boldsymbol{C}^{-1}\boldsymbol{m}^T \end{vmatrix}},$$

provided that the determinant in the denominator is non-zero. The weights depend linearly on $\mu_V$.

## Proof

Here we need to find the minimum of (5.16) subject to two constraints (5.14) and (5.15). We take

$$G(\boldsymbol{w},\lambda,\mu) = \boldsymbol{w}\boldsymbol{C}\boldsymbol{w}^T - \lambda\boldsymbol{u}\boldsymbol{w}^T - \mu\boldsymbol{m}\boldsymbol{w}^T,$$

where $\lambda$ and $\mu$ are Lagrange multipliers. The partial derivatives of $G$ with respect to the weights $w_i$ equated to zero give a necessary condition for a minimum, $2\boldsymbol{w}\boldsymbol{C} - \lambda\boldsymbol{u} - \mu\boldsymbol{m} = 0$, which implies that

$$\boldsymbol{w} = \frac{\lambda}{2}\boldsymbol{u}\boldsymbol{C}^{-1} + \frac{\mu}{2}\boldsymbol{m}\boldsymbol{C}^{-1}.$$

Substituting this into the constraints (5.14) and (5.15), we obtain a system of linear equations

$$\begin{aligned} 1 &= \frac{\lambda}{2}\boldsymbol{u}\boldsymbol{C}^{-1}\boldsymbol{u}^T + \frac{\mu}{2}\boldsymbol{u}\boldsymbol{C}^{-1}\boldsymbol{m}^T, \\ \mu_V &= \frac{\lambda}{2}\boldsymbol{m}\boldsymbol{C}^{-1}\boldsymbol{u}^T + \frac{\mu}{2}\boldsymbol{m}\boldsymbol{C}^{-1}\boldsymbol{m}^T, \end{aligned}$$

to be solved for $\lambda$ and $\mu$. The asserted formula follows by substituting the solution into the expression for $\boldsymbol{w}$. □

## Example 5.10

(3 securities) Consider three securities with expected returns, standard deviations of returns and correlations between returns

$$\begin{aligned} &\mu_1 = 0.10, \quad \sigma_1 = 0.28, \quad \rho_{12} = \rho_{21} = -0.10, \\ &\mu_2 = 0.15, \quad \sigma_2 = 0.24, \quad \rho_{23} = \rho_{32} = \phantom{-}0.20, \\ &\mu_3 = 0.20, \quad \sigma_3 = 0.25, \quad \rho_{31} = \rho_{13} = \phantom{-}0.25. \end{aligned}$$

We arrange the $\mu_i$'s into a one-row matrix $\boldsymbol{m}$ and 1's into a one-row matrix $\boldsymbol{u}$,

$$\boldsymbol{m} = \begin{bmatrix} 0.10 & 0.15 & 0.20 \end{bmatrix}, \quad \boldsymbol{u} = \begin{bmatrix} 1 & 1 & 1 \end{bmatrix}.$$

Next we compute the entries $c_{ij} = \rho_{ij}\sigma_i\sigma_j$ of the covariance matrix $\boldsymbol{C}$, and find the inverse matrix to $\boldsymbol{C}$,

$$\boldsymbol{C} \cong \begin{bmatrix} 0.0784 & -0.0067 & 0.0175 \\ -0.0067 & 0.0576 & 0.0120 \\ 0.0175 & 0.0120 & 0.0625 \end{bmatrix}, \quad \boldsymbol{C}^{-1} \cong \begin{bmatrix} 13.954 & 2.544 & -4.396 \\ 2.544 & 18.548 & -4.274 \\ -4.396 & -4.274 & 18.051 \end{bmatrix}$$

From Proposition 5.9 we can compute the weights in the minimum variance portfolio. Since

$$\begin{aligned}\boldsymbol{u}\boldsymbol{C}^{-1} &\cong \left[\begin{array}{ccc} 12.102 & 16.818 & 9.382 \end{array}\right], \\ \boldsymbol{u}\boldsymbol{C}^{-1}\boldsymbol{u}^T &\cong 38.302,\end{aligned}$$

we obtain

$$\boldsymbol{w} = \frac{\boldsymbol{u}\boldsymbol{C}^{-1}}{\boldsymbol{u}\boldsymbol{C}^{-1}\boldsymbol{u}^T} \cong \left[\begin{array}{ccc} 0.316 & 0.439 & 0.245 \end{array}\right].$$

The expected return and standard deviation of this portfolio are

$$\mu_V = \boldsymbol{m}\boldsymbol{w}^T \cong 0.146, \quad \sigma_V = \sqrt{\boldsymbol{w}\boldsymbol{C}\boldsymbol{w}^T} \cong 0.162.$$

The minimum variance line can be computed using Proposition 5.10. To this end we compute

$$\begin{aligned}\boldsymbol{u}\boldsymbol{C}^{-1} &\cong \left[\begin{array}{ccc} 12.102 & 16.818 & 9.382 \end{array}\right], \\ \boldsymbol{m}\boldsymbol{C}^{-1} &\cong \left[\begin{array}{ccc} 0.898 & 2.182 & 2.530 \end{array}\right], \\ \boldsymbol{u}\boldsymbol{C}^{-1}\boldsymbol{u}^T &\cong 38.302, \quad \boldsymbol{m}\boldsymbol{C}^{-1}\boldsymbol{m}^T \cong 0.923, \\ \boldsymbol{u}\boldsymbol{C}^{-1}\boldsymbol{m}^T &= \boldsymbol{m}\boldsymbol{C}^{-1}\boldsymbol{u}^T \cong 5.609.\end{aligned}$$

Substituting these into the formula for $\boldsymbol{w}$ in Proposition 5.10, we obtain the weights in the portfolio with minimum variance among all portfolios with expected return $\mu_V$:

$$\boldsymbol{w} \cong \left[\begin{array}{ccc} 1.578 - 8.614\mu_V & 0.845 - 2.769\mu_V & -1.422 + 11.384\mu_V \end{array}\right].$$

The standard deviation of this portfolio is

$$\sigma_V = \sqrt{\boldsymbol{w}\boldsymbol{C}\boldsymbol{w}^T} \cong \sqrt{0.237 - 2.885\mu_V + 9.850\mu_V^2}.$$

## *Exercise 5.12*

Among all attainable portfolios constructed using three securities with expected returns $\mu_1 = 0.20$, $\mu_2 = 0.13$, $\mu_3 = 0.17$, standard deviations of returns $\sigma_1 = 0.25$, $\sigma_2 = 0.28$, $\sigma_3 = 0.20$, and correlations between returns $\rho_{12} = 0.30$, $\rho_{23} = 0.00$, $\rho_{31} = 0.15$, find the minimum variance portfolio. What are the weights in this portfolio? Also compute the expected return and standard deviation of this portfolio.

## *Exercise 5.13*

Among all attainable portfolios with expected return $\mu_V = 20\%$ constructed using the three securities in Exercise 5.12 find the portfolio with the smallest variance. Compute the weights and the standard deviation of this portfolio.

## Example 5.11

(3 securities visualised) There are two convenient ways to visualise all portfolios that can be constructed from the three securities in Example 5.10. One is presented in Figure 5.6. Here two of the three weights, namely $w_2$ and $w_3$,

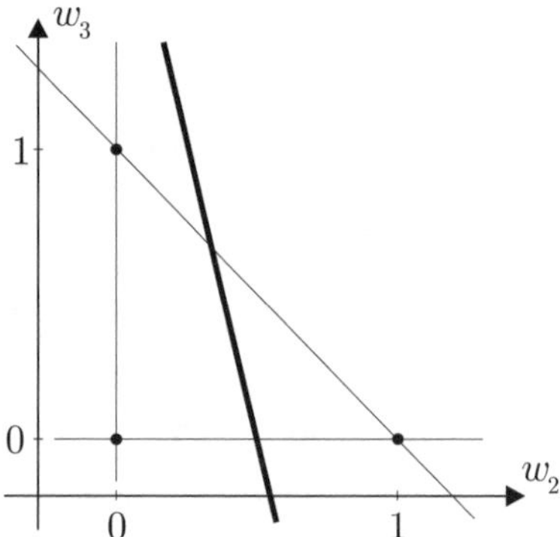


**Figure 5.6** Attainable portfolios on the $w_2, w_3$ plane

are used as parameters. The remaining weight is given by $w_1 = 1 - w_2 - w_3$. (Of course any other two weights can also be used as parameters.) Each point on the $w_2, w_3$ plane represents a different portfolio. The vertices of the triangle represent the portfolios consisting of only one of the three securities. For example, the vertex with coordinates $(1, 0)$ corresponds to weights $w_1 = 0$, $w_2 = 1$ and $w_3 = 0$, that is, represents a portfolio with all money invested in security number 2. The lines through the vertices correspond to portfolios consisting of two securities only. For example, the line through $(1, 0)$ and $(0, 1)$ corresponds to portfolios containing securities 2 and 3 only. Points inside the triangle, including the boundaries, correspond to portfolios without short selling. For example, $(\frac{2}{5}, \frac{1}{2})$ represents a portfolio with 10% of the initial funds invested in security 1, 40% in security 2, and 50% in security 3. Points outside the triangle correspond to portfolios with one or two of the three securities shorted. The minimum variance line is a straight line because of the linear dependence of the weights on the expected return. It is represented by the bold line in Figure 5.6.

Figure 5.7 shows another way to visualise attainable portfolios by plotting the expected return of a portfolio against the standard deviation. This is sometimes called the risk–expected return graph. The three points indicated in this picture correspond to portfolios consisting of only one of the three securities. For instance, the portfolio with all funds invested in security 2 is represented by the point $(0.24, 0.15)$. The lines passing through a pair of these three points correspond to portfolios consisting of just two securities. These are the two-security lines studied in detail in Section 5.2. For example, all portfolios containing securities 2 and 3 only lie on the line through $(0.24, 0.15)$ and $(0.25, 0.20)$. The three points and the lines passing through them correspond to the vertices of the triangle and the straight lines passing through them in Figure 5.6. The shaded area (both dark and light), including the boundary, represents portfolios that can be constructed from the three securities, that is, all attainable portfolios. The boundary, shown as a bold line, is the minimum variance line. The shape of it is known as the *Markowitz bullet*. The darker part of the shaded area corresponds to the interior of the triangle in Figure 5.6, that is, it represents portfolios without short selling.

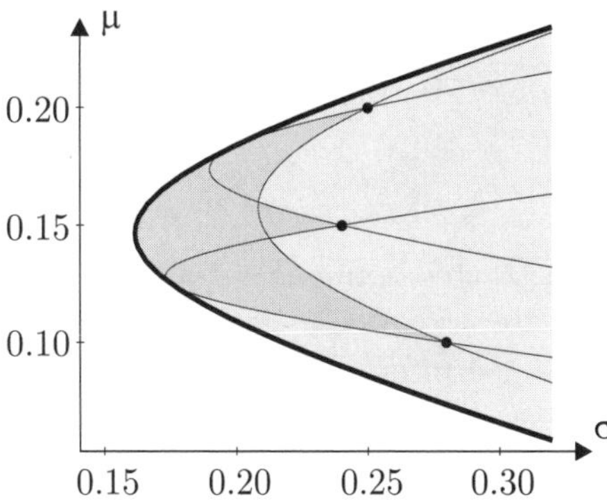


**Figure 5.7** Attainable portfolios on the $\sigma, \mu$ plane

It is instructive to imagine how the whole $w_2, w_3$ plane in Figure 5.6 is mapped onto the shaded area representing all attainable portfolios in Figure 5.7. Namely, the $w_2, w_3$ plane is folded along the minimum variance line, being simultaneously warped and stretched to attain the shape of the Markowitz bullet. This means, in particular, that pairs of points on opposite sides of the minimum variance line on the $w_2, w_3$ plane are mapped into single points on the $\sigma, \mu$ plane. In other words, each point inside the shaded area in Figure 5.7 corresponds to two different portfolios. However, each point on the minimum variance line corresponds to a single portfolio.

## Example 5.12

(3 securities without short selling) For the same three securities as in Examples 5.10 and 5.11, Figure 5.8 shows what happens if no short selling is allowed. All portfolios without short selling are represented by the interior and boundary of the triangle on the $w_1, w_2$ plane and by the shaded area with boundary on the $\sigma, \mu$ plane. The minimum variance line without short selling is shown as a bold line in both plots. For comparison, the minimum variance line with short selling is shown as a broken line.

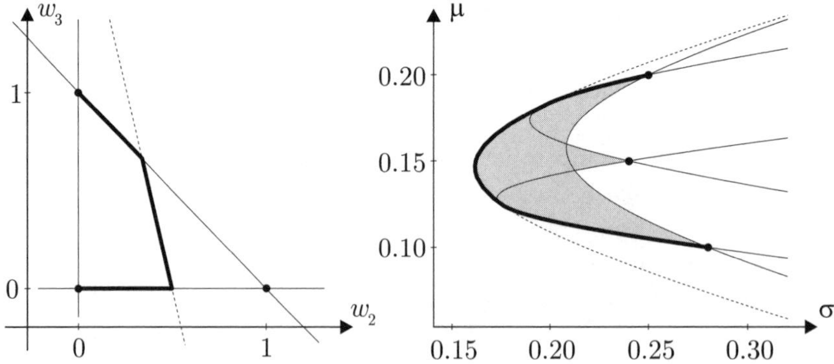


**Figure 5.8** Portfolios without short selling

*Exercise 5.14*

For portfolios constructed with and without short selling from the three securities in Exercise 5.12 compute the minimum variance line parametrised by the expected return and sketch it a) on the $w_2, w_3$ plane and b) on the $\sigma, \mu$ plane. Also sketch the set of all attainable portfolios with and without short selling.

## 5.3.2 Efficient Frontier

Given the choice between two securities a rational investor will, if possible, choose that with higher expected return and lower standard deviation, that is, lower risk. This motivates the following definition.

### Definition 5.1

We say that a security with expected return $\mu_1$ and standard deviation $\sigma_1$ *dominates* another security with expected return $\mu_2$ and standard deviation $\sigma_2$ whenever

$$\mu_1 \geq \mu_2 \quad \text{and} \quad \sigma_1 \leq \sigma_2.$$

This definition readily extends to portfolios, which can of course be considered as securities in their own right.

### Remark 5.4

Given two securities such that one dominates the other, the dominated security may appear quite redundant on first sight. Nevertheless, it can also be of some use. Employing the techniques of Section 5.2, it may be possible to construct portfolios consisting of the two securities with smaller risk than either of the securities, as in Figure 5.9, in which the security with $\sigma_2, \mu_2$ is dominated by that with $\sigma_1, \mu_1$.

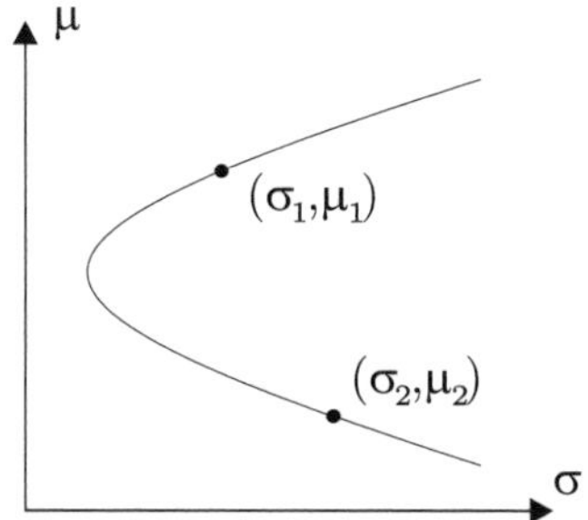


**Figure 5.9** Reduction of risk using a dominated security

## Definition 5.2

A portfolio is called *efficient* if there is no other portfolio, except itself, that dominates it. The set of efficient portfolios among all attainable portfolios is called the *efficient frontier*.

Every rational investor will choose an efficient portfolio, always preferring a dominating portfolio to a dominated one. However, different investors may select different portfolios on the efficient frontier, depending on their individual preferences. Given two efficient portfolios with $\mu_1 \leq \mu_2$ and $\sigma_1 \leq \sigma_2$, a cautious person may prefer that with lower risk $\sigma_1$ and lower expected return $\mu_1$, while others may choose a portfolio with higher risk $\sigma_2$, regarding the higher expected return $\mu_2$ as compensation for increased risk.

In particular, an efficient portfolio has the highest expected return among all attainable portfolios with the same standard deviation (the same risk), and has the lowest standard deviation (the lowest risk) among all attainable portfolios with the same expected return. As a result, the efficient frontier must be a subset of the minimum variance line. To understand the structure of the efficient frontier we shall first study the minimum variance line in more detail and then select a suitable subset.

## Proposition 5.11

Take any two different portfolios on the minimum variance line, with weights $\boldsymbol{w}'$ and $\boldsymbol{w}''$. Then the minimum variance line consists of portfolios with weights

$c\boldsymbol{w}' + (1-c)\boldsymbol{w}''$ for any $c \in \mathbb{R}$ and only of such portfolios.

## Proof

By Proposition 5.10 the minimum variance line consists of portfolios whose weights are given by a certain linear function of the expected return $\mu_V$ on the portfolio, $\boldsymbol{w} = \boldsymbol{a}\mu_V + \boldsymbol{b}$. If $\boldsymbol{w}'$ and $\boldsymbol{w}''$ are the weights of two different portfolios on the minimum variance line, then $\boldsymbol{w}' = \boldsymbol{a}\mu_{V'} + \boldsymbol{b}$ and $\boldsymbol{w}'' = \boldsymbol{a}\mu_{V''} + \boldsymbol{b}$ for some $\mu_{V'} \neq \mu_{V''}$. Because numbers of the form $c\mu_{V'} + (1-c)\mu_{V''}$ for $c \in \mathbb{R}$ exhaust the whole real line, it follows that portfolios with weights $c\boldsymbol{w}' + (1-c)\boldsymbol{w}''$ for $c \in \mathbb{R}$ exhaust the whole minimum variance line. □

This proposition is important. It means that the minimum variance line has the same shape as the set of portfolios constructed from two securities, studied in great detail in Section 5.2. It also means that the shape of the minimum variance line on the $\sigma, \mu$ plane (the Markowitz bullet), which we have seen so far for portfolios constructed from two or three securities, will in fact be the same for any number of securities.

Once the shape of the minimum variance line is understood, distinguishing the efficient frontier is easy, also in the case of $n$ securities. This is illustrated in Figure 5.10. The efficient frontier consists of all portfolios on the minimum variance line whose expected return is greater than or equal to the expected return on the minimum variance portfolio.

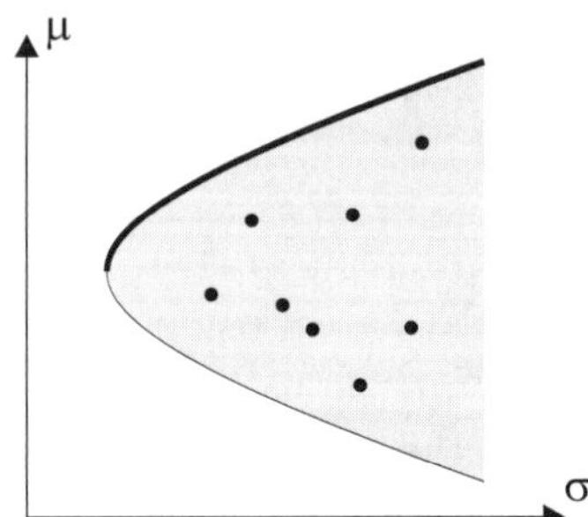


**Figure 5.10** Efficient frontier constructed from several securities

The next proposition provides a property of the efficient frontier which will prove useful in the Capital Asset Pricing Model.

## Proposition 5.12

The weights $\boldsymbol{w}$ of any portfolio belonging to the efficient frontier (except for the minimum variance portfolio) satisfy the condition

$$\gamma \boldsymbol{w}\boldsymbol{C} = \boldsymbol{m} - \mu \boldsymbol{u} \tag{5.17}$$

for some real numbers $\gamma > 0$ and $\mu$.

## Proof

Let $\boldsymbol{w}$ be the weights of a portfolio, other than the minimum variance portfolio, belonging to the efficient frontier. The portfolio has expected return $\mu_V = \boldsymbol{m}\boldsymbol{w}^T$ and standard deviation $\sigma_V = \sqrt{\boldsymbol{w}\boldsymbol{C}\boldsymbol{w}^T}$. On the $\sigma, \mu$ plane we draw the tangent line to the efficient frontier through the point representing the portfolio. This line will intersect the vertical axis at some point with coordinate $\mu$, the gradient of the line being $\dfrac{\boldsymbol{m}\boldsymbol{w}^T - \mu}{\sqrt{\boldsymbol{w}\boldsymbol{C}\boldsymbol{w}^T}}$. This gradient is maximal among all lines passing through the point on the vertical axis with coordinate $\mu$ and intersecting the set of attainable portfolios. The maximum is to be taken over all weights $\boldsymbol{w}$ subject to the constraint $\boldsymbol{u}\boldsymbol{w}^T = 1$. We put

$$F(\boldsymbol{w}, \lambda) = \frac{\boldsymbol{m}\boldsymbol{w}^T - \mu}{\sqrt{\boldsymbol{w}\boldsymbol{C}\boldsymbol{w}^T}} - \lambda \boldsymbol{u}\boldsymbol{w}^T,$$

where $\lambda$ is a Lagrange multiplier. A necessary condition for a constrained maximum is that the partial derivatives of $F$ with respect to the weights should be zero. This gives

$$\boldsymbol{m} - \lambda \sigma_V \boldsymbol{u} = \frac{\mu_V - \mu}{\sigma_V^2} \boldsymbol{w}\boldsymbol{C}.$$

Multiplying by $\boldsymbol{w}^T$ on the right and using the constraint, we find that $\lambda = \frac{\mu}{\sigma_V}$. For $\gamma = \frac{\mu_V - \mu}{\sigma_V^2}$ this gives the asserted condition. Because the tangent line has positive slope, we have $\mu_V > \mu$, that is, $\gamma > 0$. □

## Remark 5.5

An interpretation of $\gamma$ and $\mu$ follows clearly from the proof: $\gamma\sigma_V$ is the gradient of the tangent line to the efficient frontier at the point representing the given portfolio, $\mu$ being the intercept of this tangent line on the $\sigma, \mu$ plane.

### *Exercise 5.15*

In a market consisting of the three securities in Exercise 5.12, consider the portfolio on the efficient frontier with expected return $\mu_V = 21\%$. Compute the values of $\gamma$ and $\mu$ such that the weights $\boldsymbol{w}$ in this portfolio satisfy $\gamma \boldsymbol{w}\boldsymbol{C} = \boldsymbol{m} - \mu \boldsymbol{u}$.

## 5.4 Capital Asset Pricing Model

In the days when computers where slow it was difficult to use portfolio theory. For a market with $n = 1,000$ traded securities the covariance matrix $\boldsymbol{C}$ will have $n^2 = 1,000,000$ entries. To find the efficient frontier we have to compute the inverse matrix $\boldsymbol{C}^{-1}$, which is computationally intensive. Accurate estimation of $\boldsymbol{C}$ may pose considerable problems in practice. The Capital Asset Pricing Model (CAPM) provides a solution that is much more efficient computationally, does not involve an estimate of $\boldsymbol{C}$, but offers a deep, even if somewhat oversimplified, insight into some fundamental economic issues.

Within the CAPM it is assumed that every investor uses the same values of expected returns, standard deviation and correlations for all securities, making investment decisions based only on these values. In particular, every investor will compute the same efficient frontier on which to select his or her portfolio. However, investors may differ in their attitude to risk, selecting different portfolios on the efficient frontier.

### 5.4.1 Capital Market Line

Form now on we shall assume that a risk-free security is available in addition to $n$ risky securities. The return on the risk-free security will be denoted by $r_F$. The standard deviation is of course zero for the risk-free security.

Consider a portfolio consisting of the risk-free security and a specified risky security (possibly a portfolio of risky securities) with expected return $\mu_1$ and standard deviation $\sigma_1 > 0$. By Proposition 5.7 all such portfolios form a broken line on the $\sigma, \mu$ plane consisting of two rectilinear half-lines, see Figure 5.5. By taking portfolios containing the risk-free security and a security with $\sigma_1, \mu_1$ anywhere in the attainable set represented by the Markowitz bullet on the $\sigma, \mu$ plane, we can construct any portfolio between the two half-lines shown in Figure 5.11. The efficient frontier of this new set of portfolios, which may contain the risk-free security, is the upper half-line tangent to the Markowitz bullet and passing through the point with coordinates $0, r_F$. According to the assumptions of the CAPM, every rational investor will select his or her portfolio on this half-line, called the *capital market line*. This argument works as long as the risk-free return $r_F$ is not too high, so the upper half-line is tangent to the bullet. (If $r_F$ is too high, then the upper half-line will no longer be tangent to the bullet.)

The tangency point with coordinates $\sigma_M, \mu_M$ plays a special role. Every portfolio on the capital market line can be constructed from the risk-free security and the portfolio with standard deviation $\sigma_M$ and expected return $\mu_M$.

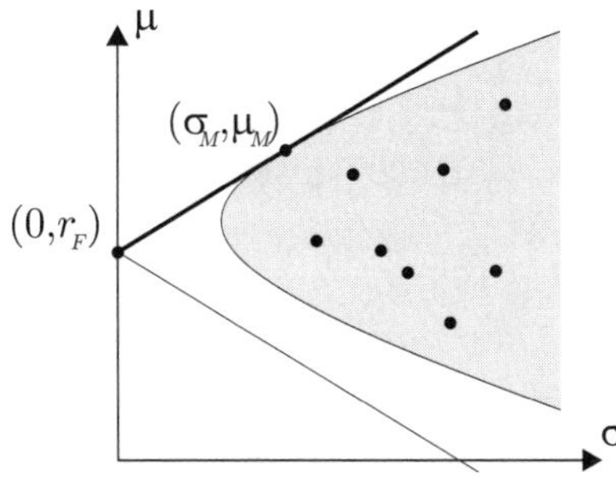


**Figure 5.11** Efficient frontier for portfolios with a risk-free security

Since every investor will select a portfolio on the capital market line, everyone will be holding a portfolio with the same relative proportions of risky securities. But this means that the portfolio with standard deviation $\sigma_M$ and expected return $\mu_M$ has to contain all risky securities with weights equal to their relative share in the whole market. Because of this property it is called the *market portfolio*. In practice the market portfolio is approximated by a suitable stock exchange index.

The capital market line joining the risk-free security and the market portfolio satisfies the equation

$$\mu = r_F + \frac{\mu_M - r_F}{\sigma_M}\sigma. \tag{5.18}$$

For a portfolio on the capital market line with risk $\sigma$ the term $\frac{\mu_M - r_F}{\sigma_M}\sigma$ is called the *risk premium*. This additional return above the risk-free level provides compensation for exposure to risk.

## Example 5.13

We shall apply Proposition 5.12 to compute the market portfolio for a toy market consisting of the three securities in Example 5.10 and a risk-free security with return $r_F = 5\%$. The weights $\boldsymbol{w}$ in the market portfolio, which belongs to the efficient frontier, satisfy condition (5.17), which implies that

$$\gamma \boldsymbol{w} = (\boldsymbol{m} - \mu \boldsymbol{u})\boldsymbol{C}^{-1}.$$

From the proof of Proposition 5.12 we know that $\mu = r_F$ because the capital market line, tangent to the efficient frontier at the point representing the market portfolio, intersects the $\mu$ axis at $r_F$. Substituting the numerical values from Example 5.10, we find that

$$\gamma \boldsymbol{w} \cong \left[\begin{array}{ccc} 0.293 & 1.341 & 2.061 \end{array}\right].$$

Since $\boldsymbol{w}$ must satisfy (5.14), it follows that $\gamma \cong 3.694$ and the weights in the market portfolio are

$$\boldsymbol{w} \cong \begin{bmatrix} 0.079 & 0.363 & 0.558 \end{bmatrix}.$$

*Exercise 5.16*

Suppose that the risk-free return is $r_F = 5\%$. Compute the weights in the market portfolio constructed from the three securities in Exercise 5.11. Also compute the expected return and standard deviation of the market portfolio.

### 5.4.2 Beta Factor

It is important to understand how the return $K_V$ on a given portfolio or a single security will react to trends affecting the whole market. To this end we can plot the values of $K_V$ for each market scenario against those of the return $K_M$ on the market portfolio and compute the *line of best fit*, also known as the *regression line* or the *characteristic line*. In Figure 5.12 the values of $K_M$ are marked along the $x$ axis and the values of $K_V$ along the $y$ axis. The equation of the line of best fit will be

$$y = \beta_V x + \alpha_V.$$

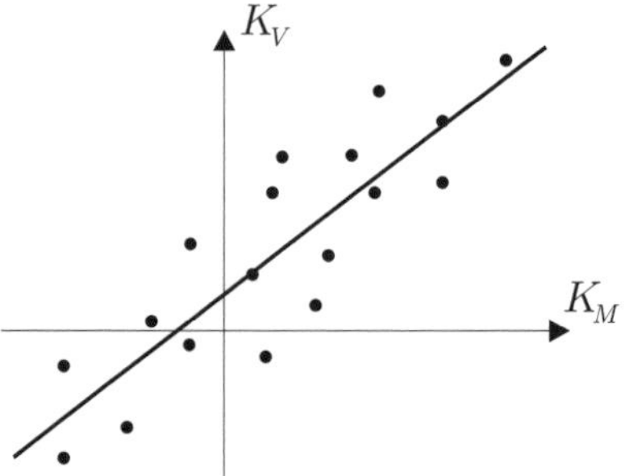


**Figure 5.12** Line of best fit

For any given $\beta$ and $\alpha$ the values of the random variable $\alpha + \beta K_M$ can be regarded as predictions for the return on the given portfolio. The difference $\varepsilon = K_V - (\alpha + \beta K_M)$ between the actual return $K_V$ and the predicted return

$\alpha + \beta K_M$ is called the *residual random variable*. The condition defining the line of best fit is that

$$E(\varepsilon^2) = E(K_V^2) - 2\beta E(K_V K_M) + \beta^2 E(K_M^2) + \alpha^2 - 2\alpha E(K_V) + 2\alpha\beta E(K_M)$$

as a function of $\beta$ and $\alpha$ should attain its minimum at $\beta = \beta_V$ and $\alpha = \alpha_V$. In other words, the line of best fit should lead to predictions that are as close as possible to the true values of $K_V$. A necessary condition for a minimum is that the partial derivatives with respect to $\beta$ and $\alpha$ should be zero at $\beta = \beta_V$ and $\alpha = \alpha_V$. This leads to the system of linear equations

$$\alpha_V E(K_M) + \beta_V E(K_M^2) = E(K_V K_M),$$
$$\alpha_V + \beta_V E(K_M) = E(K_V),$$

which can be solved to find the gradient $\beta_V$ and intercept $\alpha_V$ of the line of best fit,

$$\beta_V = \frac{\text{Cov}(K_V, K_M)}{\sigma_M^2}, \qquad \alpha_V = \mu_V - \beta_V \mu_M.$$

Here we employ the usual notation $\mu_V = E(K_V)$, $\mu_M = E(K_M)$ and $\sigma_M^2 = \text{Var}(K_M)$.

### *Exercise 5.17*

Suppose that the returns $K_V$ on a given portfolio and $K_M$ on the market portfolio take the following values in different market scenarios:

| Scenario | Probability | Return $K_V$ | Return $K_M$ |
|---|---|---|---|
| $\omega_1$ | 0.1 | −5% | 10% |
| $\omega_2$ | 0.3 | 0% | 14% |
| $\omega_3$ | 0.4 | 2% | 12% |
| $\omega_3$ | 0.2 | 4% | 16% |

Compute the gradient $\beta_V$ and intercept $\alpha_V$ of the line of best fit.

### Definition 5.3

We call

$$\beta_V = \frac{\text{Cov}(K_V, K_M)}{\sigma_M^2}$$

the *beta factor* of the given portfolio or individual security.

The beta factor is an indicator of expected changes in the return on a particular portfolio or individual security in response to the behaviour of the market as a whole. Since $\mu_V = \beta_V \mu_M + \alpha_V$, the return on a security with a positive beta factor tends to increase as the return on the market portfolio increases, while the return on a security with a negative beta factor tends to increase if the return on the market portfolio goes down.

In what follows we discuss another interpretation of the beta factor. The risk $\sigma_V^2 = \mathrm{Var}(K_V)$ of a security or portfolio can be written as

$$\sigma_V^2 = \mathrm{Var}(\varepsilon_V) + \beta_V^2 \sigma_M^2.$$

This formula is easy to verify upon substituting the expression $\varepsilon_V = K_V - (\alpha_V + \beta_V K_M)$ for the residual random variable. The first term $\mathrm{Var}(\varepsilon_V)$ is called the *residual variance* or *diversifiable risk*. It vanishes for the market portfolio, $\mathrm{Var}(\varepsilon_M) = 0$. This part of risk can 'diversified away' by investing in the market portfolio. The second term $\beta_V^2 \sigma_M^2$ is called the *systematic* or *undiversifiable risk*. The market portfolio involves only this kind of risk. The beta factor $\beta_V$ can be regarded as a measure of systematic risk associated with a security or portfolio.

This interpretation of the beta factor is of crucial importance. In the CAPM systematic risk, measured by $\beta_V$, will be linked to the expected return $\mu_V$ and hence to the pricing of individual securities and portfolios: The higher the systematic risk, the higher the return required by investors as a premium for exposure to this kind of risk. However, diversifiable risk will attract no additional premium, having no effect on $\mu_V$. This is because diversifiable risk can be eliminated by spreading an investment in a portfolio of many securities and, in particular, by investing in the market portfolio. The next section is devoted to establishing the link between $\beta_V$ and $\mu_V$.

*Exercise 5.18*

Show that the beta factor $\beta_V$ of a portfolio consisting of $n$ securities with weights $w_1, \ldots, w_n$ is given by $\beta_V = w_1\beta_1 + \cdots + w_n\beta_n$, where $\beta_1, \ldots, \beta_n$ are the beta factors of the securities.

### 5.4.3 Security Market Line

Consider an arbitrary portfolio with weights $\boldsymbol{w}_V$. The weights in the market portfolio will be denoted by $\boldsymbol{w}_M$. The market portfolio belongs to the efficient frontier of the attainable set of portfolios consisting of risky securities. Thus, by Proposition 5.12

$$\gamma \boldsymbol{w}_M \boldsymbol{C} = \boldsymbol{m} - \mu \boldsymbol{u}$$

for some numbers $\gamma > 0$ and $\mu$. The beta factor of the portfolio with weights $\boldsymbol{w}_V$ can, therefore, be written as

$$\beta_V = \frac{\operatorname{Cov}(K_V, K_M)}{\sigma_M^2} = \frac{\boldsymbol{w}_M \boldsymbol{C} \boldsymbol{w}_V^T}{\boldsymbol{w}_M \boldsymbol{C} \boldsymbol{w}_M^T} = \frac{\gamma(\boldsymbol{m} - \mu \boldsymbol{u})\boldsymbol{w}_V^T}{\gamma(\boldsymbol{m} - \mu \boldsymbol{u})\boldsymbol{w}_M^T} = \frac{\mu_V - \mu}{\mu_M - \mu}.$$

To find $\mu$ consider the risk-free security, with return $r_F$ and beta factor $\beta_F = 0$. Substituting $\beta_F$ and $r_F$ for $\beta_V$ and $\mu_V$ in the above equation, we find that $\mu = r_F$. We have proved the following remarkable property.

## Theorem 5.13

The expected return $\mu_V$ on a portfolio (or an individual security) is a linear function of the beta coefficient $\beta_V$ of the portfolio,

$$\mu_V = r_F + (\mu_M - r_F)\beta_V. \tag{5.19}$$

The expected return plotted against the beta coefficient of any portfolio or individual security will form a straight line on the $\beta, \mu$ plane, called the *security market line*. This is shown in Figure 5.13, in which the security market line is plotted next to the capital market line for comparison. A number of different portfolios and individual securities are indicated by dots in both graphs.

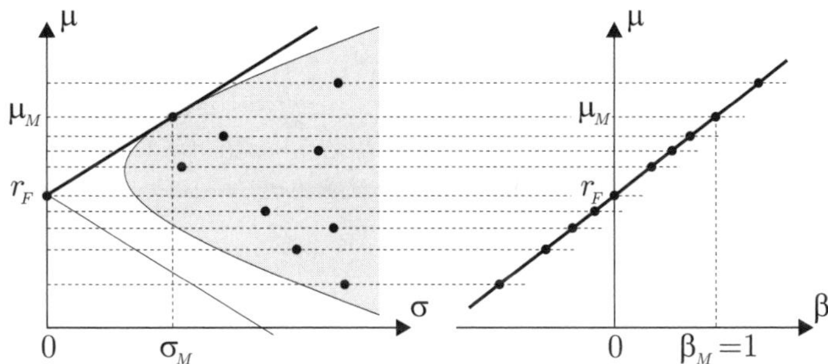


**Figure 5.13** Capital market line and security market line

Similarly as in formula (5.18) for the capital market line, the term $(\mu_M - r_F)\beta_V$ in (5.19) is the *risk premium*, interpreted as compensation for exposure to systematic risk. However, (5.18) applies only to portfolios on the capital market line, whereas (5.19) is much more general: It applies to *all* portfolios and individual securities.

### *Exercise 5.19*

Show that the characteristic lines of all securities intersect at a common point in the CAPM. What are the coordinates of this point?

The CAPM describes a state of equilibrium in the market. Everyone is holding a portfolio of risky securities with the same weights as the market portfolio. Any trades that may be executed by investors will only affect their split of funds between the risk-free security and the market portfolio. As a result, the demand and supply of all securities will be balanced. This will remain so as long as the estimates of expected returns and beta factors satisfy (5.19).

However, as soon as some new information about the market becomes available to investors, it may affect their estimates of expected returns and beta factors. The new estimated values may no longer satisfy (5.19). Suppose, for example, that

$$\mu_V > r_F + (\mu_M - r_F)\beta_V$$

for a particular security. In this case investors will want to increase their relative position in this security, which offers a higher expected return than required as compensation for systematic risk. Demand will exceed supply, the price of the security will begin to rise and the expected return will decline. On the other hand, if the reverse inequality

$$\mu_V < r_F + (\mu_M - r_F)\beta_V$$

holds, investors will want to sell the security. In this case supply will exceed demand, the price will fall and the expected return will increase. This will continue until the prices and with them the expected returns of all securities settle at a new level, restoring equilibrium.

The above inequalities are important in practice. They send a clear signal to investors whether any particular security is underpriced or, respectively, overpriced, that is, whether it should be bought or sold.

# 6 Forward and Futures Contracts

## 6.1 Forward Contracts

A *forward contract* is an agreement to buy or sell an asset on a fixed date in the future, called the *delivery time*, for a price specified in advance, called the *forward price*. The party to the contract who agrees to sell the asset is said to be taking a *short forward position*. The other party, obliged to buy the asset at delivery, is said to have a *long forward position*. The principal reason for entering into a forward contract is to become independent of the unknown future price of a risky asset. There are a variety of examples: a farmer wishing to fix the sale price of his crops in advance, an importer arranging to buy foreign currency at a fixed rate in the future, a fund manager who wants to sell stock for a price known in advance. A forward contract is a direct agreement between two parties. It is typically settled by physical delivery of the asset on the agreed date. As an alternative, settlement may sometimes be in cash.

Let us denote the time when the forward contract is exchanged by 0, the delivery time by $T$, and the forward price by $F(0,T)$. The time $t$ market price of the underlying asset will be denoted by $S(t)$. No payment is made by either party at time 0, when the forward contract is exchanged. At delivery the party with a long forward position will benefit if $F(0,T) < S(T)$. They can buy the asset for $F(0,T)$ and sell it for the market price $S(T)$, making an instant profit of $S(T) - F(0,T)$. Meanwhile, the party holding a short forward position will suffer a loss of $S(T) - F(0,T)$ because they will have to sell below the market price. If $F(0,T) > S(T)$, then the situation will be reversed. The payoffs at delivery are $S(T) - F(0,T)$ for a long forward position and $F(0,T) - S(T)$ for a short position; see Figure 6.1.

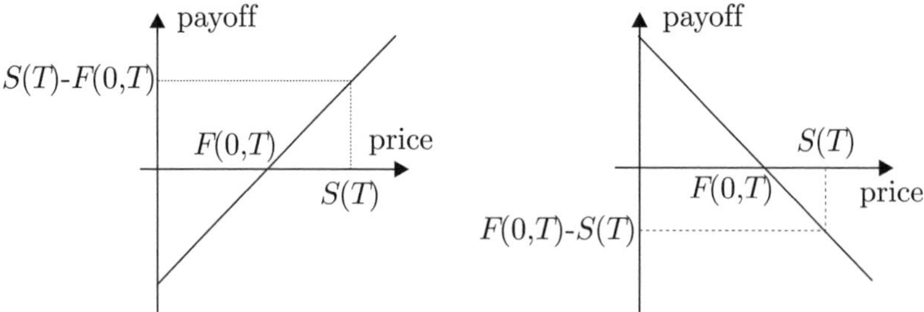


**Figure 6.1** Payoff for long and short forward positions at delivery

If the contract is initiated at time $t < T$ rather than 0, then we shall write $F(t,T)$ for the forward price, the payoff at delivery being $S(T) - F(t,T)$ for a long forward position and $F(t,T) - S(T)$ for a short position.

### 6.1.1 Forward Price

The No-Arbitrage Principle makes it possible to obtain formulae for the forward prices of assets of various kinds. We begin with the simplest case.

**Stock Paying No Dividends.** Consider a security that can be stored at no cost and brings no profit (except perhaps for capital gains arising from random price fluctuations). A typical example is a stock paying no dividends. We shall denote by $r$ the risk-free rate under continuous compounding and assume that it is constant throughout the period in question.

An alternative to taking a long forward position in stock with delivery at time $T$ and forward price $F(0,T)$ is to borrow $S(0)$ dollars to buy the stock at time 0 and keep it until time $T$. The amount $S(0)\mathrm{e}^{rT}$ to be paid to settle the loan with interest at time $T$ is a natural candidate for the forward price $F(0,T)$. The following theorem makes this intuitive argument formal.

## Theorem 6.1

For a stock paying no dividends the forward price is

$$F(0,T) = S(0)\mathrm{e}^{rT}, \tag{6.1}$$

where $r$ is a constant risk-free interest rate under continuous compounding. If the contract is initiated at time $t \leq T$, then

$$F(t,T) = S(t)\mathrm{e}^{r(T-t)}. \tag{6.2}$$

## Proof

We shall prove formula (6.1). Suppose that $F(0,T) > S(0)e^{rT}$. In this case, at time 0

- borrow the amount $S(0)$ until time $T$;
- buy one share for $S(0)$;
- take a short forward position, that is, agree to sell one share for $F(0,T)$ at time $T$.

Then, at time $T$

- sell the stock for $F(0,T)$;
- pay $S(0)e^{rT}$ to clear the loan with interest.

This will bring a risk-free profit of

$$F(0,T) - S(0)e^{rT} > 0,$$

contrary to the No-Arbitrage Principle. Next, suppose that $F(0,T) < S(0)e^{rT}$. In this case we construct the opposite strategy to the one above. At time 0

- sell short one share for $S(0)$;
- invest the proceeds at the risk-free rate;
- enter into a long forward contract with forward price $F(0,T)$.

Then, at time $T$

- cash the risk-free investment with interest, collecting $S(0)e^{rT}$ dollars;
- buy the stock for $F(0,T)$ using the forward contract;
- close out the short position in stock by returning it to the owner.

You will end up with a positive amount

$$S(0)e^{rT} - F(0,T) > 0,$$

again a contradiction with the No-Arbitrage Principle.

The proof of (6.2) is similar. Simply replace 0 by $t$, observing that the time elapsed between exchanging the forward contract and delivery is now $T-t$. □

In a market with restrictions on short sales of stock the inequality $F(0,T) < S(0)e^{rT}$ does not necessarily lead to arbitrage opportunities.

### *Exercise 6.1*

Suppose that $S(0) = 17$ dollars, $F(0,1) = 18$ dollars, $r = 8\%$, and short-selling requires a 30% security deposit attracting interest at $d = 4\%$. Is there an arbitrage opportunity? Find the highest rate $d$ for which there is no arbitrage opportunity.

### *Exercise 6.2*

Suppose that the price of stock on 1 April 2000 turns out to be 10% lower than it was on 1 January 2000. Assuming that the risk-free rate is constant at $r = 6\%$, what is the percentage drop of the forward price on 1 April 2000 as compared to that on 1 January 2000 for a forward contract with delivery on 1 October 2000?

### Remark 6.1

In the case considered here we always have $F(t,T) = S(t)\mathrm{e}^{r(T-r)} > S(t)$. The difference $F(t,T) - S(t)$, which is called the *basis*, converges to 0 as $t \nearrow T$.

### Remark 6.2

Under periodic compounding the forward price is given by

$$F(0,T) = S(0)(1 + \frac{r}{m})^{mT}.$$

In terms of zero-coupon bond prices, this formula becomes

$$F(0,T) = S(0)B(0,T)^{-1}.$$

The last formula is in fact more general, requiring no assumption about constant interest rates.

**Including Dividends.** We shall generalise the formula for the forward price to cover assets that generate income during the lifetime of the forward contract. The income may be in the form of dividends or a convenience yield. We shall also cover the case when the asset involves some costs (called the cost of carry), such as storage or insurance, by treating the costs as negative income.

Suppose that the stock is to pay a dividend div at an intermediate time $t$ between initiating the forward contract and delivery. At time $t$ the stock price will drop by the amount of the dividend paid. The formula for the forward price, which involves the present stock price, can be modified by subtracting the present value of the dividend.

### Theorem 6.2

The forward price of a stock paying dividend div at time $t$, where $0 < t < T$, is

$$F(0,T) = [S(0) - \mathrm{e}^{-rt}\mathrm{div}]\mathrm{e}^{rT}. \tag{6.3}$$

## Proof

Suppose that

$$F(0,T) > [S(0) - \mathrm{e}^{-rt}\mathrm{div}]\mathrm{e}^{rT}.$$

We shall construct an arbitrage strategy. At time 0

- enter into a short forward contract with forward price $F(0,T)$ and delivery time $T$;
- borrow $S(0)$ dollars and buy one share.

At time $t$

- cash the dividend div and invest it at the risk-free rate for the remaining time $T-t$.

At time $T$

- sell the share for $F(0,T)$;
- pay $S(0)\mathrm{e}^{rT}$ to clear the loan with interest and collect $\mathrm{e}^{r(T-t)}\mathrm{div}$.

The final balance will be positive:

$$F(0,T) - S(0)\mathrm{e}^{rT} + \mathrm{e}^{r(T-t)}\mathrm{div} > 0,$$

a contradiction with the No-Arbitrage Principle. On the other hand, suppose that

$$F(0,T) < [S(0) - \mathrm{e}^{-rt}\mathrm{div}]\mathrm{e}^{rT}.$$

In this case, at time 0

- enter into a long forward contract with forward price $F(0,T)$ and delivery at time $T$;
- sell short one share and invest the proceeds $S(0)$ at the risk-free rate.

At time $t$

- borrow div dollars and pay a dividend to the stock owner.

At time $T$

- buy one share for $F(0,T)$ and close out the short position in stock;
- cash the risk-free investment with interest, collecting the amount $S(0)\mathrm{e}^{rT}$, and pay $\mathrm{e}^{r(T-t)}\mathrm{div}$ to clear the loan with interest.

The final balance will again be positive,

$$-F(0,T) + S(0)\mathrm{e}^{rT} - \mathrm{e}^{r(T-t)}\mathrm{div} > 0,$$

completing the proof. □

The formula can easily be generalised to the case when dividends are paid more than once:

$$F(0,T) = [S(0) - \text{div}_0]e^{rT}, \tag{6.4}$$

where $\text{div}_0$ is the present value of all dividends due during the lifetime of the forward contract.

### *Exercise 6.3*

Consider a stock whose price on 1 January is \$120 and which will pay a dividend of \$1 on 1 July 2000 and \$2 on 1 October 2000. The interest rate is 12%. Is there an arbitrage opportunity if on 1 January 2000 the forward price for delivery of the stock on 1 November 2000 is \$131? If so, compute the arbitrage profit.

### *Exercise 6.4*

Suppose that the risk-free rate is 8%. However, as a small investor, you can invest money at 7% only and borrow at 10%. Does either of the strategies in the proof of Proposition 6.2 give an arbitrage profit if $F(0,1) = 89$ and $S(0) = 83$ dollars, and a \$2 dividend is paid in the middle of the year, that is, at time $1/2$?

**Dividend Yield.** Dividends are often paid continuously at a specified rate, rather than at discrete time instants. For example, in a case of a highly diversified portfolio of stocks it is natural to assume that dividends are paid continuously rather than to take into account frequent payments scattered throughout the year. Another example is foreign currency, attracting interest at the corresponding rate.

We shall first derive a formula for the forward price in the case of foreign currency. Let the price of one British pound in New York be $P(t)$ dollars, and let the risk-free interest rates for investments in British pounds and US dollars be $r_{\text{GBP}}$ and $r_{\text{USD}}$, respectively. Let us compare the following strategies:

A: Invest $P(0)$ dollars at the rate $r_{\text{USD}}$ for time $T$.

B: Buy 1 pound for $P(0)$ dollars, invest it for time $T$ at the rate $r_{\text{GBP}}$, and take a short position in $e^{r_{\text{GBP}}T}$ pound sterling forward contracts with delivery time $T$ and forward price $F(0,T)$.

Both strategies require the same initial outlay, so the final values should be also the same:

$$P(0)e^{r_{\text{USD}}T} = e^{r_{\text{GBP}}T}F(0,T).$$

It follows that

$$F(0,T) = P(0)e^{(r_{\text{USD}} - r_{\text{GBP}})T}. \tag{6.5}$$

Next, suppose that a stock pays dividends continuously at a rate $r_{\text{div}} > 0$, called the (continuous) *dividend yield*. If the dividends are reinvested in the stock, then an investment in one share held at time 0 will increase to become $e^{r_{\text{div}}T}$ shares at time $T$. (The situation is similar to continuous compounding.) Consequently, in order to have one share at time $T$ we should begin with $e^{-r_{\text{div}}T}$ shares at time 0. This observation is used in the arbitrage proof below.

## Theorem 6.3

The forward price for stock paying dividends continuously at a rate $r_{\text{div}}$ is

$$F(0,T) = S(0)e^{(r-r_{\text{div}})T}. \tag{6.6}$$

## Proof

Suppose that

$$F(0,T) > S(0)e^{(r-r_{\text{div}})T}.$$

In this case, at time 0

- enter into a short forward contract;
- borrow the amount $S(0)e^{-r_{\text{div}}T}$ to buy $e^{-r_{\text{div}}T}$ shares.

Between time 0 and $T$ collect the dividends paid continuously, reinvesting them in the stock. At time $T$ you will have 1 share, as explained above. At that time

- sell the share for $F(0,T)$, closing out the short forward position;
- pay $S(0)e^{(r-r_{\text{div}})T}$ to clear the loan with interest.

The final balance $F(0,T) - S(0)e^{(r-r_{\text{div}})T} > 0$ will be your arbitrage profit. Now suppose that

$$F(0,T) < S(0)e^{(r-r_{\text{div}})T}.$$

If this is the case, then at time 0

- take a long forward position;
- sell short a fraction $e^{-r_{\text{div}}T}$ of a share investing the proceeds $S(0)e^{-r_{\text{div}}T}$ risk free.

Between time 0 and $T$ you will need to pay dividends to the stock owner, raising cash by shorting the stock. Your short position in stock will thus increase to 1 share at time $T$. At that time

- buy one share for $F(0,T)$ and return it to the owner, closing out the long forward position and the short position in stock;
- receive $S(0)e^{(r-r_{\text{div}})T}$ from the risk-free investment.

Again you will end up with a positive amount $S(0)e^{(r-r_{\text{div}})T} - F(0,T) > 0$, contrary to the No-Arbitrage Principle. □

In general, if the contract is initiated at time $t < T$, then

$$F(t,T) = S(t)\mathrm{e}^{(r-r_{\mathrm{div}})(T-t)}. \tag{6.7}$$

*Exercise 6.5*

A US importer of German cars wants to arrange a forward contract to buy euros in half a year. The interest rates for investments in US dollars and euros are $r_{\mathrm{USD}} = 4\%$ and $r_{\mathrm{EUR}} = 3\%$, respectively, the current exchange rate being 0.9834 euros to a dollar. What is the forward price of euros expressed in dollars (that is, the forward exchange rate)?

### 6.1.2 Value of a Forward Contract

Every forward contract has value zero when initiated. As time goes by, the price of the underlying asset may change. Along with it, the value of the forward contract will vary and will no longer be zero, in general. In particular, the value of a long forward contract will be $S(T) - F(0,T)$ at delivery, which may turn out to be positive, zero or negative. We shall derive formulae to capture the changes in the value of a forward contract.

Suppose that the forward price $F(t,T)$ for a forward contract initiated at time $t$, where $0 < t < T$, is higher than $F(0,T)$. This is good news for an investor with a long forward position initiated at time 0. At time $T$ such an investor will gain $F(t,T) - F(0,T)$ as compared to an investor entering into a new long forward contract at time $t$ with the same delivery date $T$. To find the value of the original forward position at time $t$ all we have to do is to discount this gain back to time $t$. This discounted amount would be received (or paid, if negative) by the investor with a long position should the forward contract initiated at time 0 be closed out at time $t$, that is, prior to delivery $T$. This intuitive argument needs to be supported by a rigorous arbitrage proof.

Theorem 6.4

For any $t$ such that $0 \le t \le T$ the time $t$ value of a long forward contract with forward price $F(0,T)$ is given by

$$V(t) = [F(t,T) - F(0,T)]\mathrm{e}^{-r(T-t)}. \tag{6.8}$$

## Proof

Suppose that

$$V(t) < [F(t,T) - F(0,T)]e^{-r(T-t)}.$$

If so, then at time $t$

- borrow the amount $V(t)$ to enter into a long forward contract with forward price $F(0,T)$ and delivery time $T$;
- initiate a short forward position with forward price $F(t,T)$, at no cost.

Next, at time $T$

- close out the forward contracts collecting (or paying, if negative) the amounts $S(T) - F(0,T)$ for the long position and $-S(T) + F(t,T)$ for the short position;
- pay back the loan with interest amounting to $V(t)e^{r(T-t)}$ in total.

The final balance $F(t,T) - F(0,T) - V(t)e^{r(T-t)} > 0$ will be your arbitrage profit.

We leave the case when

$$V(t) > [F(t,T) - F(0,T)]e^{-r(T-t)}$$

as an exercise. □

### *Exercise 6.6*

Show that $V(t) > [F(t,T) - F(0,T)]e^{-r(T-t)}$ leads to an arbitrage opportunity.

Observe that $V(0) = 0$, which is the initial value of the forward contract, and $V(T) = S(T) - F(0,T)$ (since $F(T,T) = S(T)$), which is the terminal payoff.

For a stock paying no dividends formula (6.8) gives

$$V(t) = [S(t)e^{r(T-t)} - S(0)e^{rT}]e^{-r(T-t)} = S(t) - S(0)e^{rt}. \tag{6.9}$$

The message is: If the stock price grows at the same rate as a risk-free investment, then the value of the forward contract will be zero. Growth above the risk-free rate results in a gain for the holder of a long forward position.

## Remark 6.3

Consider a contract with delivery price $X$ rather than $F(0,T)$. The value of this contract at time $t$ will be given by (6.8) with $F(0,T)$ replaced by $X$,

$$V_X(t) = [F(t,T) - X]e^{-r(T-t)}.$$

Such a contract may have non-zero value initially. In the case of a stock paying no dividends

$$V_X(0) = [F(0,T) - X]\mathrm{e}^{-rT} = S(0) - X\mathrm{e}^{-rT}. \tag{6.10}$$

For a stock paying one dividend between times 0 and $T$ the initial value of the contract is

$$V_X(0) = S(0) - \mathrm{div}_0 - X\mathrm{e}^{-rT},$$

$\mathrm{div}_0$ being the value of the dividend discounted to time 0. For a stock paying dividends continuously at a rate $r_{\mathrm{div}}$, the initial value of the contract is

$$V_X(0) = S(0)\mathrm{e}^{-r_{\mathrm{div}}T} - X\mathrm{e}^{-rT}.$$

*Exercise 6.7*

Suppose that the price of a stock is \$45 at the beginning of the year, the risk-free rate is 6%, and a \$2 dividend is to be paid after half a year. For a long forward position with delivery in one year, find its value after 9 months if the stock price at that time turns out to be a) \$49, b) \$51.

## 6.2 Futures

One of the two parties to a forward contract will be losing money. There is always a risk of default by the party suffering a loss. Futures contracts are designed to eliminate such risk.

We assume for a while that time is discrete with steps of length $\tau$, typically a day.

Just like a forward contract, a *futures contract* involves an underlying asset and a specified time of delivery, a stock with prices $S(n)$ for $n = 0, 1, \ldots$ and time $T$, say. In addition to the usual stock prices, the market dictates the so-called *futures prices* $f(n,T)$ for each step $n = 0, 1, \ldots$ such that $n\tau \leq T$. These prices are unknown at time 0, except for $f(0,T)$, and we shall treat them as random variables.

As in the case of a forward contract, it costs nothing to initiate a futures position. The difference lies in the cash flow during the lifetime of the contract. A long forward contract involves just a single payment $S(T) - F(0,T)$ at delivery. A futures contract involves a random cash flow, known as *marking to market*. Namely, at each time step $n = 1, 2, \ldots$ such that $n\tau \leq T$ the holder of a long futures position will receive the amount

$$f(n,T) - f(n-1,T)$$

if positive, or will have to pay it if negative. The opposite payments apply for a short futures position. The following two conditions are imposed:

1. The futures price at delivery is $f(T,T) = S(T)$.
2. At each time step $n = 0, 1, \ldots$ such that $n\tau \leq T$ the value of a futures position is zero. (At each step $n \geq 1$ this value is computed after marking to market.)

The second condition means that, in particular, it costs nothing to close, open or alter a futures position at any time step between 0 and $T$.

## Remark 6.4

To ensure that the obligations involved in a futures position are fulfilled, certain practical regulations are enforced. Each investor entering into a futures contract has to pay a deposit, called the *initial margin*, which is kept by the clearing house as collateral. In the case of a long futures position the amount $f(n,T) - f(n-1,T)$ is added to the deposit if positive or subtracted if negative at each time step $n$, typically once a day. (The opposite amount is added or subtracted for a short futures position.) Any excess that builds up above the initial margin can be withdrawn by the investor. On the other hand, if the deposit drops below a certain level, called the *maintenance margin*, the clearing house will issue a *margin call*, requesting the investor to make a payment and restore the deposit to the level of the initial margin. A futures position can be closed at any time, in which case the deposit will be returned to the investor. In particular, the futures position will be closed immediately by the clearing house if the investor fails to respond to a margin call. As a result, the risk of default is eliminated.

## Example 6.1

Suppose that the initial margin is set at 10% and the maintenance margin at 5% of the futures price. The table below shows a scenario with futures prices $f(n,T)$. The columns labelled 'margin 1' and 'margin 2' show the deposit at the beginning and at the end of each day, respectively. The 'payment' column contains the amounts paid to top up the deposit (negative numbers) or withdrawn (positive numbers).

| $n$ | $f(n,T)$ | cash flow | margin 1 | payment | margin 2 |
|---|---|---|---|---|---|
| 0 | 140 | opening: | 0 | −14 | 14 |
| 1 | 138 | − 2 | 12 | 0 | 12 |
| 2 | 130 | − 8 | 4 | − 9 | 13 |
| 3 | 140 | +10 | 23 | + 9 | 14 |
| 4 | 150 | +10 | 24 | + 9 | 15 |
| | | closing: | 15 | +15 | 0 |
| | | | total: | 10 | |

On day 0 a futures position is opened and a 10% deposit paid. On day 1 the futures price drops by \$2, which is subtracted from the deposit. On day 2 the futures price drops further by \$8, triggering a margin call because the deposit falls below 5%. The investor has to pay \$9 to restore the deposit to the 10% level. On day 3 the forward price increases and \$9 is withdrawn, leaving a 10% margin. On day 4 the forward price goes up again, allowing the investor to withdraw another \$9. At the end of the day the investor decides to close the position, collecting the balance of the deposit. The total of all payments is \$10, the increase in the futures price between day 0 and 4.

Remark 6.5

An important feature of the futures market is liquidity. This is possible due to standardisation and the presence of a clearing house. Only futures contracts with particular delivery dates are traded. Moreover, futures contracts on commodities such as gold or timber specify standardised delivery arrangements as well as standardised physical properties of the assets. The clearing house acts as an intermediary, matching the total of a large number of short and long futures positions of various sizes. The clearing house also maintains the margin deposit for each investor to eliminate the risk of default. This is in contrast to forward contracts negotiated directly between two parties.

### 6.2.1 Pricing

We shall show that in some circumstances the forward and the futures prices are the same. Let $r$ be the risk-free rate under continuous compounding.

Theorem 6.5

If the interest rate is constant, then $f(0,T) = F(0,T)$.

## Proof

Suppose for simplicity that marking to market is performed at just two intermediate time instants $0 < t_1 < t_2 < T$. The argument below can readily be extended to cover more frequent marking to market.

Take a long forward position with forward price $F(0,T)$ and invest the amount of $\mathrm{e}^{-rT}F(0,T)$ risk free. At time $T$ close the risk-free investment, collecting the amount $F(0,T)$, purchase one share for $F(0,T)$ using the forward contract, and sell the share for the market price $S(T)$. Your final wealth will be $S(T)$.

Our goal is to replicate this payoff by a suitable strategy using futures contracts. At time 0

- we open a fraction $\mathrm{e}^{-r(T-t_1)}$ of a long futures position (at no cost);
- we invest the amount $\mathrm{e}^{-rT}f(0,T)$ risk free (this investment will grow to $v_0 = f(0,T)$ at time $T$).

At time $t_1$

- we receive (or pay) the amount $\mathrm{e}^{-r(T-t_1)}[f(t_1,T) - f(0,T)]$ as a result of marking to market;
- we invest (or borrow, depending on the sign) $\mathrm{e}^{-r(T-t_1)}[f(t_1,T) - f(0,T)]$ (this investment will grow to $v_1 = f(t_1,T) - f(0,T)$ at time $T$);
- we increase our long futures position to $\mathrm{e}^{-r(T-t_2)}$ of a contract (at no cost).

At time $t_2$

- we cash (or pay) $\mathrm{e}^{-r(T-t_2)}[f(t_2,T) - f(t_1,T)]$ as a result of marking to market;
- we invest (or borrow, depending on the sign) $\mathrm{e}^{-r(T-t_2)}[f(t_2,T) - f(t_1,T)]$ (this investment will grow to $v_2 = f(t_2,T) - f(t_1,T)$ at time $T$);
- we increase the long futures position to 1 (at no cost).

At time $T$

- we close the risk-free investment, collecting the amount $v_0 + v_1 + v_2 = f(t_2,T)$;
- we close the futures position, receiving (or paying) the amount $S(T) - f(t_2,T)$.

The final wealth will be $S(T)$, as before. Therefore, to avoid arbitrage, the initial investments initiating both strategies have to be the same, that is,

$$\mathrm{e}^{-rT}F(0,T) = \mathrm{e}^{-rT}f(0,T),$$

which proves the claim. □

This construction cannot be performed if the interest rate changes unpredictably. However if interest rate changes are known in advance, the argument can be suitably modified and the equality between the futures and forward prices remains valid.

In an economy with constant interest rates $r$ we obtain a simple structure of futures prices,

$$f(t,T) = S(t)e^{r(T-t)} \tag{6.11}$$

if the stock pays no dividends. The futures prices are random, but this is caused entirely by the randomness of the prices of the underlying asset. If the futures prices depart from the values given by the above formula, it is a reflection of the market's view of future interest rate changes.

*Exercise 6.8*

Suppose the interest rate $r$ is constant. Given $S(0)$, find the price $S(1)$ of the stock after one day such that the marking to market of futures with delivery in 3 months is zero on that day.

This exercise shows an important benchmark for the profitability of a futures position: An investor who wants to take advantage of a predicted increase in the price of stock above the risk-free rate should enter into a long futures position. A short futures position will bring a profit should the stock price go down or increase below the risk-free rate.

### 6.2.2 Hedging with Futures

**The Basis.** One relatively simple way to hedge an exposure to stock price variations is to enter a forward contract. However, a contract of this kind may not be readily available, not to mention the risk of default. Another possibility is to hedge using the futures market, which is well-developed, liquid and protected from the risk of default.

Example 6.2

Let $S(0) = 100$ dollars and let the risk-free rate be constant at $r = 8\%$. Assume that marking to market takes place once a month, the time step being $\tau = 1/12$. Suppose that we wish to sell the stock after 3 months. To hedge the exposure to stock price variations we enter into one short futures contract on the stock with delivery in 3 months. The payments resulting from marking to market are invested (or borrowed), attracting interest at the risk-free rate. The results for two different stock price scenarios are displayed below. The column labelled 'm2m' represents the payments due to marking to market and the last column shows the interest accrued up to the delivery date.

Scenario 1

| $n$ | $S(n)$ | $f(n, 3/12)$ | m2m | interest |
|---|---|---|---|---|
| 0 | 100 | 102.02 | | |
| 1 | 102 | 103.37 | −1.35 | −0.02 |
| 2 | 101 | 101.67 | +1.69 | +0.01 |
| 3 | 105 | 105.00 | −3.32 | 0.00 |
| | | total: | −2.98 | −0.01 |

In this scenario we sell the stock for \$105.00, but marking to market brings losses, reducing the sum to $105.00 - 2.98 - 0.01 = 102.01$ dollars. Note that if the marking to market payments were not invested at the risk-free rate, then the realized sum would be $105.00 - 2.98 = 102.02$ dollars, that is, exactly equal to the futures price $f(0, 3/12)$.

Scenario 2

| $n$ | $S(n)$ | $f(n, 3/12)$ | m2m | interest |
|---|---|---|---|---|
| 0 | 100 | 102.02 | | |
| 1 | 98 | 99.31 | +2.70 | +0.04 |
| 2 | 97 | 97.65 | +1.67 | +0.01 |
| 3 | 92 | 92.00 | +5.65 | 0.00 |
| | | total: | +10.02 | +0.05 |

In this case we sell the stock for \$92.00 and benefit from marking to market along with the interest earned, bringing the final sum to $92.00 + 10.02 + 0.05 = 102.07$ dollars. Without the interest the final sum would be $92.00 + 10.02 = 102.02$ dollars, once again exactly the futures price $f(0, 3/12)$.

In reality the calculations in Example 6.2 are slightly more complicated because of the presence of the initial margin, which we have neglected for simplicity. Some limitations come from the standardisation of futures contracts. As a result, a difficulty may arise in matching the terms of the contract to our needs. For example, the exercise dates for futures are typically certain fixed days in four specified months in a year, for example the third Friday in March, June, September and December. If we want to close out our investment at the end of April, we will need to hedge with futures contracts with delivery date beyond the end of April, for example, in June.

## Example 6.3

Suppose we wish to sell stock after 2 months and we hedge using futures with delivery in 3 months (we work in the same scenarios as in Example 6.2):

Scenario 1

| $n$ | $S(n)$ | $f(n,3/12)$ | m2m | interest |
|---|---|---|---|---|
| 0 | 100 | 102.02 | | |
| 1 | 102 | 103.37 | −1.35 | −0.01 |
| 2 | 101 | 101.67 | 1.69 | 0.00 |
| | | total: | 0.34 | −0.01 |

We sell the stock for \$101.00, which together with marking to market and interest will give \$101.33.

Scenario 2

| $n$ | $S(n)$ | $f(n,3/12)$ | m2m | interest |
|---|---|---|---|---|
| 0 | 100 | 102.02 | | |
| 1 | 98 | 99.31 | 2.70 | 0.02 |
| 2 | 97 | 97.65 | 1.67 | 0.00 |
| | | total: | 4.37 | 0.02 |

In this case we sell the stock for \$97.00, and together with marking to market and interest obtain \$101.39.

We almost hit the target, which is the futures price $f(0,2) \cong 101.34$ dollars, that is, the value of \$100 compounded at the risk-free rate.

## Remark 6.6

The difference between the spot and futures prices is called the *basis* (as for forward contracts):

$$b(t,T) = S(t) - f(t,T).$$

(Sometimes the basis is defined as $f(t,T) - S(t)$.) The basis converges to zero as $t \to T$, since $f(T,T) = S(T)$. In a market with constant interest rates it is given explicitly by

$$b(t,T) = S(t)(1 - \mathrm{e}^{r(T-t)}),$$

being negative for $t < T$. If the asset pays dividends at a rate $r_{\mathrm{div}} > r$, then the basis is positive:

$$b(t,T) = S(t)(1 - \mathrm{e}^{(r-r_{\mathrm{div}})(T-t)}).$$

Going back to the problem of designing a hedge, suppose that we wish to sell an asset at time $t < T$. To protect ourselves against a decrease in the asset price, at time 0 we can short a futures contract with futures price $f(0,T)$. At time $t$ we shall receive $S(t)$ from selling the asset plus the cash flow $f(0,T) - f(t,T)$ due to marking to market (for simplicity, we neglect any intermediate cash flow, assuming that $t$ is the first instance when marking to market takes place), that is, we obtain

$$f(0,T) + S(t) - f(t,T) = f(0,T) + b(t,T).$$

The price $f(0,T)$ is known at time 0, so the risk involved in the hedging position will be related to the unknown level of the basis. This uncertainty is mainly concerned with unknown future interest rates.

If the goal of a hedger is to minimise risk, it may be best to use a certain optimal hedge ratio, that is to enter into $N$ futures contracts, with $N$ not necessarily equal to the number of shares of the underlying asset held. To see this compute the risk as measured by the variance of the basis $b_N(t,T) = S(t) - Nf(t,T)$:

$$\mathrm{Var}(b_N(t,T)) = \sigma^2_{S(t)} + N^2\sigma^2_{f(t,T)} - 2N\sigma_{S(t)}\sigma_{f(t,T)}\rho_{S(t)f(t,T)},$$

where $\rho_{S(t)f(t,T)}$ is the correlation coefficient between the spot and futures prices, and $\sigma_{S(t)}, \sigma_{f(t,T)}$ are the standard deviations. The variance is a quadratic function in $N$ and has a minimum at

$$N = \rho_{S(t)f(t,T)}\frac{\sigma_{S(t)}}{\sigma_{f(t,T)}},$$

which is the optimal hedge ratio.

### *Exercise 6.9*

Find the optimal hedge ratio if the interest rates are constant.

**Futures on Stock Index.** A stock exchange index is a weighted average of a selection of stock prices with weights proportional to the market capitalisation of stocks. An index of this kind will be approximately proportional to the value of the market portfolio (see Chapter 5) if the chosen set of stocks is large enough. For example, the Standard and Poor Index S&P500 is computed using 500 stocks, representing about 80% of trade at the New York Stock Exchange. For the purposes of futures markets the index can be treated as a security. This is because the index can be identified with a portfolio, even though in practice transaction costs would impede trading in this portfolio. The futures prices $f(n,T)$, expressed in index points, are assumed to satisfy the same conditions as before. Marking to market is given by the difference $f(n,T) - f(n-1,T)$

multiplied by a fixed amount (\$500 for futures on S&P500). If the number of stocks included in the index is large, it is possible and convenient to assume that the index is an asset with dividends paid continuously.

### *Exercise 6.10*

Suppose that the value of a stock exchange index is 13,500, the futures price for delivery in 9 months is 14,100 index points, and the interest rate is 8%. Find the dividend yield.

Our goal in this section is to study applications of index futures for hedging based on the Capital Asset Pricing Model introduced in Chapter 5. As we know, see (5.19), the expected return on a portfolio over a time step of length $\tau$ is given by

$$\mu_V = r_F + (\mu_M - r_F)\beta_V,$$

where $\beta_V$ is the beta coefficient of the portfolio, $\mu_M$ is the expected return on the market portfolio and $r_F$ is the risk-free return over one time step. By $V(n)$ we shall denote the value of the portfolio at the $n$th time step. We assume for simplicity that the index is equal to the value of the market portfolio, so that the futures prices are given by

$$f(n,T) = M(n)(1 + r_F)^{T-n},$$

$M(n)$ being the value of the market portfolio at the $n$th time step. (Here we use discrete time and ordinary returns together with periodic compounding in the spirit of Portfolio Theory.)

We can form a new portfolio with value $\widetilde{V}(n)$ by supplementing the original portfolio with $N$ short futures contracts on the index with delivery time $T$. The initial value $\widetilde{V}(0)$ of the new portfolio is the same as the value $V(0)$ of the original portfolio, since it costs nothing to initiate a futures contract. The value

$$\widetilde{V}(n) = V(n) - N(f(n,T) - f(n-1,T))$$

of the new portfolio at the $n$th step includes the marking to market cash flow. The return on the new portfolio over the first step is

$$K_{\widetilde{V}} = \frac{\widetilde{V}(1) - \widetilde{V}(0)}{\widetilde{V}(0)} = \frac{V(1) - N(f(1,T) - f(0,T)) - V(0)}{V(0)}.$$

We shall show that the beta coefficient $\beta_{\widetilde{V}}$ of the new portfolio can be modified arbitrarily by a suitable choice of the futures position $N$.

## Proposition 6.6

If

$$N = (\beta_V - a)\frac{(1+r_F)V(0)}{f(0,T)},$$

then $\beta_{\widetilde{V}} = a$ for any given number $a$.

## Proof

We shall compute the beta coefficient from the definition:

$$\begin{aligned}\beta_{\widetilde{V}} &= \mathrm{Cov}(K_{\widetilde{V}}, K_M)/\sigma_M^2 \\ &= \mathrm{Cov}(K_V, K_M)/\sigma_M^2 - \frac{1}{V(0)}\mathrm{Cov}(N(f(1,T)-f(0,T)), K_M)/\sigma_M^2,\end{aligned}$$

where $K_M$ is the return on the market portfolio and $K_V$ the return on the portfolio without futures. Since $\mathrm{Cov}(f(0,T), K_M) = 0$ and covariance is linear with respect to each argument,

$$\mathrm{Cov}(N(f(1,T)-f(0,T)), K_M) = N\mathrm{Cov}(f(1,T), K_M).$$

Inserting the futures price $f(1,T) = M(1)(1+r_F)^{T-1}$, we have

$$\mathrm{Cov}(f(1,T), K_M) = (1+r_F)^{T-1}\mathrm{Cov}(M(1), K_M).$$

Again by the linearity of covariance in each argument

$$\mathrm{Cov}(M(1), K_M) = M(0)\mathrm{Cov}(\frac{M(1)-M(0)}{M(0)}, K_M) = M(0)\sigma_M^2.$$

Subsequent substitutions give

$$\beta_{\widetilde{V}} = \beta_V - \frac{(1+r_F)^{T-1}NM(0)}{V(0)} = \beta_V - N\frac{f(0,T)}{V(0)(1+r_F)},$$

which implies the asserted property. □

## Corollary 6.7

If $a = 0$, then $\mu_{\widetilde{V}} = r_F$.

## Example 6.4

Suppose that the index drops from $M(0) = 890$ down to $M(1) = 850$, that is, by 4.49% within one time step. Suppose further that the risk-free rate is 1%.

This means that the futures prices on the index (with delivery after 3 steps) are

$$f(0,3) = M(0)(1+r_F)^3 = 890 \times 1.01^3 \cong 916.97,$$
$$f(1,3) = M(1)(1+r_F)^3 = 850 \times 1.01^2 \cong 867.09.$$

Consider a portfolio with $\beta_V = 1.5$ and initial value $V(0) = 100$ dollars. This portfolio will have negative expected return

$$\begin{aligned}\mu_V &= r_F + (\mu_M - r_F)\beta_V \\ &\cong 1\% + (-4.49\% - 1\%)1.5 \cong -7.24\%.\end{aligned}$$

To construct a new portfolio with $\beta_{\widetilde{V}} = 0$ we can supplement the original portfolio with

$$N = \beta_V \frac{(1+r_F)V(0)}{f(0,3)} \cong 1.5 \times \frac{1.01 \times 100}{916.97} \cong 0.1652$$

short forward contracts on the index with delivery after 3 steps.

Suppose that the actual return on the original portfolio during the first time step happens to be equal to the expected return. This gives $V(1) \cong 92.76$ dollars. Marking to market gives a payment of

$$-N\left(f(1,3) - f(0,3)\right) \cong -0.1652 \times (867.09 - 916.97) \cong 8.24$$

dollars due to the holder of $N \cong 0.1652$ short forward contracts. This makes the new portfolio worth

$$\widetilde{V}(1) = V(1) - N\left(f(1,3) - f(0,3)\right) \cong 92.76 + 8.24 = 101.00$$

dollars at time 1, matching the risk-free growth exactly.

### *Exercise 6.11*

Perform the same calculations in the case when the index increases from 890 to 920.

### Remark 6.7

The ability to adjust the beta of a portfolio is valuable to investors who may wish either to reduce or to magnify the systematic risk. For example, suppose that an investor is able to design a portfolio with superior average performance to that of the market. By entering into a futures position such that the beta of the resulting portfolio is zero, the investor will be hedged against adverse movements of the market. This is crucial in the event of recession, so that the superior performance of the portfolio as compared to the market can be turned into a profit despite a decline in the market. On the other hand, should the market show some growth, the expected return on the hedged portfolio will be reduced by comparison because the futures position will result in a loss.

It needs to be emphasized that this type of hedging with futures works only on average. In particular, setting the beta coefficient to zero will not make the investment risk-free.

Let us conclude this chapter with a surprising application of index futures.

## Example 6.5

In emerging markets short sales are rarely available. This was the case in Poland in the late 1990's. However, index futures were traded. Due to the fact that one of the indices (WIG20) was composed of 20 stocks only, it was possible to manufacture a short sale of any stock among those 20 by entering into a short futures position on the index, combined with purchasing a suitable portfolio of the remaining 19 stocks. With a larger number of stocks comprising the index the transaction costs would have been too high to make such a construction practicable.

# 7
# Options: General Properties

In Chapters 1 and 4 we have seen simple examples of call and put options in a one-step discrete-time setting. Here we shall establish some fundamental properties of options, looking at them from a wider perspective and using continuous time. Nevertheless, many conclusions will also be valid in discrete time. Chapter 8 will be devoted to pricing and hedging options.

## 7.1 Definitions

A *European call option* is a contract giving the holder the right to buy an asset, called the *underlying*, for a price $X$ fixed in advance, known as the *exercise price* or *strike price*, at a specified future time $T$, called the *exercise* or *expiry time*. A *European put option* gives the right to sell the underlying asset for the strike price $X$ at the exercise time $T$.

An *American call* or *put option* gives the right to buy or, respectively, to sell the underlying asset for the strike price $X$ at any time between now and a specified future time $T$, called the *expiry time*. In other words, an American option can be exercised at any time up to and including expiry.

The term 'underlying asset' has quite general scope. Apart from typical assets such as stocks, commodities or foreign currency, there are options on stock indices, interest rates, or even on the snow level at a ski resort. Some underlying assets may be impossible to buy or sell. The option is then cleared in cash in a fashion which resembles settling a bet. For example, the holder of a European call option on the Standard and Poor Index (see page 141) with strike price 800 will gain if the index turns out to be 815 on the exercise date. The writer of the option will have to pay the holder an amount equal to the difference $815 - 800 = 15$ multiplied by a fixed sum of money, say by \$100. No payment will be due if the index turns out to be lower than 800 on the exercise date.

An option is determined by its payoff, which for a European call is

$$\begin{cases} S(T) - X & \text{if } S(T) > X, \\ 0 & \text{otherwise.} \end{cases}$$

This payoff is a random variable, contingent on the price $S(T)$ of the underlying on the exercise date $T$. (This explains why options are often referred to as *contingent claims*.) It is convenient to use the notation

$$x^+ = \begin{cases} x & \text{if } x > 0, \\ 0 & \text{otherwise.} \end{cases}$$

for the *positive part* of a real number $x$. Then the payoff of a European call option can be written as $(S(T) - X)^+$. For a put option the payoff is $(X - S(T))^+$.

Since the payoffs are non-negative, a premium must be paid to buy an option. If no premium had to be paid, an investor purchasing an option could under no circumstances lose money and would in fact make a profit whenever the payoff turned out to be positive. This would be contrary to the No-Arbitrage Principle. The premium is the market price of the option.

Establishing bounds and some general properties for option prices is the primary goal of the present chapter. The next chapter will be devoted to detailed techniques of computing these prices. We assume that options are freely traded, that is, can readily be bought and sold at the market price. The prices of calls and puts will be denoted by $C^{\mathrm{E}}, P^{\mathrm{E}}$ for European options and $C^{\mathrm{A}}, P^{\mathrm{A}}$ for American options, respectively. The same constant interest rate $r$ will apply for lending and borrowing money without risk, and continuous compounding will be used.

## Example 7.1

On 22 March 1997 European calls on Rolls-Royce stock with strike price 220 pence to be exercised on 22 May 1997 traded at 19.5 pence at the London International Financial Futures Exchange (LIFFE). Suppose that the purchase of such an option was financed by a loan at 5.23% compounded continuously, so that $19.5e^{0.0523 \times \frac{2}{12}} \cong 19.67$ pence would have to be paid back on the exercise date. The investment would bring a profit if the stock price turned out to be higher than $220 + 19.67 = 239.67$ pence on the exercise date.

### *Exercise 7.1*

Find the stock price on the exercise date for a European put option with strike price \$36 and exercise date in three months to produce a profit of \$3 if the option is bought for \$4.50, financed by a loan at 12% compounded continuously.

The gain of an option buyer (writer) is the payoff modified by the premium $C^{\mathrm{E}}$ or $P^{\mathrm{E}}$ paid (received) for the option. At time $T$ the gain of the buyer of a European call is $(S(T)-X)^+ - C^{\mathrm{E}}\mathrm{e}^{rT}$, where the time value of the premium is taken into account. For the buyer of a European put the gain is $(X-S(T))^+ - P^{\mathrm{E}}\mathrm{e}^{rT}$. These gains are illustrated in Figure 7.1. For the writer of an option the gains are $C^{\mathrm{E}}\mathrm{e}^{rT} - (S(T)-X)^+$ for a call and $P^{\mathrm{E}}\mathrm{e}^{rT} - (X-S(T))^+$ for a put option. Note that the potential loss for a buyer of a call or put is always limited to the premium paid. For a writer of an option the loss can be much higher, even unbounded in the case of a call option.

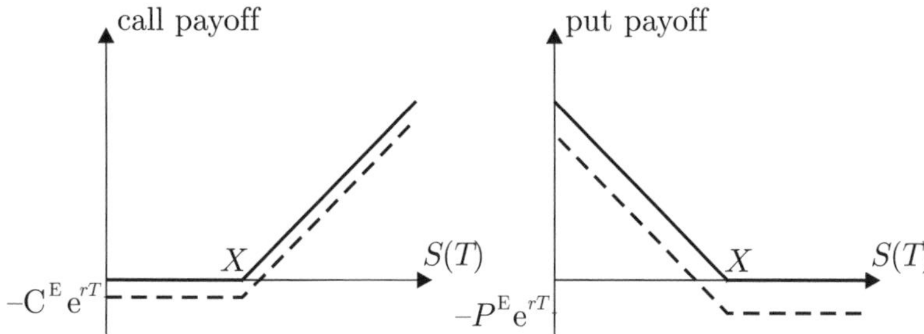


**Figure 7.1** Payoffs (solid lines) and gains (broken lines) for a buyer of European calls and puts

### *Exercise 7.2*

Find the expected gain (or loss) for a holder of a European call option with strike price \$90 to be exercised in 6 months if the stock price on the exercise date may turn out to be \$87, \$92 or \$97 with probability $\frac{1}{3}$ each, given that the option is bought for \$8, financed by a loan at 9% compounded continuously.

## 7.2 Put-Call Parity

In this section we shall make an important link between the prices of European call and put options.

Consider a portfolio constructed by writing and selling one put and buying one call option, both with the same strike price $X$ and exercise date $T$. Adding the payoffs of the long position in calls and the short position in puts, we obtain the payoff of a long forward contract with forward price $X$ and delivery time $T$. Indeed, if $S(T) \geq X$, then the call will pay $S(T) - X$ and the put will be worthless. If $S(T) < X$, then the call will be worth nothing and the writer of the put will need to pay $X - S(T)$. In either case, the value of the portfolio will be $S(T) - X$ at expiry, the same as for the long forward position, see Figure 7.2. As a result, the current value of such a portfolio of options should be that of the forward contract, which is $S(0) - Xe^{-rT}$, see Remark 6.3. This motivates the theorem below. Even though the theorem follows from the above intuitive argument, we shall give a different proof with a view to possible generalisations.

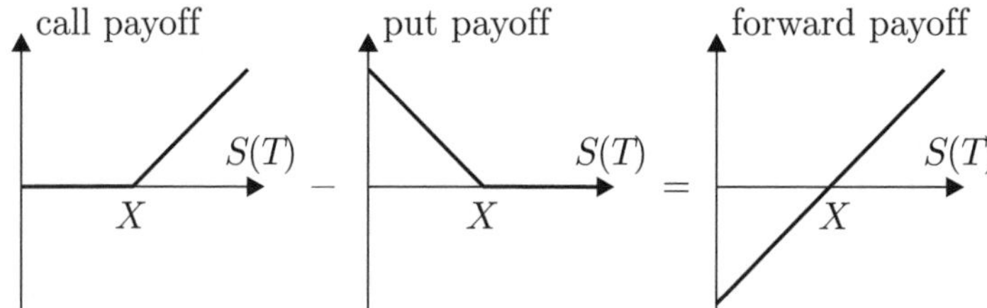


**Figure 7.2** Long forward payoff constructed from calls and puts

### Theorem 7.1 (Put-Call Parity)

For a stock that pays no dividends the following relation holds between the prices of European call and put options, both with exercise price $X$ and exercise time $T$:

$$C^{\mathrm{E}} - P^{\mathrm{E}} = S(0) - Xe^{-rT}. \tag{7.1}$$

### Proof

Suppose that

$$C^{\mathrm{E}} - P^{\mathrm{E}} > S(0) - Xe^{-rT}. \tag{7.2}$$

In this case an arbitrage strategy can be constructed as follows: At time 0

- buy one share for $S(0)$;

- buy one put option for $P^{\mathrm{E}}$;
- write and sell one call option for $C^{\mathrm{E}}$;
- invest the sum $C^{\mathrm{E}} - P^{\mathrm{E}} - S(0)$ (or borrow, if negative) on the money market at the interest rate $r$.

The balance of these transactions is 0. Then, at time $T$

- close out the money market position, collecting (or paying, if negative) the sum $(C^{\mathrm{E}} - P^{\mathrm{E}} - S(0))\mathrm{e}^{rT}$;
- sell the share for $X$ either by exercising the put if $S(T) \leq X$ or settling the short position in calls if $S(T) > X$.

The balance will be $(C^{\mathrm{E}} - P^{\mathrm{E}} - S(0))\mathrm{e}^{rT} + X$, which is positive by (7.2), contradicting the No-Arbitrage Principle.

Now suppose that

$$C^{\mathrm{E}} - P^{\mathrm{E}} < S(0) - X\mathrm{e}^{-rT}. \tag{7.3}$$

Then the following reverse strategy will result in arbitrage: At time 0

- sell short one share for $S(0)$;
- write and sell a put option for $P^{\mathrm{E}}$;
- buy one call option for $C^{\mathrm{E}}$;
- invest the sum $S(0) - C^{\mathrm{E}} + P^{\mathrm{E}}$ (or borrow, if negative) on the money market at the interest rate $r$.

The balance of these transactions is 0. At time $T$

- close out the money market position, collecting (or paying, if negative) the sum $(S(0) - C^{\mathrm{E}} + P^{\mathrm{E}})\mathrm{e}^{rT}$;
- buy one share for $X$ either by exercising the call if $S(T) > X$ or settling the short position in puts if $S(T) \leq X$, and close the short position in stock.

The balance will be $(S(0) - C^{\mathrm{E}} + P^{\mathrm{E}})\mathrm{e}^{rT} - X$, positive by (7.3), once again contradicting the No-Arbitrage Principle. □

### *Exercise 7.3*

Suppose that a stock paying no dividends is trading at \$15.60 a share. European calls on the stock with strike price \$15 and exercise date in three months are trading at \$2.83. The interest rate is $r = 6.72\%$, compounded continuously. What is the price of a European put with the same strike price and exercise date?

### *Exercise 7.4*

European call and put options with strike price \$24 and exercise date in six months are trading at \$5.09 and \$7.78. The price of the underlying stock is \$20.37 and the interest rate is 7.48%. Find an arbitrage opportunity.

## Remark 7.1

We can make a simple but powerful observation based on Theorem 7.1: The prices of European calls and puts depend in the same way on any variables absent in the put-call parity relation (7.1). In other words, the difference of these prices does not depend on such variables. As an example, consider the expected return on stock If the price of a call should grow along with the expected return, which on first sight seems consistent with intuition because higher stock prices mean higher payoffs on calls, then the price of a put would also grow. The latter, however, contradicts common sense because higher stock prices mean lower payoffs on puts. Because of this, one could argue that put and call prices should be independent of the expected return on stock. We shall see that this is indeed the case once the Black–Scholes formula is derived for call and put options in Chapter 8.

Following the argument presented at the beginning of this section, we can reformulate put-call parity as follows:

$$C^{\mathrm{E}} - P^{\mathrm{E}} = V_X(0), \tag{7.4}$$

where $V_X(0)$ is the value of a long forward contract, see (6.10). Note that if $X$ is equal to the theoretical forward price $S(0)\mathrm{e}^{rT}$ of the asset, then the value of the forward contract is zero, $V_X(0) = 0$, and so $C^{\mathrm{E}} = P^{\mathrm{E}}$. Formula (7.4) allows us to generalise put-call parity by drawing on the relationships established in Remark 6.3. Namely, if the stock pays a dividend between times 0 and $T$, then $V_X(0) = S(0) - \mathrm{div}_0 - X\mathrm{e}^{-rT}$, where $\mathrm{div}_0$ is the present value of the dividend. It follows that

$$C^{\mathrm{E}} - P^{\mathrm{E}} = S(0) - \mathrm{div}_0 - X\mathrm{e}^{-rT}. \tag{7.5}$$

If dividends are paid continuously at a rate $r_{\mathrm{div}}$, then $V_X(0) = S(0)\mathrm{e}^{-r_{\mathrm{div}}T} - X\mathrm{e}^{-rT}$, so

$$C^{\mathrm{E}} - P^{\mathrm{E}} = S(0)\mathrm{e}^{-r_{\mathrm{div}}T} - X\mathrm{e}^{-rT}. \tag{7.6}$$

### *Exercise 7.5*

Outline an arbitrage proof of (7.5).

### *Exercise 7.6*

Outline an arbitrage proof of (7.6).

### Exercise 7.7

For the data in Exercise 6.5, find the strike price for European calls and puts to be exercised in six months such that $C^{\mathrm{E}} = P^{\mathrm{E}}$.

For American options put-call parity gives only an estimate, rather than a strict equality involving put and call prices.

## Theorem 7.2 (Put-Call Parity Estimates)

The prices of American put and call options with the same strike price $X$ and expiry time $T$ on a stock that pays no dividends satisfy

$$S(0) - X\mathrm{e}^{-rT} \geq C^{\mathrm{A}} - P^{\mathrm{A}} \geq S(0) - X.$$

## Proof

Suppose that the first inequality fails to hold, that is,

$$C^{\mathrm{A}} - P^{\mathrm{A}} - S(0) + X\mathrm{e}^{-rT} > 0.$$

Then we can write and sell a call, and buy a put and a share, financing the transactions on the money market. If the holder of the American call chooses to exercise it at time $t \leq T$, then we shall receive $X$ for the share and settle the money market position, ending up with the put and a positive amount

$$\begin{aligned} X + (C^{\mathrm{A}} - P^{\mathrm{A}} - S(0))\mathrm{e}^{rt} &= (X\mathrm{e}^{-rt} + C^{\mathrm{A}} - P^{\mathrm{A}} - S(0))\mathrm{e}^{rt} \\ &\geq (X\mathrm{e}^{-rT} + C^{\mathrm{A}} - P^{\mathrm{A}} - S(0))\mathrm{e}^{rt} > 0. \end{aligned}$$

If the call option is not exercised at all, we can sell the share for $X$ by exercising the put at time $T$ and close the money market position, also ending up with a positive amount

$$X + (C^{\mathrm{A}} - P^{\mathrm{A}} - S(0))\mathrm{e}^{rT} > 0.$$

Now suppose that

$$C^{\mathrm{A}} - P^{\mathrm{A}} - S(0) + X < 0.$$

In this case we can write and sell a put, buy a call and sell short one share, investing the balance on the money market. If the American put is exercised at time $t \leq T$, then we can withdraw $X$ from the money market to buy a share and close the short sale. We shall be left with the call option and a positive amount

$$(-C^{\mathrm{A}} + P^{\mathrm{A}} + S(0))\mathrm{e}^{rt} - X > X\mathrm{e}^{rt} - X \geq 0.$$

If the put is not exercised at all, then we can buy a share for $X$ by exercising the call at time $T$ and close the short position in stock. On closing the money market position, we shall also end up with a positive amount

$$(-C^{\mathrm{A}}+P^{\mathrm{A}}+S(0))\mathrm{e}^{rT}-X>X\mathrm{e}^{rT}-X>0.$$

The theorem, therefore, holds by the No-Arbitrage Principle. □

### *Exercise 7.8*

Modify the proof of Theorem 7.2 to show that

$$S(0)-X\mathrm{e}^{-rT}\geq C^{\mathrm{A}}-P^{\mathrm{A}}\geq S(0)-\mathrm{div}_0-X$$

for a stock paying a dividend between time 0 and the expiry time $T$, where $\mathrm{div}_0$ is the value of the dividend discounted to time 0.

### *Exercise 7.9*

Modify the proof of Theorem 7.2 to show that

$$S(0)-X\mathrm{e}^{-rT}\geq C^{\mathrm{A}}-P^{\mathrm{A}}\geq S(0)\mathrm{e}^{-r_{\mathrm{div}}T}-X$$

for a stock paying dividends continuously at a rate $r_{\mathrm{div}}$.

## 7.3 Bounds on Option Prices

First of all, we note the obvious inequalities

$$C^{\mathrm{E}}\leq C^{\mathrm{A}},\quad P^{\mathrm{E}}\leq P^{\mathrm{A}},\tag{7.7}$$

for European and American options with the same strike price $X$ and expiry time $T$. They hold because an American option gives at least the same rights as the corresponding European option.

Figure 7.3 shows a scenario of stock prices in which the payoff of a European call is zero at the exercise time $T$, whereas that of an American call will be positive if the option is exercised at an earlier time $t<T$ when the stock price $S(t)$ is higher than $X$. Nevertheless, it does not necessarily follow that the inequalities in (7.7) can be replaced by strict ones; see Section 7.3.2, where it is shown that $C^{\mathrm{E}}=C^{\mathrm{A}}$ for call options on an asset that pays no dividends.

### *Exercise 7.10*

Prove (7.7) by an arbitrage argument.

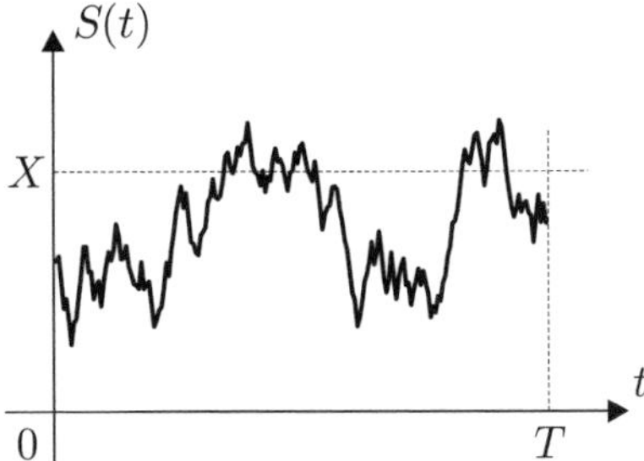


**Figure 7.3** Scenario in which an American call can bring a positive payoff, but a European call cannot

It is also obvious that the price of a call or put option has to be non-negative because an option of this kind offers the possibility of a future gain with no liability. Therefore,

$$C^{\mathrm{E}} \geq 0, \quad P^{\mathrm{E}} \geq 0.$$

Similar inequalities are of course valid for the more valuable American options. In fact the prices of options are nearly always strictly positive, except for some very special circumstances, for example, $C^{\mathrm{E}} = 0$ for a call option with strike price $X = 120$ dollars one day prior to exercise when the underlying stock is trading at \$100 and daily price movements are limited by stock exchange regulations to $\pm 10\%$.

In what follows we are going to discuss some further simple bounds for the prices of European and American options. The advantage of such bounds is that they are universal. They are independent of any particular model of stock prices and follow from the No-Arbitrage Principle alone.

### 7.3.1 European Options

We shall establish some upper and lower bounds on the prices of European call and put options.

On the one hand, observe that

$$C^{\mathrm{E}} < S(0).$$

If the reverse inequality were satisfied, that is, if $C^{\mathrm{E}} \geq S(0)$, then we could write and sell the option and buy the stock, investing the balance on the money market. On the exercise date $T$ we could then sell the stock for $\min(S(T), X)$, settling the call option. Our arbitrage profit would be $(C^{\mathrm{E}} - S(0))\mathrm{e}^{rT} + \min(S(T), X) > 0$. This proves that $C^{\mathrm{E}} < S(0)$. On the other hand, we have the lower bound

$$S(0) - Xe^{-rT} \leq C^{\mathrm{E}},$$

which follows immediately by put-call parity, since $P^{\mathrm{E}} \geq 0$. Moreover, put-call parity implies that

$$P^{\mathrm{E}} < Xe^{-rT},$$

since $C^{\mathrm{E}} < S(0)$, and

$$-S(0) + Xe^{-rT} \leq P^{\mathrm{E}},$$

since $C^{\mathrm{E}} \geq 0$.

These results are summarised in the following proposition and illustrated in Figure 7.4. The shaded areas correspond to option prices that satisfy the bounds.

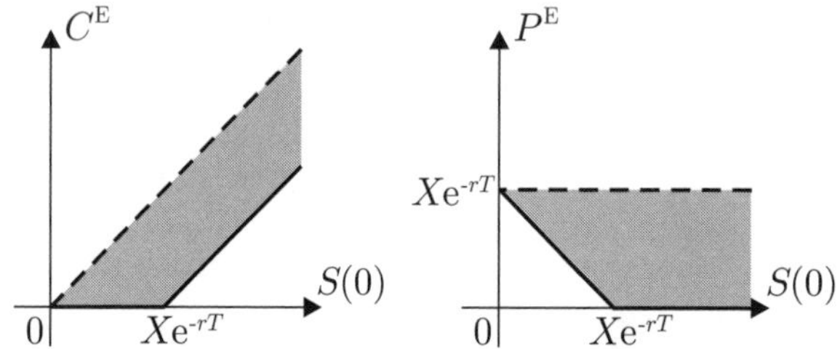


**Figure 7.4** Bounds on European call and put prices

## Proposition 7.3

The prices of European call and put options on a stock paying no dividends satisfy the inequalities

$$\max\{0, S(0) - Xe^{-rT}\} \leq C^{\mathrm{E}} < S(0),$$
$$\max\{0, -S(0) + Xe^{-rT}\} \leq P^{\mathrm{E}} < Xe^{-rT}.$$

For dividend-paying stock the bounds are

$$\max\{0, S(0) - \mathrm{div}_0 - Xe^{-rT}\} \leq C^{\mathrm{E}} < S(0) - \mathrm{div}_0,$$
$$\max\{0, -S(0) + \mathrm{div}_0 + Xe^{-rT}\} \leq P^{\mathrm{E}} < Xe^{-rT}.$$

### *Exercise 7.11*

Prove the above bounds on option prices for dividend-paying stock.

*Exercise 7.12*

For dividend-paying stock sketch the regions of call and put prices determined by the bounds.

### 7.3.2 European and American Calls on Non-Dividend Paying Stock

Consider European and American call options with the same strike price $X$ and expiry time $T$. We know that $C^{\mathrm{A}} \geq C^{\mathrm{E}}$, since the American option gives more rights than its European counterpart. If the underlying stock pays no dividends, then $C^{\mathrm{E}} \geq S(0) - X\mathrm{e}^{-rT}$ by Proposition 7.3. It follows that $C^{\mathrm{A}} > S(0) - X$ if $r > 0$. Because the price of the American option is greater than the payoff, the option will sooner be sold than exercised at time 0.

The choice of 0 as the starting time is of course arbitrary. Replacing 0 by any given $t < T$, we can show by the same argument that the American option will not be exercised at time $t$. This means that the American option will in fact never be exercised prior to expiry. This being so, it should be equivalent to the European option. In particular, their prices should be equal, leading to the following theorem.

Theorem 7.4

The prices of European and American call options on a stock that pays no dividends are equal, $C^{\mathrm{A}} = C^{\mathrm{E}}$, whenever the strike price $X$ and expiry time $T$ are the same for both options.

Proof

We already know that $C^{\mathrm{A}} \geq C^{\mathrm{E}}$, see (7.7) and Exercise 7.10. If $C^{\mathrm{A}} > C^{\mathrm{E}}$, then write and sell an American call and buy a European call, investing the balance $C^{\mathrm{A}} - C^{\mathrm{E}}$ at the interest rate $r$. If the American call is exercised at time $t \leq T$, then borrow a share and sell it for $X$ to settle your obligation as writer of the call option, investing $X$ at rate $r$. Then, at time $T$ you can use the European call to buy a share for $X$ and close your short position in stock. Your arbitrage profit will be $(C^{\mathrm{A}} - C^{\mathrm{E}})\mathrm{e}^{rT} + X\mathrm{e}^{r(T-t)} - X > 0$. If the American option is not exercised at all, you will end up with the European option and an arbitrage profit of $(C^{\mathrm{A}} - C^{\mathrm{E}})\mathrm{e}^{rT} > 0$. This proves that $C^{\mathrm{A}} = C^{\mathrm{E}}$. □

Theorem 7.4 may seem counter-intuitive at first sight. While it is possible to gain $S(t) - X$ by exercising an American call option if $S(t) > X$ at time $t < T$, this is not so with a European option, which cannot be exercised at time $t < T$. It might, therefore, appear that the American call option should be more valuable than the European one. Nevertheless, there is no contradiction. Even though a European call option cannot be exercised at time $t < T$, it can be sold for at least $S(t) - X$.

The situation is different for dividend-paying stock. Example 8.2 in the next chapter shows a case in which an American call option is worth more than its European counterpart and should be exercised prior to expiry, at least in some scenarios.

On the other hand, it often happens that an American put should be exercised prematurely even if the underlying stock pays no dividends, as in the following example.

### Example 7.2

Suppose that the stock price is \$10, the strike price of an American put expiring in one year is \$80, and the interest rate is 16%. Exercising the option now, we can gain \$70, which can be invested at 16% to become \$81.20 after one year. The value of a put option cannot possibly exceed the strike price, see (7.8), so we are definitely better off by exercising the option early.

## 7.3.3 American Options

First we consider options on non-dividend paying stock. In this case the price of an American call is equal to that of a European call, $C^{\mathrm{A}} = C^{\mathrm{E}}$, see Theorem 7.4, so it must satisfy the same bounds as in Proposition 7.3. For an American put we have

$$-S(0) + X \leq P^{\mathrm{A}}$$

because $P^{\mathrm{A}}$ cannot be less than the payoff of the option at time 0. This gives a sharper lower bound than that for a European put. However, the upper bound has to be relaxed as compared to a European put. Namely,

$$P^{\mathrm{A}} < X. \tag{7.8}$$

Indeed, if $P^{\mathrm{A}} \geq X$, then the following arbitrage strategy could be constructed: Write and sell an American put for $P^{\mathrm{A}}$ and invest this amount at the interest rate $r$. If the put is exercised at time $t \leq T$, then a share of the underlying stock will have to be bought for $X$ and can then be sold for $S(t)$. The final cash balance will be positive, $P^{\mathrm{A}}e^{rt} - X + S(t) > 0$. If the option is not exercised at all, the final balance will also be positive, $P^{\mathrm{A}}\mathrm{e}^{rT} > 0$, at expiry. These results can be summarised as follows.

### Proposition 7.5

The prices of American call and put options on a stock paying no dividends satisfy the inequalities

$$\max\{0, S(0) - X\mathrm{e}^{-rT}\} \leq C^{\mathrm{A}} < S(0),$$
$$\max\{0, -S(0) + X\} \leq P^{\mathrm{A}} < X.$$

Next we consider options on dividend-paying stock. The lower bounds for European options imply that $S(0) - \mathrm{div}_0 - X\mathrm{e}^{-rT} \leq C^{\mathrm{E}} \leq C^{\mathrm{A}}$ and $-S(0) + \mathrm{div}_0 + X\mathrm{e}^{-rT} \leq P^{\mathrm{E}} \leq P^{\mathrm{A}}$. But because the price of an American option cannot be less than its payoff at any time, we also have $S(0) - X \leq C^{\mathrm{A}}$ and $X - S(0) \leq P^{\mathrm{A}}$. Moreover, the upper bounds $C^{\mathrm{A}} < S(0)$ and $P^{\mathrm{A}} < X$ can be established in a similar manner as for non-dividend paying stock. All these inequalities can be summarised as follows: For dividend-paying stock

$$\max\{0, S(0) - \mathrm{div}_0 - X\mathrm{e}^{-rT}, S(0) - X\} \leq C^{\mathrm{A}} < S(0),$$
$$\max\{0, -S(0) + \mathrm{div}_0 + X\mathrm{e}^{-rT}, -S(0) + X\} \leq P^{\mathrm{A}} < X.$$

#### *Exercise 7.13*

Prove by an arbitrage argument that $C^{\mathrm{A}} < S(0)$ for an American call on dividend-paying stock.

## 7.4 Variables Determining Option Prices

The option price depends on a number of variables. These can be variables characterising the option, such as the strike price $X$ or expiry time $T$, variables describing the underlying asset, for example, the current price $S(0)$ or dividend rate $r_{\mathrm{div}}$, variables connected with the market as a whole such as the risk-free rate $r$, and of course the running time $t$.

We shall analyse option prices as functions of one of the variables, keeping the remaining variables constant. This is a significant simplification because usually a change in one variable is accompanied by changes in some or all of the other variables. Nevertheless, even the simplified situation will provide interesting insights.

### 7.4.1 European Options

**Dependence on the Strike Price.** We shall consider options on the same underlying asset and with the same exercise time $T$, but with different values of the strike price $X$. The call and put prices will be denoted by $C^{\mathrm{E}}(X)$ and, respectively, $P^{\mathrm{E}}(X)$ to emphasise their dependence on $X$. All remaining variables such as the exercise time $T$, running time $t$ and the underlying asset price $S(0)$ will be kept fixed for the time being.

#### Proposition 7.6

If $X' < X''$, then

$$C^{\mathrm{E}}(X') \geq C^{\mathrm{E}}(X''),$$
$$P^{\mathrm{E}}(X') \leq P^{\mathrm{E}}(X'').$$

This means that $C^{\mathrm{E}}(X)$ is a non-increasing and $P^{\mathrm{E}}(X)$ a non-decreasing function of $X$.

These inequalities are obvious. The right to buy at a lower price is more valuable than the right to buy at a higher price. Similarly, it is better to sell an asset at a higher price than at a lower one.

#### *Exercise 7.14*

Give a rigorous arbitrage argument to prove the inequalities in Proposition 7.6.

#### Proposition 7.7

If $X' < X''$, then

$$C^{\mathrm{E}}(X') - C^{\mathrm{E}}(X'') \leq \mathrm{e}^{-rT}\left(X'' - X'\right),$$
$$P^{\mathrm{E}}(X'') - P^{\mathrm{E}}(X') \leq \mathrm{e}^{-rT}\left(X'' - X'\right).$$

#### Proof

By put-call parity (7.1)

$$C^{\mathrm{E}}(X') - P^{\mathrm{E}}(X') = S(0) - X'\mathrm{e}^{-rT},$$
$$C^{\mathrm{E}}(X'') - P^{\mathrm{E}}(X'') = S(0) - X''\mathrm{e}^{-rT}.$$

Subtracting, we get

$$\left(C^{\mathrm{E}}(X') - C^{\mathrm{E}}(X'')\right) + \left(P^{\mathrm{E}}(X'') - P^{\mathrm{E}}(X')\right) = (X'' - X')\mathrm{e}^{-rT}.$$

Since, by Proposition 7.6, both terms on the left-hand side are non-negative, neither of them can exceed the right-hand side. □

## Remark 7.2

In the language of mathematics the inequalities mean that the call and put prices as functions of the strike price satisfy the Lipschitz condition with constant $\mathrm{e}^{-rT} < 1$,

$$\begin{aligned} |C^{\mathrm{E}}(X'') - C^{\mathrm{E}}(X')| &\le \mathrm{e}^{-rT}|X'' - X'|, \\ |P^{\mathrm{E}}(X'') - P^{\mathrm{E}}(X')| &\le \mathrm{e}^{-rT}|X'' - X'|. \end{aligned}$$

In particular, the slope of the graph of the option price as a function of the strike price is less than 45°. This is illustrated in Figure 7.5 for a call option.

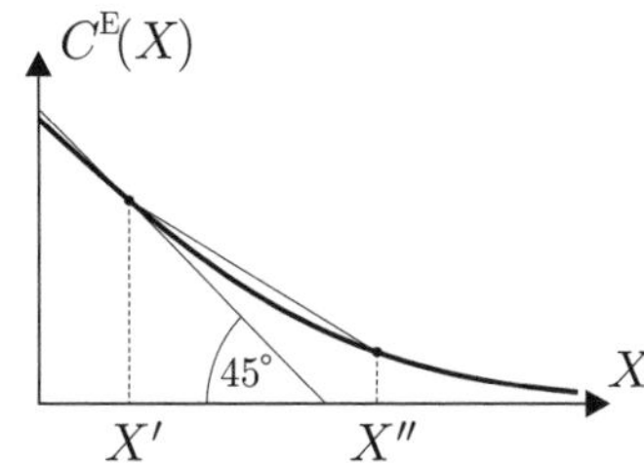


**Figure 7.5** Lipschitz property of call prices $C^{\mathrm{E}}(X)$

## Proposition 7.8

Let $X' < X''$ and let $\alpha \in (0, 1)$. Then

$$\begin{aligned} C^{\mathrm{E}}(\alpha X' + (1-\alpha)X'') &\le \alpha C^{\mathrm{E}}(X') + (1-\alpha)C^{\mathrm{E}}(X''), \\ P^{\mathrm{E}}(\alpha X' + (1-\alpha)X'') &\le \alpha P^{\mathrm{E}}(X') + (1-\alpha)P^{\mathrm{E}}(X''). \end{aligned}$$

In other words, $C^{\mathrm{E}}(X)$ and $P^{\mathrm{E}}(X)$ are convex functions of $X$.

## Proof

For brevity, we put $X = \alpha X' + (1-\alpha)X''$. Suppose that

$$C^{\mathrm{E}}(X) > \alpha C^{\mathrm{E}}(X') + (1-\alpha)C^{\mathrm{E}}(X'').$$

We can write and sell an option with strike price $X$, and purchase $\alpha$ options with strike price $X'$ and $1-\alpha$ options with strike price $X''$, investing the balance $C^{\mathrm{E}}(X) - \left(\alpha C^{\mathrm{E}}(X') + (1-\alpha)C^{\mathrm{E}}(X'')\right) > 0$ without risk. If the option with strike price $X$ is exercised at expiry, then we shall have to pay $(S(T)-X)^+$. We can raise the amount $\alpha\,(S(T)-X')^+ + (1-\alpha)\,(S(T)-X'')^+$ by exercising $\alpha$ calls with strike $X'$ and $1-\alpha$ calls with strike $X''$. In this way we will realise an arbitrage profit because of the following inequality, which is easy to verify (the details are left to the reader, see Exercise 7.15):

$$(S(T)-X)^+ \leq \alpha\,(S(T)-X')^+ + (1-\alpha)\,(S(T)-X'')^+ . \tag{7.9}$$

Convexity for put options follows from that for calls by put-call parity (7.1). Alternatively, an arbitrage argument can be given along similar lines as for call options. □

### *Exercise 7.15*

Verify inequality (7.9).

## Remark 7.3

According to Proposition 7.8, $C^{\mathrm{E}}(X)$ and $P^{\mathrm{E}}(X)$ are convex functions of $X$. Geometrically, this means that if two points on the graph of the function are joined with a straight line, then the graph of the function between the two points will lie below the line. This is illustrated in Figure 7.6 for call prices.

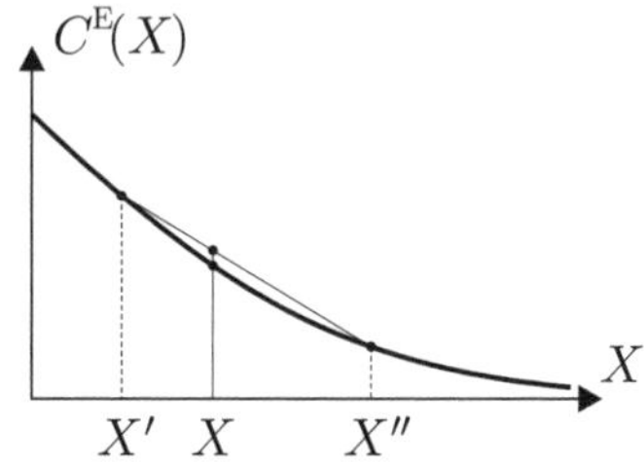


**Figure 7.6** Convexity of call prices $C^{\mathrm{E}}(X)$

**Dependence on the Underlying Asset Price.** The current price $S(0)$ of the underlying asset is given by the market and cannot be altered. However, we can consider an option on a portfolio consisting of $x$ shares, worth $S = xS(0)$. The payoff of a European call with strike price $X$ on such a portfolio to be exercised at time $T$ will be $(xS(T)-X)^+$. For a put the payoff will be $(X - xS(T))^+$. We shall study the dependence of option prices on $S$. Assuming that all remaining variables are fixed, we shall denote the call and put prices by $C^{\mathrm{E}}(S)$ and $P^{\mathrm{E}}(S)$.

## Remark 7.4

Even though options on a portfolio of stocks are of little practical significance, the functions $C^{\mathrm{E}}(S)$ and $P^{\mathrm{E}}(S)$ are important because they also reflect the dependence of option prices on very sudden changes of the price of the underlying such that the remaining variables remain almost unaltered.

## Proposition 7.9

If $S' < S''$, then

$$C^{\mathrm{E}}(S') \leq C^{\mathrm{E}}(S''),$$
$$P^{\mathrm{E}}(S') \geq P^{\mathrm{E}}(S''),$$

that is, $C^{\mathrm{E}}(S)$ is a non-decreasing function and $P^{\mathrm{E}}(S)$ a non-increasing function of $S$.

## Proof

Suppose that $C^{\mathrm{E}}(S') > C^{\mathrm{E}}(S'')$ for some $S' < S''$, where $S' = x'S(0)$ and $S'' = x''S(0)$. We can write and sell a call on a portfolio with $x'$ shares and buy a call on a portfolio with $x''$ shares, the two options sharing the same strike price $X$ and exercise time $T$, and we can invest the balance $C^{\mathrm{E}}(S') - C^{\mathrm{E}}(S'')$ without risk. Since $x' < x''$, the payoffs satisfy $(x'S(T) - X)^+ \leq (x''S(T) - X)^+$. If the option sold is exercised at time $T$, we can, therefore, exercise the other option to cover our liability and will be left with an arbitrage profit.

The inequality for puts follows by a similar arbitrage argument. □

### *Exercise 7.16*

Prove the inequality in Proposition 7.9 for put options.

## Proposition 7.10

Suppose that $S' < S''$. Then

$$C^{\mathrm{E}}(S'') - C^{\mathrm{E}}(S') \leq S'' - S',$$
$$P^{\mathrm{E}}(S') - P^{\mathrm{E}}(S'') \leq S'' - S'.$$

## Proof

We employ put-call parity (7.1):

$$C^{\mathrm{E}}(S'') - P^{\mathrm{E}}(S'') = S'' - X\mathrm{e}^{-rT},$$
$$C^{\mathrm{E}}(S') - P^{\mathrm{E}}(S') = S' - X\mathrm{e}^{-rT}.$$

Subtracting, we get

$$(C^{\mathrm{E}}(S'') - C^{\mathrm{E}}(S')) + (P^{\mathrm{E}}(S') - P^{\mathrm{E}}(S'')) = S'' - S'.$$

Both terms on the left-hand side are non-negative by Proposition 7.9, so neither can exceed the right-hand side. □

## Remark 7.5

A consequence of Proposition 7.10 is that the slope of the straight line joining two points on the graph of the call or put price as a function of $S$ is less than $45^\circ$. This is illustrated in Figure 7.7 for call options. In other words, the call and

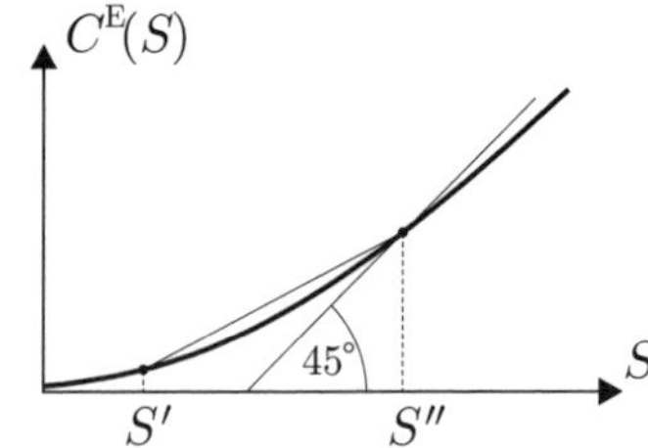


**Figure 7.7** Lipschitz property of call prices $C^{\mathrm{E}}(S)$

put prices $C^{\mathrm{E}}(S)$ and $P^{\mathrm{E}}(S)$ satisfy the Lipschitz condition with constant 1,

$$\left|C^{\mathrm{E}}(S'') - C^{\mathrm{E}}(S')\right| \leq |S'' - S'|,$$
$$\left|P^{\mathrm{E}}(S'') - P^{\mathrm{E}}(S')\right| \leq |S'' - S'|.$$

## Proposition 7.11

Let $S' < S''$ and let $\alpha \in (0,1)$. Then

$$C^{\mathrm{E}}(\alpha S' + (1-\alpha)S'') \leq \alpha C^{\mathrm{E}}(S') + (1-\alpha)C^{\mathrm{E}}(S''),$$
$$P^{\mathrm{E}}(\alpha S' + (1-\alpha)S'') \leq \alpha P^{\mathrm{E}}(S') + (1-\alpha)P^{\mathrm{E}}(S'').$$

This means that the call and put prices are convex functions of $S$.

## Proof

We put $S = \alpha S' + (1-\alpha)S''$ for brevity. Let $S' = x'S(0)$, $S'' = x''S(0)$ and $S = xS(0)$, so $x = \alpha x' + (1-\alpha)\,x''$. Suppose that

$$C^{\mathrm{E}}(S) > \alpha C^{\mathrm{E}}(S') + (1-\alpha)C^{\mathrm{E}}(S'').$$

We write and sell a call on a portfolio with $x$ shares, and purchase $\alpha$ calls on a portfolio with $x'$ shares and $1-\alpha$ calls on a portfolio with $x''$ shares, investing the balance $C^{\mathrm{E}}(S) - \alpha C^{\mathrm{E}}(S') - (1-\alpha)C^{\mathrm{E}}(S'')$ without risk. If the option sold is exercised at time $T$, then we shall have to pay $(xS(T) - X)^+$. To cover this liability we can exercise the other options. Since

$$(xS(T) - X)^+ \leq \alpha\,(x'S(T) - X)^+ + (1-\alpha)\,(x''S(T) - X)^+ \,,$$

this is an arbitrage strategy.

The inequality for put options can be proved by a similar arbitrage argument or using put-call parity. □

### 7.4.2 American Options

In general, American options have similar properties to their European counterparts. One difficulty is the absence of put-call parity; we only have the weaker estimates in Theorem 7.2. In addition, we have to take into account the possibility of early exercise.

**Dependence on the Strike Price**. We shall denote the call and put prices by $C^{\mathrm{A}}(X)$ and $P^{\mathrm{A}}(X)$ to emphasise the dependence on $X$, keeping any other variables fixed.

The following proposition is obvious for the same reasons as for European options: Higher strike price makes the right to buy less valuable and the right to sell more valuable.

## Proposition 7.12

If $X' < X''$, then

$$C^{\mathrm{A}}(X') \geq C^{\mathrm{A}}(X''),$$
$$P^{\mathrm{A}}(X') \leq P^{\mathrm{A}}(X'').$$

*Exercise 7.17*

Give a rigorous arbitrage proof of Proposition 7.12.

## Proposition 7.13

Suppose that $X' < X''$. Then

$$C^{\mathrm{A}}(X') - C^{\mathrm{A}}(X'') \leq X'' - X',$$
$$P^{\mathrm{A}}(X'') - P^{\mathrm{A}}(X') \leq X'' - X'.$$

## Proof

Suppose that $X' < X''$, but $C^{\mathrm{A}}(X') - C^{\mathrm{A}}(X'') > X'' - X'$. We write and sell a call with strike price $X'$, buy a call with strike price $X''$ and invest the balance $C^{\mathrm{A}}(X') - C^{\mathrm{A}}(X'')$ without risk. If the written option is exercised at time $t \leq T$, then we shall have to pay $(S(t) - X')^+$. Exercising the other option immediately, we shall receive $(S(t) - X'')^+$. Observe that

$$(S(t) - X'')^+ - (S(t) - X')^+ \geq -(X'' - X').$$

Together with the risk-free investment, amounting to more than $X'' - X'$, we shall therefore end up with a positive amount, realising an arbitrage profit.

The proof is similar for put options. □

## Theorem 7.14

Suppose that $X' < X''$ and let $\alpha \in (0, 1)$. Then

$$C^{\mathrm{A}}(\alpha X' + (1 - \alpha)X'') \leq \alpha C^{\mathrm{A}}(X') + (1 - \alpha)C^{\mathrm{A}}(X''),$$
$$P^{\mathrm{A}}(\alpha X' + (1 - \alpha)X'') \leq \alpha P^{\mathrm{A}}(X') + (1 - \alpha)P^{\mathrm{A}}(X'').$$

## Proof

For brevity, we put $X = \alpha X' + (1 - \alpha)X''$. Suppose that

$$C^{\mathrm{A}}(X) > \alpha C^{\mathrm{A}}(X') + (1 - \alpha)C^{\mathrm{A}}(X'').$$

We write an option with strike price $X$ and buy $\alpha$ options with strike price $X'$ and $(1 - \alpha)$ options with strike price $X''$, investing without risk the positive balance of these transactions. If the written option is exercised at time $t \leq T$, then we exercise both options held. If the option is not exercised at all, we do not need to do anything. In this way we shall achieve arbitrage because

$$(S(t) - X)^+ \leq \alpha (S(t) - X')^+ + (1 - \alpha)(S(t) - X'')^+.$$

The proof for put options is similar. □

**Dependence on the Underlying Asset Price.** Once again, we shall consider options on a portfolio of $x$ shares. The prices of American calls and puts on such a portfolio will be denoted by $C^{\mathrm{A}}(S)$ and $P^{\mathrm{A}}(S)$, where $S = xS(0)$ is the value of the portfolio, all remaining variables being fixed. The payoffs at time $t$ are $(xS(t) - X)^+$ for calls and $(X - xS(t))^+$ for puts.

## Proposition 7.15

If $S' < S''$, then

$$C^{\mathrm{A}}(S') \le C^{\mathrm{A}}(S''),$$
$$P^{\mathrm{A}}(S') \ge P^{\mathrm{A}}(S'').$$

## Proof

Suppose that $C^{\mathrm{A}}(S') > C^{\mathrm{A}}(S'')$ for some $S' < S''$, where $S' = x'S(0)$ and $S'' = x''S(0)$. We can write and sell a call on a portfolio with $x'$ shares and buy a call on a portfolio with $x''$ shares, both options having the same strike price $X$ and expiry time $T$. The balance $C^{\mathrm{A}}(S') - C^{\mathrm{A}}(S'')$ of these transactions can be invested without risk. If the written option is exercised at time $t \le T$, then we can meet the liability by exercising the other option immediately. Because $x' < x''$, the payoffs satisfy $(x'S(t) - X)^+ \le (x''S(t) - X)^+$. As a result, this strategy will provide an arbitrage opportunity.

The proof is similar for put options. □

## Proposition 7.16

Suppose that $S' < S''$. Then

$$C^{\mathrm{A}}(S'') - C^{\mathrm{A}}(S') \le S'' - S',$$
$$P^{\mathrm{A}}(S') - P^{\mathrm{A}}(S'') \le S'' - S'.$$

## Proof

The inequality for calls follows from Theorem 7.4 and Proposition 7.10.

For puts, suppose that $P^{\mathrm{A}}(S') - P^{\mathrm{A}}(S'') > S'' - S'$ for some $S' < S''$, where $S' = x'S(0)$ and $S'' = x''S(0)$. We buy $x'' - x' > 0$ shares, buy a put on a portfolio of $x''$ shares, and sell a put on a portfolio of $x'$ shares, both puts with the same strike price $X$ and expiry $T$. The cash balance of these transactions is $-(S'' - S') - P^{\mathrm{A}}(S'') + P^{\mathrm{A}}(S') > 0$. Should the holder of the put on $x'$ shares choose to exercise it at time $t \le T$, we shall need to pay $(X - x'S(t))^+$. By selling $x'' - x'$ shares and exercising the option on $x''$ shares at time $t$, we can raise enough cash to settle this liability:

$$(x'' - x')\, S(t) + (X - x''S(t))^+ \geq (X - x'S(t))^+ ,$$

since $x'' > x'$. If the put on $x'$ shares is not exercised at all, we need to take no action. In any case, the initial profit plus interest is ours to keep, resulting in an arbitrage opportunity. □

## Proposition 7.17

Let $S' < S''$ and let $\alpha \in (0, 1)$. Then

$$C^{\mathrm{A}}(\alpha S' + (1-\alpha)S'') \leq \alpha C^{\mathrm{A}}(S') + (1-\alpha)C^{\mathrm{A}}(S''),$$
$$P^{\mathrm{A}}(\alpha S' + (1-\alpha)S'') \leq \alpha P^{\mathrm{A}}(S') + (1-\alpha)P^{\mathrm{A}}(S'').$$

## Proof

Let $S = \alpha S' + (1-\alpha)S''$ and let $S' = x'S(0)$, $S'' = x''S(0)$ and $S = xS(0)$. Suppose that

$$C^{\mathrm{A}}(S) > \alpha C^{\mathrm{A}}(S') + (1-\alpha)C^{\mathrm{A}}(S'').$$

We can write and sell a call on a portfolio with $x$ shares, and purchase $\alpha$ calls on a portfolio with $x'$ shares and $1-\alpha$ calls on a portfolio with $x''$ shares, all three options sharing the same strike price $X$ and expiry time $T$. The positive balance $C^{\mathrm{A}}(S) - \alpha C^{\mathrm{A}}(S') - (1-\alpha)C^{\mathrm{A}}(S'')$ of these transactions can be invested without risk. If the written option is exercised at time $t \leq T$, then we shall have to pay $(xS(t) - X)^+$, where $x = \alpha x' + (1-\alpha)\, x''$. We can exercise the other two options to cover the liability. This is an arbitrage strategy because

$$(xS(t) - X)^+ \leq \alpha\, (x'S(t) - X)^+ + (1-\alpha)\, (x''S(t) - X)^+ .$$

The proof for put options is similar. □

**Dependence on the Expiry Time.** For American options we can also formulate a general result on the dependence of their prices on the expiry time $T$. To emphasise this dependence, we shall now write $C^{\mathrm{A}}(T)$ and $P^{\mathrm{A}}(T)$ for the prices of American calls and puts, assuming that all other variables are fixed.

## Proposition 7.18

If $T' < T''$, then

$$C^{\mathrm{A}}(T') \leq C^{\mathrm{A}}(T''),$$
$$P^{\mathrm{A}}(T') \leq P^{\mathrm{A}}(T'').$$

### Proof

Suppose that $C^{\mathrm{A}}(T') > C^{\mathrm{A}}(T'')$. We write and sell one option expiring at time $T'$ and buy one with the same strike price but expiring at time $T''$, investing the balance without risk. If the written option is exercised at time $t \leq T'$, we can exercise the other option immediately to cover our liability. The positive balance $C^{\mathrm{A}}(T') - C^{\mathrm{A}}(T'') > 0$ invested without risk will be our arbitrage profit.

The argument is the same for puts. □

## 7.5 Time Value of Options

The following convenient terminology is often used. We say that at time $t$ a call option with strike price $X$ is

- *in the money* if $S(t) > X$,
- *at the money* if $S(t) = X$,
- *out of the money* if $S(t) < X$.

Similarly, for a put option we say that it is

- *in the money* if $S(t) < X$,
- *at the money* if $S(t) = X$,
- *out of the money* if $S(t) > X$.

Also convenient, though less precise, are the terms *deep in the money* and *deep out of the money*, which mean that the difference between the two sides in the respective inequalities is considerable.

An American option in the money will bring a positive payoff if exercised immediately, whereas an option out of the money will not. We use the same terms for European options, though their meaning is different: Even if the option is currently in the money, it may no longer be so on the exercise date, when the payoff may well turn out to be zero. A European option in the money is no more than a promising asset.

### Definition 7.1

At time $t \leq T$ the *intrinsic value* of a call option with strike price $X$ is equal to $(S(t) - X)^+$. The intrinsic value of a put option with the same strike price is $(X - S(t))^+$.

We can see that the intrinsic value is zero for options out of the money or at the money. Options in the money have positive intrinsic value. The price of an option at expiry $T$ coincides with the intrinsic value. The price of an American option prior to expiry may be greater than the intrinsic value because of the possibility of future gains. The price of a European option prior to the exercise time may be greater or smaller than the intrinsic value.

## Definition 7.2

The *time value* of an option is the difference between the price of the option and its intrinsic value, that is,

$$\begin{aligned} &C^{\mathrm{E}}(t)-(S(t)-X)^{+} && \text{for a European call,}\\ &P^{\mathrm{E}}(t)-(X-S(t))^{+} && \text{for a European put,}\\ &C^{\mathrm{A}}(t)-(S(t)-X)^{+} && \text{for an American call,}\\ &P^{\mathrm{A}}(t)-(X-S(t))^{+} && \text{for an American put.}\end{aligned}$$

## Example 7.3

Let us examine some typical data. Suppose that the current price of stock is \$125.23 per share. Consider the following:

| | Intrinsic Value | | Time Value | | Option Price | |
|---|---|---|---|---|---|---|
| Srike Price | Call | Put | Call | Put | Call | Put |
| 110 | 15.23 | 0.00 | 3.17 | 2.84 | 18.40 | 2.84 |
| 120 | 5.23 | 0.00 | 7.04 | 6.46 | 12.27 | 6.46 |
| 130 | 0.00 | 5.23 | 6.78 | 4.41 | 6.78 | 9.64 |

An American call option with strike price \$110 is in the money and has \$15.23 intrinsic value. The option price must be at least equal to the intrinsic value, since the option may be exercised immediately. Typically, the price will be higher than the intrinsic value because of the possibility of future gains. On the other hand, a put option with strike price \$110 will be out of the money and its intrinsic value will be zero. The positive price of the put is entirely due to the possibility of future gains. Similar relationships for other strike prices can be seen in the table.

The time value of a European call as a function of $S$ is shown in Figure 7.8. It can never be negative, and for large values of $S$ it exceeds the difference $X - X\mathrm{e}^{-rT}$. This is because of the inequality $C^{\mathrm{E}}(S) \geq S - X\mathrm{e}^{-rT}$, see Proposition 7.3.

The market value of a European put may be lower than its intrinsic value, that is, the time value may be negative, see Figure 7.9. This may be so only if the put option is in the money, $S < X$, and it should be deep in the money.

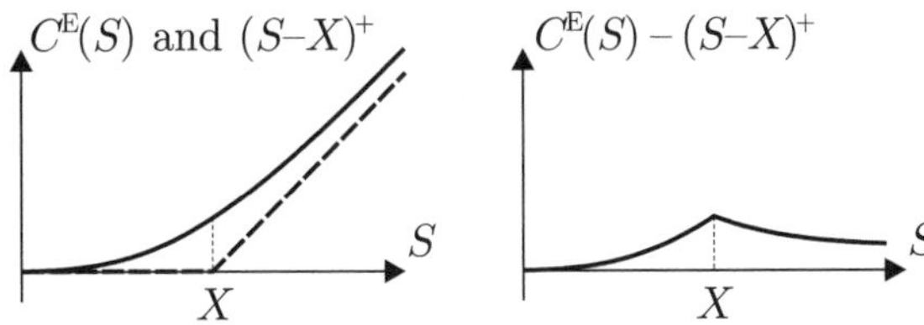


**Figure 7.8** Time value $C^{\mathrm{E}}(S) - (S - X)^+$ of a European call option

For a European option we have to wait until the exercise time $T$ to realise the payoff. The risk that the stock price will rise above $X$ in the meantime may be considerable, which reduces the value of the option.

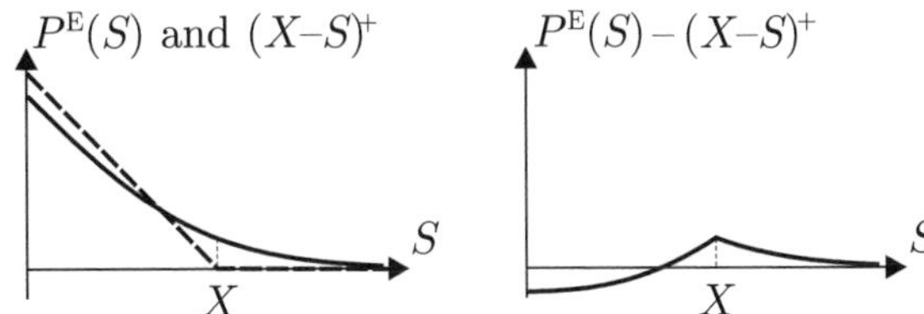


**Figure 7.9** Time value $P^{\mathrm{E}}(S) - (X - S)^+$ of a European put option

The time value of an American call option is the same as that of a European call (if there are no dividends) and Figure 7.8 applies. For an American put a typical graph of the time value is shown in Figure 7.10.

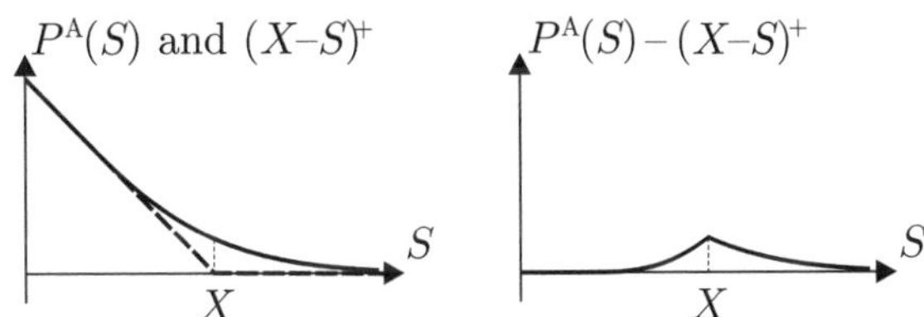


**Figure 7.10** Time value $C^{\mathrm{A}}(S) - (S - X)^+$ of an American put option

Figures 7.8, 7.9 and 7.10 also illustrate the following assertion.

## Proposition 7.19

For any European or American call or put option with strike price $X$, the time value attains its maximum at $S = X$.

## Proof

We shall present an argument for European calls. For $S \leq X$ the intrinsic value of the option is zero. Since $C^{\mathrm{E}}(S)$ is an increasing function of $S$ by Proposition 7.9, this means that the time value is an increasing function of $S$ for $S \leq X$. On the other hand, $C^{\mathrm{E}}(S'') - C^{\mathrm{E}}(S') \leq S'' - S'$ for any $S' < S''$ by Proposition 7.10. It follows that $C^{\mathrm{E}}(S'') - (S'' - X)^+ \leq C^{\mathrm{E}}(S') - (S' - X)^+$ if $X \leq S' < S''$, which means that the time value is a decreasing function of $S$ for $S \geq X$. As a result, the time value has a maximum at $S = X$.

The proof for other options is similar. □

### *Exercise 7.18*

Prove Proposition 7.19 for put options.

# 8
# Option Pricing

By a *European derivative security* or *contingent claim* with stock $S$ as the underlying asset we mean a random variable of the form $D(T) = f(S(T))$, where $f$ is a given function, called the *payoff*. This is a direct generalisation of a call option with $f(S) = (S - X)^+$, a put option with $f(S) = (X - S)^+$, or a forward contract with $f(S) = S - X$ (for the long position).

We have already learnt the basic method of pricing options in the one-step model (see Section 1.6) based on replicating the option payoff. Not surprisingly, this idea extends to a general binomial tree model constructed out of such one-step two-state building blocks. Developing this extension will be our primary task in this chapter.

### Theorem 8.1

Suppose that for any contingent claim $D(T)$ there exists a replication strategy, that is, an admissible strategy $x(t), y(t)$ with final value $V(T) = D(T)$. Then the price $D(0)$ of the contingent claim at time 0 must be equal to that of the replicating strategy, $V(0) = D(0)$.

### Proof

The proof is just a modification of that of Proposition 1.3. If $D(0) > V(0)$, then we write the derivative security and take a long position in the strategy. Our obligation will be covered by the strategy, the difference $D(0) - V(0)$ being our arbitrage profit. If $D(0) < V(0)$, then we take the opposite positions, with $V(0) - D(0)$ the resulting arbitrage profit. □

Replication also solves the problem of hedging the position of the option writer. If the cash received for the option is invested in the replicating strategy, then all the risk involved in writing the option will be eliminated.

In this chapter we shall gradually develop such pricing methods for options, starting with a comprehensive analysis of the one-step binomial model, which will then be extended to a multi-step model. Finally, the Black–Scholes formula in continuous time will be introduced.

## 8.1 European Options in the Binomial Tree Model

### 8.1.1 One Step

This simple case was discussed in Chapter 1. Here we shall reiterate the ideas in a more general setting: We shall be pricing general derivative securities and not just call or put options. This will enable us to extend the approach to the multi-step model.

We assume that the random stock price $S(1)$ at time 1 may take two values denoted by

$$\begin{cases} S^{\mathrm{u}} = S(0)(1+u), \\ S^{\mathrm{d}} = S(0)(1+d), \end{cases}$$

with probabilities $p$ and $1-p$, respectively. To replicate a general derivative security with payoff $f$ we need to solve the system of equations

$$\begin{cases} x(1)S^{\mathrm{u}} + y(1)(1+r) = f(S^{\mathrm{u}}), \\ x(1)S^{\mathrm{d}} + y(1)(1+r) = f(S^{\mathrm{d}}), \end{cases}$$

for $x(1)$ and $y(1)$. This gives

$$x(1) = \frac{f(S^{\mathrm{u}}) - f(S^{\mathrm{d}})}{S^{\mathrm{u}} - S^{\mathrm{d}}},$$

which is the replicating position in stock, called the *delta* of the option. We also find the money market position

$$y(1) = -\frac{(1+d)f(S^{\mathrm{u}}) - (1+u)f(S^{\mathrm{d}})}{(u-d)(1+r)}.$$

The initial value of the replicating portfolio is $x(1)S(0)+y(1)$. By Theorem 8.1

$$\begin{aligned} D(0) &= x(1)S(0)+y(1) \\ &= \frac{f(S^{\mathrm{u}})-f(S^{\mathrm{d}})}{u-d} - \frac{(1+d)f(S^{\mathrm{u}})-(1+u)f(S^{\mathrm{d}})}{(u-d)(1+r)}. \end{aligned} \tag{8.1}$$

### *Exercise 8.1*

Show that the price of a call option grows with $u$, the other variables being kept constant. Analyse the impact of a change of $d$ on the option price.

### *Exercise 8.2*

Find a formula for the price $C^{\mathrm{E}}(0)$ of a call option if $r=0$ and $S(0)=X=1$ dollar. Compute the price for $u=0.05$ and $d=-0.05$, and also for $u=0.01$ and $d=-0.19$. Draw a conclusion about the relationship between the variance of the return on stock and that on the option.

Recall the notion of the risk-neutral probability, given by

$$p_* = \frac{r-d}{u-d}, \tag{8.2}$$

which turns the discounted stock price process $(1+r)^{-n}S(n)$ into a martingale, see Chapter 3.

### Theorem 8.2

The expectation of the discounted payoff computed with respect to the risk-neutral probability is equal to the present value of the contingent claim,

$$D(0) = E_*\left((1+r)^{-1}f(S(1))\right). \tag{8.3}$$

## Proof

This is an immediate consequence of (8.1):

$$\begin{aligned} D(0) &= \frac{f(S^{\mathrm{u}})-f(S^{\mathrm{d}})}{u-d} + \frac{(1+u)f(S^{\mathrm{d}})-(1+d)f(S^{\mathrm{u}})}{(u-d)\,(1+r)} \\ &= \frac{1}{1+r}\left(\frac{(r-d)f(S^{\mathrm{u}})}{(u-d)} + \frac{(u-r)f(S^{\mathrm{d}})}{u-d}\right) \\ &= \frac{1}{1+r}\left(p_* f(S^{\mathrm{u}}) + (1-p_*)f(S^{\mathrm{d}})\right) \\ &= E_*\left((1+r)^{-1} f(S(1))\right), \end{aligned}$$

as claimed. □

### *Exercise 8.3*

Find the initial value of the portfolio replicating a call option if proportional transaction costs are incurred whenever the underlying stock is sold. (No transaction costs apply when the stock is bought.) Compare this value with the case free of such costs. Assume that $S(0) = X = 100$ dollars, $u = 0.1$, $d = -0.1$ and $r = 0.05$, admitting transaction costs at $c = 2\%$ (the seller receiving 98% of the stock value).

### *Exercise 8.4*

Let $S(0) = 75$ dollars and let $u = 0.2$ and $d = -0.1$. Suppose that you can borrow money at 12%, but the rate for deposits is lower at 8%. Find the values of the replicating portfolios for a put and a call. Is the answer consistent with the put and call prices following from Theorem 8.2?

## 8.1.2 Two Steps

We begin with two time steps. The stock price $S(2)$ has three possible values

$$S^{\mathrm{uu}} = S(0)(1+u)^2, \quad S^{\mathrm{ud}} = S(0)(1+u)(1+d), \quad S^{\mathrm{dd}} = S(0)(1+d)^2,$$

and $S(1)$ has two values

$$S^{\mathrm{u}} = S(0)(1+u), \quad S^{\mathrm{d}} = S(0)(1+d),$$

at the nodes of the tree in Figure 8.1 marked by the corresponding sequences of letters u and d.

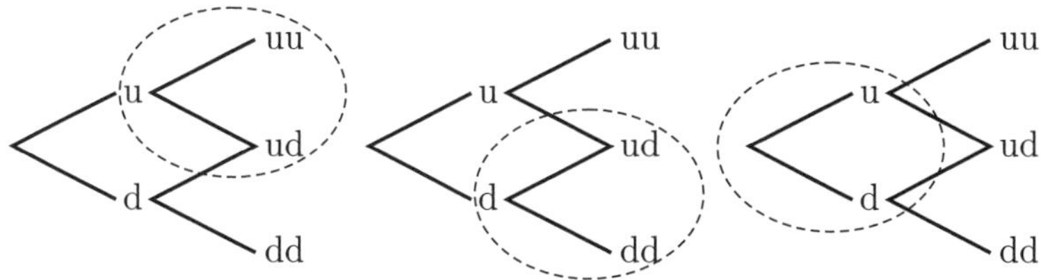


**Figure 8.1** Branchings in the two-step binomial tree

For each of the three subtrees in Figure 8.1 we can use the one-step replication procedure as described above. At time 2 the derivative security is represented by its payoff,

$$D(2) = f(S(2)),$$

which has three possible values. The derivative security price $D(1)$ has two values

$$\frac{1}{1+r}\left[p_* f(S^{\mathrm{uu}}) + (1-p_*)\, f(S^{\mathrm{ud}})\right], \qquad \frac{1}{1+r}\left[p_* f(S^{\mathrm{du}}) + (1-p_*)\, f(S^{\mathrm{dd}})\right],$$

found by the one-step procedure applied to the two subtrees at nodes u and d. This gives

$$\begin{aligned} D(1) &= \frac{1}{1+r}\left[p_* f(S(1)(1+u)) + (1-p_*)\, f(S(1)(1+d))\right] \\ &= g(S(1)), \end{aligned}$$

where

$$g(x) = \frac{1}{1+r}\left[p_* f(x(1+u)) + (1-p_*) f(x(1+d))\right].$$

As a result, $D(1)$ can be regarded as a derivative security expiring at time 1 with payoff $g$. (Though it cannot be exercised at time 1, the derivative security can be sold for $D(1) = g(S(1))$.) This means that the one-step procedure can be applied once again to the single subtree at the root of the tree. We have, therefore,

$$D(0) = \frac{1}{1+r}\left[p_* g(S(0)(1+u)) + (1-p_*)\, g(S(0)(1+d))\right].$$

It follows that

$$\begin{aligned} D(0) &= \frac{1}{1+r}\left[p_* g(S^{\mathrm{u}}) + (1-p_*)\, g(S^{\mathrm{d}})\right] \\ &= \frac{1}{(1+r)^2}\left[p_*^2 f(S^{\mathrm{uu}}) + 2p_*\,(1-p_*)\, f(S^{\mathrm{ud}}) + (1-p_*)^2\, f(S^{\mathrm{dd}})\right]. \end{aligned}$$

The last expression in square brackets is the risk-neutral expectation of $f(S(2))$. This proves the following result.

## Theorem 8.3

The expectation of the discounted payoff computed with respect to the risk-neutral probability is equal to the present value of the derivative security,

$$D(0) = E_*\left((1+r)^{-2} f(S(2))\right).$$

### *Exercise 8.5*

Let $S(0) = 120$ dollars, $u = 0.2$, $d = -0.1$ and $r = 0.1$. Consider a call option with strike price $X = 120$ dollars and exercise time $T = 2$. Find the option price and the replicating strategy.

### *Exercise 8.6*

Using the data in the previous exercise, find the price of a call and the replicating strategy if a 15 dollar dividend is paid at time 1.

### 8.1.3 General $N$-Step Model

The extension of the results above to a multi-step model is straightforward. Beginning with the payoff at the final step, we proceed backwards, solving the one-step problem repeatedly. Here is the procedure for the three-step model:

$$\begin{aligned}
D(3) &= f(S(3)),\\
D(2) &= \frac{1}{1+r}\left[p_* f(S(2)(1+u)) + (1-p_*) f(S(2)(1+d))\right]\\
&= g(S(2)),\\
D(1) &= \frac{1}{1+r}\left[p_* g(S(1)(1+u)) + (1-p_*) g(S(1)(1+d))\right]\\
&= h(S(1)),\\
D(0) &= \frac{1}{1+r}\left[p_* h(S(0)(1+u)) + (1-p_*) h(S(0)(1+d))\right],
\end{aligned}$$

where

$$\begin{aligned}
g(x) &= \frac{1}{1+r}\left[p_* f(x(1+u)) + (1-p_*) f(x(1+d))\right],\\
h(x) &= \frac{1}{1+r}\left[p_* g(x(1+u)) + (1-p_*) g(x(1+d))\right].
\end{aligned}$$

It follows that

$$\begin{aligned}
D(0) &= \frac{1}{1+r}\left[p_* h(S^{\mathrm{u}}) + (1-p_*)h(S^{\mathrm{d}}))\right] \\
&= \frac{1}{(1+r)^2}\left[p_*^2 g(S^{\mathrm{uu}}) + 2p_*(1-p_*)g(S^{\mathrm{ud}}) + (1-p_*)^2 g(S^{\mathrm{dd}}))\right] \\
&= \frac{1}{(1+r)^3}\left[p_*^3 f(S^{\mathrm{uuu}}) + 3p_*^2(1-p_*)f(S^{\mathrm{uud}})\right. \\
&\qquad\qquad \left. +3p_*(1-p_*)^2 f(S^{\mathrm{udd}}) + (1-p_*)^3 f(S^{\mathrm{ddd}}))\right].
\end{aligned}$$

The emerging pattern is this: Each term in the square bracket is characterised by the number $k$ of upward stock price movements. This number determines the power of $p_*$ and the choice of the payoff value. The power of $1-p_*$ is the number of downward price movements, equal to $3-k$ in the last expression, and $N-k$ in general, where $N$ is the number of steps. The coefficients in front of each term give the number of scenarios (paths through the tree) that lead to the corresponding payoff, equal to $\binom{N}{k} = \frac{N!}{k!(N-k)!}$, the number of $k$-element combinations out of $N$ elements. For example, there are three paths through the 3-step tree leading to the node udd.

As a result, in the $N$-step model

$$D(0) = \frac{1}{(1+r)^N}\sum_{k=0}^{N}\binom{N}{k}p_*^k(1-p_*)^{N-k} f\Big(S(0)(1+u)^k(1+d)^{N-k}\Big). \tag{8.4}$$

The expectation of $f(S(N))$ under the risk-neutral probability can readily be recognised in this formula. The result can be summarised as follows.

## Theorem 8.4

The value of a European derivative security with payoff $f(S(N))$ in the $N$-step binomial model is the expectation of the discounted payoff under the risk-neutral probability:

$$D(0) = E_*\Big((1+r)^{-N} f(S(N))\Big).$$

## Remark 8.1

There is no need to know the actual probability $p$ to compute $D(0)$. This remarkable property of the option price is important in practice, as the value of $p$ may be difficult to estimate from market data. Instead, the formula for $D(0)$ features $p_*$, the risk-neutral probability, which may have nothing in common with $p$, but is easy to compute from (8.2).

### 8.1.4 Cox–Ross–Rubinstein Formula

The payoff for a call option with strike price $X$ satisfies $f(x) = 0$ for $x \leq X$, which reduces the number of terms in (8.4). The summation starts with the least $m$ such that

$$S(0)(1+u)^m(1+d)^{N-m} > X.$$

Hence

$$C^{\mathrm{E}}(0) = (1+r)^{-N} \sum_{k=m}^{N} \binom{N}{k} p_*^k (1-p_*)^{N-k} \Big( S(0)(1+u)^k(1+d)^{N-k} - X \Big).$$

This can be written as

$$C^{\mathrm{E}}(0) = x(1)S(0) + y(1),$$

relating the option price to the initial replicating portfolio $x(1), y(1)$, where

$$x(1) = (1+r)^{-N} \sum_{k=m}^{N} \binom{N}{k} p_*^k (1-p_*)^{N-k}(1+u)^k(1+d)^{N-k},$$

$$y(1) = -X(1+r)^{-N} \sum_{k=m}^{N} \binom{N}{k} p_*^k (1-p_*)^{N-k}.$$

The expression for $x(1)$ can be rewritten as

$$x(1) = \sum_{k=m}^{N} \binom{N}{k} \left( p_* \frac{1+u}{1+r} \right)^k \left( (1-p_*) \frac{1+d}{1+r} \right)^{N-k} = \sum_{k=m}^{N} \binom{N}{k} q^k (1-q)^{N-k},$$

where

$$q = p_* \frac{1+u}{1+r}.$$

(Note that $p_* \frac{1+u}{1+r}$ and $(1-p_*)\frac{1+d}{1+r}$ add up to one.) Similar formulae can be derived for put options, either directly or using put-call parity.

These important results are summarised in the following theorem, in which $\Phi(m, N, p)$ denotes the cumulative binomial distribution with $N$ trials and probability $p$ of success in each trial,

$$\Phi(m, N, p) = \sum_{k=0}^{m} \binom{N}{k} p^k (1-p)^{N-k}.$$

### Theorem 8.5 (Cox–Ross–Rubinstein Formula)

In the binomial model the price of a European call and put option with strike price $X$ to be exercised after $N$ time steps is given by

$$C^{\mathrm{E}}(0) = S(0)\left[1 - \Phi(m-1, N, q)\right] - (1+r)^{-N} X \left[1 - \Phi(m-1, N, p_*)\right],$$
$$P^{\mathrm{E}}(0) = -S(0)\Phi(m-1, N, q) + (1+r)^{-N} X \Phi(m-1, N, p_*).$$

The initial replicating portfolio $x(1), y(1)$ is given by

| | $x(1)$ | $y(1)$ |
|---|---|---|
| for a call | $1 - \Phi(m-1, N, q)$ | $-(1+r)^{-N} X \left[1 - \Phi(m-1, N, p_*)\right]$ |
| for a put | $-\Phi(m-1, N, q)$ | $(1+r)^{-N} X \Phi(m-1, N, p_*)$ |

#### *Exercise 8.7*

Let $S(0) = 50$ dollars, $r = 5\%$, $u = 0.3$ and $d = -0.1$. Find the price of a European call and put with strike price $X = 60$ dollars to be exercised after $N = 3$ time steps.

#### *Exercise 8.8*

Let $S(0) = 50$ dollars, $r = 0.5\%$, $u = 0.01$ and $d = -0.01$. Find $m$, $x(1)$, and the price $C^{\mathrm{E}}(0)$ of a European call option with strike $X = 60$ dollars to be exercised after $N = 50$ time steps.

#### *Exercise 8.9*

Consider the scenario in which stock goes up at each step. At which step will the delta of a European call become 1?

## 8.2 American Options in the Binomial Tree Model

Even the formulation of a precise mathematical definition of an American type contingent claim presents some difficulties. Nevertheless, the informal description is simple: The option can be exercised at any time step $n$ such that $0 \leq n \leq N$, with payoff $f(S(n))$. Of course, it can be exercised only once. The price of an American option at time $n$ will be denoted by $D^{\mathrm{A}}(n)$.

To begin with, we shall analyse an American option expiring after 2 time steps. Unless the option has already been exercised, at expiry it will be worth

$$D^{\mathrm{A}}(2) = f(S(2)),$$

where we have three values depending on the values of $S(2)$. At time 1 the option holder will have the choice to exercise immediately, with payoff $f(S(1))$, or to wait until time 2, when the value of the American option will become $f(S(2))$. The value of waiting can be computed by treating $f(S(2))$ as a one-step European contingent claim to be priced at time 1, which gives the value

$$\frac{1}{1+r}\left[p_* f(S(1)(1+u)) + (1-p_*) f(S(1)(1+d))\right]$$

at time 1. In effect, the option holder has the choice between the latter value or the immediate payoff $f(S(1))$. The American option at time 1 will, therefore, be worth the higher of the two,

$$\begin{aligned} D^{\mathrm{A}}(1) &= \max\left\{ f(S(1)), \frac{1}{1+r}\left[p_* f(S(1)(1+u)) + (1-p_*) f(S(1)(1+d))\right] \right\} \\ &= f_1(S(1)) \end{aligned}$$

(a random variable with two values), where

$$f_1(x) = \max\left\{ f(x), \frac{1}{1+r}\left[p_* f(x(1+u)) + (1-p_*) f(x(1+d))\right] \right\}.$$

A similar argument gives the American option value at time 0,

$$D^{\mathrm{A}}(0) = \max\left\{ f(S(0)), \frac{1}{1+r}\left[p_* f_1(S(0)(1+u)) + (1-p_*) f_1(S(0)(1+d))\right] \right\}.$$

## Example 8.1

To illustrate the above procedure we consider an American put option with strike price $X = 80$ dollars expiring at time 2 on a stock with initial price $S(0) = 80$ dollars in a binomial model with $u = 0.1$, $d = -0.05$ and $r = 0.05$. (We consider a put, as we know that there is no difference between American and European call options, see Theorem 7.4.) The stock values are

| $n$ | 0 | | 1 | | 2 |
|---|---|---|---|---|---|
| | | | | | 96.80 |
| | | | 88.00 | $<$ | |
| $S(n)$ | 80.00 | $<$ | | | 83.60 |
| | | | 76.00 | $<$ | |
| | | | | | 72.20 |

The price of the American put will be denoted by $P^{\mathrm{A}}(n)$ for $n = 0, 1, 2$. At expiry the payoff will be positive only in the scenario with two downward stock price movements,

| $n$ | 0 | | 1 | | 2 |
|---|---|---|---|---|---|
| | | | | | 0.00 |
| | | | ? | < | |
| $P^{\mathrm{A}}(n)$ | ? | < | | | 0.00 |
| | | | ? | < | |
| | | | | | 7.80 |

At time 1 the option writer can choose between exercising the option immediately or waiting until time 2. In the up state at time 1 the immediate payoff and the value of waiting are both zero. In the down state the immediate payoff is 4 dollars, while the value of waiting is $1.05^{-1} \times \frac{1}{3} \times 7.8 \cong 2.48$ dollars. The option holder will choose the higher value (exercising the option in the down state at time 1). This gives the time 1 values of the American put,

| $n$ | 0 | | 1 | | 2 |
|---|---|---|---|---|---|
| | | | | | 0.00 |
| | | | 0.00 | < | |
| $P^{\mathrm{A}}(n)$ | ? | < | | | 0.00 |
| | | | 4.00 | < | |
| | | | | | 7.80 |

At time 0 the choice is, once again, between the payoff, which is zero, or the value of waiting, which is $1.05^{-1} \times \frac{1}{3} \times 4 \cong 1.27$ dollars. Taking the higher of the two completes the tree of option prices,

| $n$ | 0 | | 1 | | 2 |
|---|---|---|---|---|---|
| | | | | | 0.00 |
| | | | 0.00 | < | |
| $P^{\mathrm{A}}(n)$ | 1.27 | < | | | 0.00 |
| | | | 4.00 | < | |
| | | | | | 7.80 |

For comparison, the price of a European put is $P^{\mathrm{E}}(0) = 1.05^{-1} \times \frac{1}{3} \times 2.48 \cong 0.79$ dollars, clearly less than the American put price $P^{\mathrm{A}}(0) \cong 1.27$ dollars.

This can be generalised, leading to the following definition.

## Definition 8.1

An *American derivative security* or *contingent claim* with payoff function $f$ expiring at time $N$ is a sequence of random variables defined by backward induction:

$$\begin{aligned}
D^{\mathrm{A}}(N) &= f(S(N)), \\
D^{\mathrm{A}}(N-1) &= \max\Big\{f(S(N-1)), \frac{1}{1+r}[p_* f(S(N-1)(1+u)) \\
&\quad + (1-p_*)f(S(N-1)(1+d))]\Big\} =: f_{N-1}(S(N-1)), \\
D^{\mathrm{A}}(N-2) &= \max\Big\{f(S(N-2)), \frac{1}{1+r}[p_* f_{N-1}(S(N-2)(1+u)) \\
&\quad + (1-p_*)f_{N-1}(S(N-2)(1+d))]\Big\} =: f_{N-2}(S(N-2)), \\
&\vdots \\
D^{\mathrm{A}}(1) &= \max\Big\{f(S(1)), \frac{1}{1+r}[p_* f_2(S(1)(1+u)) \\
&\quad + (1-p_*)f_2(S(1)(1+d))]\Big\} =: f_1(S(1)), \\
D^{\mathrm{A}}(0) &= \max\Big\{f(S(0)), \frac{1}{1+r}[p_* f_1(S(0)(1+u)) \\
&\quad + (1-p_*)f_1(S(0)(1+d))]\Big\}.
\end{aligned}$$

### *Exercise 8.10*

Compute the value of an American put expiring at time 3 with strike price $X = 62$ dollars on a stock with initial price $S(0) = 60$ dollars in a binomial model with $u = 0.1$, $d = -0.05$ and $r = 0.03$.

### *Exercise 8.11*

Compare the prices of an American call and a European call with strike price $X = 120$ dollars expiring at time 2 on a stock with initial price $S(0) = 120$ dollars in a binomial model with $u = 0.2$, $d = -0.1$ and $r = 0.1$.

## Example 8.2

The last exercise can be modified to show that the equality of European and American call prices may not hold if a dividend is paid. Suppose that a dividend of 14 dollars is paid at time 2. Otherwise, we shall use the same data as in

Exercise 8.11. The ex-dividend stock prices are

| $n$ | 0 | | 1 | | 2 |
|---|---|---|---|---|---|
| | | | | | 158.80 |
| | | | 144.00 | $<$ | |
| $S(n)$ | 120.00 | $<$ | | | 115.60 |
| ex-div | | | 108.00 | $<$ | |
| | | | | | 83.20 |

The corresponding European and American call values will be

| $n$ | 0 | | 1 | | 2 |
|---|---|---|---|---|---|
| | | | | | 38.80 |
| | | | | | 38.80 |
| | | | 23.52 | $<$ | |
| | | | **24.00** | | |
| $C^{\mathrm{E}}(n)$ | 14.25 | $<$ | | | 0.00 |
| $C^{\mathrm{A}}(n)$ | 14.55 | | | | 0.00 |
| | | | 0.00 | $<$ | |
| | | | 0.00 | | |
| | | | | | 0.00 |
| | | | | | 0.00 |

The American call should be exercised early in the up state at time 1 with payoff 24 dollars (bold figures), which is more than the value of holding the option to expiry. As a result, the price of the American call is higher than that of the European call.

*Exercise 8.12*

Compute the prices of European and American puts with exercise and strike price $X = 14$ dollars expiring at time 2 on a stock with $S(0) = 12$ dollars in a binomial model with $u = 0.1$, $d = -0.05$ and $r = 0.02$, assuming that a dividend of 2 dollars is paid at time 1.

## 8.3 Black–Scholes Formula

We shall present an outline of the main results for European call and put options in continuous time, culminating in the famous Black–Scholes formula. Our treatment of continuous time is a compromise lacking full mathematical rigour, which would require a systematic study of *Stochastic Calculus*, a topic treated in detail in more advanced texts. In place of this, we shall exploit an analogy with the discrete time case.

As a starting point we take the continuous time model of stock prices developed in Chapter 3 as a limit of suitably scaled binomial models with time steps going to zero. In the resulting continuous time model the stock price is given by

$$S(t) = S(0)\mathrm{e}^{mt+\sigma W(t)}, \tag{8.5}$$

where $W(t)$ is the standard Wiener process (Brownian motion), see Section 3.3.2. This means, in particular, that $S(t)$ has the log normal distribution.

Consider a European option on the stock expiring at time $T$ with payoff $f(S(T))$. As in the discrete-time case, see Theorem 8.4, the time 0 price $D(0)$ of the option ought to be equal to the expectation of the discounted payoff $\mathrm{e}^{-rT}f(S(T))$,

$$D(0) = E_*\left(\mathrm{e}^{-rT}f(S(T))\right), \tag{8.6}$$

under a risk-neutral probability $P_*$ that turns the discounted stock price process $\mathrm{e}^{-rt}S(t)$ into a martingale. Here we shall accept this formula without proof, by analogy with the discrete time result. (The proof is based on an arbitrage argument combined with a bit of Stochastic Calculus, the latter beyond the scope of this book.)

What is the risk-neutral probability $P_*$, then? A necessary condition is that the expectation of the discounted stock prices $\mathrm{e}^{-rt}S(t)$ should be constant (independent of $t$), just like in the discrete time case, see (3.5).

Let us compute this expectation using the real market probability $P$. Since $W(t)$ is normally distributed with mean 0 and variance $t$, it has density $\frac{1}{\sqrt{2\pi t}}\mathrm{e}^{-\frac{x^2}{2t}}$ under probability $P$. As a result,

$$\begin{aligned}
E\left(\mathrm{e}^{-rt}S(t)\right) &= S(0)E\left(\mathrm{e}^{\sigma W(t)+(m-r)t}\right)\\
&= S(0)\int_{-\infty}^{\infty}\mathrm{e}^{\sigma x+(m-r)t}\frac{1}{\sqrt{2\pi t}}\mathrm{e}^{-\frac{x^2}{2t}}\,\mathrm{d}x\\
&= S(0)\mathrm{e}^{(m-r+\frac{1}{2}\sigma^2)t}\int_{-\infty}^{\infty}\frac{1}{\sqrt{2\pi t}}\mathrm{e}^{-\frac{(x-\sigma t)^2}{2t}}\,\mathrm{d}x\\
&= S(0)\mathrm{e}^{(m-r+\frac{1}{2}\sigma^2)t}\int_{-\infty}^{\infty}\frac{1}{\sqrt{2\pi t}}\mathrm{e}^{-\frac{y^2}{2t}}\,\mathrm{d}y\\
&= S(0)\mathrm{e}^{(m-r+\frac{1}{2}\sigma^2)t}.
\end{aligned}$$

If $m+\frac{1}{2}\sigma^2 \neq r$, then the expectation $E(\mathrm{e}^{-rt}S(t)) = S(0)\mathrm{e}^{(m-r+\frac{1}{2}\sigma^2)t}$ clearly depends on $t$, so $S(t)$ cannot be a martingale under $P$.

However, the calculations above suggest a modification $P_*$ of $P$ that would make the corresponding expectation $E_*(\mathrm{e}^{-rt}S(t))$ independent of $t$ by eliminating the exponential factor $\mathrm{e}^{(m-r+\frac{1}{2}\sigma^2)t}$. Namely, if $P$ can be replaced by a probability $P_*$ such that $V(t) = W(t) + \left(m - r + \frac{1}{2}\sigma^2\right)t/\sigma$ (rather than $W(t)$ itself) becomes a Wiener process under $P_*$, then the exponential factor $e^{(m-r+\frac{1}{2}\sigma^2)t}$ will be eliminated from the final expression. (The existence of such a probability $P_*$ follows from an advanced result in Stochastic Calculus, the so-called *Girsanov theorem.*) Indeed, since $V(t)$ has density $\frac{1}{\sqrt{2\pi t}}e^{-\frac{x^2}{2t}}$ under $P_*$, that is, it is normally distributed with mean 0 and variance $t$, it follows that

$$\begin{aligned} E_*\left(e^{-rt}S(t)\right) &= S(0)E_*\left(e^{\sigma W(t)+(m-r)t}\right) \\ &= S(0)E_*\left(e^{\sigma V(t)-\frac{1}{2}\sigma^2 t}\right) \\ &= S(0)\int_{-\infty}^{\infty} e^{\sigma x - \frac{1}{2}\sigma^2 t}\frac{1}{\sqrt{2\pi t}}e^{-\frac{x^2}{2t}}\,dx \\ &= S(0)\int_{-\infty}^{\infty} \frac{1}{\sqrt{2\pi t}}e^{-\frac{(x-\sigma t)^2}{2t}}\,dx \\ &= S(0)\int_{-\infty}^{\infty} \frac{1}{\sqrt{2\pi t}}e^{-\frac{y^2}{2t}}\,dy = S(0). \end{aligned}$$

The fact that $E_*(e^{-rt}S(t)) = S(0)$ does not depend on time $t$ is a necessary condition for the discounted price process $e^{-rt}S(t)$ to be a martingale under $P_*$. To show that $e^{-rt}S(t)$ is indeed a martingale under $P_*$ we need in fact to verify the stronger condition

$$E_*\left(e^{-rt}S(t)|S(u)\right) = e^{-ru}S(u) \tag{8.7}$$

for any $t \geq u \geq 0$, involving the conditional expectation of $e^{-rt}S(t)$ given $S(u)$. So far we have dealt with conditional expectation where the condition was given in terms of a discrete random variable, see Section 3.2.2. Here, however, the condition is expressed in terms of $S(u)$, a random variable with continuous distribution. In this case the precise mathematical meaning of (8.7) is that for every $a > 0$

$$E_*\left(e^{-rt}S(t)1_{S(u)<a}\right) = E_*\left(e^{-ru}S(u)1_{S(u)<a}\right), \tag{8.8}$$

where $1_{S(u)<a}$ is the *indicator random variable*, equal to 1 if $S(u) < a$ and to 0 if $S(u) \geq a$.

### Exercise 8.13

Verify equality (8.8).

### Exercise 8.14

Find the density of $W(t)$ under the risk-neutral probability $P_*$.

Above we have identified the risk-neutral probability $P_*$. Now we shall consider a European call option on the stock with strike price $X$ to be exercised at time $T$. The general formula (8.6) for the price of an option becomes

$$C^{\mathrm{E}}(0) = E_*\left(\mathrm{e}^{-rT}(S(T)-X)^+\right).$$

Let us compute this expectation. Because $V(T) = W(t) + \left(m - r + \frac{1}{2}\sigma^2\right)\frac{t}{\sigma}$ for $t \geq 0$ is a Wiener process under $P_*$, the random variable $V(T) = W(T) + \left(m - r + \frac{1}{2}\sigma^2\right)\frac{T}{\sigma}$ is normally distributed with mean 0 and variance $T$, that is, it has density $\frac{1}{\sqrt{2\pi T}}\mathrm{e}^{-\frac{x^2}{2T}}$. As a result,

$$\begin{aligned}
C^{\mathrm{E}}(0) &= E_*\left(\mathrm{e}^{-rT}(S(T)-X)^+\right) \\
&= E_*\left(\left(S(0)\mathrm{e}^{\sigma V(t)-\frac{1}{2}\sigma^2 T} - X\mathrm{e}^{-rT}\right)^+\right) \\
&= \int_{-d_2\sqrt{T}}^{\infty}\left(S(0)\mathrm{e}^{\sigma x-\frac{1}{2}\sigma^2 T} - X\mathrm{e}^{-rT}\right)\frac{1}{\sqrt{2\pi T}}\mathrm{e}^{-\frac{x^2}{2T}}\,\mathrm{d}x \\
&= S(0)\int_{-d_1}^{\infty}\frac{1}{\sqrt{2\pi}}\mathrm{e}^{-\frac{y^2}{2}}\,\mathrm{d}y - X\mathrm{e}^{-rT}\int_{-d_2}^{\infty}\frac{1}{\sqrt{2\pi}}\mathrm{e}^{-\frac{y^2}{2}}\,\mathrm{d}y \\
&= S(0)N(d_1) - X\mathrm{e}^{-rT}N(d_2),
\end{aligned}$$

where

$$d_1 = \frac{\ln\frac{S(0)}{X} + \left(r + \frac{1}{2}\sigma^2\right)T}{\sigma\sqrt{T}}, \qquad d_2 = \frac{\ln\frac{S(0)}{X} + \left(r - \frac{1}{2}\sigma^2\right)T}{\sigma\sqrt{T}}, \tag{8.9}$$

and where

$$N(x) = \int_{-\infty}^{x}\frac{1}{\sqrt{2\pi}}\mathrm{e}^{-\frac{y^2}{2}}\,\mathrm{d}y = \int_{-x}^{\infty}\frac{1}{\sqrt{2\pi}}\mathrm{e}^{-\frac{y^2}{2}}\,\mathrm{d}y \tag{8.10}$$

is the normal distribution function.

What we have just derived is the celebrated Black–Scholes formula for European call options. The choice of time 0 to compute the price of the option is arbitrary. In general, the option price can be computed at any time $t < T$, in which case the time remaining before the option is exercised will be $T - t$. Substituting $t$ for 0 and $T - t$ for $T$ in the above formulae, we thus obtain the following result.

## Theorem 8.6 (Black–Scholes Formula)

The time $t$ price of a European call with strike price $X$ and exercise time $T$, where $t < T$, is given by

$$C^{\mathrm{E}}(t) = S(t)N(d_1) - X\mathrm{e}^{-r(T-t)}N(d_2)$$

with

$$d_1 = \frac{\ln \frac{S(t)}{X} + \left(r + \frac{1}{2}\sigma^2\right)(T-t)}{\sigma\sqrt{T-t}}, \quad d_2 = \frac{\ln \frac{S(t)}{X} + \left(r - \frac{1}{2}\sigma^2\right)(T-t)}{\sigma\sqrt{T-t}}. \tag{8.11}$$

### *Exercise 8.15*

Derive the Black–Scholes formula

$$P^{\mathrm{E}}(t) = X\mathrm{e}^{-r(T-t)}N(-d_2) - S(t)N(-d_1),$$

with $d_1$ and $d_2$ given by (8.11), for the price of a European put with strike $X$ and exercise time $T$.

## Remark 8.2

Observe that the Black–Scholes formula contains no $m$. It is a property analogous to that in Remark 8.1, and of similar practical significance: There is no need to know $m$ to work out the price of a European call or put option in continuous time.

It is interesting to compare the Black–Scholes formula for the price of a European call with the Cox–Ross–Rubinstein formula. There is close analogy between the terms. Apart from the obvious correspondence between the continuous and discrete time discount factors $\mathrm{e}^{-rT}$ and $(1+r)^{-N}$, the binomial and normal distribution terms appearing in these formulae are also related to one another. The precise relationship comes from a version of the *Central Limit Theorem*: It can be shown that the option price given by the Cox–Ross–Rubinstein formula tends to that in the Black–Scholes formula in the continuous time limit described in Chapter 3.

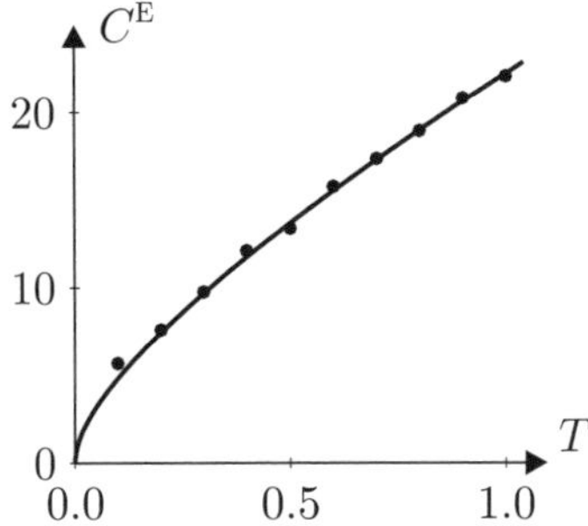


**Figure 8.2** Option price $C^{\mathrm{E}}$ in continuous and discrete time models as a function of time $T$ remaining before the option is exercised

Rather than looking at the details of this limit, we just refer to Figure 8.2 for illustration. It shows the price $C^{\mathrm{E}}$ of a European call with strike $X = 100$ on a stock with $S(0) = 100$, $\sigma = 0.3$ and $m = 0.2$. (Though $m$ is irrelevant for the Black–Scholes formula, it still features in the discrete time approximation.) The continuous compounding interest rate is taken to be $r = 0.2$. The option price is computed in two ways, as a function of the time $T$ remaining before the option is exercised:

a) (*solid line*) from the Black–Scholes formula for $T$ between 0 and 1;

b) (*dots*) using the Cox–Ross–Rubinstein formula with $T$ increasing from 0 to 1 in $N = 10$ steps of duration $\tau = 0.1$ each; the discrete growth rates for each step are computed using formulae (3.7).

Even with as few as 10 steps there is remarkably good agreement between the discrete and continuous time formulae.

# 9
# Financial Engineering

This chapter shows some applications of derivative securities to managing the risk exposure in various situations. The presentation will be by means of examples and mini case studies. Even though these are concerned with very particular circumstances, the methods are applicable to a wide range of tasks handled by financial managers.

First, we shall present methods for eliminating or reducing the risk involved in writing options. This is a problem faced by financial institutions who issue and sell derivative securities, but may not wish to bear the accompanying risk. Such institutions are typically satisfied by the commission charged for their services, without taking an active position in the market.

Next, we shall analyse methods of reducing undesirable risk stemming from certain business activities. Our case studies will be concerned with foreign exchange risk. It is possible to deal in a similar way with the risk resulting from unexpected future changes of various market variables such as commodity prices, interest rates or stock prices. We shall introduce a measure of risk called Value at Risk (VaR), which has recently become very popular. Derivative securities will be used to design portfolios with a view to reducing this kind of risk.

Finally, we shall consider an application of options to manufacturing a levered investment, for which increased risk will be accompanied by high expected return.

## 9.1 Hedging Option Positions

The writer of a European call option is exposed to risk, as the option may end up in the money. The risk profile for a call writer is $C^{\mathrm{E}}\mathrm{e}^{rT}-(S(T)-X)^{+}$, where $C^{\mathrm{E}}\mathrm{e}^{rT}$ is the value at the exercise time $T$ of the premium $C^{\mathrm{E}}$ received for the option and invested without risk. Theoretically, the loss to the writer may be unlimited. For a put option the risk profile has the form $P^{\mathrm{E}}\mathrm{e}^{rT}-(X-S(T))^{+}$, with limited loss, though still possibly very large compared to the premium $P^{\mathrm{E}}$ received. We shall see how to eliminate or at least reduce this risk over a short time horizon by taking a suitable position in the underlying asset and, if necessary, also in other derivative securities written on the same asset.

In practice it is impossible to hedge in a perfect way by designing a single portfolio to be held for the whole period up to the exercise time $T$. The hedging portfolio will need to be modified whenever the variables affecting the option change with time. In a realistic case of non-zero transaction costs these modifications cannot be performed too frequently and some compromise strategy may be required. Nevertheless, here we shall only discuss hedging over a single short time interval, neglecting transaction costs.

### 9.1.1 Delta Hedging

The value of a European call or put option as given by the Black–Scholes formula clearly depends on the price of the underlying asset. This can be seen in a slightly broader context.

Consider a portfolio whose value depends on the current stock price $S = S(0)$ and is hence denoted by $V(S)$. Its dependence on $S$ can be measured by the derivative $\frac{\mathrm{d}}{\mathrm{d}S}V(S)$, called the *delta* of the portfolio. For small price variations from $S$ to $S+\varDelta S$ the value of the portfolio will change by

$$\varDelta V(S) \cong \frac{\mathrm{d}}{\mathrm{d}S}V(S)\times \varDelta S.$$

The principle of *delta hedging* is based on embedding derivative securities in a portfolio, the value of which does not alter too much when $S$ varies. This can be achieved by ensuring that the delta of the portfolio is equal to zero. Such a portfolio is called *delta neutral*.

We take a portfolio composed of stock, bonds and the hedged derivative security, its value given by

$$V(S) = xS + y + zD(S),$$

where the derivative security price is denoted by $D(S)$ and a bond with current value 1 is used. Specifically, suppose that a single derivative security has been written, that is, $z = -1$. Then

$$\frac{\mathrm{d}}{\mathrm{d}S}V(S) = x - \frac{\mathrm{d}}{\mathrm{d}S}D(S).$$

The last term $\frac{\mathrm{d}}{\mathrm{d}S}D(S)$, which is the *delta* of the derivative security, can readily be computed if the model of stock prices is specified, so that an explicit formula for $D(S)$ is available.

## Proposition 9.1

Denote the European call option price in the Black–Scholes model by $C^{\mathrm{E}}(S)$. The delta of the option is given by

$$\frac{\mathrm{d}}{\mathrm{d}S}C^{\mathrm{E}}(S) = N(d_1),$$

where $N(x)$ is the normal distribution function given by (8.10) and $d_1$ is defined by (8.9).

## Proof

The price $S = S(0)$ appears in three places in the Black–Scholes formula, see Theorem 8.6, so the differentiation requires a bit of work, with plenty of nice cancellations in due course, and is left to the reader. Bear in mind that the derivative $\frac{\mathrm{d}}{\mathrm{d}S}C^{\mathrm{E}}(S)$ is computed at time $t = 0$. □

### *Exercise 9.1*

Find a similar expression for the delta $\frac{\mathrm{d}}{\mathrm{d}S}P^{\mathrm{E}}(S)$ of a European put option in the Black–Scholes model.

For the remainder of this section we shall consider a European call option within the Black–Scholes model. By Proposition 9.1 the portfolio $(x, y, z) = (N(d_1), y, -1)$, where the position in stock $N(d_1)$ is computed for the initial stock price $S = S(0)$, has delta equal to zero for any money market position $y$. Consequently, its value

$$V(S) = N(d_1)S + y - C^{\mathrm{E}}(S)$$

does not vary much under small changes of the stock price about the initial value. It is convenient to choose $y$ so that the initial value of the portfolio is equal to zero. By the Black–Scholes formula for $C^{\mathrm{E}}(S)$ this gives

$$y = -X\mathrm{e}^{-Tr}N(d_2),$$

with $d_2$ is given by (8.9).

Let us analyse the following example, which will subsequently be expanded and modified. Suppose that the risk-free rate is 8% and consider a 90-day call option with strike price $X = 60$ dollars written on a stock with current price $S = 60$ dollars. Assume that the stock volatility is $\sigma = 30\%$. The Black–Scholes formula gives the option price $C^{\mathrm{E}} = 4.14452$ dollars, the delta of the option being equal to 0.581957.

Suppose that we write and sell 1,000 call options, cashing a premium of \$4,144.52. To construct the hedge we buy 581.96 shares for \$34,917.39, borrowing \$30,772.88. Our portfolio will be $(x, y, z)$ with $x = 581.96$, $y = -30,772.88$, $z = -1,000$ and with total value zero. (While it might be more natural mathematically to consider a single option with $z = -1$, in practice options are traded in batches.)

We shall analyse the value of the portfolio after one day by considering some possible scenarios. The time to expiry will then be 89 days. Suppose that the stock volatility and the risk-free rate do not vary, and consider the following three scenarios of stock price movements:

1. The stock price remains unaltered, $S(\frac{1}{365}) = 60$ dollars. A single option is now worth \$4.11833, so our liability due to the short position in options is reduced. Our debt on the money market is increased by the interest due. The position in stock is worth the same as initially. The balance on day one is

| | |
|---|---:|
| stock | 34,917.39 |
| money | −30,779.62 |
| options | −4,118.33 |
| TOTAL | **19.45** |

   Without hedging ($x = 0$, $y = 4,118.33$, $z = -1,000$) our wealth would have been \$27.10, that is, we would have benefited from the reduced value of the option and the interest due on the premium invested without risk.

2. The stock price goes up to $S(\frac{1}{365}) = 61$ dollars. A single option is now worth \$4.72150, which is more than initially. The unhedged (naked) position would have suffered a loss of \$576.07. On the other hand, for a holder of a delta neutral portfolio the loss on the options is almost completely balanced out by the increase in the stock value:

| | |
|---|---:|
| stock | 35,499.35 |
| money | −30,779.62 |
| options | −4,721.50 |
| TOTAL | **−1.77** |

3. The stock price goes down to $S(\frac{1}{365}) = 59$ dollars. The value of the written options decreases, a single option now being worth \$3.55908. The value of the stock held decreases too. The portfolio brings a small loss:

| | |
|---|---|
| stock | 34, 335.44 |
| money | −30, 779.62 |
| options | −3, 559.08 |
| TOTAL | **−3.26** |

   In this scenario it would have been much better not to have hedged at all, since then we would have gained \$586.35.

It may come as a surprise that the hedging portfolio brings a profit when the stock price remains unchanged. As we shall see later in Exercise 9.5, a general rule is at work here.

### *Exercise 9.2*

Find the stock price on day one for which the hedging portfolio attains its maximum value.

### *Exercise 9.3*

Suppose that 50,000 puts with exercise date in 90 days and strike price $X = 1.80$ dollars are written on a stock with current price $S(0) = 1.82$ dollars and volatility $\sigma = 14\%$. The risk-free rate is $r = 5\%$. Construct a delta neutral portfolio and compute its value after one day if the stock price drops to $S(\frac{1}{365}) = 1.81$ dollars.

Going back to our example, let us collect the values $V$ of the delta neutral portfolio for various stock prices after one day as compared to the values $U$ of the unhedged position:

| $S$ | $V$ | $U$ |
|---|---|---|
| 58.00 | −71.35 | 1, 100.22 |
| 58.50 | −31.56 | 849.03 |
| 59.00 | −3.26 | 586.35 |
| 59.50 | 13.69 | 312.32 |
| 60.00 | 19.45 | 27.10 |
| 60.50 | 14.22 | −269.11 |
| 61.00 | −1.77 | −576.07 |
| 61.50 | −28.24 | −893.53 |
| 62.00 | −64.93 | −1, 221.19 |

Now, let us see what happens if the stock price changes are considerable:

| $S$ | $V$ | $U$ |
|---|---|---|
| 50 | $-2,233.19$ | $3,594.03$ |
| 55 | $-554.65$ | $2,362.79$ |
| 60 | $19.45$ | $27.10$ |
| 65 | $-481.60$ | $-3,383.73$ |
| 70 | $-1,765.15$ | $-7,577.06$ |

If we fear that such large changes might happen, the above hedge is not a satisfactory solution. If we do not hedge, at least we have a gamble with a positive outcome whenever the stock price goes down. Meanwhile, no matter whether the stock price goes up or down, the delta neutral portfolio may bring losses, though considerably smaller than the naked position.

Let us see what can happen if some other variables, in addition to the stock price, change after one day:

1. Suppose that the interest rate increases to 9% with volatility as before. Some loss will result from an increase in the option value. The interest on the cash loan due on day one is not affected because the new rate will only have an effect on the interest payable on the second day or later. The values of the hedging portfolio are given in the second column in the table below.
2. Now suppose that $\sigma$ grows to 32%, with the interest rate staying at the original level of 8%. The option price will increase considerably, which is not compensated by the stock position even if the stock price goes up. The results are given in the third column in the following table:

| $S$ | $V$ | |
|---|---|---|
| | $r = 9\%, \sigma = 30\%$ | $r = 8\%, \sigma = 32\%$ |
| 58.00 | $-133.72$ | $-299.83$ |
| 58.50 | $-97.22$ | $-261.87$ |
| 59.00 | $-72.19$ | $-234.69$ |
| 59.50 | $-58.50$ | $-218.14$ |
| 60.00 | $-55.96$ | $-212.08$ |
| 60.50 | $-64.38$ | $-216.33$ |
| 61.00 | $-83.51$ | $-230.68$ |
| 61.50 | $-113.07$ | $-254.90$ |
| 62.00 | $-152.78$ | $-288.74$ |

As we can see, in some circumstances delta hedging may be far from satisfactory. We need to improve the stability of hedging when the underlying asset price changes considerably and/or some other variables change simultaneously. In what follows, after introducing some theoretical tools we shall return again to the current example.

### *Exercise 9.4*

Find the value of the delta neutral portfolio in Exercise 9.3 if the risk-free rate of interest decreases to 3% on day one.

## 9.1.2 Greek Parameters

We shall define so-called *Greek parameters* describing the sensitivity of a portfolio with respect to the various variables determining the option price. The strike price $X$ and expiry date $T$ are fixed once the option is written, so we have to analyse the four remaining variables $S$, $t$, $r$, $\sigma$.

Let us write the value of a general portfolio containing stock and some contingent claims based on this stock as a function $V(S,t,\sigma,r)$ of these variables and denote

$$\begin{aligned}\mathrm{delta}_V &= \frac{\partial V}{\partial S},\\ \mathrm{gamma}_V &= \frac{\partial^2 V}{\partial S^2},\\ \mathrm{theta}_V &= \frac{\partial V}{\partial t},\\ \mathrm{vega}_V &= \frac{\partial V}{\partial \sigma},\\ \mathrm{rho}_V &= \frac{\partial V}{\partial r}.\end{aligned}$$

For small changes $\Delta S$, $\Delta t$, $\Delta\sigma$, $\Delta r$ of the variables we have the following approximate equality (by the Taylor formula):

$$\begin{aligned}\Delta V \cong\ & \mathrm{delta}_V \times \Delta S + \mathrm{theta}_V \times \Delta t + \mathrm{vega}_V \times \Delta\sigma + \mathrm{rho}_V \times \Delta r\\ &+ \frac{1}{2}\mathrm{gamma}_V \times (\Delta S)^2.\end{aligned}$$

Hence, a way to immunise a portfolio against small changes of a particular variable is to ensure that the corresponding Greek parameter is equal to zero. For instance, to hedge against volatility movements we should construct a *vega neutral* portfolio, with vega equal to zero. To retain the benefits of delta hedging, we should design a portfolio with both delta and vega equal to zero (*delta-vega neutral*). A *delta-gamma neutral* portfolio will be immune against larger changes of the stock price. Examples of such hedging portfolios will be examined below.

The Black–Scholes formula allows us to compute the derivatives explicitly for a single option. For a European call we have

$$\begin{aligned}
\text{delta}_{C^{\text{E}}} &= N(d_1), \\
\text{gamma}_{C^{\text{E}}} &= \frac{1}{S\sigma\sqrt{2\pi T}}\mathrm{e}^{-\frac{d_1^2}{2}}, \\
\text{theta}_{C^{\text{E}}} &= -\frac{S\sigma}{2\sqrt{2\pi T}}\mathrm{e}^{-\frac{d_1^2}{2}} - rX\mathrm{e}^{-rT}N(d_2), \\
\text{vega}_{C^{\text{E}}} &= \frac{S\sqrt{T}}{\sqrt{2\pi}}e^{-\frac{d_1^2}{2}}, \\
\text{rho}_{C^{\text{E}}} &= TX\mathrm{e}^{-rT}N(d_2).
\end{aligned}$$

(The Greek parameters are computed at time $t = 0$.)

## Remark 9.1

It is easy to see from the above that

$$\text{theta}_{C^{\text{E}}} + rS\,\text{delta}_{C^{\text{E}}} + \frac{1}{2}\sigma^2 S^2 \text{gamma}_{C^{\text{E}}} = rC^{\text{E}}.$$

In general, the price $D$ of any European derivative security can be shown to satisfy the *Black–Scholes equation*

$$\frac{\partial D}{\partial t} + rS\frac{\partial D}{\partial S} + \frac{1}{2}\sigma^2 S^2 \frac{\partial^2 D}{\partial S^2} = rD.$$

### *Exercise 9.5*

Show that a delta neutral portfolio with initial value zero hedging a single call option will gain in value with time if the stock price, volatility and risk-free rate remain unchanged.

### *Exercise 9.6*

Derive formulae for the Greek parameters of a put option.

### 9.1.3 Applications

To show some possibilities offered by Greek parameters we consider hedging the position of a writer of European call options.

**Delta-Gamma Hedging.** The construction is based on making both delta and gamma zero. A portfolio of the form $(x, y, z)$ is insufficient for this. Given the position in options, say $z = -1,000$, there remains only one parameter that can be adjusted, namely the position $x$ in the underlying. This allows us to make the delta of the portfolio zero. To make the gamma also equal to zero an additional degree of freedom is needed. To this end we consider another option on the same underlying stock, for example, a call expiring after 60 days, $\widehat{T} = 60/365$, with strike price $\widehat{X} = 65$, and construct a portfolio $(x, y, z, \widehat{z})$, where $\widehat{z}$ is a position in the additional option. The other variables are as in the previous examples: $r = 8\%$, $\sigma = 30\%$, $S(0) = 60$.

Let us sum up all the information about the prices and selected Greek parameters (we also include vega, which will be used later):

| option | time to expiry | strike price | option price | delta | gamma | vega |
|---|---|---|---|---|---|---|
| original | 90/365 | 60 | 4.14452 | 0.581957 | 0.043688 | 11.634305 |
| additional | 60/365 | 65 | 1.37826 | 0.312373 | 0.048502 | 8.610681 |

We choose $x$ and $\widehat{z}$ so that the delta and gamma of the portfolio are zero,

$$\begin{aligned} \text{delta}_V &= x - 1,000\,\text{delta}_{C^{\text{E}}} + \widehat{z}\,\text{delta}_{\widehat{C}^{\text{E}}} = 0, \\ \text{gamma}_V &= -1,000\,\text{gamma}_{C^{\text{E}}} + \widehat{z}\,\text{gamma}_{\widehat{C}^{\text{E}}} = 0, \end{aligned}$$

and the money position $y$ so that the value of the portfolio is zero,

$$V(S) = xS + y - 1,000C^{\text{E}}(S) + \widehat{z}\widehat{C}^{\text{E}}(S) = 0.$$

This gives the following system of equations:

$$\begin{aligned} x - 581.957 + 0.312373\,\widehat{z} &= 0, \\ -43.688 + 0.048502\,\widehat{z} &= 0, \end{aligned}$$

with solution $x \cong 300.58$, $\widehat{z} \cong 900.76$. It follows that $y \cong -15,131.77$. That is, we take long positions in stock and the additional option, and a short cash position. (We already have a short position $z = -1,000$ in the original option.)

After one day, if stock goes up, the original option will become more expensive, increasing our liability, which will be set off by increases in the value of stock and the additional options held. The reverse happens if the stock price declines. Our money debt increases in either case by the interest due after one day. The values of the portfolio are given below (for comparison we also recall the values of the delta neutral portfolio):

| $S(\frac{1}{365})$ | delta-gamma | delta |
|---|---|---|
| 58.00 | −2.04 | −71.35 |
| 58.50 | 0.30 | −31.56 |
| 59.00 | 1.07 | −3.26 |
| 59.50 | 0.81 | 13.69 |
| 60.00 | 0.02 | 19.45 |
| 60.50 | −0.79 | 14.22 |
| 61.00 | −1.11 | −1.77 |
| 61.50 | −0.49 | −28.24 |
| 62.00 | 1.52 | −64.93 |

We can see that we are practically safe within the given range of stock prices. For larger changes we are also in a better position as compared with delta hedging:

| $S(\frac{1}{365})$ | delta-gamma | delta |
|---|---|---|
| 50 | −614.08 | −2, 233.19 |
| 55 | −78.22 | −554.65 |
| 60 | 0.02 | 19.45 |
| 65 | 63, 13 | −481.60 |
| 70 | 440.81 | −1, 765.15 |

As predicted, a delta-gamma neutral portfolio offers better protection against stock price changes than a delta neutral one.

**Delta-Vega Hedging.** Next we shall hedge against an increase in volatility, while retaining cover against small changes in the stock price. This will be achieved by constructing a delta-vega neutral portfolio containing, as before, an additional option. The conditions imposed are

$$\begin{aligned} \text{delta}_V &= x - 1,000\,\text{delta}_{C^{\text{E}}} + \widehat{z}\,\text{delta}_{\widehat{C}^{\text{E}}} = 0, \\ \text{vega}_V &= -1,000\,\text{vega}_{C^{\text{E}}} + \widehat{z}\,\text{vega}_{\widehat{C}^{\text{E}}} = 0. \end{aligned}$$

They lead to the system of equations

$$\begin{aligned} x - 581.957 + 0.312373\,\widehat{z} &= 0, \\ -1,1634.305 + 8.610681\,\widehat{z} &= 0, \end{aligned}$$

with an approximate solution $x \cong 159.89$, $\widehat{z} \cong 1,351.15$. The corresponding money position is $y \cong -7,311.12$.

Suppose that the volatility increases to $\sigma = 32\%$ on day one. Let us compare the results for delta-vega and delta hedging:

| $S(1/365)$ | delta-vega | delta |
|---|---|---|
| 58.00 | −5.90 | −299.83 |
| 58.50 | −12.81 | −261.87 |
| 59.00 | −16.05 | −234.69 |
| 59.50 | −14.99 | −218.14 |
| 60.00 | −9.06 | −212.08 |
| 60.50 | 2.27 | −216.33 |
| 61.00 | 19.52 | −230.68 |
| 61.50 | 43.17 | −254.90 |
| 62.00 | 73.62 | −288.74 |

*Exercise 9.7*

Using the data in our ongoing example (stock price \$60, volatility 30%, interest rate 8%), construct a delta-rho neutral portfolio to hedge a short position of 1,000 call options expiring after 90 days with strike price \$60, taking as an additional component a call option expiring after 120 days with strike price \$65. Analyse the sensitivity of the portfolio value to stock price variations if the interest rate goes up to 9% after one day, comparing with the previous results. What will happen if the interest rate jumps to 15%?

The examples above illustrate the variety of possible hedging strategies. The choice between them depends on individual aims and preferences. We have not touched upon questions related to transaction costs or long term hedging. Nor have we discussed the optimality of the choice of an additional derivative instrument. Portfolios based on three Greek parameters would require yet another derivative security as a component. They could provide comprehensive cover, though their performance might deteriorate if the variables remain unchanged. In addition, they might prove expensive if transaction costs were included.

## 9.2 Hedging Business Risk

We begin by introducing an alternative measure of risk, related to an intuitive understanding of risk as the size and likelihood of a possible loss.

### 9.2.1 Value at Risk

Let us present the basic idea using a simple example. We buy a share of stock for $S(0) = 100$ dollars to sell it after one year. The selling price $S(1)$ is random. We shall suffer a loss if $S(1) < 100\mathrm{e}^r$, where $r$ is the risk-free rate under continuous compounding. (The purchase can either be financed by a loan, or, if the initial sum is already at our disposal, we take into account the foregone opportunity of a risk-free investment.) What is the probability of a loss being less than a given amount, for example,

$$P(100\mathrm{e}^r - S(1) < 20) = ?$$

Let us reverse the question and fix the probability, 95% say. Now we seek an amount such that the probability of a loss not exceeding this amount is 95%. This is referred to as *Value at Risk* at 95% confidence level and denoted by VaR. (Other confidence levels can also be used.) So, VaR is an amount such that

$$P(100\mathrm{e}^r - S(1) < \mathrm{VaR}) = 95\%.$$

It should be noted that the majority of textbooks neglect the time value of money in this context, stating the definition of VaR only for $r = 0$.

#### Example 9.1

Suppose that the distribution of the stock price is log normal, the logarithmic return $k = \ln(S(1)/S(0))$ having normal distribution with mean $m = 12\%$ and standard deviation $\sigma = 30\%$. With probability 95% the return will satisfy $k > m + x\sigma \cong -37.50\%$, where $N(x) \cong 5\%$, so $x \cong -1.645$. (Here $N(x)$ is the normal distribution function (8.10) with mean 0 and variance 1.) Hence with probability 95% the future price $S(1)$ will satisfy

$$S(1) > S(0)\mathrm{e}^{m+x\sigma} \cong 68.83 \text{ dollars},$$

and so, given that $r = 8\%$,

$$\mathrm{VaR} = S(0)\mathrm{e}^r - S(0)\mathrm{e}^{m+x\sigma} \cong 39.50 \text{ dollars}.$$

#### *Exercise 9.8*

Evaluate VaR at 95% confidence level for a one-year investment of \$1,000 into euros if the interest rate for risk-free investments in euros is $r_{\mathrm{EUR}} = 4\%$ and the exchange rate from euros into US dollars follows the log normal distribution with $m = 1\%$ and $\sigma = 15\%$. Take into account the foregone opportunity of investing dollars without risk, given that the risk-free interest rate for dollars is $r_{\mathrm{USD}} = 5\%$.

### *Exercise 9.9*

Suppose that $\$1,000$ is invested in European call options on a stock with current price $S(0) = 60$ dollars. The options expire after 6 months with strike price $X = 40$ dollars. Assume that $\sigma = 30\%$, $r = 8\%$, and the expected logarithmic return on stock is 12%. Compute VaR after 6 months at 95% confidence level. Find the final wealth if the stock price grows at the expected rate. Find the stock price level that will be exceeded with 5% probability and compute the corresponding final payoff.

## 9.2.2 Case Study

We shall discuss a number of ways in which VaR can be managed with the aid of derivative securities. The methods will be illustrated by a simple example of business activity.

### Case 9.1

A company manufactures goods in the UK for sale in the USA. The investment to start production is 5 million pounds. Additional funds can be raised by borrowing British pounds at 16% to finance a hedging strategy. The rate of return demanded by investors, bearing in mind the risk involved, is 25%. The sales are predicted to generate 8 million dollars at the end of the year. The costs are 3 million pounds per year. The interest rates are 8% for dollars and 11% for pounds (here we assume continuous compounding). The current rate of exchange is 1.6 dollars to a pound. The volatility of the logarithmic return on the rate of exchange is estimated at $\sigma = 15\%$. The company pays 20% tax on earnings.

First note that to satisfy the expectations of investors the company should be able to achieve a profit of 1.25 million pounds a year to pay the dividend. A lower profit would mean a dividend lower than required, with the shortfall regarded as a loss from the point of view of the investors. The profit depends on the rate of exchange $d$ at the end of the year, hence some risk emerges. (We assume that the other values will be as predicted.)

To begin with, suppose that no action is taken to manage the risk.

1. **Unhedged Position.** If the exchange rate $d$ turns out to be 1.6 dollars to a pound at the end of the year, then the net earnings will be 1.6 million

pounds, as shown in the following statement (all amounts in pounds):

| | |
|---|---:|
| sales | 5,000,000 |
| costs | −3,000,000 |
| earnings before tax | 2,000,000 |
| tax | −400,000 |
| earnings after tax | 1,600,000 |
| dividend | −1,250,000 |
| result | 350,000 |

The surplus income will be 0.35 million pounds.

However, if the exchange rate $d$ becomes 2 dollars to a pound, the dividend will in fact have to be reduced and the investors will end up with a loss of 0.45 million pounds (taking the full dividend as a hypothetical cost):

| | |
|---|---:|
| sales | 4,000,000 |
| costs | −3,000,000 |
| earnings before tax | 1,000,000 |
| tax | −200,000 |
| earnings after tax | 800,000 |
| dividend | −1,250,000 |
| result | −450,000 |

Let us compute VaR. We assume that the rate of exchange has log normal distribution of the following form

$$d(t) = d(0) \exp\left( (r_{USD} - r_{GBP} - \frac{1}{2}\sigma^2)t + \sigma\sqrt{t}N \right)$$

where $N$ has the standard normal distribution.[1] With probability 95%, $N$ will not exceed 1.6449, which corresponds to an exchange rate $d = d(1) \cong 1.9650$ dollars to a pound. The statement for this borderline rate of exchange will be as follows (all amounts rounded to the nearest pound):

| | |
|---|---:|
| sales | 4,071,290 |
| costs | −3,000,000 |
| earnings before tax | 1,071,290 |
| tax | −214,258 |
| earnings after tax | 857,032 |
| dividend | −1,250,000 |
| result | −392,968 |

[1] See Etheridge (2002), Sect. 5.3.

As a result, VaR $\cong$ 392,968 dollars. The final result as a function of the exchange rate $d$ is

$$\begin{aligned} b(d) &= 80\% \times \left(\frac{8,000,000}{d} - 3,000,000\right) - 1,250,000 \\ &= \frac{6,400,000}{d} - 3,650,000. \end{aligned}$$

The break even exchange rate, which solves $b(d) = 0$, is approximately equal to 1.7534 dollars to a pound. In an optimistic scenario in which the pound weakens, for example, down to 1.5 dollars, the final balance will be about £616,667.

The question is how to manage this risk exposure.

2. **Forward Contract.** The easiest solution would be to fix the exchange rate in advance by entering into a long forward contract. The forward rate is $d(0)e^{r_{USD}-r_{GBP}} = 1.6 \times e^{-3\%} \cong 1.5527$ dollars to a pound. As a result, the company can obtain the following statement with guaranteed surplus, but no possibility of further gains should the exchange rate become more favourable:

| | |
|---|---:|
| sales | 5,152,273 |
| costs | −3,000,000 |
| earnings before tax | 2,152,273 |
| tax | −430,455 |
| net income | 1,721,818 |
| dividend | −1,250,000 |
| result | 471,818 |

3. **Full Hedge with Options.** Options can be used to ensure that the rate of exchange is capped at a certain level, whilst the benefits associated with favourable exchange rate movements are retained. However, this may be costly because of the premium paid for options.

   The company can buy call options on the pound. A European call to buy one pound with strike price 1.6 dollars to a pound will cost \$0.0669.[2] Suppose that the company buys 5 million of such options, paying £209,069, an amount they have to borrow at 16%. The interest is tax deductible,

[2] For options on currencies the Black–Scholes formula of Section 8.3 applies with $S(0) = d(0)\exp(-r_{GBP})$, $r = r_{USD}$, $t = 1$.

making the loan less costly. Nevertheless, the final result is disappointing:

| | |
|---|---:|
| sales | 5,000,000 |
| costs | −3,000,000 |
| earnings before interest and tax | 2,000,000 |
| interest | −33,451 |
| earnings before tax | 1,966,549 |
| tax | −393,310 |
| net income | 1,573,239 |
| loan repaid | −209,069 |
| dividend | −1,250,000 |
| result | 114,170 |

If the exchange rate drops to 1.5 dollars to a pound, the options will not be exercised and the sum obtained from sales will reach £5,333,333, with a positive final result of £380,837. This strategy leads to a better result than the hedge involving a forward contract only if the rate of exchange drops below 1.4687 dollars to a pound.

4. **Partial Hedge with Options.** To reduce the cost of options the company can hedge partially by buying call options to cover only a fraction of the dollar amount from sales. Suppose that the company buys 2,500,000 units of the same call option as above, paying a half of the previous premium. A half of the revenue is then exposed to risk. To find VaR at 95% confidence level we assume that this sum is exchanged at 1.9650 dollars to a pound, as in the case of an unhedged position, the other half being exchanged at the exercise price:

| | |
|---|---:|
| sales | 4,535,645 |
| costs | −3,000,000 |
| earnings before interest and tax | 1,535,645 |
| interest | −16,726 |
| earnings before tax | 1,518,919 |
| tax | −303,784 |
| net income | 1,215,136 |
| loan repaid | −104,534 |
| dividend | −1,250,000 |
| result | −139,399 |

If the exchange rate drops to 1.5 dollars to a pound, the investors will have a surplus of £498,752.

5. **Combination of Options and Forward Contracts.** Finally, let us investigate what happens if the company hedges with both kinds of derivatives. Half of their position will be hedged with options. In the worst case scenario they will buy pounds for half of their dollar revenue at the rate of 1.6 dollars to a pound, the remaining half being exchanged at the forward rate of 1.5527 dollars to a pound. The outcome is shown below, where we summarise the resulting VaR for all strategies considered (the result below is equal to minus VaR):

| strategy | 1 | 2 | 3 | 4 | 5 |
|---|---|---|---|---|---|
| result | $-392,968$ | $471,818$ | $114,170$ | $-139,399$ | $292,994$ |

These values are computed at 95% confidence level, corresponding to the exchange rate of 1.9887 dollars to a pound.

Clearly, VaR provides only partial information about possible outcomes of various strategies. Figure 9.1 shows the graphs of the final result as a function of the exchange rate $d$ for each of the above strategies. The graphs are labelled by the strategy number as above. The strategy using a forward contract (strat-

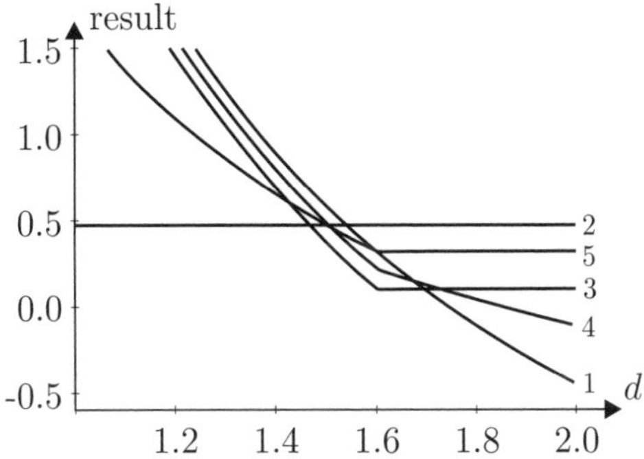


**Figure 9.1** Comparison of various strategies

egy 2) appears to be the safest one. An adventurous investor who strongly believes that the pound will weaken considerably may prefer to remain uncovered (strategy 1). A variety of middle-of-the-road strategies are also available. The probability distribution of the exchange rate $d$ should also be taken into account when examining the graphs.

# 9.3 Speculating with Derivatives

## 9.3.1 Tools

Options can be used as building blocks to design sophisticated investment instruments. We shall consider an investor with specific views on the future behaviour of stock prices and willing to take risks. Our task will be to design a portfolio of securities with a prescribed payoff profile that would satisfy this kind of investor.

Suppose that the investor expects the stock price to rise and wants to gamble on that. One simple way is to buy a call option. An option with strike price $X'$ close to the current stock price is considerably cheaper than the stock itself, creating a risky leverage position, as will be seen in the case study to follow. The premium may be reduced by selling a call option with strike price $X'' > X'$. In this way we can build a so-called *bull spread* with payoff shown in Figure 9.2. This strategy will bring a good return if stock price increases are moderate.

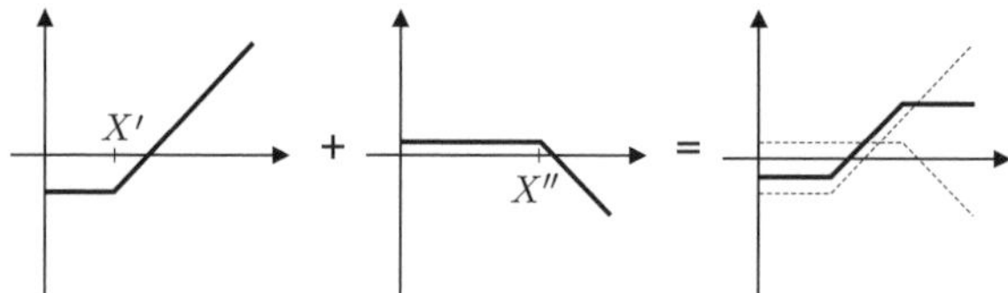


**Figure 9.2** Bull spread

Using put options with strike prices $X' < X''$, selling the former and purchasing the latter, we can construct a *bear spread* with positive payoff for low future stock prices, see Figure 9.3. This may be employed by an investor who expects a moderate decline in the stock price.

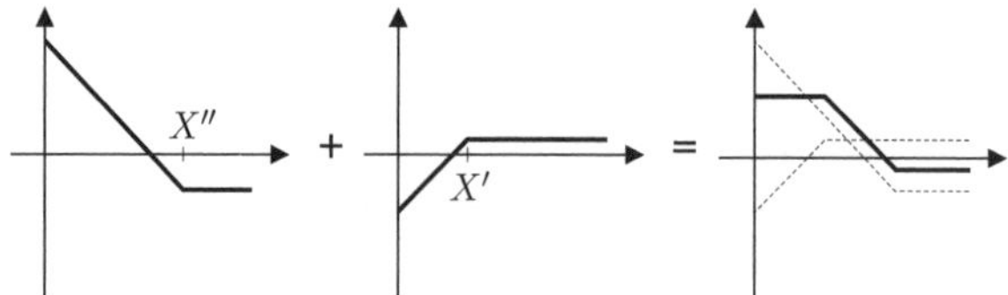


**Figure 9.3** Bear spread

An investor who believes that the stock price will stay unaltered or change insignificantly may choose a *butterfly*. It is constructed from three call options with strike prices $X' < X'' < X'''$. Two calls are bought, one with strike $X'$ and one with strike $X'''$, and two calls with strike price $X''$ are sold. Figure 9.4

shows the case when $X''$ is the average of the other two strike prices. *Reversed butterfly* is the opposite strategy, bringing profits when the stock price changes. (We have already come across the butterfly in the proof of Proposition 7.8.)

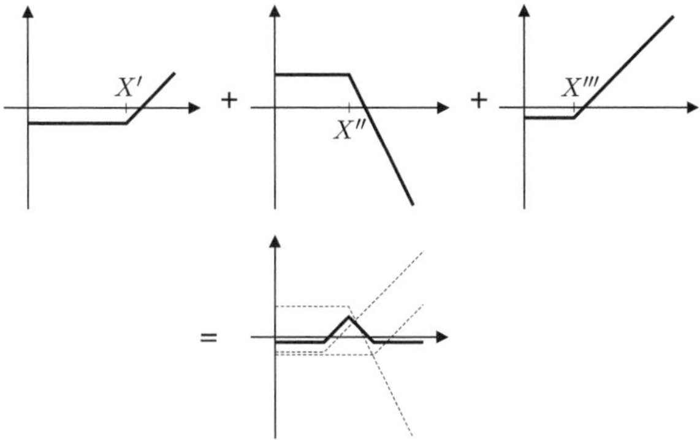


**Figure 9.4** Butterfly

Finally, we observe that any continuous payoff function consisting of straight line segments can be manufactured from put and call options. Figure 9.5 outlines the step-by-step decomposition of a target profile into a portfolio of options with various strike price values. The number of options for each strike price is chosen to match the slopes of the target profile. Such a construction is sufficient for practical purposes because any continuous payoff function can be approximated by straight line segments.

### 9.3.2 Case Study

We shall combine the portfolio theory techniques with the tools described above. We have in mind an investor with specific views on the future prices of assets, who is prepared to accept some risk in order to increase expected return.

#### Case 9.2

An investor with $\$15,000$ believes that a certain stock price should rise during the next month, with expected annualised return $\mu_S = 31\%$. The current stock price is $S(0) = 60$ dollars. Call options expiring in 20 days with strike price \$60 are available at \$2.112. The effective risk-free rate is 12%.

To analyse this case we shall use the binomial model, assuming that trading takes place once a day and that the market probabilities are the same for up

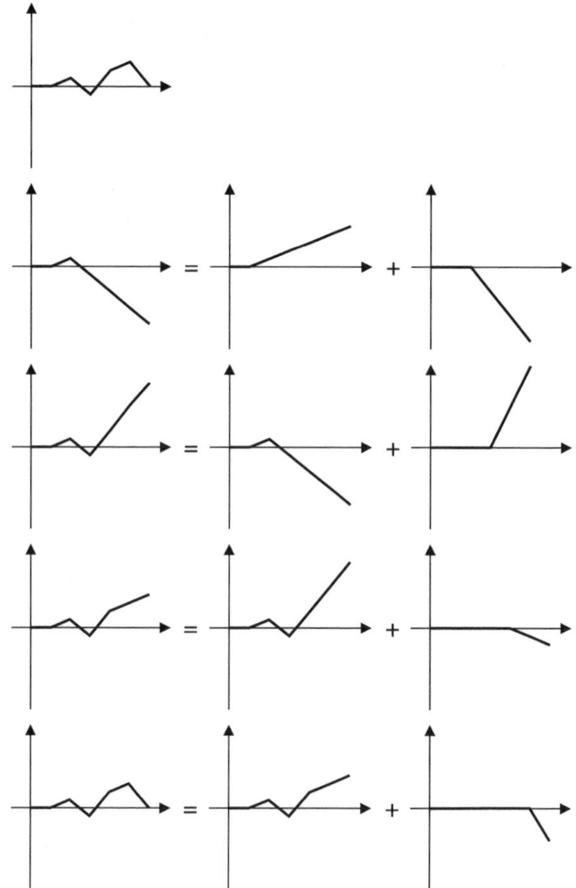


**Figure 9.5** Decomposition of a target payoff into options

and down price jumps. We also assume for simplicity that there are 360 days in a year. The risk-free return over 20 days is $r_F \cong 0.6316\%$. (Implied by the effective rate of 12%.) The \$15,000 invested without risk would become \$15,094.74 at the end of the 20-day period. Consider the following risky investments:

1. **Stock.** An investment in stock should bring an expected return of $\mu_S \cong 1.5115\%$. (Equivalent to 31% annually.) Buying 250 shares, the investor would expect to end up with \$15,226.72 after 20 days. The risk can be estimated from the option price, see below.

2. **Call Options.** A more risky alternative is to buy call options. The return

is random and depends on the stock price after 20 days,

$$K_C = \frac{(S(20/365) - 60)^+ - C}{C}.$$

To compute the expected return on an option we can find the parameters of the binomial model consistent with the option price and the expected return on stock, assuming that the market probability of up and down price movements is 1/2. First we find the risk-free return over a single day,

$$r = (1 + 12\%)^{\frac{1}{360}} - 1 \cong 0.0315\%.$$

Then we write down a condition on the up and down daily stock returns such that the expected annual return is 31%,

$$\frac{u + d}{2} = (1 + 31\%)^{\frac{1}{360}} - 1 \cong 0.075\%.$$

The call price gives another condition for $u$ and $d$, and we finally arrive at the following values:[3]

$$u \cong 1.8571\%, \quad d \cong -1.7070\%.$$

Now we can compute the standard deviation for the period in question (using the actual market probabilities $p_k = \binom{20}{k}0.5^{20}$, $k = 0, 1, \ldots, 20$),

$$\sigma_S \cong 8.0962\%.$$

Finally, we compute the expected return and risk of the investment in options,

$$\mu_C \cong 14.8453\%, \quad \sigma_C \cong 153.9693\%.$$

The return is impressive, but so is the risk. Observe that with probability 0.4119 the investor can lose all his or her money.

3. **Forward Contracts.** The forward price is approximately \$60.38. Suppose that entering into a forward contract requires a 20% deposit of the initial stock price, that is, \$12 per share. The investor can afford to enter into 1,250 forward contracts. The expected return and risk in the binomial model are

$$\mu_F \cong 4.3993\%, \quad \sigma_F \cong 40.4811\%.$$

Note that if the stock price falls below \$48.38, the investor will lose the deposit and suffer an additional loss, resulting in a return below $-100\%$.

[3] Take any value of $u$, compute the corresponding 21 stock price values after 20 days, the option payoffs, risk-neutral probability, and finally the option price. Using the Goal Seek facility in a spreadsheet application (or trial and error), find the value of $u$ such that the option price is as given.

4. **Options Combined with Risk-Free Investment.** The risk can be adjusted to an arbitrary level if options are combined with a risk-free asset. Suppose that the investor is willing to accept similar risk to the stock investment. Investing 94.7417% of the capital without risk and the remainder in options, the investor can construct a portfolio with the same standard deviation as that for the stock. The expected return on the portfolio is slightly lower than that on stock,

$$\mu_P \cong 1.3790\%, \quad \sigma_P \cong 8.0962\%.$$

## Remark 9.2

The slope of the line connecting the risk-free asset $F$ with any other portfolio $A$ on the $(\sigma, \mu)$ plane is given by $\frac{\mu_A - r_F}{\sigma_A}$, called the *market price of risk*. It can be used to compare different portfolios: Those with steep slope are preferable. We can see that the above risky investments have similar values of the market price of risk, about 0.1 in each case. (These values would in fact be identical if the Black–Scholes model were used for stock prices.)

The advantage of the investment in a portfolio of options and risk-free assets can be seen if we consider VaR, given in the table below for two different confidence levels (chosen to be compatible with the probabilities in the binomial model). On the other hand, VaR would be disastrously high if the whole amount were invested only in options: The investor could lose everything at the given confidence levels.

| Investment | Stock | Call options | Forwards | Calls with risk-free asset |
|---|---|---|---|---|
| Market price of risk | 0.1087 | 0.0923 | 0.0931 | 0.0923 |
| VaR at 94.23% | \$1,931.78 | \$15,000.00 | \$9,753.85 | \$788.75 |
| VaR at 99.41% | \$2,836.84 | \$15,000.00 | \$14,279.27 | \$788.75 |

## Case 9.3

An analyst researching the company has come to the conclusion that the stock price after 20 days will not fall below \$58 or raise above \$66. All market parameters remain as in Case 9.2. From the point of view of the analyst, compare the expected return and risk for stock, options and a bull spread with strike prices \$58 and \$60.

We shall build a simple model reflecting the analysts's point of view. Additional information obtained by the analyst will result in modified probabilities as compared to the market probability $P$. (We assume, as before, that the market probability of up and down movements is 1/2 in each step.) Namely, the probability $Q$ assigned by the analyst will be the market probability $P$ conditioned by the event $58 \leq S(20) \leq 66$. In particular,

$$\begin{aligned} Q(S(20) = x) &= P(S(20) = x | 58 \leq S(20) \leq 66) \\ &= \begin{cases} \frac{P(S(20)=x)}{P(58 \leq S(20) \leq 66)} & \text{if } 58 \leq x \leq 66, \\ 0 & \text{if } x < 50 \text{ or } x > 66. \end{cases} \end{aligned}$$

As a result, the analyst will arrive at the following values:

1. **Stock.** Under the modified probability $Q$

$$\mu_S \cong 2.6788\%, \quad \sigma_S \cong 3.9257\%.$$

2. **Call Options.** Take a call with strike price $X = 58$ dollars. Hence $C^{\mathrm{E}} \cong 3.2923$ dollars (this price is found in the binomial model without any restriction on the range of stock prices after 20 days). For an investment in options we find that

$$\mu_C \cong 9.5693\%, \quad \sigma_C \cong 71.5441\%.$$

3. **Bull Spread.** Construct the spread by purchasing a call with strike \$58 and selling a call with strike \$60. The premium paid for the former is \$3.2923, hence a single spread costs \$1.1803. The expected return and risk are

$$\mu_{\text{bull}} \cong 38.4094\%, \quad \sigma_{\text{bull}} \cong 52.3997\%.$$

4. **Bull Spread Combined with Risk-Free Asset.** Investing 94.5809% of the capital in the risk-free asset and the remainder in a bull spread, we can construct a portfolio $P$ with the same expected return as stock, but lower risk,

$$\mu_P \cong 2.6788\%, \quad \sigma_P \cong 2.8396\%.$$

From the point of view of VaR, we consider the worst case scenario (among those admitted by the investor) when $S(20) \cong 58.59$ dollars, which may happen with conditional probability 0.2597. In this scenario each of the above investments will bring a loss, which can be regarded as VaR at 74.03% confidence level. The values of VaR and the market price of risk are collected below:

| Investment | Stock | Call options | Bull spread | Bull spread with risk-free asset |
|---|---|---|---|---|
| Market price of risk | 0.5 | 0.1 | 0.7 | 0.7 |
| VaR at 74.03% | \$447 | \$12,409 | \$7,602 | \$412 |

The bull spread combined with risk-free will clearly be preferable to the other investments as it has the highest market price of risk and lowest VaR.

### *Exercise 9.10*

Check the above computations and consider a modification such that the bull spread is constructed by buying a call with strike price \$60 and selling a call with strike price \$62. Compute the expected return, risk and VaR.

### *Exercise 9.11*

Within the framework of the binomial model used above consider an analyst who has reasons to believe that the stock price will fall, but no more than 20% after 20 days. For a bear spread with strikes \$56 and \$58 constructed from put options compute the expected return, risk, and VaR for the worst possible outcome.

# 10
# Variable Interest Rates

This chapter begins with a model in which the interest rates implied by bonds do not depend on maturity. If the rates are deterministic, then they must be constant and the model turns out to be too simple to describe any real-life situation. In an extension allowing random changes of interest rates the problem of risk management will be dealt with by introducing a mathematical tool called the *duration* of bond investments. Finally, we shall show that maturity-dependent rates cannot be deterministic either, preparing the motivation and notation for the next chapter, in which a model of stochastic rates will be explored.

As in Chapter 2, $B(t,T)$ will denote the price at time $t$ (the running time) of a zero-coupon unit bond maturing at time $T$ (the maturity time). The dependence on two time variables gives rise to some difficulties in mathematical models of bond prices. These prices are exactly what is needed to describe the time value of money. In Chapter 2 we saw how bond prices imply the interest rate, under the assumption that the rate is constant. Here, we want to relax this restriction, allowing variable interest rates.

In this chapter and the next one time will be discrete, though some parts of the theory can easily be extended to continuous time. We shall fix a time step $\tau$, writing $t = \tau n$ for the running time and $T = \tau N$ for the maturity time. In the majority of examples we shall take either $\tau = \frac{1}{12}$ or $\tau = 1$. The notation $B(n, N)$ will be employed instead of $B(t,T)$ for the price of a zero-coupon unit bond. We shall use continuous compounding, bearing in mind that it simplifies notation and makes it possible to handle time steps of any length consistently.

## 10.1 Maturity-Independent Yields

The present value of a zero-coupon unit bond determines an interest rate called the *yield* and denoted by $y(0)$ to emphasise the fact that it is computed at time 0:

$$B(0,N) = \mathrm{e}^{-N\tau y(0)}.$$

For a different running time instant $n$ such that $0 < n < N$ the implied yield may in general be different from $y(0)$. For each such $n$ we thus have a number $y(n)$ satisfying

$$B(n,N) = \mathrm{e}^{-(N-n)\tau y(n)}.$$

Generally (and in most real cases), a bond with different maturity $N$ will imply a different yield. Nevertheless, in this section we consider the simplified situation when $y(n)$ is independent of $N$, that is, bonds with different maturities generate the same yield. Independence of maturity will be relaxed later in Section 10.2.

### Proposition 10.1

If the yield $y(n)$ for some $n > 0$ were known at time 0, then $y(0) = y(n)$ or else an arbitrage strategy could be found.

### Proof

Suppose that $y(0) < y(n)$. (We need to know not only $y(0)$ but also $y(n)$ at time 0 to decide whether or not this inequality holds.)

- Borrow a dollar for the period between 0 and $n+1$ and deposit it for the period between 0 and $n$, both at the rate $y(0)$. (The yield can be regarded as the interest rate for deposits and loans.)
- At time $n$ withdraw the deposit with interest, $\mathrm{e}^{n\tau y(0)}$ in total, and invest this sum for a single time step at the rate $y(n)$. At time $n+1$ this brings $\mathrm{e}^{n\tau y(0)+\tau y(n)}$. The initial loan requires repayment of $\mathrm{e}^{(n+1)\tau y(0)}$, leaving a positive balance $\mathrm{e}^{n\tau y(0)}(\mathrm{e}^{\tau y(n)} - \mathrm{e}^{\tau y(0)})$, which is the arbitrage profit.

The reverse inequality $y(0) > y(n)$ can be dealt with in a similar manner. □

#### *Exercise 10.1*

Let $\tau = \frac{1}{12}$. Find arbitrage if the yields are independent of maturity, and unit bonds maturing at time 6 (half a year) are traded at $B(0,6) = 0.9320$ dollars and $B(3,6) = 0.9665$ dollars, both prices being known at time 0.

As a consequence of Proposition 10.1, if the yield is independent of maturity and deterministic (that is, $y(n)$ is known in advance for any $n \geq 0$), then it must be constant, $y(n) = y$ for all $n$. This is the situation in Chapter 2, where all the bond prices were determined by a single interest rate. The yield $y(n) = y$, independent of $n$, is then equal to the constant risk-free interest rate denoted previously by $r$.

Historical bond prices show a different picture: The yields implied by the bond prices recorded in the past clearly vary with time. In an arbitrage-free model, to admit yields varying with time but independent of maturity we should allow them to be random, so it is impossible to predict in advance whether $y(n)$ will be higher or lower than $y(0)$.

We assume, therefore, that at each time instant the yield $y(n)$ is a positive random number independent of the maturity of the underlying bond.

Our goal is to analyse the return on a bond investment and the imminent risk arising from random changes of interest rates. Suppose that we intend to invest a certain sum of money $P$ for a fixed period of $N$ time steps. If the yield $y$ remains constant, then, as observed in Chapter 2, our terminal wealth will be $Pe^{N\tau y}$. This will be our benchmark for designing strategies hedged against unpredictable interest rate movements.

### 10.1.1 Investment in Single Bonds

If we invest in zero-coupon bonds and keep them to maturity, the rate of return is guaranteed, since the final payment is fixed in advance and is not affected by any future changes of interest rates. However, if we choose to close out our investment prior to maturity by selling the bonds, we face the risk that the interest rates may change in the meantime with an adverse effect on the final value of the investment.

#### Example 10.1

Suppose we invest in bonds for a period of six months. Let $\tau = \frac{1}{12}$. We buy a number of unit bonds that will mature after one year, paying $B(0, 12) = 0.9300$ for each. This price implies a rate $y(0) \cong 7.26\%$. Since we are going to sell the bonds at time $n = 6$, we are concerned with the price $B(6, 12)$ or, equivalently, with the corresponding rate $y(6)$. Let us discuss some possible scenarios:

1. The rate is stable, $y(6) = 7.26\%$. The bond price is $B(6, 12) \cong 0.9644$ and the logarithmic return on the investment is 3.63%, a half of the interest rate, in line with the additivity of logarithmic returns.
2. The rate decreases to $y(6) = 6.26\%$, say. (The convention is that 0.01% is

one *basis point*, so here the rate drops by 100 basis points.) Then $B(6,12) \cong 0.9692$, which is more than in scenario 1. As a result, we are going to earn more, achieving a logarithmic return of 4.13%.

3. The rate increases to $y(6) = 8.26\%$. In this case the logarithmic return on our investment will be 3.13%, which is lower than in scenario 1, the bond price being $B(6,12) \cong 0.9596$.

We can see a pattern here: One is better off if the rate drops and worse off if the rate increases. A general formula for the return on this kind of investment is easy to find.

Suppose that the initial yield $y(0)$ changes randomly to become $y(n) \neq y(0)$ at time $n$. Hence

$$B(0,N) = \mathrm{e}^{-y(0)\tau N}, \quad B(n,N) = \mathrm{e}^{-y(n)\tau(N-n)},$$

and the return on an investment closed at time $n$ will be

$$k(0,n) = \ln \tfrac{B(n,N)}{B(0,N)} = \ln \mathrm{e}^{y(0)\tau N - y(n)\tau(N-n)} = y(0)\tau N - y(n)\tau(N-n).$$

We can see that the return decreases as the rate $y(n)$ increases. The impact of a rate change on the return depends on the timing. For example, if $\tau = \frac{1}{12}$, $N = 12$ and $n = 6$, then a rate increase of 120 basis points will reduce the return by 0.6% as compared to the case when the rate remains unchanged.

### Exercise 10.2

Let $\tau = \frac{1}{12}$. Invest \$100 in six-month zero-coupon bonds trading at $B(0,6) = 0.9400$ dollars. After six months reinvest the proceeds in bonds of the same kind, now trading at $B(6,12) = 0.9368$ dollars. Find the implied interest rates and compute the number of bonds held at each time. Compute the logarithmic return on the investment over one year.

### Exercise 10.3

Suppose that $B(0,12) = 0.8700$ dollars. What is the interest rate after 6 months if an investment for 6 months in zero-coupon bonds gives a logarithmic return of 14% ?

### Exercise 10.4

In this exercise we take a finer time scale with $\tau = \frac{1}{360}$. (A year is assumed to have 360 days here.) Suppose that $B(0,360) = 0.9200$ dollars, the rate remains unchanged for the first six months, goes up by 200 basis points on day 180, and remains at this level until the end of the year. If a bond is bought at the beginning of the year, on which day should it be sold to produce a logarithmic return of 4.88% or more?

An investment in coupon bonds is more complicated. Even if the bond is kept to maturity, the coupons are paid in the meantime and can be reinvested. The return on such an investment depends on the interest rates prevailing at the times when the coupons are due. First consider the relatively simple case of an investment terminated as soon as the first coupon is paid.

## Example 10.2

Let us invest the sum of \$1,000 in 4-year bonds with face value \$100 and \$10 annual coupons. A coupon bond of this kind can be regarded as a collection of four zero-coupon bonds maturing after 1, 2, 3 and 4 years with face value \$10, \$10, \$10 and \$110, respectively. Suppose that such coupon bonds trade at \$91.78, which can be expressed as the sum of the prices of the four zero-coupon bonds,

$$91.78 = 10\mathrm{e}^{-y(0)} + 10\mathrm{e}^{-2y(0)} + 10\mathrm{e}^{-3y(0)} + 110\mathrm{e}^{-4y(0)}.$$

(The length of a time step is $\tau = 1$.) This equation can be solved to find the yield, $y(0) \cong 12\%$. We can afford to buy 10.896 coupon bonds. After one year we cash the coupons, collecting \$108.96, and sell the bonds, which are now 3-year coupon bonds. Consider three scenarios:

1. After one year the interest rate remains unchanged, $y(1) = 12\%$, the coupon bonds being valued at

   $$10\mathrm{e}^{-0.12} + 10\mathrm{e}^{-2\times 0.12} + 110\mathrm{e}^{-3\times 0.12} \cong 93.48$$

   dollars, and we shall receive $108.96 + 1,018.52 \cong 1,127.48$ dollars in total.
2. The rate drops to 10%. As a result, the coupon bonds will be worth

   $$10\mathrm{e}^{-0.1} + 10\mathrm{e}^{-2\times 0.1} + 110\mathrm{e}^{-3\times 0.1} \cong 98.73$$

   dollars each. We shall end up with \$1,184.63.
3. The rate goes up to 14%, the coupon bonds trading at \$88.53. The final value of our investment will be \$1,073.51.

### *Exercise 10.5*

Find the rate $y(1)$ such that the logarithmic return on the investment in Example 10.2 will be a) 12%, b) 10%, c) 14%.

If the lifetime of our investment exceeds one year, we will be facing the problem of reinvesting coupons. In the following example we assume that the coupons are used to purchase the same bond.

## Example 10.3

We begin as in Example 10.2, but our intention is to terminate the investment after 3 years. After one year we reinvest the coupons obtained in the same, now a 3-year, coupon bond. Consider the following scenarios after one year:

1. The rate remains the same for the period of our investment, $y(0) = y(1) = y(2) = y(3) = 12\%$. The bond price is \$93.48, so for the \$108.96 received from coupons we can buy 1.17 additional bonds, increasing the number of bonds held to 12.06. We can monitor the value of our investment by simply multiplying the number of bonds held by the current bond price. We repeat this in the following year. After three years we cash the coupons and sell the bonds, the final value of the investment being \$1,433.33. This number will be used as a benchmark for other scenarios. Observe that

$$1,433.33 \cong 1,000e^{3\times 12\%},$$

the same as the value after 3 years of \$1,000 invested on zero-coupon bonds. The building blocks of our investment are summarised in the table below.

| Year | 0 | 1 | 2 | 3 |
|---|---|---|---|---|
| Rate | 12% | 12% | 12% | 12% |
| PV of coupon 1 | \$8.87 | \$10.00 | | |
| PV of coupon 2 | \$7.87 | \$8.87 | \$10.00 | |
| PV of coupon 3 | \$6.98 | \$7.87 | \$8.87 | \$10.00 |
| PV of coupon 4 | \$6.19 | \$6.98 | \$7.87 | \$8.87 |
| PV of face value | \$61.88 | \$69.77 | \$78.66 | \$88.69 |
| Bond price | \$91.78 | \$93.48 | \$95.40 | \$97.56 |
| Cashed coupons | | \$108.96 | \$120.60 | \$133.26 |
| Additional bonds | | 1.17 | 1.26 | |
| Number of bonds | 10.90 | 12.06 | 13.33 | |
| Value of investment | \$1,000.00 | \$1,127.50 | \$1,271.25 | \$1,433.33 |

2. Suppose that the rate goes down by 2% after one year and then remains at the new level. The drop of the rate results in an increase of all bond prices. The number of additional bonds that can be bought for the coupons is lower than in scenario 1. Nevertheless, the final value of the investment is

higher because so is the price at which we sell the bonds after three years.

| Year | 0 | 1 | 2 | 3 |
|---|---|---|---|---|
| Rate | 12% | 10% | 10% | 10% |
| PV of coupon 1 | \$8.87 | \$10.00 | | |
| PV of coupon 2 | \$7.87 | \$9.05 | \$10.00 | |
| PV of coupon 3 | \$6.98 | \$8.19 | \$9.05 | \$10.00 |
| PV of coupon 4 | \$6.19 | \$7.41 | \$8.19 | \$9.05 |
| PV of face value | \$61.88 | \$74.08 | \$81.87 | \$90.48 |
| Bond price | \$91.78 | \$98.73 | \$99.11 | \$99.53 |
| Cashed coupons | | \$108.96 | \$119.99 | \$132.10 |
| Additional bonds | | 1.10 | 1.21 | |
| Number of bonds | 10.90 | 12.00 | 13.21 | |
| Value of investment | \$1,000.00 | \$1,184.65 | \$1,309.25 | \$1,446.94 |

3. If the rate increases to 14% and stays there, the bonds will be cheaper than in Scenario 1. The final value of the investment will be disappointing.

| Year | 0 | 1 | 2 | 3 |
|---|---|---|---|---|
| Rate | 12% | 14% | 14% | 14% |
| PV of coupon 1 | \$8.87 | \$10.00 | | |
| PV of coupon 2 | \$7.87 | \$8.69 | \$10.00 | |
| PV of coupon 3 | \$6.98 | \$7.56 | \$8.69 | \$10.00 |
| PV of coupon 4 | \$6.19 | \$6.57 | \$7.56 | \$8.69 |
| PV of face value | \$61.88 | \$65.70 | \$75.58 | \$86.94 |
| Bond price | \$91.78 | \$88.53 | \$91.83 | \$95.63 |
| Cashed coupons | | \$108.96 | \$121.26 | \$134.46 |
| Additional bonds | | 1.23 | 1.32 | |
| Number of bonds | 10.90 | 12.13 | 13.45 | |
| Value of investment | \$1,000.00 | \$1,073.53 | \$1,234.85 | \$1,420.41 |

As a motivation for certain theoretical notions, consider the above investment, with the same possible scenarios, but involving a specially designed security, a coupon bond with annual coupons paying \$32, all other parameters remaining unchanged. The results are as follows:

| Scenario | Value after 3 years |
|---|---|
| 12%, 12%, 12%, 12% | \$1,433.33 |
| 12%, 10%, 10%, 10% | \$1,433.68 |
| 12%, 14%, 14%, 14% | \$1,433.78 |

It is remarkable that any change in interest rates improves the result of our investment. We do not lose if the rates change unfavourably. On the other hand, we do not gain in other circumstances. This is explained by the fact, that a certain parameter of the bond, called duration and defined below, is exactly equal to the lifetime of our investment. In some sense, the bond behaves approximately like a zero-coupon bond with prescribed maturity.

*Exercise 10.6*

Check the numbers given in the above tables.

*Exercise 10.7*

Compute the value after three years of \$1,000 invested in a 4-year bond with \$32 annual coupons and \$100 face value if the rates in consecutive years are as follows:

Scenario 1: $12\%, 11\%, 12\%, 12\%$;

Scenario 2: $12\%, 13\%, 12\%, 12\%$.

Design a spreadsheet and experiment with various interest rates.

### 10.1.2 Duration

We have seen that variable interest leads to uncertainty as to the future value of an investment in bonds. This may be undesirable, or even unacceptable, for example for a pension fund manager. We shall introduce a tool which makes it possible to immunise such an investment, at least in the special situation of maturity-independent rates considered in this section.

For notational simplicity we denote the current yield $y(0)$ by $y$. Consider a coupon bond with coupons $C_1, C_2, \ldots, C_N$ payable at times $0 < \tau n_1 < \tau n_2 < \ldots < \tau n_N$ and face value $F$, maturing at time $\tau n_N$. Its current price is given by

$$P(y) = C_1 \mathrm{e}^{-\tau n_1 y} + C_2 \mathrm{e}^{-\tau n_2 y} + \cdots + (C_N + F)\mathrm{e}^{-\tau n_N y}. \tag{10.1}$$

The *duration* of the coupon bond is defined to be

$$D(y) = \frac{\tau n_1 C_1 \mathrm{e}^{-\tau n_1 y} + \tau n_2 C_2 \mathrm{e}^{-\tau n_2 y} + \cdots + \tau n_N (C_N + F)\mathrm{e}^{-\tau n_N y}}{P(y)}. \tag{10.2}$$

The numbers $C_1 \mathrm{e}^{-\tau n_1 y}/P(y), C_2 \mathrm{e}^{-\tau n_2 y}/P(y), \ldots, (C_N + F)\mathrm{e}^{-\tau n_N y}/P(y)$ are non-negative and add up to one, so they may be regarded as weights or probabilities. It can be said that the duration is a weighted average of future payment times. The duration of any future cash flow can be defined in a similar manner.

Duration measures the sensitivity of the bond price to changes in the interest rate. To see this we compute the derivative of the bond price with respect to $y$,

$$\frac{\mathrm{d}}{\mathrm{d}y}P(y) = -\tau n_1 C_1 \mathrm{e}^{-\tau n_1 y} - \tau n_2 C_2 \mathrm{e}^{-\tau n_2 y} - \cdots - \tau n_N (C_N + F)\mathrm{e}^{-\tau n_N y},$$

which gives

$$\frac{\mathrm{d}}{\mathrm{d}y}P(y) = -D(y)P(y).$$

The last formula is sometimes taken as the definition of duration.

## Example 10.4

A 6-year bond with \$10 annual coupons, \$100 face value and yield of 6% has a duration of 4.898 years. A 6-year bond with the same coupons and yield, but with \$500 face value, will have a duration of 5.671 years. The duration of any zero-coupon bond is equal to its lifetime.

### *Exercise 10.8*

A 2-year bond with \$100 face value pays a \$6 coupon each quarter and has 11% yield. Compute the duration.

### *Exercise 10.9*

What should be the face value of a 5-year bond with 10% yield, paying \$10 annual coupons to have duration 4? Find the range of durations that can be obtained by altering the face value, as long as a coupon cannot exceed the face value. If the face value is fixed, say \$100, find the level of coupons for the duration to be 4. What durations can be manufactured in this way?

### *Exercise 10.10*

Show that $P$ is a convex function of $y$.

If we invest in a bond with the intention to close the investment at time $t$, then the future value of the money invested in a single bond will be $P(y)\mathrm{e}^{ty}$, provided that the interest rate remains unchanged (being equal to the initial yield $y(0)$). To see how sensitive this amount is to interest rate changes compute the derivative with respect to $y$,

$$\frac{\mathrm{d}}{\mathrm{d}y}(P(y)\mathrm{e}^{ty}) = \left(\frac{\mathrm{d}}{\mathrm{d}y}P(y)\right)\mathrm{e}^{ty} + tP(y)\mathrm{e}^{ty} = (t - D(y))P(y)\mathrm{e}^{ty}.$$

If the duration of the bond is exactly $t$, then

$$\frac{\mathrm{d}}{\mathrm{d}y}(P(y)\mathrm{e}^{ty}) = 0.$$

If the derivative is zero at some point, then the graph of the function is 'flat' near this point. This means that small changes of the rate will have little effect on the future value of the investment.

### 10.1.3 Portfolios of Bonds

If a bond of desirable duration is not available, it may be possible to create a synthetic one by investing in a suitable portfolio of bonds of different durations.

#### Example 10.5

If the initial interest rate is 14%, then a 4-year bond with annual coupons $C = 10$ and face value $F = 100$ has duration 3.44 years. A zero-coupon bond with $F = 100$ and $N = 1$ has duration 1. A portfolio consisting of two bonds, one of each kind, can be regarded as a single bond with coupons $C_1 = 110$, $C_2 = C_3 = C_4 = 10$, $F = 100$. Its duration can be computed using the general formula (10.2), which gives 2.21 years.

We shall derive a formula for the duration of a portfolio in terms of the durations of its components. Denote by $P_A(y)$ and $P_B(y)$ the values of two bonds $A$ and $B$ with durations $D_A(y)$ and $D_B(y)$. Take a portfolio consisting of $a$ bonds $A$ and $b$ bonds $B$, its value being $aP_A(y) + bP_B(y)$. The task of finding the duration of the portfolio will be divided into two steps:

1. Find the duration of a portfolio consisting of $a$ bonds of type $A$. We shall write $aA$ to denote such a portfolio. Its price is obviously $aP_A(y)$. Since

$$\frac{\mathrm{d}}{\mathrm{d}y}(aP_A(y)) = -D_A(y)(aP_A(y)),$$

it follows that

$$D_{aA}(y) = D_A(y).$$

This is clear if we examine the cash flow of $aA$. Each coupon and the face value are multiplied by $a$, which cancels out in the computation of duration directly from (10.2).

2. Find the duration of a portfolio consisting of one bond $A$ and one bond $B$, which will be denoted by $A + B$. The price of this portfolio is $P_A(y) + P_B(y)$.

Differentiating the last expression, we obtain

$$\begin{aligned}\frac{\mathrm{d}}{\mathrm{d}y}(P_A(y)+P_B(y)) &= \frac{\mathrm{d}}{\mathrm{d}y}P_A(y)+\frac{\mathrm{d}}{\mathrm{d}y}P_B(y)\\ &= -D_A(y)P_A(y)-D_B(y)P_B(y).\end{aligned}$$

The last term can be written as $-D_{A+B}(y)(P_A(y)+P_B(y))$ if we put

$$D_{A+B}(y)=D_A(y)\frac{P_A(y)}{P_A(y)+P_B(y)}+D_B(y)\frac{P_B(y)}{P_A(y)+P_B(y)}.$$

This means that $D_{A+B}(y)$ is a linear combination of $D_A(y)$ and $D_B(y)$, the coefficients being the percentage weights of each bond in the portfolio.

From the above considerations we obtain the general formula

$$D_{aA+bB}(y)=D_A(y)w_A+D_B(y)w_B,$$

where

$$w_A=\frac{aP_A(y)}{aP_A(y)+bP_B(y)},\quad w_B=\frac{bP_A(y)}{aP_A(y)+bP_B(y)},$$

are the percentage weights of individual bonds.

If we allow negative values of $a$ or $b$ (which corresponds to writing a bond instead of purchasing it, in other words, to borrowing money instead of investing), then, given two durations $D_A\neq D_B$, the duration $D$ of the portfolio can take any value because $w_B=1-w_A$ and

$$D=D_Aw_A+D_B(1-w_A)=D_B+w_A(D_A-D_B).$$

The value of $D$ can even be negative, which corresponds to a negative cash flow, that is, sums of money to be paid rather than received.

## Example 10.6

Let $D_A=1$ and $D_B=3$. We wish to invest \$1,000 for 6 months. For the duration to match the lifetime of the investment we need $0.5=w_A+3w_B$. Since $w_A+w_B=1$, it follows that $w_B=-0.25$ and $w_A=1.25$. With $P_A=0.92$ dollars and $P_B=1.01$ dollars, we invest \$1,250 in $\frac{1250}{0.92}\cong 1,358.70$ bonds $A$ and we issue $\frac{250}{1.01}\cong 247.52$ bonds $B$.

### *Exercise 10.11*

Find the number of bonds of type $A$ and $B$ to be bought if $D_A=2$, $D_B=3.4$, $P_A=0.98$, $P_B=1.02$ and you need a portfolio worth \$5,000 with duration 6.

*Exercise 10.12*

Invest $\$1,000$ in a portfolio of bonds with duration 2 using 1-year zero-coupon bonds with \$100 face value and 4-year bonds with \$15 annual coupons and \$100 face value that trade at \$102.

A portfolio with duration matching the investment lifetime is insensitive to small changes of interest rates. However in practice we shall have to modify the portfolio if, for example, the investment is for 3 years and one of the bonds is a zero-coupon bond expiring after one year. In addition, the duration may, as we shall see below, go off the target. As a result, it will become necessary to update the portfolio during the lifetime of the investment. This is the subject of the next subsection.

### 10.1.4 Dynamic Hedging

Even if a portfolio is selected with duration matching the desired investment lifetime, this will only be valid at the initial instant, since duration changes with time as well as with the interest rate.

Example 10.7

Take a 5-year bond with \$10 annual coupons and \$100 face value. If $y = 10\%$, then the duration will be about 4.16 years. Before the first coupon is paid the duration decreases in line with time: After 6 months it will be 3.66, and after 9 months $4.16 - 0.75 = 3.31$. If the duration matches our investment's lifetime and the interest rates do not change, no action will be necessary until a coupon becomes payable. As soon as the first coupon is paid after one year, the bond will become a 4-year one with duration 3.48, no longer consistent with the investment lifetime.

*Exercise 10.13*

Assuming that the interest rate does not change, show that before the first coupon is paid the duration after time $t$ will $D - t$, where $D$ is the duration computed at time 0.

The next example shows the impact of the interest rate on duration.

## Example 10.8

The bond in Example 10.7 will have duration 4.23 if $y = 6\%$, and 4.08 if $y = 14\%$.

### *Exercise 10.14*

Show that the duration of a 2-year bond with annual coupons decreases as the yield increases.

Duration will now be applied to design an investment strategy immune to interest rate changes. This will be done by monitoring the position at the end of each year, or more frequently if needed. For clarity of exposition we restrict ourselves to an example.

Set the lifetime of the investment to be 3 years and the target value to be \$100, 000. Suppose that the interest rate is 12% initially. We invest \$69, 767.63, which would be the present value of \$100, 000 if the interest rate remained constant.

We restrict our attention to two instruments, a 5-year bond $A$ with \$10 annual coupons and \$100 face value, and a 1-year zero-coupon bond $B$ with the same face value. We assume that a new bond of type $B$ is always available. In subsequent years we shall combine it with bond $A$.

At time 0 the bond prices are \$90.27 and \$88.69, respectively. We find $D_A \cong 4.12$ and the weights $w_A \cong 0.6405$, $w_B \cong 0.3595$ which give a portfolio with duration 3. We split the initial sum according to the weights, spending \$44, 687.93 to buy $a \cong 495.05$ bonds $A$ and \$25, 079.70 to buy $b \cong 282.77$ bonds $B$. Consider some possible scenarios of future interest rate changes.

1. After one year the rate increases to 14%. The value of our portfolio is the sum of:
   - the first coupons of bonds $A$: \$4, 950.51,
   - the face value of cashed bonds $B$: \$28, 277.29,
   - the market value of bonds $A$ held, which are now 4-year bonds selling at \$85.65: \$42, 403.53.

   This gives \$75, 631.32 altogether. The duration of bonds $A$ is now 3.44. The desired duration is 2, so we find $w_A \cong 0.4094$ and $w_B \cong 0.5906$ and arrive at the number of bonds to be held in the portfolio: 361.53 bonds $A$ and 513.76 bonds $B$. (This means that we have to sell 133.52 bonds $A$ and buy 513.76 new bonds $B$.)

   a) After two years the rate drops to 9%. To compute our wealth we add:
      - the coupons of $A$: \$3, 615.30,

- the face values of $B$: \$51,376.39,
- the market value of $A$, selling at \$101.46: \$36,682.22.

The result is \$91,673.92. We invest all the money in bonds $B$, since the required duration is now 1. (The payoff of these bonds is guaranteed next year.) We can afford to buy 1,003.07 bonds $B$ selling at \$91.39. The terminal value of the investment will be about **\$100,307**.

b) After two years the rate goes up to 16%. We cash the same amount as above for coupons and zero-coupon bonds, but bonds $A$ are now cheaper, selling at \$83.85, so we have less money in total: \$85,305.68. However, the zero-coupon bonds are now cheap as well, selling at \$85.21, and we can afford to buy 1,001.07 of them, ending up with **\$100,107**.

2. After one year the rate drops to 9%. In a similar way as before, we arrive at the current value of the investment by adding the coupons of $A$, the face value of $B$ and the market value of bonds $A$ held, obtaining \$83,658.73. Then we find the weights $w_A \cong 0.4013$, $w_B \cong 0.5987$, determining our new portfolio of 329.56 bonds $A$ and 548.04 bonds $B$. (We have to sell 165.50 bonds $A$ and buy 548.04 new bonds $B$.)

   a) After two years the rate goes up to 14%. We cash \$3,295.55 from the coupons of $A$, which together with the \$54,803.77 obtained from $B$ and the market value of \$29,174.39 of bonds $A$ gives \$87,273.72 in total. We buy 1003.89 new zero-coupon bonds $B$, ending up with **\$100,389** after 3 years.

   b) After two years the rate drops to 6%. Our wealth will then be \$94,405.29, we can afford to buy 1,002.43 bonds $B$, and the final value of our investment will be **\$100,243**.

As we can see, we end up with more than \$100,000 in each scenario.[1]

### *Exercise 10.15*

Design an investment of \$20,000 in a portfolio of duration 2 years consisting of two kinds of coupon bonds maturing after 2 years, with annual coupons, bond $A$ with \$20 coupons and \$100 face value, and bond $B$ with \$5 coupons and \$500 face value, given that the initial rate is 8%. How much will this investment be worth after 2 years?

[1] It can be shown that the future value at time $t$ of a bond investment with duration equal to $t$ has a minimum if the rate $y$ remains unchanged. This means that rate jumps in a model with yields independent of maturity lead to arbitrage. In an arbitrage-free model with rate jumps, the yields must therefore depend on maturity.

## 10.2 General Term Structure

Here we shall discuss a model of bond prices without the condition that the yield should be independent of maturity.

The prices $B(n, N)$ of zero-coupon unit bonds with various maturities determine a family of yields $y(n, N)$ by

$$B(n, N) = \mathrm{e}^{-(N-n)\tau y(n,N)}.$$

Note that the yields have to be positive, since $B(n, N)$ has to be less than 1 for $n < N$. The function $y(n, N)$ of two variables $n < N$ is called the *term structure of interest rates*. The yields $y(0, N)$ dictated by the current prices are called the *spot rates*.

The *initial term structure* $y(0, N)$ formed by the spot rates is a function of one variable $N$. Typically, it is an increasing function, but other graphs have also been observed in financial markets. In particular, the initial term structure may be *flat*, that is, the yields may be independent of $N$, which is the case considered in the previous section.

### *Exercise 10.16*

If $B(0, 6) = 0.96$ dollars, find $B(0, 3)$ and $B(0, 9)$ such that the initial term structure is flat.

The price of a coupon bond as the present value of future payments can be written using the spot rates in the following way:

$$P = C_1 \mathrm{e}^{-\tau n_1 y(0,n_1)} + C_2 \mathrm{e}^{-\tau n_2 y(0,n_2)} + \cdots + (C_N + F)\mathrm{e}^{-\tau n_N y(0,n_N)} \quad (10.3)$$

for a bond with coupons $C_1, C_2, \ldots, C_N$ due at times $0 < \tau n_1 < \tau n_2 < \cdots < \tau n_N$ and with face value $F$, maturing at time $\tau n_N$.

Despite the fact that for a coupon bond we cannot use a single rate for discounting future payments, such a rate can be introduced just as an artificial quantity. It is called the *yield to maturity*, and is defined to be the number $y$ solving the equation

$$P = C_1 \mathrm{e}^{-\tau n_1 y} + C_2 \mathrm{e}^{-\tau n_2 y} + \cdots + (F + C_N)\mathrm{e}^{-\tau n_N y}.$$

Yield to maturity provides a convenient simple description of coupon bonds and is quoted in the financial press. Of course, if the interest rates are independent of maturity, then this formula is the same as (10.1).

## Remark 10.1

To determine the initial term structure we need the prices of zero-coupon bonds. However, for longer maturities (typically over one year) only coupon bonds may be traded, making it necessary to decompose coupon bonds into zero-coupon bonds with various maturities. This can be done by applying formula (10.3) repeatedly to find the yield with the longest maturity, given the bond price and all the yields with shorter maturities. This procedure was recognised by the U.S. Treasury, who in 1985 introduced a programme called STRIPS (Separate Trading of Registered Interest and Principal Securities), allowing an investor to keep the required cash payments (for certain bonds) by selling the rest (the 'stripped' bond) back to the Treasury.

## Example 10.9

Suppose that a one-year zero-coupon bond with face value \$100 is trading at \$91.80 and a two-year bond with \$10 annual coupons and face value \$100 is trading at \$103.95. This gives the following equations for the yields

$$\begin{aligned} 91.80 &= 100\mathrm{e}^{-y(0,1)}, \\ 103.95 &= 10\mathrm{e}^{-y(0,1)} + 110\mathrm{e}^{-2y(0,2)}. \end{aligned}$$

From the first equation we obtain $y(0,1) \cong 8.56\%$. On substituting this into the second equation, we find $y(0,2) \cong 7.45\%$. As a result, the price of the 'stripped' two-year bond, a zero-coupon bond maturing in two years with face value \$100, will be $100\mathrm{e}^{-2y(0,2)} \cong 86.16$ dollars. Given the price of a three-year coupon bond, we could then evaluate $y(0,3)$, and so on.

Going back to our general study of bonds, let us consider a deterministic term structure (thus known in advance with certainty). The next proposition indicates that this, in fact, is not realistic.

## Proposition 10.2

If the term structure is deterministic, then the No-Arbitrage Principle implies that

$$B(0,N) = B(0,n)B(n,N). \tag{10.4}$$

## Proof

If $B(0,N) < B(0,n)B(n,N)$, then:

- Buy a bond maturing at time $N$ and write a fraction $B(n,N)$ of a bond maturing at $n$. (Here we use the assumption that the future bond prices are known today.) This gives $B(0,n)B(n,N) - B(0,N)$ dollars now.
- At time $n$ settle the written bonds, raising the required sum of $B(n,N)$ by issuing a single unit bond maturing at $N$.
- At time $N$ close the position, retaining the initial profit.

The reverse inequality $B(0,N) > B(0,n)B(n,N)$ can be dealt with in a similar manner, by adopting the opposite strategy. □

Employing the representation of bond prices in terms of yields, we have

$$B(n,N) = \frac{B(0,N)}{B(0,n)} = \mathrm{e}^{\tau n y(0,n) - \tau N y(0,N)}.$$

This would mean that all bonds prices (and so the whole term structure) are determined by the initial term structure. However, it is clear that one cannot expect this to hold in real bond markets. In particular, this relation is not supported by historical data.

This shows that assuming deterministic bond prices would go too far in reducing the complexity of the model. We have no choice but to allow the future term structure to be random, only the initial term structure being known with certainty. In what follows, future bond prices will be random, as will be the quantities determined by them.

### 10.2.1 Forward Rates

We begin with an example showing how to secure in advance the interest rate for a deposit to be made or a loan to be taken at some future time.

#### Example 10.10

Suppose that the business plan of your company will require taking a loan of \$100,000 one year from now in order to purchase new equipment. You expect to have the means to repay the loan after another year. You would like to arrange the loan today at a fixed interest rate, rather than to gamble on future rates. Suppose that the spot rates are $y(0,1) = 8\%$ and $y(0,2) = 9\%$ (with $\tau = 1$). You buy 1,000 one-year bonds with \$100 face value, paying $100{,}000\mathrm{e}^{-8\%} \cong 92{,}311.63$ dollars. This sum is borrowed for 2 years at 9%. After one year you will receive the \$100,000 from the bonds, and after two years you can settle the loan with interest, the total amount to pay being $92{,}311.63\mathrm{e}^{2\times 9\%} \cong 110{,}517.09$ dollars. Thus, the interest rate on the constructed future loan will be $\ln(110,517.09/100,000) \cong 10\%$. Financial intermediaries may simplify your task by offering a so-called Forward Rate Agreement and perform the above construction of the loan on your behalf.

### *Exercise 10.17*

Explain how a deposit of \$50,000 for six months can be arranged to start in six months and find the rate if $y(0,6) = 6\%$ and $y(0,12) = 7\%$, where $\tau = \frac{1}{12}$.

In general, the *initial forward rate* $f(0,M,N)$ is an interest rate such that

$$B(0,N) = B(0,M)\mathrm{e}^{-(N-M)\tau f(0,M,N)},$$

so

$$f(0,M,N) = -\frac{1}{\tau(N-M)}\ln\frac{B(0,N)}{B(0,M)} = -\frac{\ln B(0,N) - \ln B(0,M)}{\tau(N-M)}.$$

Note that this rate is deterministic, since it is worked out using the present bond prices. It can be conveniently expressed in terms of the initial term structure. Insert into the above expression the bond prices as determined by the yields, $B(0,N) = \mathrm{e}^{-\tau N y(0,N)}$ and $B(0,M) = \mathrm{e}^{-\tau M y(0,M)}$, to get

$$f(0,M,N) = \frac{Ny(0,N) - My(0,M)}{N-M}. \tag{10.5}$$

### *Exercise 10.18*

Suppose that the following spot rates are provided by central London banks (LIBOR, the London Interbank Offer Rate, is the rate at which money can be deposited; LIBID, the London Interbank Bid Rate, is the rate at which money can be borrowed):

| Rate | LIBOR | LIBID |
|---|---|---|
| 1 month | 8.41% | 8.59% |
| 2 months | 8.44% | 8.64% |
| 3 months | 9.01% | 9.23% |
| 6 months | 9.35% | 9.54% |

As a bank manager acting for a customer who wishes to arrange a loan of \$100,000 in a month's time for a period of 5 months, what rate could you offer and how would you construct the loan? Suppose that another institution offers the possibility of making a deposit for 4 months, starting 2 months from now, at a rate of 10.23%. Does this present an arbitrage opportunity? All rates stated in this exercise are continuous compounding rates.

As time passes, the bond prices will change and, consequently, so will the forward rates. The *forward rate over the interval* $[M, N]$ *determined at time* $n < M < N$ is defined by

$$B(n,N) = B(n,M)\mathrm{e}^{-(N-M)\tau f(n,M,N)},$$

that is,

$$f(n,M,N) = -\frac{\ln B(n,N) - \ln B(n,M)}{(N-M)\tau}.$$

The *instantaneous forward rates* $f(n,N) = f(n,N,N+1)$ are the forward rates over a one-step interval. Typically, when $\tau$ is one day, the instantaneous forward rates correspond to overnight deposits or loans. The formula for the forward rate

$$f(n,N) = -\frac{\ln B(n,N+1) - \ln B(n,N)}{\tau} \tag{10.6}$$

will enable us to reconstruct the bond prices, given the forward rates at a particular time $n$.

## Example 10.11

Let $\tau = \frac{1}{12}$, $n = 0$, $N = 0, 1, 2, 3$, and suppose that the bond prices are

$$\begin{aligned} B(0,1) &= 0.9901, \\ B(0,2) &= 0.9828, \\ B(0,3) &= 0.9726. \end{aligned}$$

Then we have the following implied yields

$$\begin{aligned} y(0,1) &\cong 11.94\%, \\ y(0,2) &\cong 10.41\%, \\ y(0,3) &\cong 11.11\%, \end{aligned}$$

and forward rates

$$\begin{aligned} f(0,0) &\cong 11.94\%, \\ f(0,1) &\cong \ \ 8.88\%, \\ f(0,2) &\cong 12.52\%. \end{aligned}$$

Observe that, using the formula for the forward rates, we get

$$\exp(-(0.1194 + 0.0888 + 0.1252)/12) \cong 0.9726 = B(0,3)$$

which illustrates the next proposition.

## Proposition 10.3

The bond price is given by

$$B(n,N)=\exp\{-\tau(f(n,n)+f(n,n+1)+\cdots+f(n,N-1))\}.$$

## Proof

For this purpose note that

$$f(n,n)=-\frac{\ln B(n,n+1)}{\tau},$$

since $B(n,n)=1$, so

$$B(n,n+1)=\exp\{-\tau f(n,n)\}.$$

Next,

$$f(n,n+1)=-\frac{\ln B(n,n+2)-\ln B(n,n+1)}{\tau}$$

and, after inserting the expression for $B(n,n+1)$,

$$B(n,n+2)=\exp\{-\tau(f(n,n)+f(n,n+1))\}.$$

Repeating this a number of times, we arrive at the required general formula. □

We have a simple representation of the forward rates in terms of the yields:

$$f(n,N)=(N+1-n)y(n,N+1)-(N-n)y(n,N). \tag{10.7}$$

In particular,

$$f(n,n)=y(n,n+1),$$

resulting in the intuitive formula

$$y(n,N)=\frac{f(n,n)+f(n,n+1)+\cdots+f(n,N-1)}{N-n}.$$

## Example 10.12

We can clearly see from the above formulae that if the term structure is flat, that is, $y(n,N)$ is independent of $N$, then $f(n,N)=y(n,N)$. Now consider an example of $f(n,N)$ increasing with $N$ for a fixed $n$, and compute the corresponding yields

$$\begin{aligned} f(0,0)&=8.01\%, & y(0,1)&=8.01\%,\\ f(0,1)&=8.03\%, & y(0,2)&=8.02\%,\\ f(0,2)&=8.08\%, & y(0,3)&=8.04\%. \end{aligned}$$

We can see that the yields also increase. (See Exercise 10.20 below for a generalisation of this.)

However, the forward rates do not have to increase with maturity even if the yields do:

$$\begin{aligned} f(0,0) &= 9.20\%, & y(0,1) &= 9.20\%, \\ f(0,1) &= 9.80\%, & y(0,2) &= 9.50\%, \\ f(0,2) &= 9.56\%, & y(0,3) &\cong 9.52\%. \end{aligned}$$

### Exercise 10.19

Can a forward rate be negative?

### Exercise 10.20

Prove that if $f(n,N)$ increases with $N$, then the same is true for $y(n,N)$.

## 10.2.2 Money Market Account

The *short rate* is defined by $r(n) = f(n,n)$. An alternative expression is $r(n) = y(n,n+1)$, so this is a rate valid for one step starting at time $n$. The short rates are unknown in advance, except for the current one, $r(0)$. It is important to distinguish between $r(n)$ and $f(0,n)$. Both rates apply to a single step from time $n$ to $n+1$, but the former is random, whereas the latter is known at the present moment and determined by the initial term structure.

The money market account denoted by $A(n)$, $n \geq 1$, is defined by

$$A(n) = \exp\{\tau(r(0) + r(1) + \cdots + r(n-1))\}$$

with $A(0) = 1$, and represents the value at time $n$ of one dollar invested in an account attracting interest given by the short rate under continuous compounding. For example, if $\tau = \frac{1}{365}$, then the interest is given by the overnight rate.

The money market account defined in Chapter 2 was a deterministic sequence independent of the particular way the initial dollar is invested. Here $A(n)$ is random and, as will be seen below, in general different from $\exp\{\tau n y(0,n)\}$, the latter being deterministic and constructed by using zero-coupon bonds maturing at time $n$.

### Example 10.13

In the setting introduced in Example 10.11, suppose that the bond prices change as follows:

$$\begin{aligned}
&B(0,1) = 0.9901, \\
&B(0,2) = 0.9828, \quad B(1,2) = 0.9947, \\
&B(0,3) = 0.9726, \quad B(1,3) = 0.9848, \quad B(2,3) = 0.9905.
\end{aligned}$$

The corresponding yields are

$$\begin{aligned}
&y(0,1) \cong 11.94\%, \\
&y(0,2) \cong 10.41\%, \quad y(1,2) \cong 6.38\%, \\
&y(0,3) \cong 11.11\%, \quad y(1,3) \cong 9.19\%, \quad y(2,3) \cong 11.45\%.
\end{aligned}$$

The forward rates are

$$\begin{aligned}
&f(0,0) \cong 11.94\%, \\
&f(0,1) \cong \ \ 8.88\%, \quad f(1,1) \cong \ \ 6.38\%, \\
&f(0,2) \cong 12.52\%, \quad f(1,2) \cong 12.00\%, \quad f(2,2) \cong 11.45\%.
\end{aligned}$$

We can read off the short rates and compute the values of the money market account

$$\begin{aligned}
& && A(0) = 1, \\
&r(0) = f(0,0) \cong 11.94\%, && A(1) \cong 1.0100, \\
&r(1) = f(1,1) \cong \ \ 6.38\%, && A(2) \cong 1.0154, \\
&r(2) = f(2,2) \cong 11.45\%, && A(3) \cong 1.0251.
\end{aligned}$$

### *Exercise 10.21*

Which bond prices in Example 10.13 can be altered so that the values of the money market remain unchanged?

### *Exercise 10.22*

Using the data in Example 10.13, compare the logarithmic return on an investment in the following securities over the period from 0 to 3: a) zero-coupon bonds maturing at time 3; b) single-period zero-coupon bonds; c) the money market account.

# 11
# Stochastic Interest Rates

This chapter is devoted to modelling the time evolution of random interest rates. We adopt an approach similar to the binomial model of stock prices in Chapter 3. Modelling the evolution of interest rates can be reduced to modelling the evolution of the bond prices, since the latter determine the former. We begin with some properties that a model of bond prices should satisfy, emphasising the differences between bonds and stock.

First, let us recall that the evolution of interest rates or bond prices is described by functions of two variables, the running time and the maturity time, whereas stock prices are functions of just one variable, the running time.

Second, there are many ways of describing the term structure: bond prices, implied yields, forward rates, short rates. Bond prices and yields are clearly equivalent, being linked by a simple formula. Bond prices and forward rates are also equivalent. The short rates are different, easier to handle, but the problem of reconstructing the term structure emerges. This may be non-trivial, since short rates usually carry less information.

Third, the model needs to match the initial data. For a stock this is just the current price. In the case of bonds the whole initial term structure is given, imposing more restrictions on the model, which has to be consistent with all currently available market information.

Fourth, bonds become non-random at maturity. This is in sharp contrast with stock prices. The fact that a bond gives a sure dollar at maturity has to be included in the model.

Finally, the dependence of yields on maturity must be quite special. Bonds with similar maturities will typically behave in a similar manner. In statistical terms this means that they are strongly positively correlated.

## 11.1 Binomial Tree Model

The shape of the tree will be similar to that in Section 3.2. However, to facilitate the necessary level of sophistication of the model, it has to be more complex. Namely, the probabilities and returns will depend on the position in the tree. We need suitable notation to distinguish between different positions.

By a *state* we mean a finite sequence of consecutive up or down movements. The state depends, first of all, on time or, in other words, on the number of steps. We shall use sequences of letters u and d of various lengths, the length corresponding to the time elapsed (the number of steps from the root of the tree). At time 1 we have just two states $s_1$ = u or d, at time 2 four states $s_2$ = ud, dd, du, or uu. We shall write $s_2 = s_1$u or $s_1$d, meaning that we go up or, respectively, down at time 2, having been at $s_1$ at time 1. In general, $s_{n+1} = s_n$u or $s_n$d.

The probabilities will be allowed to depend on particular states. We write $p(s_n)$ to denote the probability of going up at time $n+1$, having started at state $s_n$ at time $n$. At the first step the probability of going up will be denoted by $p$ without an argument. In Figure 11.1 we have $p = 0.3$, $p(\text{u}) = 0.1$, $p(\text{d}) = 0.4$, $p(\text{uu}) = 0.4$, $p(\text{ud}) = 0.2$, $p(\text{du}) = 0.5$, $p(\text{dd}) = 0.4$.

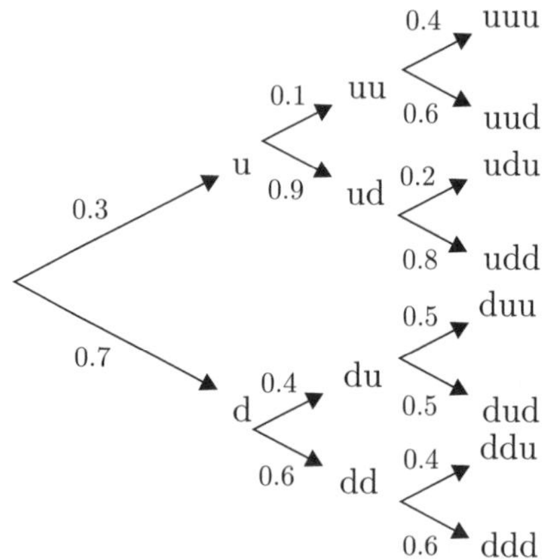


**Figure 11.1** States and probabilities

Let us fix a natural number $N$ as the time horizon. It will be the upper bound of the maturities of all the bonds considered. The states $s_N$ at time $N$ represent the complete scenarios of bond price movements.

Next, we shall describe the evolution of bond prices. At time 0 we are given the initial bond prices for all maturities up to $N$, that is, a sequence of $N$ numbers

$$B(0,1), B(0,2), B(0,3), \ldots, B(0,N-1), B(0,N).$$

At time 1 one of the prices becomes redundant, namely the first bond matures and only the remaining $N-1$ bonds are still being traded. We introduce randomness by allowing two possibilities distinguished by the states u and d, so we have two sequences

$$\begin{aligned}&B(1,2;\mathrm{u}), B(1,3,\mathrm{u}), \ldots, B(1,N-1;\mathrm{u}), B(1,N;\mathrm{u}),\\ &B(1,2;\mathrm{d}), B(1,3;\mathrm{d}), \ldots, B(1,N-1;\mathrm{d}), B(1,N;\mathrm{d}).\end{aligned}$$

At time 2 we have four states and four sequences of length $N-2$:

$$\begin{aligned}&B(2,3,\mathrm{uu}), \ldots, B(2,N-1;\mathrm{uu}), B(2,N;\mathrm{uu}),\\ &B(2,3;\mathrm{ud}), \ldots, B(2,N-1;\mathrm{ud}), B(2,N;\mathrm{ud}),\\ &B(2,3;\mathrm{du}), \ldots, B(2,N-1;\mathrm{du}), B(2,N;\mathrm{du}),\\ &B(2,3;\mathrm{dd}), \ldots, B(2,N-1;\mathrm{dd}), B(2,N;\mathrm{dd}).\end{aligned}$$

We do not require that the ud and du prices coincide, which was the case for stock prices movements in Section 3.2.

This process continues in the same manner. At each step the length of the sequence decreases by one and the number of sequences doubles. At time $N-1$ we have just single numbers, $2^{N-1}$ of them,

$$B(N-1,N;s_{N-1})$$

indexed by all possible states $s_{N-1}$. The tree structure breaks down here because the last movement is certain: The last bond matures, becoming a sure dollar at time $N$, $B(N,N;s_N)=1$ for all states.

## Example 11.1

A particular evolution of bond prices for $N=3$, with monthly steps ($\tau=\frac{1}{12}$) is given in Figure 11.2. The prices of three bonds with maturities 1, 2, and 3 are shown.

The evolution of bond prices can be described be means of returns. Suppose we have reached state $s_{n-1}$ and the bond price $B(n-1,N;s_{n-1})$ becomes known. Then we can write

$$\begin{aligned}B(n,N;s_{n-1}\mathrm{u}) &= B(n-1,N;s_{n-1})\exp\{k(n,N;s_{n-1}\mathrm{u})\},\\ B(n,N;s_{n-1}\mathrm{d}) &= B(n-1,N;s_{n-1})\exp\{k(n,N;s_{n-1}\mathrm{d})\},\end{aligned}$$

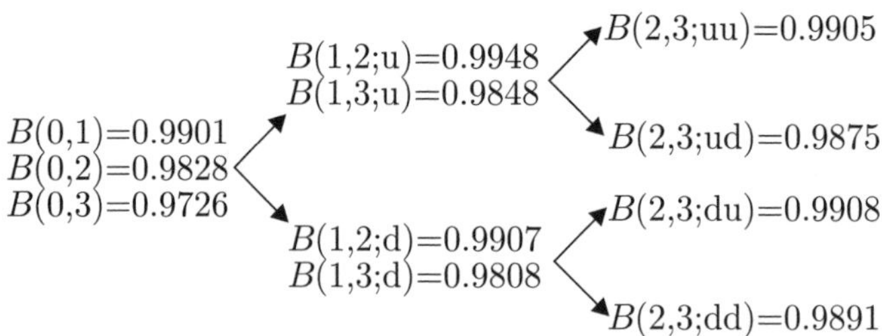


**Figure 11.2** Evolution of bond prices in Example 11.1

implicitly defining the logarithmic returns

$$k(n, N; s_{n-1}\mathrm{u}) = \ln \frac{B(n, N; s_{n-1}\mathrm{u})}{B(n-1, N; s_{n-1})},$$
$$k(n, N; s_{n-1}\mathrm{d}) = \ln \frac{B(n, N; s_{n-1}\mathrm{d})}{B(n-1, N; s_{n-1})}.$$

We assume here that $k(n, N; s_{n-1}\mathrm{u}) \geq k(n, N; s_{n-1}\mathrm{d})$.

## Remark 11.1

Note that there are some places in the tree where the returns are non-random given the state $s_{n-1}$ is known. Namely,

$$k(n, n; s_{n-1}\mathrm{u}) = k(n, n; s_{n-1}\mathrm{d}) = \ln \frac{1}{B(n-1, n; s_{n-1})},$$

since $B(n, n; s_n) = 1$ for all $s_n$.

## Example 11.2

From the data in Example 11.1 we extract the prices of bonds with maturity 3, completing the picture with the final value 1. The tree shown in Figure 11.3

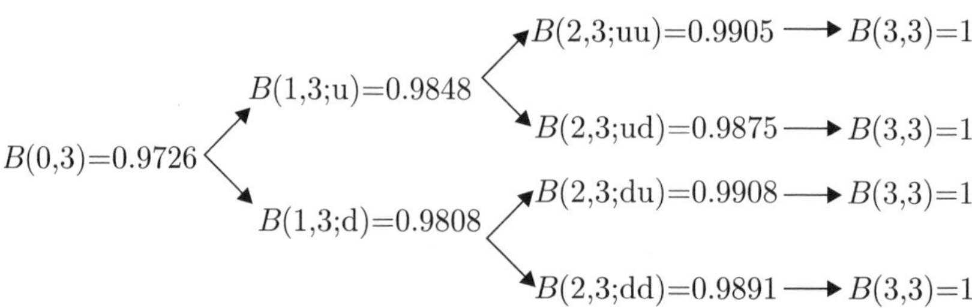


**Figure 11.3** Prices of the bond maturing at time 3 in Example 11.2

describes the random evolution of a single bond purchased at time 0 for 0.9726. The returns are easy to compute, for instance

$$k(2,3;\mathrm{ud}) = \ln \frac{B(2,3;\mathrm{ud})}{B(1,3;\mathrm{u})} \cong 0.27\%.$$

The results are gathered in Figure 11.4. (Recall that the length of each step is one month.)

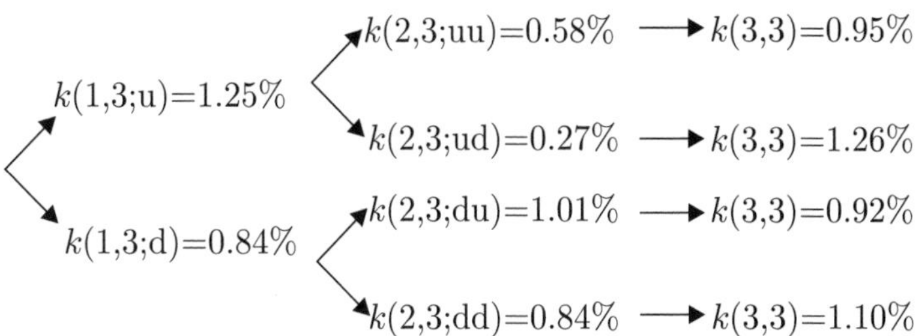


**Figure 11.4** Returns on the bond maturing at time 3 in Example 11.2

### *Exercise 11.1*

For the tree of weekly returns shown in Figure 11.5 construct the tree of bond prices and fill in the missing returns.

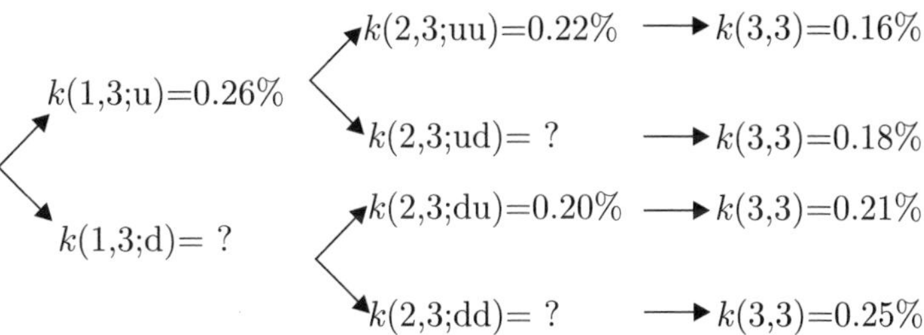


**Figure 11.5** Returns in Exercise 11.1

The evolution of bond prices is in perfect correspondence with the evolution of implied yields to maturity. Namely,

$$y(n,m;s_n) = \frac{1}{\tau(m-n)} \ln \frac{1}{B(n,m;s_n)}$$

with the same tree structure as for bond prices. In particular, the final yields are non-random given that the state $s_{n-1}$ at the penultimate step is known. Note that the words 'up' and 'down' lose their meaning here because the yield goes down as the bond price goes up. Nevertheless, we keep the original indicators u and d.

## Example 11.3

We continue Example 11.1 and find the yields, bearing in mind that $\tau = \frac{1}{12}$. The results are collected in Figure 11.6.

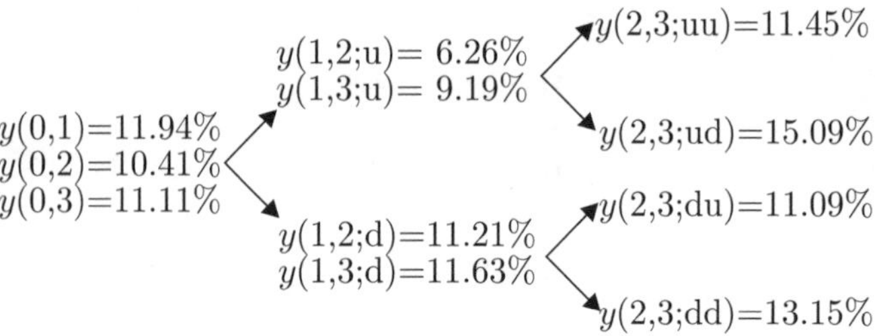


**Figure 11.6** Yields in Example 11.3

### *Exercise 11.2*

Take the returns in Exercise 11.1 and find the yield $y(0,3)$. What is the general relationship between the returns and yields to maturity? Can you complete the missing returns without computing the bond prices?

Now consider the instantaneous forward rates. At the initial time 0 there are $N$ forward rates

$$f(0,0), f(0,1), f(0,2), \ldots, f(0,N-1)$$

generated by the initial bond prices. Note that the first number is the short rate $r(0) = f(0,0)$. For all subsequent steps the current bond prices imply the forward rates. Formula (10.6) applied to random bond prices allows us to find the random evolution of forward rates:

$$f(n,N;s_n) = -\frac{\ln B(n,N+1;s_n) - \ln B(n,N;s_n)}{\tau}. \tag{11.1}$$

At time 1 we have two possible sequences of $N-1$ forward rates obtained from two sequences of bond prices

$$f(1,1;\mathrm{u}), f(1,2;\mathrm{u}), \ldots, f(1,N-1;\mathrm{u}),$$
$$f(1,1;\mathrm{d}), f(1,2;\mathrm{d}), \ldots, f(1,N-1;\mathrm{d}).$$

At time 2 we have four sequences of $N-2$ forward rates, and so on. At time $N-1$ we have $2^{N-1}$ single numbers $f(N-1, N-1; s_{N-1})$.

## Example 11.4

Using (11.1), we can evaluate the forward rates for the data in Example 11.1. For instance,

$$f(1,2;\mathrm{u}) = -\frac{\ln B(1,3;\mathrm{u}) - \ln B(1,2;\mathrm{u})}{\tau}.$$

Alternatively, we can use the yields found in Example 11.3 along with formula (10.7):

$$f(1,2;\mathrm{u}) = 2y(1,3;\mathrm{u}) - y(1,2;\mathrm{u}).$$

The results are gathered in Figure 11.7.

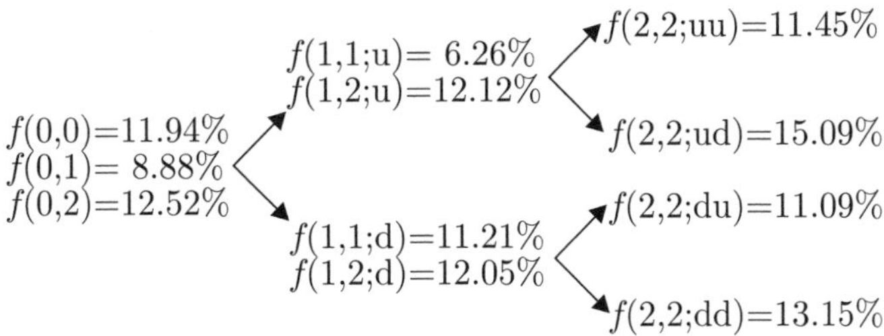


**Figure 11.7** Forward rates in Example 11.4

The information contained in forward rates is sufficient to reconstruct the bond prices, as was shown in Proposition 10.3.

### *Exercise 11.3*

Suppose a tree of forward rates is given as in Figure 11.8. Find the corresponding bond prices (using one-month steps).

The short rates are just special cases of forward rates,

$$r(n; s_n) = f(n, n; s_n)$$

for $n \geq 1$, with deterministic $r(0) = f(0,0)$. The short rates are also given by $r(n; s_n) = y(n, n+1; s_n)$, $n \geq 1$, and $r(0) = y(0,1)$, that is, by the rates of return on a bond maturing at the next step. This is obvious from the relations between the forward rates and yields.

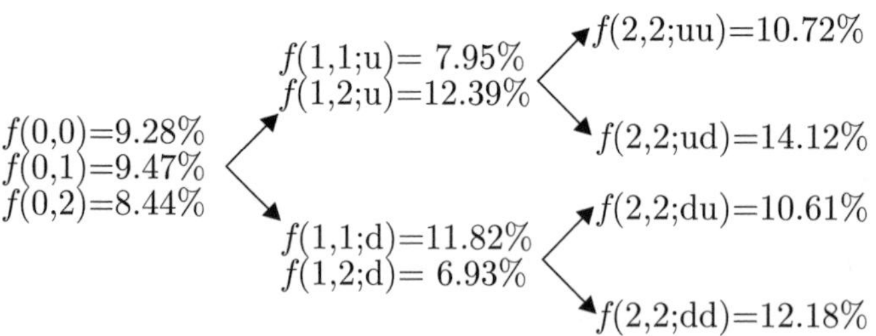


**Figure 11.8** Forward rates in Exercise 11.3

We are now ready to describe the money market account. It starts with $A(0) = 1$. The next value

$$A(1) = \exp(\tau r(0))$$

is still deterministic. It becomes random at subsequent steps. At time 2 there are two values depending on the states at time 1:

$$A(2; \mathrm{u}) = \exp(\tau(r(0) + r(1; \mathrm{u})) = A(1) \exp\{\tau r(1; \mathrm{u})\},$$
$$A(2; \mathrm{d}) = \exp(\tau(r(0) + r(1; \mathrm{d})) = A(1) \exp\{\tau r(1; \mathrm{d})\}.$$

Next, for example,

$$A(3; \mathrm{ud}) = \exp(\tau(r(0) + r(1; \mathrm{u}) + r(2; \mathrm{ud})) = A(2; \mathrm{u}) \exp\{\tau r(2; \mathrm{ud})\}.$$

In general,

$$A(n+1; s_{n-1}\mathrm{u}) = A(n; s_{n-1}) \exp\{\tau r(n; s_{n-1}\mathrm{u})\},$$
$$A(n+1; s_{n-1}\mathrm{d}) = A(n; s_{n-1}) \exp\{\tau r(n; s_{n-1}\mathrm{d})\}.$$

*Exercise 11.4*

Find the evolution of the money market account if the forward rates are the same as in Exercise 11.3.

For bond investments the money market account plays the same role as the risk-free component of investment strategies on the stock market in earlier chapters. It is used to discount future cash flows when valuing bonds and derivative securities, as will be shown below.

## 11.2 Arbitrage Pricing of Bonds

Suppose that we are given the binomial tree of bond prices $B(n, N; s_n)$ for a bond maturing at the fixed time horizon $N$. In addition, we are given the money market process $A(n; s_{n-1})$. As was mentioned in the introduction to this chapter, the prices of other bonds cannot be completely arbitrary. We shall show that the prices $B(n, M; s_n)$ for $M < N$ can be replicated by means of bonds with maturity $N$ and the money market. As a consequence of the No-Arbitrage Principle, the prices of $B(n, M; s_n)$ will have to be equal to the values of the corresponding replicating strategies.

### Example 11.5

Consider the data in Example 11.1. At the first step the short rate is deterministic, being implied by the price $B(0, 1)$. The first two values of the money market account are $A(0) = 1$ and $A(1) = 1.01$. As the underlying instrument we take the bond maturing at time 3. The prices of this bond at time 0 and 1 are given in Figure 11.9, along with the prices of the bond maturing at time 2. We can find a portfolio $(x, y)$, with $x$ being the number of bonds of maturity 3

| | | |
|---|---|---|
| | | $B$(1,2;u)=0.9948<br>$B$(1,3;u)=0.9848 |
| $B$(0,2)=0.9828<br>$B$(0,3)=0.9726 | ↗<br>↘ | |
| | | $B$(1,2;d)=0.9907<br>$B$(1,3;d)=0.9808 |

**Figure 11.9** Bond prices from Example 11.1

and $y$ the position in the money market, such that the value of this portfolio matches the time 1 prices of the bond maturing at time 2. To this end we solve the following system of equations

$$0.9848x + 1.01y = 0.9948,$$
$$0.9808x + 1.01y = 0.9907,$$

obtaining $x = 1$ and $y \cong 0.0098$. The value of this portfolio at time 0 is $1 \times B(0, 3) + 0.0098 \times A(0) \cong 0.9824$, which is *not* equal to $B(0, 2)$. The prices in Figure 11.9 provide an arbitrage opportunity:

- Sell a bond maturing at time 2 for \$0.9828 and buy the portfolio constructed above for \$0.9824.
- Whatever happens at time 1, the value of the portfolio will be sufficient to buy the bond back, the initial balance \$0.0004 being the arbitrage profit.

The model in Example 11.1 turns out to be *inconsistent with the No-Arbitrage Principle* and has to be rectified. We can only adjust some of the future prices, since the present prices of all bonds are dictated by the market. It is easy to see that by taking $B(1,2;\mathrm{u}) = 0.9958$ with $B(1,2;\mathrm{d})$ unchanged, or by letting $B(1,2;\mathrm{d}) = 0.9913$ with $B(1,2;\mathrm{u})$ unchanged, we can eliminate the arbitrage opportunity. Of course, there are many other ways of repairing the model by a simultaneous change of both values of $B(1,2)$. Let us put $B(1,2;\mathrm{d}) = 0.9913$ and leave $B(1,2;\mathrm{u})$ unchanged. The rectified tree of bond prices is shown in Figure 11.10 and the corresponding yields in Figure 11.11.

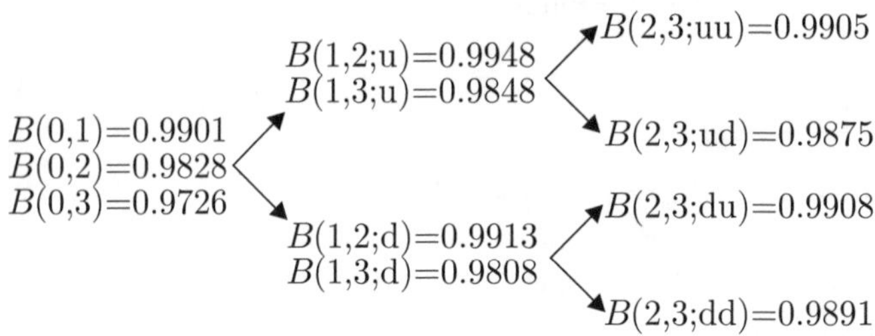


**Figure 11.10** Rectified tree of bond prices in Example 11.5

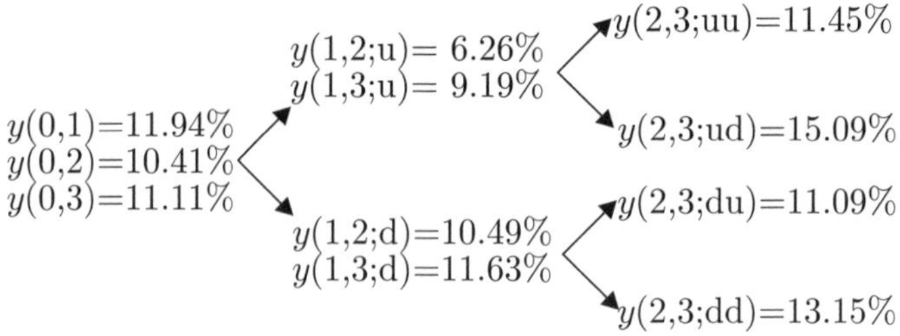


**Figure 11.11** Rectified tree of yields in Example 11.5

## Remark 11.2

The process of rectifying bond prices in Example 11.5 bears some resemblance to the pricing of general derivative securities described in Chapter 8. The role of the derivative security is played by the bond maturing at time 2. The bond maturing at time 3 plays the role of the underlying security. The difference is that the present price of the bond of maturity 2 is fixed and we can only adjust the future prices in the model to eliminate arbitrage. At this stage we are concerned only with building consistent models rather than with pricing securities.

### Exercise 11.5

Evaluate the prices of a bond maturing at time 2 given a tree of prices of a bond maturing at time 3 and short rates as shown in Figure 11.12, with $\tau = 1/12$.

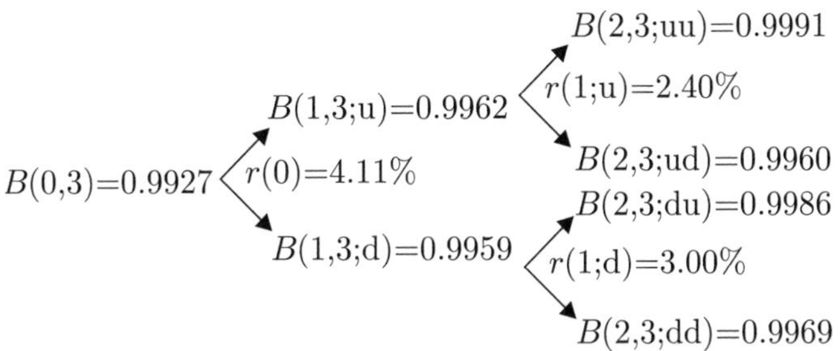


**Figure 11.12** Bond prices and short rates in Exercise 11.5

We can readily generalize Example 11.5. The underlying bond matures at time $N$ and we can find the structure of prices of any bond maturing at $M < N$. The replication proceeds backwards step-by-step starting from time $M$, for which $B(M, M; s_M) = 1$ in each state $s_M$. The first step is easy: for each state $s_{M-1}$ we take a portfolio with $x = 0$ and $y = 1/A(M; s_{M-1})$, since the bond becomes risk free one step prior to maturity.

Next, consider time $M-2$. For any state $s_{M-2}$ we find $x = x(M-1; s_{M-2})$, the number of bonds maturing at $N$, and $y = y(M-1; s_{M-2})$, the position in the money market, by solving the system

$$xB(M-1, N; s_{M-2}\mathrm{u}) + yA(M-1; s_{M-2}) = B(M-1, M; s_{M-2}\mathrm{u}),$$
$$xB(M-1, N; s_{M-2}\mathrm{d}) + yA(M-1; s_{M-2}) = B(M-1, M; s_{M-2}\mathrm{d}).$$

In this way we can find the prices at time $M-2$ of the bond maturing at time $M$,

$$B(M-2, M; s_{M-3}\mathrm{u}) = xB(M-2, N; s_{M-3}\mathrm{u}) + yA(M-2; s_{M-3}),$$
$$B(M-2, M; s_{M-3}\mathrm{d}) = xB(M-2, N; s_{M-3}\mathrm{d}) + yA(M-2; s_{M-3}).$$

We can iterate the replication process moving backwards through the tree.

### Remark 11.3

Replication is possible if a no-arbitrage condition analogous to Condition 3.2 is satisfied for the binomial tree. Here the condition $u > r > d$ of Chapter 3 is replaced by

$$k(n,N;s_{n-1}\mathrm{u}) > \tau r(n-1;s_{n-1}) > k(n,N;s_{n-1}\mathrm{d}). \tag{11.2}$$

Any future cash flow can be replicated in a similar fashion. Consider, for example, a coupon bond with fixed coupons.

## Example 11.6

Take a coupon bond maturing at time 2 with face value $F = 100$, paying coupons $C = 10$ at times 1 and 2. We price the future cash flow by using the zero-coupon bond maturing at time 3 as the underlying security. The coupon bond price $P$ at a particular time will not include the coupon due (the so-called ex-coupon price). Assume that the structure of the bond prices is as in Figure 11.10.

Consider time 1. In state u the short rate is determined by the price $B(1,2;\mathrm{u}) = 0.9948$, so we have $r(1;\mathrm{u}) \cong 6.26\%$. Hence $P(1;\mathrm{u}) \cong 109.43$. In state d we use $B(1,2;\mathrm{d}) = 0.9913$ to find $r(1;\mathrm{d}) \cong 10.49\%$ and $P(1;\mathrm{d}) \cong 109.04$.

Consider time 0. The cash flow at time 1 which we are to replicate includes the coupon due, so it is given by $P(1;\mathrm{u}) + 10 \cong 119.43$ and $P(1;\mathrm{d}) + 10 \cong 119.04$. The short rate $r(0) \cong 11.94\%$ determines the money market account as in Example 11.5, $A(1) = 1.01$, and we find $x \cong 96.25$, $y \cong 24.40$. Hence $P(0) \cong 118.01$ is the present price of the coupon bond.

An alternative is to use the spot yields: $y(0,1) \cong 11.94\%$ and $y(0,2) \cong 10.41\%$ to discount the future payments with the same result: $118.01 \cong 10 \times \exp(-\frac{1}{12} \times 11.94\%) + 110 \times \exp(-\frac{2}{12} \times 10.41\%)$.

In general,

$$\begin{aligned} P(0) &= C_1 \exp\{-\tau y(0,1)\} + C_2 \exp\{-2\tau y(0,2)\} \\ &\quad + \cdots + (C_N + F)\exp\{-N\tau y(0,N)\}. \end{aligned} \tag{11.3}$$

(For simplicity we include all time steps, so $C_k = 0$ at the time steps $k$ when no coupon is paid.) At each time $k$ when a coupon is paid, the cash flow is the sum of the (deterministic) coupon and the (stochastic) price of the remaining bond:

$$\begin{aligned} C_k + P(k;s_k) &= C_k + C_{k+1}\exp\{-\tau y(k,k+1;s_k)\} \\ &\quad + \cdots + (C_n + F)\exp\{-\tau(n-k)y(k,n;s_k)\}. \end{aligned}$$

Quite often the coupons depend on other quantities. In this way a coupon bond may become a derivative security. An important benchmark case is described below, where the coupons are computed as fractions of the face value.

These fractions, defining the *coupon rate*, are obtained by converting the short rate to an equivalent discrete compounding rate. In practice, when $\tau$ is one day, the coupon rate will be the overnight LIBOR rate.

### Proposition 11.1

A coupon bond maturing at time $N$ with random coupons

$$C_k(s_{k-1}) = (\exp\{\tau r(k-1; s_{k-1})\} - 1)F \tag{11.4}$$

for $0 < k \leq N$ is trading *at par*. (That is, the price $P(0)$ is equal to the face value $F$.)

### Proof

Fix time $N-1$ and a state $s_{N-1}$. In this state the value $P(N-1; s_{N-1})$ of the bond is $F + C_N(s_{N-1})$ discounted at the short rate, which gives $P(N-1; s_{N-1}) = F$ if the coupon is expressed by (11.4). Proceeding backwards through the tree and applying the same argument for each state, we finally arrive at $P(0) = F$. □

#### *Exercise 11.6*

Find the coupons of a bond trading at par and maturing at time 2, given the yields as in Example 11.5, see Figure 11.11.

## 11.2.1 Risk-Neutral Probabilities

In Chapter 3 we have learnt that the stock price $S(n)$ at time $n$ is equal to the expectation under the risk-neutral probability of the stock price $S(n+1)$ at time $n+1$ discounted to time $n$. The situation is similar in the binomial model of interest rates.

The discount factors are determined by the money market account, or, in other words, by the short rates. In general, they are random, being of the form $\exp\{-\tau r(n; s_n)\}$.

Suppose that state $s_n$ has occurred at time $n$. The short rate determining the time value of money for the next step is now known with certainty. Consider a bond maturing at time $N$ with $n < N-1$. We are given the bond price $B(n, N; s_n)$ and two possible values at the next step, $B(n+1, N; s_n\mathrm{u})$ and $B(n+1, N; s_n\mathrm{d})$. These values represent a random variable, which will be denoted by $B(n+1, N; s_n\cdot)$. If $n = N-1$, then the bond matures at the next step $N$, when it has just one price independent of the state, namely the face value. We are looking for a probability $p_*$ such that

$$B(n, N; s_n) = [p_* B(n+1, N; s_n\mathrm{u}) + (1-p_*) B(n+1, N; s_n\mathrm{d})] \times \exp\{-\tau r(n; s_n)\}. \tag{11.5}$$

This equation can be solved for $p_*$, which in principle depends on $n$, $N$ and $s_n$. (As will turn out soon, see Proposition 11.2, $p_*$ is in fact independent of maturity $N$.) Recalling the definition of logarithmic returns, we have

$$B(n+1, N; s_{n+1}) = B(n, N; s_n) \exp\{k(n+1, N; s_{n+1})\},$$

which gives

$$p_*(n, N; s_n) = \frac{\exp\{\tau r(n; s_n)\} - \exp\{k(n+1, N; s_n\mathrm{d})\}}{\exp\{k(n+1, N; s_n\mathrm{u})\} - \exp\{k(n+1, N; s_n\mathrm{d})\}}. \tag{11.6}$$

These numbers are called the *risk-neutral* or *martingale probabilities*. Condition (11.2) for the lack of arbitrage can now be written as

$$0 < p_*(n, N; s_n) < 1.$$

## Example 11.7

We shall find the tree of risk-neutral probabilities $p_*(n, 3; s_n)$ for $n = 0, 1$, using the rectified data in Example 11.5 (the bond prices as shown in Figure 11.10).

First we compute the returns on the money market. The simplest way is to use the yields (Figure 11.11). With $\tau = \frac{1}{12}$ we have $\tau r(n; s_n) = y(n, n+1; s_n)/12$, $n = 0, 1$, which gives the following values:

$$\begin{array}{lcl} & & \tau r(1;\mathrm{u}) = 0.521\% \\ \tau r(0) = 0.995\% & < & \\ & & \tau r(1;\mathrm{d}) = 0.874\% \end{array}$$

Next, we find the returns $k(1, 3; s_1)$ and $k(2, 3; s_2)$ on bonds. For example, if $s_2 = \mathrm{ud}$, then $k(2, 3; \mathrm{ud}) = \ln(\frac{0.9875}{0.9848})$. The results are collected below:

$$\begin{array}{llcl} & & & k(2,3;\mathrm{uu}) = 0.58\% \\ & k(1,3;\mathrm{u}) = 1.25\% & < & \\ / & & & k(2,3;\mathrm{ud}) = 0.27\% \\ & & & \\ \backslash & & & k(2,3;\mathrm{du}) = 1.01\% \\ & k(1,3;\mathrm{d}) = 0.84\% & < & \\ & & & k(2,3;\mathrm{dd}) = 0.84\% \end{array}$$

We can see that the no-arbitrage conditions are satisfied: $0.84\% < 0.99\% < 1.25\%$, $0.27\% < 0.52\% < 0.58\%$ and $0.84\% < 0.87\% < 1.01\%$.

Finally, we find the desired probabilities by a direct application of (11.6): $p_*(0) = 0.3813$, $p_*(1;\mathrm{u}) = 0.8159$, $p_*(1;\mathrm{d}) = 0.1811$, see Figure 11.13.

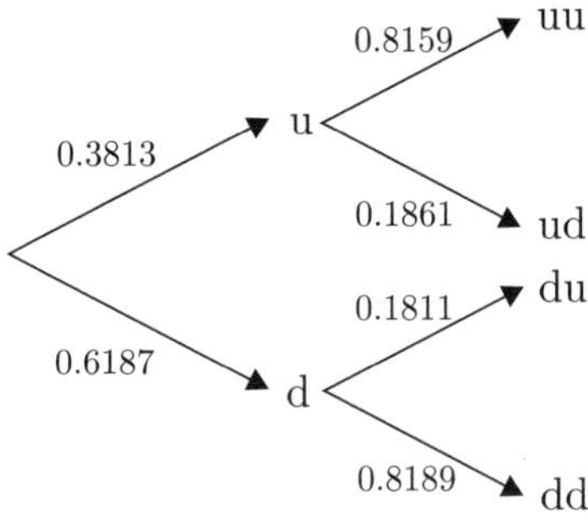


**Figure 11.13** Risk-neutral probabilities in Example 11.7

A crucial observation about the model is this: Pricing via replication is equivalent to pricing by means of the risk-neutral probability. This follows from the No-Arbitrage Principle and applies to any cash flow, even a random one, where the amounts depend on the states. This opens a way to pricing absolutely any security by means of the expectation with respect to the probabilities $p_*(n, N; s_n)$. The expectation is computed step-by-step, starting at the last one and proceeding backwards through the tree.

## Example 11.8

Consider a coupon bond maturing at $N = 2$ with face value $F = 100$ and with coupons equal to 5% of the current value of the bond, paid at times 1 and 2. In particular, the coupon at maturity is $C_2 = 5$ in each state. Using the risk-neutral probabilities from Example 11.7, we can find the bond values at time 1. In the up state we have the discounted value of 105 due at maturity using the short rate $r(1;\mathrm{u}) \cong 6.26\%$, which gives 104.4540. In the same way in the down state we obtain 104.0865. Now we add 5% coupons, so the amounts due at time 1 become 109.6767 in the up state and 109.2908 in the down state. Using the risk-neutral probabilities, we find the present value of the bond: $108.3545 \cong (0.3813 \times 109.6767 + 0.6187 \times 109.2908)/1.01$.

### *Exercise 11.7*

Use the risk-neutral probabilities in Example 11.7 to find the present value of the following random cash flow: At time 2 we receive \$20 in the state uu, \$10 in the states ud and du, and nothing in the state dd. No payments are due at other times.

### *Exercise 11.8*

Find an arbitrage opportunity for the bond prices in Figure 11.14.

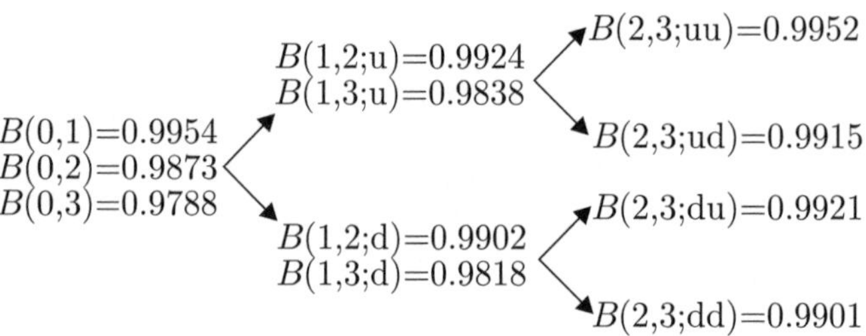


**Figure 11.14** Bond prices in Exercise 11.8

### *Exercise 11.9*

Suppose that the risk-neutral probabilities are equal to $\frac{1}{2}$ in every state. Given the following short rates, find the prices of a bond maturing at time 3 (with a one-month time step, $\tau = \frac{1}{12}$):

$$
\begin{array}{ccccc}
 & & & & r(2;\mathrm{uu}) = 8.3\% \\
 & & r(1;\mathrm{u}) = 8.5\% & < & \\
 & / & & & r(2;\mathrm{ud}) = 8.9\% \\
r(0) = 9.5\% & & & & \\
 & \backslash & & & r(2;\mathrm{du}) = 9.1\% \\
 & & r(1;\mathrm{d}) = 9.8\% & < & \\
 & & & & r(2;\mathrm{dd}) = 9.3\%
\end{array}
$$

The next proposition gives an important result, which simplifies the model significantly.

## Proposition 11.2

The lack of arbitrage implies that the risk-neutral probabilities are independent of maturity.

### Proof

Consider two bonds with maturities $M \leq N$ and fix an $n \leq M$. For each of the two bonds we have

$$
\begin{aligned}
B(n, M; s_n) &= [p_*(n, M; s_n) B(n+1, M; s_n\mathrm{u}) + (1 - p_*(n, M; s_n)) \\
&\qquad \times B(n+1, M; s_n\mathrm{d})] \exp\{-\tau r(n; s_n)\}, \qquad (11.7) \\
B(n, N; s_n) &= [p_*(n, N; s_n) B(n+1, N; s_n\mathrm{u}) + (1 - p_*(n, N; s_n)) \\
&\qquad \times B(n+1, N; s_n\mathrm{d})] \exp\{-\tau r(n; s_n)\}. \qquad (11.8)
\end{aligned}
$$

Our goal is to show that $p_*(n, M; s_n) = p_*(n, N; s_n)$ in any state $s_n$.

We can replicate the prices of the bond maturing at time $M$ by means of the bond with maturity $N$ and the money market account. Hence we find numbers $x$, $y$ such that

$$
\begin{aligned}
B(n+1, M; s_n\mathrm{u}) &= xB(n+1, N; s_n\mathrm{u}) + yA(n+1; s_n), \\
B(n+1, M; s_n\mathrm{d}) &= xB(n+1, N; s_n\mathrm{d}) + yA(n+1; s_n).
\end{aligned}
$$

The No-Arbitrage Principle implies that equalities of this kind must also hold at time $n$,

$$
\begin{aligned}
B(n, M; s_{n-1}\mathrm{u}) &= xB(n, N; s_{n-1}\mathrm{u}) + yA(n; s_{n-1}), \\
B(n, M; s_{n-1}\mathrm{d}) &= xB(n, N; s_{n-1}\mathrm{d}) + yA(n; s_{n-1}).
\end{aligned}
$$

Inserting the values of the $M$-bonds into (11.7) and using the formula for the money market account, after some algebraic transformations we obtain

$$
\begin{aligned}
B(n, N; s_n) &= [p_*(n, M; s_n) B(n+1, N; s_n\mathrm{u}) + (1 - p_*(n, M; s_n)) \\
&\qquad \times B(n+1, N; s_n\mathrm{d})] \exp\{-\tau r(n; s_n)\}.
\end{aligned}
$$

This can be solved for $p_*(n, M; s_n)$. It turns out that the solution coincides with the probability $p_*(n, N; s_n)$ implied by (11.8), as claimed. □

*Exercise 11.10*

Spot an arbitrage opportunity if the bond prices are as in Figure 11.15.

## 11.3 Interest Rate Derivative Securities

The tools introduced above make it possible to price any derivative security based on interest rates or, equivalently, on bond prices. Within the binomial tree

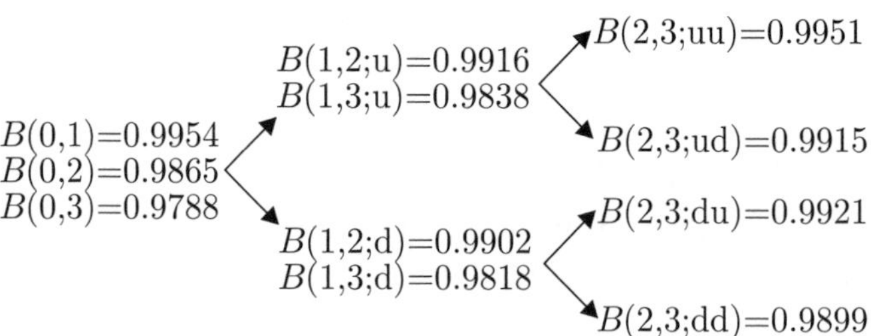


**Figure 11.15** Data for Exercise 11.10

model the cash flow associated with the derivative security can be replicated using the money market account and a bond with sufficiently long maturity. The bond does not even have to be the underlying security, since the prices of various bonds must be consistent. An alternative is to use the risk-neutral probabilities. The latter approach is often preferable to replication because of its simplicity. The equivalence of both methods should be clear in view of what has been said before.

The pricing of complex securities can essentially be reduced to finding the associated cash flows. Below we present examples of some classical interest rate contingent claims. We begin with the simplest case of options.

### 11.3.1 Options

The underlying securities for interest rate options are bonds of various kinds.

#### Example 11.9

With the bond prices as in Example 11.5 (Figure 11.10), consider a call option with exercise time 2 and strike price $X = 0.99$ on a zero-coupon bond maturing at time 3. Starting with the final payoffs shown in the last column in the table below, we move back step-by-step, computing the risk-neutral expectations of the consecutive values discounted by the appropriate short rates:

| $n = 0$ | | $n = 1$ | | $n = 2$ |
|---|---|---|---|---|
| | | | | 0.0005 |
| | | 0.00041 | < | |
| | / | | | 0 |
| 0.00024 | | | | |
| | \ | | | 0.0008 |
| | | 0.00014 | < | |
| | | | | 0 |

As a result, the price of the option is 0.00024.

### *Exercise 11.11*

Assume the structure of bond prices in Example 11.5 (Figure 11.10). Consider a coupon bond maturing at time 2 with face value $F = 100$ and coupons $C = 1$ payable at each step. Find the price of an American call option expiring at time 2 with strike price $X = 101.30$. (Include the coupon in the bond price at each step.)

Call options on bonds can be used by institutions issuing bonds to include the possibility of buying the bond back prior to maturity for a prescribed price. A bond that carries such a provision is called a *callable bond*. Its price should be reduced by the price of the attached option.

## 11.3.2 Swaps

Writing and selling a bond is a method of borrowing money. In the case of a coupon bond trading at par the principal represents the sum borrowed and the coupons represent the interest. This interest may be fixed or floating (variable). The interest is fixed if all coupons are the same. Floating interest can be realised in many ways. Here we assume that it is determined by the short rates as in (11.4). The basis for our discussion is laid by Proposition 11.1, according to which the market value of such a floating-coupon bond must be equal to its face value, the bond trading at par. For a fixed-coupon bond trading at par the size of the coupons can easily be found from (11.3). We could say that the resulting fixed coupon rate is equivalent to the variable short rate over the lifetime of the bond.

## Example 11.10

Consider a fixed-coupon bond and a floating-coupon bond, both with annual coupons, trading at par and maturing after two years with face value $F = 100$. Given that the tree of one- and two-year zero-coupon bond prices is

$$\begin{array}{ccc} & & B(1,2;\mathrm{u}) = 0.9101 \\ B(0,1) = 0.9123 & < & \\ B(0,2) = 0.8256 & & \\ & & B(1,2;\mathrm{d}) = 0.8987 \end{array}$$

where a time step is taken to be one year, $\tau = 1$, we can evaluate the coupons of the fixed- and floating-coupon bonds. The size of the floating coupons can be found from (11.4),

$$\begin{aligned} C_1 &= (B(0,1)^{-1} - 1)F \cong 9.6131, \\ C_2(\mathrm{u}) &= (B(1,2;\mathrm{u})^{-1} - 1)F \cong 9.8780, \\ C_2(\mathrm{d}) &= (B(1,2;\mathrm{d})^{-1} - 1)F \cong 11.2718. \end{aligned}$$

The fixed coupons $C$ can be found by solving equation (11.3), which takes the form

$$F = CB(0,1) + (C + F)B(0,2).$$

This gives

$$C \cong 10.0351.$$

By buying a fixed-coupon bond and selling a floating-coupon one (or the other way round, selling a fixed-coupon bond and buying a floating-coupon one) an investor can create an random cash flow with present value zero, since the two kinds of bond have the same initial price.

A company who has sold fixed-coupon bonds and is paying fixed interest may sometimes wish to switch into paying the floating rate instead. This can be realised by writing a floating-coupon bond and buying a fixed-coupon bond with the same present value. In practice, a financial intermediary will provide this service by offering a contract called a *swap*. Clearly, a swap of this kind will cost nothing to enter. Here is an example of a practical situation, where the role of the intermediary is to match the needs of two particular companies.

## Example 11.11

Suppose that company A wishes to borrow at a variable rate, whereas B prefers a fixed rate. Banks offer the following effective rates (that is, rates referring to annual compounding):

| | A | B |
|---|---|---|
| fixed | 11.40% | 13.40% |
| variable | LIBOR + 2% | LIBOR + 3% |

In this case we say that A has comparative advantage over B in the fixed rate, with B having comparative advantage over A in the variable rate. (Notwithstanding the fact that the overall credit rating of A is better, as reflected by the lower interest rates offered.) In these circumstances A should borrow at the fixed rate, B should borrow at the variable rate, and they can swap their interest payments.

Consider a principal of \$100,000 borrowed for one year and suppose that LIBOR is 10% and (just for simplicity) remains the same during the first year of the loan. If A borrows at the variable rate and B at the fixed rate, then the total interest paid will be \$25,400 between them. However, if A borrows at the fixed rate and B at the variable rate, the interest payments will be only \$24,400 in total. The difference of \$1,000 will be available to share between the two companies if they arrange to swap the rates. (In practice, this amount would be reduced by a fee charged by the intermediary arranging the deal.) If LIBOR changes to 9%, say, in the second year of the loan, so will the total interest payable, but the difference will remain at \$1,000.

How should this difference be shared between the two companies? To answer the question, we assume the term structure of interest rates determined by the prices of one- and two-year zero-coupon bonds in Example 11.10. In particular, we can identify LIBOR with the effective short rate implied by the bond prices, $B(0,1)^{-1} - 1$ in year one and $B(1,2)^{-1} - 1$ in year two. These are the same rates as those implied by the floating coupons in Example 11.10. The fixed coupons in the same example imply a rate of 10.04%.

Instead of swapping interest payments with B, company A would achieve the same result by taking a loan of \$100,000 at the fixed rate of 11.40% offered by the bank, buying 1,000 of the fixed-coupon bonds, and writing 1,000 of the floating-coupon bonds considered in Example 11.10. As a result, company A will have borrowed \$100,000 at the rate 11.40% − 10.04% + LIBOR = LIBOR + 1.36%. Compared to the variable rate of LIBOR + 2% offered to company A, this is a gain of 0.64%. On a \$100,000 loan this would mean a gain of \$640 in each year.

By a similar argument, instead of swapping with A, company B could borrow \$100,000 at the variable rate LIBOR + 3%, buy 1,000 floating-coupon bonds and write 1,000 fixed-coupon bonds. As a result, B would pay interest at LIBOR + 3% − LIBOR + 10.04% = 13.04%, a gain of 0.36% as compared to the fixed rate of 13.40% it was offered. This means a gain of \$360 in each year on an \$100,000 loan.

The result is that the \$1,000 gain should be shared as \$640 and \$360 between companies A and B.

Finally, note that the value of the swap may vary with time and state, departing from the initial value of zero. If a company wishes to enter into a swap agreement at a later time, it may purchase a *swaption*, which is a call option on the value of the swap (with prescribed strike price and expiry time).

### 11.3.3 Caps and Floors

A *cap* is a provision attached to a variable-rate bond which specifies the maximum coupon rate paid in each period over the lifetime of a loan. A *caplet* is a similar provision applied to a particular single period. In other words, a caplet is a European option on the level of interest paid or received. A cap can be thought of as a series of caplets.

#### Example 11.12

We take a loan by selling a par floating-coupon bond maturing at time 2. (That is, a bond which always has the par value, the coupons being implied by the short rates as in (11.4).) We use the bond prices and rates in Example 11.5, see Figures 11.10 and 11.11. The cash flow shown below includes the initial amount received for selling the bond together with the coupons and face value to be paid:

| $n=0$ | | $n=1$ | | $n=2$ |
|---|---|---|---|---|
| | | $-0.99990$ | — | $-100.52272$ |
| 100 | $<$ | | | |
| | | $-0.99990$ | — | $-100.87764$ |

Consider a caplet that applies at time 1 (one month) with strike interest rate of 8% (corresponding to 0.67% for a one-month period). The coupon determined by the caplet rate is 0.66889 and we modify the cash flow accordingly. At time 0 we find the bond price by discounting its time 1 value, 100.66889 in each state, that is 100 plus the coupon. This gives the following cash flow:

| $n=0$ | | $n=1$ | | $n=2$ |
|---|---|---|---|---|
| | | $-0.66889$ | — | $-100.52272$ |
| 99.67227 | $<$ | | | |
| | | $-0.66889$ | — | $-100.87764$ |

The price of the bond is reduced by the value of the caplet, that is, by 0.32773.

For a caplet at time 2 with the same strike rate the maximum size of the coupon is 0.66889, as before. In the up state we pay the original interest, exercising the caplet in the down state. The value of the bond at time 1 is not 100, since the final coupons are no longer the same as for the par bond. The time 1 prices are obtained by discounting the time 2 values. At time 0 we find the bond price by evaluating the risk-neutral expectation of the discounted values of the bond at time 1. The resulting cash flow is

| $n = 0$ | | $n = 1$ | | $n = 2$ |
|---|---|---|---|---|
| | | $-0.99990$ | — | $-100.52272$ |
| 99.87323 | < | | | |
| | | $-0.99990$ | — | $-100.66889$ |

This fixes the price of this caplet at 0.12677.

Finally, consider a cap for both times 1 and 2 with the same strike rate as above. The cash flow can be obtained in a similar manner:

| $n = 0$ | | $n = 1$ | | $n = 2$ |
|---|---|---|---|---|
| | | $-0.66889$ | — | $-100.52272$ |
| 99.54550 | < | | | |
| | | $-0.66889$ | — | $-100.66889$ |

We can see that the value of the cap, 0.45450, is the sum of the values of the caplets.

Analogously, a *floor* is a provision limiting the coupon from below. This will be of value for a bond holder. It is composed from a series of *floorlets*, each referring to a single period.

### *Exercise 11.12*

In the framework of the above example, value a floor expiring at time 2 with strike rate 8%, based on the bond prices in Example 11.5.

## 11.4 Final Remarks

We conclude this chapter with some informal remarks on possible ways in which models of the structure of bond prices can be built. This is a complex area and all we can do here is to make some general comments.

As we have seen, the theory of interest rates is more complicated than the theory of stock prices. In order to be able to price interest rate derivatives, we need a model of possible movements of bond prices for each maturity. The bond prices with different maturities have to be consistent with each other. As we have seen above, the specification of

a) a model of possible short rates,

b) a model of possible values of a bond with the longest maturity (consistent with the initial term structure)

determines the structure of possible prices of all bonds maturing earlier. An alternative approach is to specify

a) a model of possible short rates,

b) the probabilities at each state,

and, taking these probabilities as risk-neutral ones, to compute the prices of all bonds for all maturities. The latter method is conceptually simpler, especially if we take the same probability in each state. The flexibility of short rate modelling allows us to obtain sufficiently many models consistent with the initial term structure.

If so, the simplest choice of probability $1/2$ at each state of the binomial tree appears to be as good as any, and we can focus on constructing short rate models so that their parameters are consistent with historical data. A general short-rate model in discrete time can be described as follows. Let $t_n = n\tau$. Then the following relations specify a tree of the rate movements

$$r(t_{n+1}) - r(t_n) = \mu(t_n, r(t_n))\tau + \sigma(t_n, r(t_n))\xi_n$$

where $\xi_n = \pm 1$ with probability $1/2$ each, and $\mu(t,r)$, $\sigma(t,r)$ are suitably chosen functions. In the continuous time limit (in the spirit of Section 3.3.2) these relations lead to a stochastic differential equation of the form

$$\mathrm{d}r(t) = \mu(t, r(t))\mathrm{d}t + \sigma(t, r(t))\mathrm{d}w(t).$$

There are many ways in which the functions $\mu$ and $\sigma$ can be specified, but none of them is universally accepted. Here are just a few examples: $\mu(t,r) = b - ar$, $\sigma(t,r) = \sigma$ (Vasiček model), $\mu(t,r) = a(b-r)$, $\sigma(t,r) = \sigma\sqrt{r}$ (Cox–Ingersoll–Ross model), or $\mu(t,r) = \theta(t)r$, $\sigma(t,r) = \sigma r$ (Black–Derman–Toy model).

Given the short-rates, the next step is to compute the bond prices. These will depend on the functions $\mu$ and $\sigma$. Two problems may be encountered:

1. The model is too crude, for example these functions are just constants. Then we may not be able to adjust them so that the resulting bond prices agree with the initial term structure.

2. The model is too complicated, for example we take absolutely general functions $\mu$, $\sigma$. Fitting the initial term structure imposes some constraints on the parameters, but many are left free and the result is too general to be of any practical use.

These problems can be avoided if some middle-of-the-road solution is adopted.

Yet another alternative is to specify the dynamics of the entire curve of forward rates. This determines the time evolution of the term structure, with the initial term structure playing the role of initial data. This sounds conceptually simple, but the model (the Heath–Jarrow–Morton model in continuous time setting) is mathematically complex.

The literature on the subject is vast and expanding. We recommend that the reader interested in pursuing this topic should look, for example, at Pliska (1997), and Jarrow (1995) for the discrete time setting, or Björk (1998) and Chen (1996) for continuous time models.

# Solutions

## Chapter 1

**1.1** The value of the portfolio at time 0 is

$$V(0) = xS(0) + yA(0) = 1,600$$

dollars. The value of the portfolio at time 1 will be

$$V(1) = xS(1) + yA(1) = \begin{cases} 1,800 & \text{if stock goes up,} \\ 1,700 & \text{if stock goes down.} \end{cases}$$

Hence, the return on the portfolio will be

$$K_V = \frac{V(1) - V(0)}{V(0)} = \begin{cases} 0.1250 & \text{if stock goes up,} \\ 0.0625 & \text{if stock goes down,} \end{cases}$$

that is, either 12.5% or 6.25%.

**1.2** Given the same bond and stock prices as in Exercise 1.1, the value of a portfolio $(x, y)$ at time 1 will be

$$V(1) = \begin{cases} x30 + y100 & \text{if stock goes up,} \\ x20 + y100 & \text{if stock goes down.} \end{cases}$$

Thus, we obtain a system of equations

$$\begin{cases} x30 + y100 = 1,160, \\ x20 + y100 = 1,040. \end{cases}$$

The solution is $x = 12$ and $y = 8$. A portfolio with 12 shares of stock and 8 bonds will produce the desired value at time 1. The time 0 value of this portfolio is

$$V(0) = 12 \times 25 + 8 \times 90 = 1,020$$

dollars.

**1.3** An arbitrage opportunity can be realised as follows:

- Use dealer $A$ to change 1 dollar into $\frac{1}{1.5844} \cong 0.6312$ pounds.
- Use dealer $B$ to change 0.6312 pounds into $\frac{0.6312}{0.6401} \cong 0.9861$ euros.
- Use dealer $A$ to change 0.9861 euros into $0.9861 \times 1.0202 \cong 1.0060$ dollars.

The arbitrage gain will be about 0.0060 dollars.

**1.4** We want both $xS(0)$ and $yA(0)$ to be equal to a half of the initial wealth. This gives $x80 = 5,000$ and $y100 = 5,000$, so $x = 62.5$ and $y = 50$. The value of this portfolio at time 1 will be

$$V(1) = 62.5S(1) + 50A(1) = \begin{cases} 11,750 & \text{if stock goes up,} \\ 9,250 & \text{if stock goes down,} \end{cases}$$

and hence the return on this portfolio will be

$$K_V = \begin{cases} 0.175 & \text{if stock goes up,} \\ -0.075 & \text{if stock goes down.} \end{cases}$$

Now we can compute the expected return

$$E(K_V) = 0.175 \times 0.8 - 0.075 \times 0.2 = 0.125,$$

which is 12.5%, and the risk

$$\sigma_V = \sqrt{(0.175 - 0.125)^2 \times 0.8 + (-0.075 - 0.125)^2 \times 0.2} = 0.1,$$

that is, 10%.

**1.5** The following strategy will realise an arbitrage opportunity. At time 0:

- Borrow \$34.
- Buy a share of stock for \$34.
- Enter into a short forward contract with forward price \$38.60 and delivery date 1.

At time 1:

- Sell the stock for \$38.60, closing the short forward position.
- Pay $34 \times 1.12 = 38.08$ dollars to clear the loan with interest.

The balance of $38.60 - 38.08 = 0.52$ dollars will be your arbitrage profit.

**1.6** Suppose that a sterling bond promising to pay £100 at time 1 is selling for $x$ pounds at time 0. To find $x$ consider the following strategy. At time 0:

- Borrow $1.6x$ dollars and change the sum into $x$ pounds.
- Purchase a sterling bond for $x$ pounds.
- Take a short forward position to sell £100 for \$1.50 to a pound with delivery date 1.

Then, at time 1:

- Cash the bond, collecting £100.
- Close the short forward position by selling £100 for \$150.
- Repay the cash loan with interest, that is, $1.68x$ dollars in total.

The balance of all these transactions is $150 - 1.68x$ dollars, which must be equal to zero or else an arbitrage opportunity would arise. It follows that a sterling bond promising to pay £100 at time 1 must sell for $x = \frac{150}{1.68} \cong 89.29$ pounds at time 0.

**1.7** a) The payoff of a call option with strike price \$90 will be

$$C(1) = \begin{cases} 30 & \text{if stock goes up,} \\ 0 & \text{if stock goes down.} \end{cases}$$

The replicating investment into $x$ shares and $y$ bonds satisfies the system of equations

$$\begin{cases} x120 + y110 = 30, \\ x80 + y110 = \ \ 0. \end{cases}$$

The solution is $x = \frac{3}{4}$ and $y = -\frac{6}{11}$. Hence the price of the option must be

$$C(0) = \frac{3}{4} \times 100 - \frac{6}{11} \times 100 \cong 20.45$$

dollars.
b) The payoff of a call option with strike price \$110 will be

$$C(1) = \begin{cases} 10 & \text{if stock goes up,} \\ 0 & \text{if stock goes down.} \end{cases}$$

The replicating investment into $x$ shares and $y$ bonds satisfies

$$\begin{cases} x120 + y110 = 10, \\ x80 + y110 = \ \ 0. \end{cases}$$

Solving this system of equations, we find that $x = \frac{1}{4}$ and $y = -\frac{2}{11}$. Hence the price of the option is

$$C(0) = \frac{1}{4} \times 100 - \frac{2}{11} \times 100 \cong 6.82$$

dollars.

**1.8** a) The replicating investment into $x$ shares and $y$ bonds satisfies the system of equations

$$\begin{cases} x120 + y105 = 20, \\ x80 + y105 = \ \ 0, \end{cases}$$

which gives $x = \frac{1}{2}$ and $y = -\frac{8}{21}$. Hence

$$C(0) = \frac{1}{2} \times 100 - \frac{8}{21} \times 100 \cong 11.91$$

dollars.
b) In this case the replicating investment into $x$ shares and $y$ bonds satisfies

$$\begin{cases} x120 + y115 = 20, \\ x80 + y115 = \ \ 0, \end{cases}$$

so $x = \frac{1}{2}$ and $y = -\frac{8}{23}$. It follows that

$$C(0) = \frac{1}{2} \times 100 - \frac{8}{23} \times 100 \cong 15.22$$

dollars.

**1.9** We need to find an investment into $x$ shares and $y$ bonds replicating the put option, that is, such that $xS(1) + yA(1) = P(1)$, no matter whether the stock price goes up or down. This leads to the system of equations

$$\begin{cases} x120 + y110 = 0, \\ x80 + y110 = 20. \end{cases}$$

The solution is $x = -\frac{1}{2}$ and $y = \frac{6}{11}$. To replicate the put option we need to take a short position of $\frac{1}{2}$ a share in stock and to buy $\frac{6}{11}$ of a bond. The value of this investment at time 0 is

$$xS(0) + yA(0) = -\frac{1}{2} \times 100 + \frac{6}{11} \times 100 \cong 4.55$$

dollars. By a similar argument as in Proposition 1.3, it follows that $xS(0) + yA(0) = P(0)$, or else an arbitrage opportunity would arise. Therefore, the price of the put must be $P(0) \cong 4.55$ dollars.

**1.10** The investor will buy $\frac{500}{100} = 5$ shares and $\frac{500}{13.6364} \cong 36.6667$ options. Her final wealth will then be $5 \times S(1) + 36.6667 \times C(1)$, that is, $5 \times 120 + 36.6667 \times 20 \cong 1,333.33$ dollars if the price of stock goes up to \$120, or $5 \times 80 + 36.6667 \times 0 \cong 400.00$ dollars if it drops to \$80.

**1.11** a) If $p = 0.25$, then the standard deviation of the cost of buying one share is about 51.96 dollars when no option is purchased and about 25.98 dollars with the option.
b) If $p = 0.5$, then the standard deviation is 60 dollars and 30 dollars, respectively.
c) For $p = 0.75$ the standard deviation is about 51.96 dollars and 25.98 dollars, respectively.

**1.12** The standard deviation of a random variable taking values $a$ and $b$ with probabilities $p$ and $1-p$, respectively, is $|a-b|\sqrt{p(1-p)}$. If no option is involved, then the cost of buying one share will be 160 or 40 dollars, depending on whether stock goes up or down. In this case $|a-b| = |160-40| = 120$ dollars. If one option is used, then the cost will be 135 or 75 dollars, and $|a-b| = |135-75| = 60$ dollars. Clearly, the standard deviation $|a-b|\sqrt{p(1-p)}$ will be reduced by a half, no matter what $p$ is.

## Chapter 2

**2.1** The rate $r$ satisfies

$$\left(1 + \frac{61}{365} \times r\right) \times 9,000 = 9,020.$$

This gives $r \cong 0.0133$, that is, about 1.33%. The return on this investment will be

$$K(0, \frac{61}{365}) = \frac{9,020 - 9,000}{9,000} \cong 0.0022,$$

that is, about 0.22%.

**2.2** Denote the amount to be paid today by $P$. Then the return will be

$$\frac{1,000 - P}{P} = 0.02.$$

The solution is $P \cong 980.39$ dollars.

**2.3** The time $t$ satisfies

$$(1 + t \times 0.09) \times 800 = 830,$$

which gives $t \cong 0.4167$ years, that is, $0.4167 \times 365 \cong 152.08$ days. The return will be

$$K(0,t) = \frac{830 - 800}{800} = 0.0375,$$

that is, 3.75%.

**2.4** The principal $P$ to be invested satisfies

$$\left(1 + \frac{91}{365} \times 0.08\right) \times P = 1,000,$$

which gives $P \cong 980.44$ dollars.

**2.5** The time $t$ when the future value will be double the initial principal satisfies the equation

$$\left(1 + \frac{0.06}{365}\right)^{365t} = 2.$$

The solution is $t \cong 11.5534$ years. Because no interest will be paid for a fraction of the last day, this needs to be rounded up to a whole number of days, which gives 11 years and 202 days. (We disregard leap years and assume for simplicity that each year has 365 days.)

**2.6** The interest rate $r$ satisfies the equation

$$(1 + r)^{10} = 2,$$

which gives $r \cong 0.0718$, that is, about 7.18%.

**2.7** a) In the case of annual compounding the value after two years will be

$$V(2) = \left(1 + \frac{0.1}{1}\right)^{2\times 1} 100 = 121.00$$

dollars.

b) Under semi-annual compounding the value will be

$$V(2) = \left(1 + \frac{0.1}{2}\right)^{2\times 2} 100 \cong 121.55$$

dollars, which is clearly greater than in case a).

**2.8** At 15% compounded daily the deposit will grow to

$$\left(1 + \frac{0.15}{365}\right)^{1\times 365} 1,000 \cong 1,161.80$$

dollars after one year. If interest is compounded semi-annually at 15.5%, the value after one year will be

$$\left(1 + \frac{0.155}{2}\right)^{1\times 2} 1,000 \cong 1,161.01$$

dollars, which is less than in the former case.

**2.9** The initial principal $P$ satisfies the equation

$$(1+0.12)^2\,P = 1,000.$$

It follows that $P \cong 797.19$ dollars.

**2.10** a) Under daily compounding the present value is

$$100,000\left(1+\frac{0.05}{365}\right)^{-100\times 365} \cong 674.03$$

dollars.
b) If annual compounding applies, then the present value is

$$100,000\,(1+0.05)^{-100} \cong 760.45$$

dollars.

**2.11** The return will be

$$K(0,1) = \left(1+\frac{0.1}{12}\right)^{12} - 1 \cong 0.1047,$$

that is, about 10.47%.

**2.12** Using the binomial formula to expand the $m$th power, we obtain

$$\begin{aligned} K(0,1) &= (1+\frac{r}{m})^m - 1 \\ &= 1 + r + \frac{(1-\frac{1}{m})}{2!}r^2 + \cdots + \frac{(1-\frac{m-1}{m})}{m!}r^m - 1 > r \end{aligned}$$

if $m$ is an integer greater than 1.

**2.13** Denote the interest rate by $r$, the amount borrowed by $P$ and the amount of each instalment by $C$,

$$C = \frac{P}{\mathrm{PA}(r,5)} = \frac{Pr}{1-(1+r)^{-5}},$$

see Example 2.4. Let $n = 1$, 2, 3, 4 or 5. The present value of the outstanding balance after $n-1$ instalments are paid is equal to the amount borrowed reduced by the present value of the first $n-1$ instalments:

$$P - \frac{C}{1+r} - \cdots - \frac{C}{(1+r)^{n-1}} = P\frac{(1+r)^{6-n}-1}{(1+r)^5-1}.$$

The actual outstanding balance remaining after $n-1$ instalments are paid can be found by dividing the above by the discount factor $(1+r)^{-(n-1)}$, which gives

$$P\frac{(1+r)^5-(1+r)^{n-1}}{(1+r)^5-1}. \tag{S.1}$$

The interest included in the $n$th instalment is, therefore,

$$P\frac{(1+r)^5-(1+r)^{n-1}}{(1+r)^5-1}r. \tag{S.2}$$

The capital repaid as part of the $n$th instalment is the difference between the outstanding balance of the loan after the $(n-1)$st and after the $n$th instalment. By (S.1) this difference is equal to

$$P\frac{(1+r)^n-(1+r)^{n-1}}{(1+r)^5-1}=P\frac{r(1+r)^{n-1}}{(1+r)^5-1}. \tag{S.3}$$

Putting $P$ to be \$1,000 and $r$ to be 15% in (S.1), (S.2) and (S.3), we can compute the figures collected in the table:

| $t$ (years) | interest paid (\$) | capital repaid (\$) | outstanding balance (\$) |
|---|---|---|---|
| 0 | — | — | 1,000.00 |
| 1 | 150.00 | 148.32 | 851.68 |
| 2 | 127.75 | 170.56 | 681.12 |
| 3 | 102.17 | 196.15 | 484.97 |
| 4 | 72.75 | 225.57 | 259.40 |
| 5 | 38.91 | 259.40 | 0.00 |

**2.14** The amount you can afford to borrow is

$$\mathrm{PA}(18\%,10)\times 10,000=\frac{1-(1+0.18)^{-10}}{0.18}\times 10,000\cong 44,941$$

dollars.

**2.15** The present value of the balance after 40 years is

$$\mathrm{PA}(5\%,40)\times 1,200=\frac{1-(1+0.05)^{-40}}{0.05}\times 1,200\cong 20,591$$

dollars. Dividing by the discount factor $(1+0.05)^{-40}$, we find that the actual balance after 40 years will be

$$\frac{20,591}{(1+0.05)^{-40}}\cong 144,960$$

dollars.

**2.16** The annual payments will amount to

$$C=\frac{100,000}{PA(6\%,10)}\cong 13,586.80$$

dollars each. The outstanding balance to be paid to clear the mortgage after 8 years (once the 8th annual payment is made) will be

$$\mathrm{PA}(6\%,2)\times C\cong 24,909.93$$

dollars.

**2.17** Suppose that payments $C, C(1+g), C(1+g)^2,\ldots$ are made after 1 year, 2 years, 3 years, and so on. If the interest rate is constant and equal to $r$, then the present values of these payments are $C(1+r)^{-1}, C(1+g)(1+r)^{-2}, C(1+g)^2(1+r)^{-3},\ldots$ . The present value of the infinite stream of payments is, therefore,

$$\frac{C}{1+r}+\frac{C(1+g)}{(1+r)^2}+\frac{C(1+g)^2}{(1+r)^3}+\cdots=\frac{C}{r-g}.$$

The condition $g < r$ must be satisfied or otherwise the series will be divergent. Using this formula and the tail-cutting procedure, we can find that for a stream of $n$ payments

$$\frac{C}{r-g} - \frac{C(1+g)^n}{r-g}\frac{1}{(1+r)^n} = C\frac{1-\left(\frac{1+g}{1+r}\right)^n}{r-g}.$$

**2.18** The time $t$ it will take to earn \$1 in interest satisfies

$$e^{0.1t} \times 1,000,000 \cong 1,000,001.$$

This gives $t \cong 0.00001$ years, that is, 315.36 seconds.

**2.19** a) The value in year 2000 of the sum of \$24 for which Manhattan was bought in 1626 would be

$$24e^{(2000-1626)\times 0.05} \cong 3,173,350,575$$

dollars, assuming continuous compounding at 5%.
b) The same amount compounded at 5% annually would be worth

$$24(1+0.05)^{2000-1626} \cong 2,018,408,628$$

dollars in year 2000.

**2.20** \$100 deposited at 10% compounded continuously will become

$$100e^{0.1} \cong 110.52$$

dollars after one year. The same amount deposited at 10% compounded monthly will become

$$100\left(1+\frac{0.1}{12}\right)^{12} \cong 110.47$$

dollars. The difference is about \$0.05.

If the difference is to be less than \$0.01, the compounding frequency $m$ should satisfy

$$100\left(1+\frac{0.1}{m}\right)^{m} > 110.51.$$

This means that $m$ should be greater than about 55.19.

**2.21** The present value is

$$1,000,000e^{-20\times 0.06} \cong 301,194$$

dollars.

**2.22** The rate $r$ satisfies

$$950e^{0.5r} = 1,000.$$

It follows that

$$r = \frac{1}{0.5}\ln\frac{1,000}{950} \cong 0.1026,$$

that is, about 10.26%.

**2.23** The interest rate is

$$r = \frac{0.03}{2/12} = 0.18,$$

that is, 18%.

**2.24** The rate $r$ satisfies

$$e^r = \left(1 + \frac{0.12}{12}\right)^{12}.$$

The solution is $r \cong 0.1194$, about 11.94%.

**2.25** The frequency $m$ satisfies

$$\left(1 + \frac{0.2}{m}\right)^m = 1 + 0.21.$$

Whence $m = 2.0$.

**2.26** If monthly compounding at a rate $r$ applies, then $\left(1 + \frac{r}{12}\right)^{12} = 1 + r_e$ and the present value of the annuity is

$$\begin{aligned} V(0) &= \frac{C}{1 + \frac{r}{12}} + \frac{C}{\left(1 + \frac{r}{12}\right)^2} + \cdots + \frac{C}{\left(1 + \frac{r}{12}\right)^{12n}} \\ &= \frac{C}{(1 + r_e)^{1/12}} + \frac{C}{(1 + r_e)^{2/12}} + \cdots + \frac{C}{(1 + r_e)^n} \\ &= C\frac{1 - (1 + r_e)^{-n}}{(1 + r_e)^{1/12} - 1}. \end{aligned}$$

**2.27** If bimonthly compounding at a rate $r$ applies, then $\left(1 + \frac{r}{6}\right)^6 = 1 + r_e$ and the present value of the perpetuity is

$$\begin{aligned} V(0) &= \frac{C}{1 + \frac{r}{6}} + \frac{C}{\left(1 + \frac{r}{6}\right)^2} + \frac{C}{\left(1 + \frac{r}{6}\right)^3} + \cdots \\ &= \frac{C}{(1 + r_e)^{1/6}} + \frac{C}{(1 + r_e)^{2/6}} + \frac{C}{(1 + r_e)^{3/6}} + \cdots \\ &= C\frac{1}{(1 + r_e)^{1/6} - 1}. \end{aligned}$$

**2.28** We solve the equation

$$100 = 95\,(1 + r)^{\frac{1}{2}}$$

for $r$ to find the implied effective rate to be about 10.80%. If this rate remains constant, then the bond price will reach \$99 at a time $t$ such that

$$100 = 99\,(1 + r)^{\left(\frac{1}{2} - t\right)}.$$

The solution is $t \cong 0.402$ years, that is, about $0.402 \times 365 \cong 146.73$ days. The bond price will reach \$99 on day 147.

**2.29** The interest rate for annual compounding implied by the bond can be found by solving the equation

$$(1 + r)^{-(1-0.5)} = 0.9455$$

for $r$. The solution is about 11.86%. By solving the equation

$$\left(1 + \frac{r}{2}\right)^{-2(1-0.5)} = 0.9455,$$

we obtain the semi-annual rate of about 11.53%, and solving

$$e^{-r(1-0.5)} = 0.9455,$$

we find the continuous rate to be about 11.21%.

**2.30** a) If the continuous compounding rate is 8%, then the price of the bond will be

$$5e^{-0.08} + 5e^{-2\times 0.08} + 5e^{-3\times 0.08} + 105e^{-4\times 0.08} \cong 89.06$$

dollars.

b) If the rate is 5%, then the price of the bond will be

$$5e^{-0.05} + 5e^{-2\times 0.05} + 5e^{-3\times 0.05} + 105e^{-4\times 0.05} \cong 99.55$$

dollars.

**2.31** The price of the bond as a function of the continuous compounding rate $r$ can be expressed as $5e^{-r} + 5e^{-2r} + 5e^{-3r} + 105e^{-4r}$. The graph of this function is shown in Figure S.1. When $r \searrow 0$, the price approaches $5 + 5 + 5 + 105 = 120$ dollars. In the limit as $r \nearrow \infty$ the price tends to zero.

**Figure S.1** Bond price versus interest rate in Exercise 2.31

**2.32** The time $t$ price of the coupon bond in Examples 2.9 and 2.10 is

$$\begin{array}{rl}
10e^{r(t-1)} + 10e^{r(t-2)} + 10e^{r(t-3)} + 10e^{r(t-4)} + 110e^{r(t-5)} & \text{if } 0 \le t < 1, \\
10e^{r(t-2)} + 10e^{r(t-3)} + 10e^{r(t-4)} + 110e^{r(t-5)} & \text{if } 1 \le t < 2, \\
10e^{r(t-3)} + 10e^{r(t-4)} + 110e^{r(t-5)} & \text{if } 2 \le t < 3, \\
10e^{r(t-4)} + 110e^{r(t-5)} & \text{if } 3 \le t < 4, \\
110e^{r(t-5)} & \text{if } 4 \le t < 5.
\end{array}$$

The graph is shown in Figure S.2.

**2.33** In Figure S.2 we can see that the bond price will reach \$95 for the first time during year one, when the bond price is given by $10e^{r(t-1)} + 10e^{r(t-2)} + 10e^{r(t-3)} + 10e^{r(t-4)} + 110e^{r(t-5)}$. Putting $r = 0.12$, we can find the desired time $t$ when the price will reach \$95 by solving the equation

$$10e^{r(t-1)} + 10e^{r(t-2)} + 10e^{r(t-3)} + 10e^{r(t-4)} + 110e^{r(t-5)} = 95.$$

This gives $t \cong 0.4257$ years or 155.4 days.

**2.34** Since the bond is trading at par, its initial price is the same as the face value $F = 100$. The implied continuous compounding rate $r$ can be found by solving the equation

$$8e^{-r} + 8e^{-2r} + 108e^{-3r} = 100.$$

This gives $r \cong 0.0770$ or 7.70%.

**Figure S.2** Coupon bond price versus time in Exercise 2.32

**2.35** By solving the equation

$$(1+r)^{-1} = 0.89$$

we find that $r \cong 0.1236$, that is, the effective rate implied by the bond is about 12.36%. The price of the bond after 75 days will be

$$B(75/365, 1) = B(0,1)(1+r)^{\frac{75}{365}} = 0.89\,(1+0.1236)^{\frac{75}{365}} \cong 0.9115$$

and the return will be

$$K(0, 75/365) = \frac{B(75/365,1) - B(0,1)}{B(0,1)} \cong \frac{0.9115 - 0.89}{0.89} \cong 0.0242,$$

about 2.42%.

**2.36** The initial price of a six-month unit bond is $e^{-0.5r}$, where $r$ denotes the implied continuous rate. If the bond is to produce a 7% return over six months, then

$$\frac{1 - e^{-0.5r}}{e^{-0.5r}} = 0.07,$$

which gives $r \cong 0.1353$, or 13.53%.

**2.37** The continuous rate implied by the bond satisfies

$$e^{-r} = 0.92.$$

The solution is $r \cong 0.0834$. At time $t$ the bond will be worth $0.92e^{rt}$. It will produce a 5% return at a time $t$ such that

$$\frac{0.92e^{rt} - 0.92}{0.92} = 0.05,$$

which gives $t \cong 0.5851$ years or 213.6 days.

**2.38** At time 0 we buy $1/B(0,1) = e^r$ bonds, at time 1 we increase our holdings to $e^r/B(1,2) = e^{2r}$ bonds, and generally at time $n$ we purchase $e^{(n+1)r}$ one-year bonds.

**2.39** Because the bond is trading at par and the interest rates remain constant, the price of the bond at the beginning of each year will be \$100. The sum of \$1,000 will buy 10 bonds at the beginning of year one. At the end of the year the coupons will pay $10 \times 8 = 80$ dollars, enough to buy 0.8 bonds at \$100 each. As a result, the investor will be holding $10 + 0.8 = 10.8$ bonds in year two. At the end of that year the coupons will pay $10.8 \times 8 = 86.4$ dollars and 0.864 additional bonds will be purchased at \$100 each. The number of bonds held in year three will be $10.8 + 0.864 = 11.664$, and so on.

In general, the number of bonds held in year $n$ will be

$$10\left(1+\frac{8}{100}\right)^{n-1},$$

which gives 10.0000, 10.8000, 11.6640, 12.5971, 13.6049 bonds held in years one to five.

# Chapter 3

**3.1** The tree representing the scenarios and price movements in Example 3.1 is shown in Figure S.3.

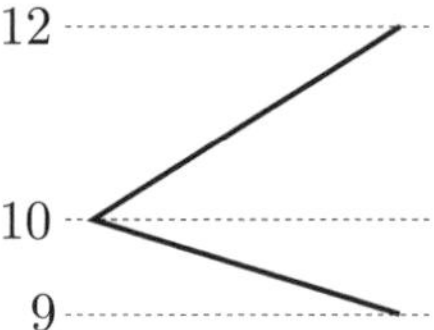


**Figure S.3** Tree of price movements in Example 3.1

**3.2** The tree representing the scenarios and price movements is shown in Figure S.4. There are altogether eight scenarios represented by the paths through the tree leading from the 'root' on the left towards the rightmost branch tips.

**3.3** We can use (3.1) to find

| Scenario | $S(0)$ | $S(1)$ | $S(2)$ | $S(3)$ |
|---|---|---|---|---|
| $\omega_1$ | 45.00 | 49.50 | 51.98 | 46.78 |
| $\omega_2$ | 45.00 | 47.25 | 51.98 | 57.17 |
| $\omega_3$ | 45.00 | 47.25 | 42.53 | 46.78 |

The tree is shown in Figure S.5.

**3.4** When dividends are payable, formula (3.1) becomes

$$S(n) = S(n-1)(1+K(n)) - \mathrm{div}(n),$$

which gives

| Scenario | $S(0)$ | $S(1)$ | $S(2)$ | $S(3)$ |
|---|---|---|---|---|
| $\omega_1$ | 45.00 | 48.50 | 49.93 | 43.93 |
| $\omega_2$ | 45.00 | 46.25 | 49.88 | 53.86 |
| $\omega_3$ | 45.00 | 46.25 | 40.63 | 43.69 |

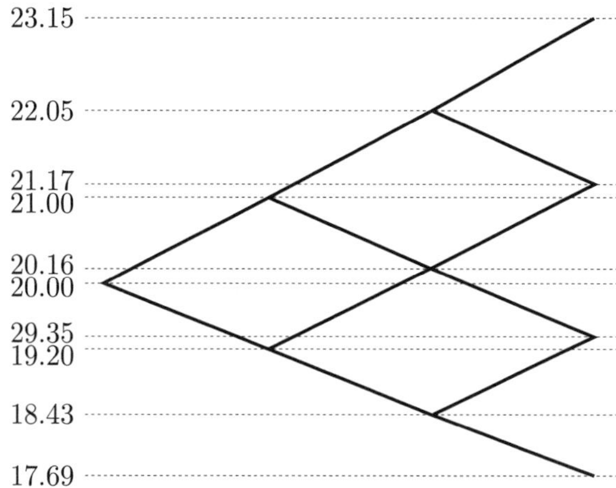


**Figure S.4** Tree of price movements in Exercise 3.2

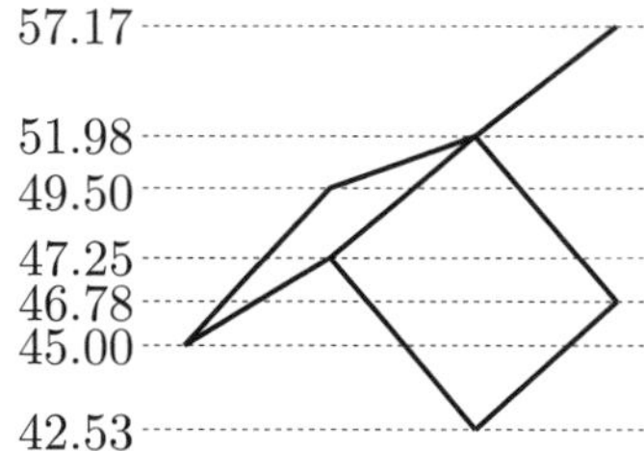


**Figure S.5** Tree of price movements in Exercise 3.3

**3.5** The return over two time steps as compared to the sum of one-step returns can take the following values:

| Scenario | $K(0,2)$ | $K(1)+K(2)$ |
|---|---|---|
| $\omega_1$ | 15.50% | 15.00% |
| $\omega_2$ | 15.50% | 15.00% |
| $\omega_3$ | −5.50% | −5.00% |

Over three time steps we have

| Scenario | $K(0,3)$ | $K(1)+K(2)+K(3)$ |
|---|---|---|
| $\omega_1$ | 3.95% | 5.00% |
| $\omega_2$ | 27.05% | 25.00% |
| $\omega_3$ | 3.95% | 5.00% |

The sum of one-step returns tends to be larger then the return over the total interval if the sign of one-step returns alternates.

**3.6** First find $K(0,2)$ and then the one-step returns $K(1) = K(2) = K$ from the relation $1 + K(0,2) = (1+K)^2$ (assuming that $1 + K > 0$):

| Scenario | $K(0,2)$ | $K(1) = K(2)$ |
|---|---|---|
| $\omega_1$ | 17.14% | 8.23% |
| $\omega_2$ | −8.57% | −4.38% |
| $\omega_3$ | −20.00% | −10.56% |

**3.7** The formula

$$1 + K(0,2) = (1 + K(1))\,(1 + K(2))$$

can be used to find $K(2)$. For example, the following scenarios and values of $K(2)$ are consistent with the conditions of Exercise 3.7:

| Scenario | $K(0,2)$ | $K(1)$ | $K(2)$ |
|---|---|---|---|
| $\omega_1$ | 21.00% | 10.00% | 10.00% |
| $\omega_2$ | 10.00% | 10.00% | 0.00% |
| $\omega_3$ | −1.00% | −10.00% | 10.00% |

This is not the only possible solution. Another one can be obtained from the above by changing scenario $\omega_2$ to

| Scenario | $K(0,2)$ | $K(1)$ | $K(2)$ |
|---|---|---|---|
| $\omega_2$ | 10.00% | −10.00% | 22.22% |

with the other two scenarios unaltered.

**3.8** For the three scenarios in Example 3.2 we find

| Scenario | $k(1)$ | $k(2)$ | $k(0,2)$ |
|---|---|---|---|
| $\omega_1$ | 5.31% | 3.39% | 8.70% |
| $\omega_2$ | 5.31% | −10.92% | −5.61% |
| $\omega_3$ | −5.61% | 1.90% | −3.70% |

In all three cases $k(0,2) = k(1) + k(2)$.

**3.9** Let $K$ denote the return in the third scenario. If the expected return is equal to 6%, then

$$\frac{1}{2} \times (-5\%) + \frac{1}{4} \times 6\% + \frac{1}{4} \times K = 6\%.$$

Solving for $K$, we find that the return in the third scenario must be 28%.

**3.10** First, compute the returns $K(1)$, $K(2)$ and $K(0,2)$ in each scenario:

| Scenario | $K(1)$ | $K(2)$ | $K(0,2)$ |
|---|---|---|---|
| $\omega_1$ | 10.00% | 9.09% | 20.00% |
| $\omega_2$ | 5.00% | −4.76% | 0.00% |
| $\omega_3$ | −10.00% | 11.11% | 0.00% |

It follows that

$$\begin{aligned}
E(K(1)) &\cong 0.25 \times 10.00\% + 0.25 \times 5.00\% - 0.5 \times 10.00\% \cong -1.25\%,\\
E(K(2)) &\cong 0.25 \times \phantom{1}9.09\% - 0.25 \times 4.76\% + 0.5 \times 11.11\% \cong \phantom{-}6.64\%,\\
E(K(0,2)) &\cong 0.25 \times 20.00\% + 0.25 \times 0.00\% + 0.5 \times \phantom{1}0.00\% \cong \phantom{-}5.00\%.
\end{aligned}$$

Clearly,

$$(1 + E(K(1)))(1 + E(K(2))) \cong 1.0530 \neq 1.0500 \cong 1 + E(K(0,2)).$$

**3.11** Since the quarterly returns $K(1), K(2), K(3), K(4)$ are independent and identically distributed,

$$E(K(1)) = E(K(2)) = E(K(3)) = E(K(4))$$

and

$$1 + E(K(0,3)) = (1 + E(K(1))^3,$$
$$1 + E(K(0,4)) = (1 + E(K(1))^4.$$

Thus, if $E(K(0,3)) = 12\%$, then the expected quarterly return $E(K(1)) \cong 3.85\%$ and the expected annual return $E(K(0,4)) \cong 16.31\%$.

**3.12** By Condition 3.1 the random variables

$$\frac{S(1)}{S(0)} = 1 + K(1), \quad \frac{S(2)}{S(1)} = 1 + K(2), \quad \frac{S(3)}{S(2)} = 1 + K(3) \qquad \text{(S.4)}$$

are independent, each taking two values $1 + d$ and $1 + u$ with probabilities $p$ and $1 - p$, respectively.

The price $S(2)$, which is the product of $S(0)$ and the first two of these random variables, takes up to four values corresponding to the four price movement scenarios, that is, paths through the two-step tree of stock prices shown in Figure 3.3 (in which $S(0) = 1$ for simplicity). Among these four values of $S(2)$ there are in fact only three different ones,

$$S(2) = \begin{cases} S(0)(1+u)^2 & \text{with probability } p^2, \\ S(0)(1+u)(1+d) & \text{with probability } 2p(1-p), \\ S(0)(1+d)^2 & \text{with probability } (1-p)^2. \end{cases}$$

The price $S(3)$, which is the product of $S(0)$ and the three independent random variables in (S.4), takes up to eight values corresponding to the eight price movement scenarios, that is, paths through the three-step tree of stock prices in Figure 3.4 (with $S(0) = 1$ for simplicity). Among these eight values of $S(3)$ there are only four different ones,

$$S(3) = \begin{cases} S(0)(1+u)^3 & \text{with probability } p^3, \\ S(0)(1+u)^2(1+d) & \text{with probability } 3p^2(1-p), \\ S(0)(1+u)(1+d)^2 & \text{with probability } 3p(1-p)^2, \\ S(0)(1+d)^3 & \text{with probability } (1-p)^3. \end{cases}$$

**3.13** The top values of $S(1)$ and $S(2)$ can be used to find $u$:

$$u = \frac{92 - 87}{87} \cong 0.0575.$$

Next, $u$ and the top value of $S(1)$ give the value of $S(0)$:

$$S(0) \cong \frac{87}{1 + 0.0575} \cong 82.27$$

dollars. Finally, $d$ is determined by $S(0)$ and the bottom value of $S(1)$:

$$d \cong \frac{76 - 82.27}{82.27} \cong -0.0762.$$

**3.14** Given the continuous risk-free rate of 14% and the time step $\tau = 1/12$, we find the one-step return

$$r = e^{0.14/12} - 1 \cong 0.0117.$$

By Condition 3.2, $u > r \cong 0.0117$. This means that the middle value $S(0)(1+u)(1+d)$ of $S(2)$ must be no less than about $22(1+0.0117)(1-0.01) \cong 22.04$ dollars.

**3.15** Consider the system of equations

$$S(0)(1+u)^2 = 32,$$
$$S(0)(1+u)(1+d) = 28,$$
$$S(0)(1+d)^2 = x.$$

It follows that

$$\frac{32}{28} = \frac{1+u}{1+d} = \frac{28}{x}$$

and $x = 28^2/32 = 24.50$ dollars. However, the tree cannot be reconstructed uniquely. For any value $S(0) > 0$ one can find $u$ and $d$ consistent with the data.

**3.16** The values of $u$ and $d$ can be found by solving the equations

$$S(0)(1+u)^2 = 121,$$
$$S(0)(1+d)^2 = 100,$$

and selecting those solutions that satisfy $1+u > 0$ and $1+d > 0$. If $S(0) = 100$, then $u = 0.1$ and $d = 0$. If $S(0) = 104$, then $u \cong 0.0786$ and $d \cong -0.0194$.

**3.17** We only need to consider the values of $d$ between $-1$ and $r$, that is, $-1 < d < 1/10$. As $d$ increases between these two bounds, $p_*$ decreases from $11/13$ to 0. The dependence of $p_*$ on $d$ is shown in Figure S.6.

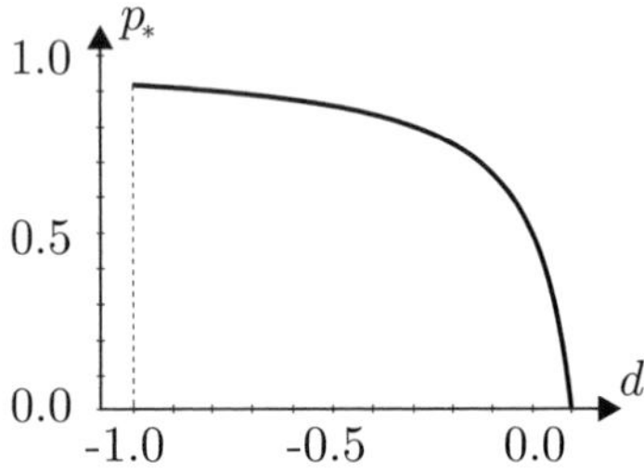


**Figure S.6** The risk-neural probability $p_*$ as a function of $d$

**3.18** By (3.4) the condition $d < r < u$ is equivalent to $d < p_*u + (1-p_*)d < u$. This, in turn, can be written as $0 < p_*(u-d) < u-d$ or, equivalently, $0 < p_* < 1$.

**3.19** By Proposition 3.5

$$E_*(S(3)|S(2) = 110) = 110(1+r) = 110(1+0.2) = 132$$

dollars.

**3.20** By Condition 3.3 the random variables $S(1)/S(0) = 1+K(1)$ and $S(2)/S(1) = 1+K(2)$ are independent, each taking three values $1+d$, $1+n$ and $1+u$ with probabilities $p$, $q$ and $1-p-q$, respectively. Therefore $S(2)$, which is the product of these two random variables and the number $S(0)$, takes up to nine values. Among these nine values there are only six different ones,

$$S(2) = \begin{cases} S(0)(1+u)^2 & \text{with probability } p^2, \\ S(0)(1+n)^2 & \text{with probability } q^2, \\ S(0)(1+d)^2 & \text{with probability } (1-p-q)^2, \\ S(0)(1+u)(1+n) & \text{with probability } 2pq, \\ S(0)(1+u)(1+d) & \text{with probability } 2p(1-p-q), \\ S(0)(1+n)(1+d) & \text{with probability } 2q(1-p-q). \end{cases}$$

**3.21** Let $p_*, q_*, 1-p_*-q_*$ be the probabilities of upward, middle and downward price movements, respectively. Condition (3.6) implies that $0.2p_* - 0.1(1-p_*-q_*) = 0$, that is, $q_* = 1-3p_*$ and $1-p_*-q_* = 2p_*$. Observe that $p_*, 1-3p_*, 2p_* \in [0,1]$ if and only if $p_* \in [0,1/3]$. It follows that $p_*, q_*, 1-p_*-q_*$ are risk-neutral probabilities if and only if $q_* = 1-3p_*$ and $p_* \in [0,1/3]$.

**3.22** Solving the system of equations

$$\begin{aligned} \ln(1+u) &= m\tau + \sigma\sqrt{\tau}, \\ \ln(1+d) &= m\tau - \sigma\sqrt{\tau}, \end{aligned}$$

we find $\sigma \cong 0.052$ and $m \cong 0.059$.

**3.23** Since $p = 1/2$ and $\xi(n)^2 = \tau$,

$$\begin{aligned} E(\xi(n)) &= \frac{1}{2}\sqrt{\tau} - \frac{1}{2}\sqrt{\tau} = 0, \\ \operatorname{Var}(\xi(n)) &= E(\xi(n)^2) - E(\xi(n))^2 = \frac{1}{2}\tau + \frac{1}{2}\tau = \tau, \\ E(k(n)) &= m\tau + \sigma E(\xi(n)) = m\tau, \\ \operatorname{Var}(k(n)) &= \sigma^2 \operatorname{Var}(\xi(n)) = \sigma^2\tau. \end{aligned}$$

**3.24** By (3.2)

$$\begin{aligned} S(1) &= S(0)\mathrm{e}^{k(1)} = S(0)\mathrm{e}^{m\tau+\sigma\xi(1)}, \\ S(2) &= S(0)\mathrm{e}^{k(1)+k(2)} = S(0)\mathrm{e}^{2m\tau+\sigma(\xi(1)+\xi(2))}. \end{aligned}$$

**3.25** Let $t = \frac{n}{N}$. Because the $\xi_N(i)$ are independent, $E(\xi_N(i)) = 0$ and $\operatorname{Var}(\xi_N(i)) = \frac{1}{N}$ for each $i = 1, 2, \ldots$, it follows that

$$\begin{aligned} E(w_N(t)) &= E(\xi_N(1) + \cdots + \xi_N(n)) \\ &= E(\xi_N(1)) + \cdots + E(\xi_N(n)) = 0, \\ \operatorname{Var}(w_N(t)) &= \operatorname{Var}(\xi_N(1) + \cdots + \xi_N(n)) \\ &= \operatorname{Var}(\xi_N(1)) + \cdots + \operatorname{Var}(\xi_N(1)) = \frac{n}{N} = t. \end{aligned}$$

# Chapter 4

**4.1** We can use the formulae in the proof of Proposition 4.1 to find

$$\begin{aligned}
y(1) &= \frac{200 - 35.24 \times 60 - 24.18 \times 20}{100} \cong -23.98, \\
V(1) &\cong 35.24 \times 65 + 24.18 \times 15 - 23.98 \times 110 \cong 15.50, \\
y(2) &= \frac{15.50 + 40.50 \times 65 - 10.13 \times 15}{110} \cong 22.69, \\
V(2) &\cong -40.50 \times 75 + 10.13 \times 25 + 22.69 \times 121 \cong -38.60.
\end{aligned}$$

**4.2** For a one-step strategy admissibility reduces to a couple of inequalities, $V(0) \geq 0$ and $V(1) \geq 0$. The first inequality can be written as

$$10x + 10y \geq 0.$$

The second inequality means that both values of the random variable $V(1)$ should be non-negative, which gives two more inequalities to be satisfied by $x$ and $y$,

$$\begin{aligned}
13x + 11y &\geq 0, \\
9x + 11y &\geq 0.
\end{aligned}$$

The set of portfolios $(x, y)$ satisfying all these inequalities is shown in Figure S.7.

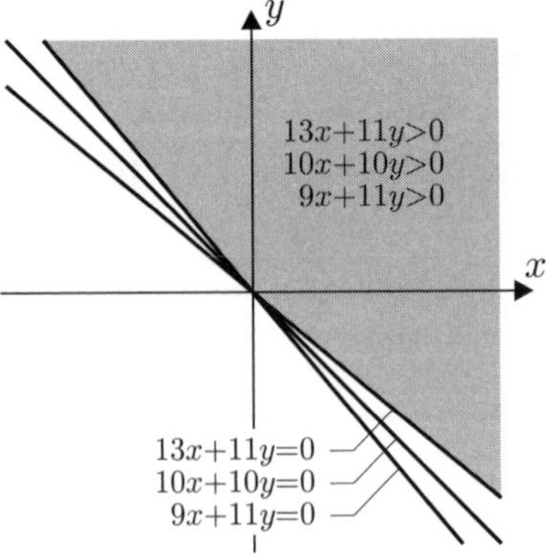


**Figure S.7** Admissible portfolios in Exercise 4.2

**4.3** Suppose that there is a self-financing predictable strategy with initial value $V(0) = 0$ and final value $0 \neq V(2) \geq 0$, such that $V(1) < 0$ with positive probability. The last inequality means that this strategy is not admissible, but we shall construct an admissible one that violates the No-Arbitrage Principle. Here is how to proceed to achieve arbitrage:

- Do not invest at all at time 0.
- At time 1 check whether the value $V(1)$ of the non-admissible strategy is negative or not. If $V(1) \geq 0$, then refrain from investing at all once again. However, if $V(1) < 0$, then take the same position in stock as in the non-admissible strategy and a risk-free position that is lower by $-V(1)$ than that in the non-admissible strategy.

This defines a predictable self-financing strategy. Its time 0 and time 1 value is 0. The value at time 2 will be

$$\begin{cases} 0 & \text{if } V(1) \geq 0, \\ V(2) - V(1) > 0 & \text{if } V(1) < 0. \end{cases}$$

This is, therefore, an admissible strategy realising an arbitrage opportunity.

**4.4** If you happen to know that an increase in stock price will be followed by a fall at the next step, then adopt this strategy:

- At time 0 do not invest in either asset.
- At time 1 check whether the stock has gone up or down. If down, then again do not invest in either asset. But if stock has gone up, then sell short one share for $S(0)u$, investing the proceeds risk-free.

Clearly, the time 0 and time 1 value of this strategy is $V(0) = V(1) = 0$. If stock goes down at the first step, then the value at time 2 will be $V(2) = 0$. But if stock goes up at the first step, then it will go down at the second step and $V(2) = S(0)u(r - d)$ will be positive, as required, since $u > r > d$. (The notation is as in Section 3.2.)

Clearly, this is not a predictable strategy, which means that no arbitrage has been achieved.

**4.5** a) If there are no short-selling restrictions, then the following strategy will realise an arbitrage opportunity:

- At time 0 do not invest at all.
- At time 1 check the price $S(1)$. If $S(1) = 120$ dollars, then once again do not invest at all. But if $S(1) = 90$ dollars, then sell short one share of the risky asset and invest the proceeds risk-free.

The time 0 and time 1 value of this admissible strategy is 0. The value at time 2 will be

$$\begin{cases} 0 & \text{in scenarios } \omega_1 \text{ and } \omega_2, \\ 3 & \text{in scenario } \omega_3, \end{cases}$$

which means that arbitrage can be achieved.

b) In a) above arbitrage has been achieved by utilising the behaviour of stock prices at the second step in scenario $\omega_2$: The return on the risky asset is lower than the risk-free return. Thus, shorting the risky asset and investing the proceeds risk-free creates arbitrage. However, when short selling of risky assets is disallowed, then this arbitrage opportunity will be beyond the reach of investors.

**4.6** The arbitrage strategy described in Solution 4.5 involves buying a fraction of a bond. If $S(1) = 90$ dollars, then one share of stock should be shorted and $\frac{9}{11}$ of a bond purchased at time 1. To obtain an arbitrage strategy involving an integer number of units of each asset, multiply these quantities by 11, that is, short sell 11 shares of stock and buy 9 bonds.

**4.7** Suppose that transaction costs of 5% apply whenever stock is bought or sold. An investor who tried to follow the strategy in Solution 4.5, short selling one share of stock at time 1 if $S(1) = 90$ dollars, would have to pay transaction costs of $90 \times 5\% = 4.50$ dollars. If the remaining amount of $90 - 4.50 = 85.50$ dollars were invested risk-free, it would be worth $85.5 \times \frac{121}{110} = 94.05$ dollars at time 2. But closing the short position in stock would cost \$96, making the final wealth negative. As a result, there is no arbitrage strategy.

**4.8** The put option gives the right (but no obligation) to sell one share of stock for the strike price $X = 110$ dollars at time 2. We consider an extended model with three assets, the stock, the money market, and the option. The unit prices of these assets are $S(n), A(n), P^{\mathrm{E}}(n)$, where $P^{\mathrm{E}}(n)$ is the market price of the put option at time $n = 0, 1, 2$. The time 2 price of the put option is

$$P^{\mathrm{E}}(2) = \max\{X - S(2), 0\}.$$

According to the Fundamental Theorem of Asset Pricing, the discounted stock and option prices $\widetilde{S}(n) = S(n)/A(n)$ and $\widetilde{P}^{\mathrm{E}}(n) = P^{\mathrm{E}}(n)/A(n)$ should form a martingale under some probability measure $P_*$, or else an arbitrage opportunity would arise. From Example 4.5 we know that there is only one probability $P_*$ turning $\widetilde{S}(n)$ into a martingale. Because of this, $\widetilde{P}^{\mathrm{E}}(n)$ must be a martingale under the same probability $P_*$. It follows that

$$P^{\mathrm{E}}(1) = \frac{A(1)}{A(2)} E_*(P^{\mathrm{E}}(2)|S(1)) \quad \text{and} \quad P^{\mathrm{E}}(0) = \frac{A(0)}{A(1)} E_*(P^{\mathrm{E}}(1)).$$

Using the values of $P_*$ for each scenario found in Example 4.5, we can compute $P^{\mathrm{E}}(1)$ and $P^{\mathrm{E}}(0)$. For example

$$\begin{aligned} P^{\mathrm{E}}(1, \omega_3) = P^{\mathrm{E}}(1, \omega_4) &= \frac{A(1)}{A(2)} \frac{P_*(\omega_3) P^{\mathrm{E}}(2, \omega_3) + P_*(\omega_4) P^{\mathrm{E}}(2, \omega_4)}{P_*(\omega_3) + P_*(\omega_4)} \\ &= \frac{110}{121} \frac{\frac{1}{25} \times 20 + \frac{1}{100} \times 30}{\frac{1}{25} + \frac{1}{100}} \cong 20.00 \end{aligned}$$

dollars. In this manner, we obtain

| Scenario | $P^{\mathrm{E}}(0)$ | $P^{\mathrm{E}}(1)$ | $P^{\mathrm{E}}(2)$ |
|---|---|---|---|
| $\omega_1$ | 1.96 | 1.21 | 0.00 |
| $\omega_2$ | 1.96 | 1.21 | 4.00 |
| $\omega_3$ | 1.96 | 20.00 | 20.00 |
| $\omega_4$ | 1.96 | 20.00 | 30.00 |

## Chapter 5

**5.1** In the first investment project

$$\begin{aligned} E(K_1) &= 0.12 \times 0.25 + 0.12 \times 0.75 = 0.12, \\ \mathrm{Var}(K_1) &= (0.12 - 0.12)^2 \times 0.25 + (0.12 - 0.12)^2 \times 0.75 = 0. \end{aligned}$$

In the second project

$$\begin{aligned} E(K_2) &= 0.11 \times 0.25 + 0.13 \times 0.75 = 0.125, \\ \mathrm{Var}(K_2) &= (0.11 - 0.125)^2 \times 0.25 + (0.13 - 0.125)^2 \times 0.75 = 0.000075. \end{aligned}$$

Finally, in the third project

$$\begin{aligned} E(K_3) &= 0.02 \times 0.25 + 0.22 \times 0.75 = 0.17, \\ \mathrm{Var}(K_3) &= (0.02 - 0.17)^2 \times 0.25 + (0.22 - 0.17)^2 \times 0.75 = 0.0075. \end{aligned}$$

The first project is the least risky one, in fact, it is risk-free. The third project involves the highest risk.

**5.2** First we put $K_2(\omega_2) = x$ and compute

$$\begin{aligned}\mathrm{Var}(K_1) &= 0.001875,\\ \mathrm{Var}(K_2) &= 0.1875x^2 + 0.015x + 0.0003.\end{aligned}$$

The two securities will have the same risk if $\mathrm{Var}(K_1) = \mathrm{Var}(K_2)$. This gives the following equation

$$0.0003 + 0.1875x^2 + 0.015x = 0.001875$$

with two solutions $x = -0.14$ or $0.06$. This means that $K_2(\omega_2) = -14\%$ or $6\%$.

**5.3** First we use the formula $\mathrm{e}^{k_i} = 1 + K_i$ for $i = 1, 2$ to compute the logarithmic returns and then work out the variance of each return:

| Scenario | Probability | $K_1$ | $K_2$ | $k_1$ | $k_2$ |
|---|---|---|---|---|---|
| $\omega_1$ | 0.5 | 10.53% | 7.23% | 10.01% | 6.98% |
| $\omega_2$ | 0.5 | 13.89% | 10.55% | 13.01% | 10.03% |
| Variance | | 0.000282 | 0.000276 | 0.000224 | 0.000232 |

We find that $\mathrm{Var}(K_1) > \mathrm{Var}(K_2)$, whereas $\mathrm{Var}(k_1) < \mathrm{Var}(k_2)$.

This is an interesting observation because it shows that greater risk as measured by $\mathrm{Var}(K)$ does not necessarily mean greater risk in the sense of $\mathrm{Var}(k)$. Nevertheless, when the rates of return are of the order of 10% or lower, the differences between these two measures of risk are tiny and can simply be ignored in financial practice. This is because the errors due to inaccurate estimation of the parameters (the probabilities and values of return rates in different scenarios) are typically greater than these differences.

**5.4** Let $x_1$ and $x_2$ be the number of shares of type 1 and 2 in the portfolio. Then

$$\begin{aligned}V(1) = x_1S_1(1) + x_2S_2(1) &= V(0)\left(w_1\frac{S_1(1)}{S_1(0)} + w_2\frac{S_2(1)}{S_2(0)}\right)\\ &= 100\left(0.25 \times \frac{48}{45} + 0.75 \times \frac{32}{33}\right) = 99.394.\end{aligned}$$

**5.5** The return on the portfolio is $K_V = w_1K_1 + w_2K_2$. This gives

$$\begin{aligned}K_V &= 0.30 \times 12\% - 0.7 \times 4\% = 0.8\% &&\text{in scenario } \omega_1,\\ K_V &= 0.30 \times 10\% + 0.7 \times 7\% = 7.9\% &&\text{in scenario } \omega_2.\end{aligned}$$

**5.6** The initial and final values of the portfolio are

$$\begin{aligned}V(0) &= x_1S_1(0) + x_2S_2(0),\\ V(1) &= x_1S_1(0)\mathrm{e}^{k_1} + x_2S_2(0)\mathrm{e}^{k_2}\\ &= V(0)\left(w_1\mathrm{e}^{k_1} + w_2\mathrm{e}^{k_2}\right).\end{aligned}$$

As a result, the return on the portfolio is

$$\mathrm{e}^{k_V} = \frac{V(1)}{V(0)} = w_1\mathrm{e}^{k_1} + w_2\mathrm{e}^{k_2}.$$

**5.7** First we find $E(K_1) = 7\%$ and $E(K_2) = 23\%$. If the expected return on the portfolio is to be $E(K_V) = 20\%$, then by (5.4) and (5.1) the weights must satisfy the system of equations

$$7w_1 + 23w_2 = 20,$$
$$w_1 + w_2 = 1.$$

The solution is $w_1 = 18.75\%$ and $w_2 = 81.25\%$.

**5.8** First, we compute $\mu_1 = 4\%$ and $\mu_2 = 16\%$ from the data in Example 5.6. Next, (5.7) and (5.1) give the system of equations

$$4w_1 + 16w_2 = 46,$$
$$w_1 + w_2 = 1,$$

for the weights $w_1$ and $w_2$. The solution is $w_1 = -2.5$ and $w_2 = 3.5$. Finally, we use (5.8) with the values $\sigma_1^2 \cong 0.0184$, $\sigma_2^2 \cong 0.0024$ and $\rho_{12} \cong -0.96309$ computed in Example 5.6 to find the risk of the portfolio:

$$\begin{aligned}\sigma_V^2 &\cong (-2.5)^2 \times 0.0184 + (3.5)^2 \times 0.0024 \\ &\quad +2 \times (-2.5) \times 3.5 \times (-0.96309) \times \sqrt{0.0184} \times \sqrt{0.0024} \\ &\cong 0.2564.\end{aligned}$$

**5.9** The returns on risky securities are non-constant random variables, that is, $K_1(\omega_1) \neq K_1(\omega_2)$ and $K_2(\omega_1) \neq K_2(\omega_2)$. Because of this, the system of equations

$$K_1(\omega_1) = aK_2(\omega_1) + b,$$
$$K_1(\omega_2) = aK_2(\omega_2) + b,$$

must have a solution $a \neq 0$ and $b$. It follows that $K_1 = aK_2 + b$.

Now, use the properties of covariance and variance to compute

$$\mathrm{Cov}(K_1, K_2) = \mathrm{Cov}(aK_2 + b, K_2) = a\mathrm{Cov}(K_2, K_2) = a\mathrm{Var}(K_2) = a\sigma_2^2,$$
$$\sigma_1^2 = \mathrm{Var}(K_1) = \mathrm{Var}(aK_2 + b) = a^2\mathrm{Var}(K_2) = a^2\sigma_2^2.$$

It follows that $\sigma_1 = |a|\,\sigma_2$ and

$$\rho_{12} = \frac{\mathrm{Cov}(K_1, K_2)}{\sigma_1\sigma_2} = \frac{a\sigma_2^2}{|a|\,\sigma_2^2} = \pm 1.$$

**5.10** Using the values $\sigma_1^2 \cong 0.0184$, $\sigma_2^2 \cong 0.0024$ and $\rho_{12} \cong -0.96309$ computed in Example 5.6, we find $s_0$ from (5.13):

$$s_0 = \frac{\sigma_1^2 - \rho_{12}\sigma_1\sigma_2}{\sigma_1^2 + \sigma_2^2 - 2\rho_{12}\sigma_1\sigma_2} \cong 0.73809.$$

This means that the weights in the portfolio with minimum risk are $w_1 = 0.73809$ and $w_2 = 0.26191$ and it involves no short selling.

**5.11** $\mu_V = 0.06$, $\sigma_V \cong 1.013$.

**5.12** The weights of the three securities in the minimum variance portfolio are $\boldsymbol{w} \cong \begin{bmatrix} 0.314 & 0.148 & 0.538 \end{bmatrix}$, the expected return on the portfolio is $\mu_V \cong 0.173$ and the standard deviation is $\sigma_V \cong 0.151$.

**5.13** The weights in the portfolio with the minimum variance among all attainable portfolios with expected return $\mu_V = 20\%$ are $\boldsymbol{w} \cong \begin{bmatrix} 0.672 & -0.246 & 0.574 \end{bmatrix}$. The standard deviation of this portfolio is $\sigma_V \cong 0.192$.

**5.14** The weights and standard deviations of portfolios along the minimum variance line, parametrised by the expected return $\mu_V$, are

$$\boldsymbol{w} \cong \begin{bmatrix} -2.027 + 13.492\mu_V & 2.728 - 14.870\mu_V & 0.298 + 1.376\mu_V \end{bmatrix},$$

$$\sigma_V = \sqrt{0.625 - 6.946\mu_V + 20.018\mu_V^2}\,.$$

This minimum variance line is presented in Figure S.8, along with the set of attainable portfolios with short selling (light shading) and without (darker shading).

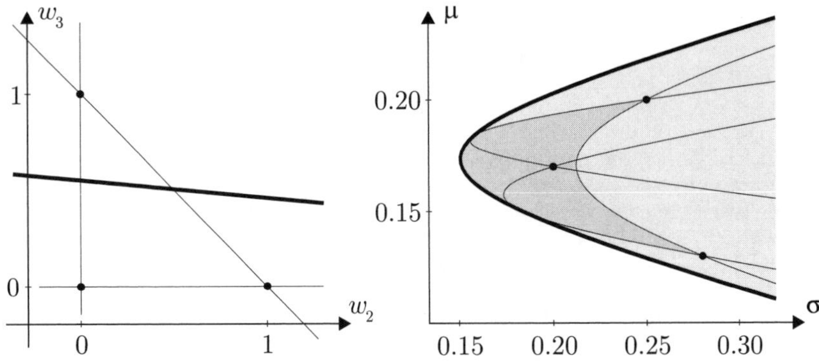


**Figure S.8** Minimum variance line and attainable portfilios on the $w_2, w_3$ and $\sigma, \mu$ planes

**5.15** Let $\boldsymbol{m}$ be the one-row matrix formed by the expected returns of the three securities. By multiplying the $\gamma \boldsymbol{w} \boldsymbol{C} = \boldsymbol{m} - \mu \boldsymbol{u}$ equality by $\boldsymbol{C}^{-1}\boldsymbol{u}^T$ and, respectively, $\boldsymbol{C}^{-1}\boldsymbol{m}^T$, we get

$$\mu_V(\boldsymbol{m} - \mu\boldsymbol{u})\boldsymbol{C}^{-1}\boldsymbol{u}^T = (\boldsymbol{m} - \mu\boldsymbol{u})\boldsymbol{C}^{-1}\boldsymbol{m}^T,$$

since $\boldsymbol{w}\boldsymbol{u}^T = 1$ and $\boldsymbol{w}\boldsymbol{m}^T = \mu_V$. This can be solved for $\mu$ to get

$$\mu = \frac{\boldsymbol{m}\boldsymbol{C}^{-1}(\boldsymbol{m}^T - \mu_V\boldsymbol{u}^T)}{\boldsymbol{u}\boldsymbol{C}^{-1}(\boldsymbol{m}^T - \mu_V\boldsymbol{u}^T)} \cong 0.142.$$

Then, $\gamma$ can be computed as follows:

$$\gamma = (\boldsymbol{m} - \mu\boldsymbol{u})\boldsymbol{C}^{-1}\boldsymbol{u}^T \cong 1.367.$$

**5.16** The market portfolio weights are $\boldsymbol{w} \cong \begin{bmatrix} 0.438 & 0.012 & 0.550 \end{bmatrix}$. The expected return on this portfolio is $\mu_M \cong 0.183$ and the standard deviation is $\sigma_M \cong 0.156$.

**5.17** $\beta_V \cong 0.857$, $\alpha_V \cong -0.102$.

**5.18** The expected return on the portfolio can be expressed as $K_V = w_1K_1 + \cdots + w_nK_n$ in terms of the expected returns on the individual securities. Because covariance is linear in each of its arguments,

$$\beta_V = \frac{\text{Cov}(K_V, K_M)}{\sigma_M^2} = w_1\frac{\text{Cov}(K_1, K_M)}{\sigma_M^2} + \cdots + w_n\frac{\text{Cov}(K_n, K_M)}{\sigma_M^2}$$
$$= w_1\beta_1 + \cdots + w_n\beta_n.$$

**5.19** The equation of the characteristic line is $y = \beta_V x + \alpha_V$, where $\beta_V$ is the beta factor of that security and $\alpha_V = \mu_V - \beta_V\mu_M$. In the CAPM the equation $\mu_V = r_F + (\mu_M - r_F)\beta_V$ of the security market line holds. Substitution into the formula for $\alpha_V$ gives $\alpha_V = r_F - r_F\beta_V$, so the equation of the characteristic line becomes $y = \beta_V(x - r_F) + r_F$. Clearly, the characteristic line of any security will pass through the point with coordinates $r_F, r_F$.

## Chapter 6

**6.1** Yes, there is an arbitrage opportunity. We enter into a long forward contract and sell short one share, investing 70% of the proceeds at 8% and paying the remaining 30% as a security deposit to attract interest at 4%. At the time of delivery the cash investments plus interest will be worth about \$18.20, out of which \$18 will need to be paid for one share to close out the short position in stock. This leaves a \$0.20 arbitrage profit.

The rates $d$ for the security deposit such that there is no arbitrage opportunity satisfy $30\% \times 17 \times e^d + 70\% \times 17 \times e^{8\%} \leq 18$. The highest such rate is $d \cong 0.1740\%$.

**6.2** We take 1 January 2000 to be time 0. By (6.2)

$$F(0, 3/4) = S(0)e^{0.06\times\frac{3}{4}}, \qquad F(1/4, 3/4) = 0.9S(0)e^{0.06\times\frac{2}{4}}.$$

It follows that the forward price drops by

$$\frac{F(0,3/4) - F(1/4,3/4)}{F(0,3/4)} = \frac{e^{\frac{3}{4}\times 6\%} - 0.9e^{\frac{1}{2}\times 6\%}}{e^{\frac{3}{4}\times 6\%}} \cong 11.34\%.$$

**6.3** The present value of the dividends is

$$\text{div}_0 = 1e^{-\frac{6}{12}\times 12\%} + 2e^{-\frac{9}{12}\times 12\%} \cong 2.77$$

dollars. The right-hand side of (6.4) is equal to

$$[S(0) - \text{div}_0]e^{rT} \cong (120 - 2.77)e^{\frac{10}{12}\times 12\%} \cong 129.56$$

dollars, which is less than the quoted forward price of \$131. As a result, there will be an arbitrage opportunity, which can be realised as follows:

- on 1 January 2000 enter into a short forward position and borrow \$120 to buy stock;
- on 1 July 2000 collect the first dividend of \$1 and invest risk-free;
- on 1 October 2000 collect the second dividend of \$2 and invest risk-free;
- on 1 November 2000 close out all positions.

You will be left with an arbitrage profit of

$$131 - 120e^{\frac{10}{12}\times 12\%} + 1e^{\frac{4}{12}\times 12\%} + 2e^{\frac{1}{12}\times 12\%} \cong 1.44$$

dollars.

**6.4** No arbitrage profit can be realised in these circumstances. Though the theoretical no-arbitrage forward price is about \$87.83, the first strategy in the proof of Proposition 6.2 brings a loss of $89 - 83e^{10\%} + 2e^{0.5\times 7\%} \cong -0.66$ dollars and the second one results in a loss of $-89 + 83e^{7\%} - 2e^{0.5\times 10\%} \cong -2.08$ dollars.

**6.5** The euro plays the role of the underlying asset with dividend yield 3%. Hence the forward price (the exchange rate) is

$$F(0, 1/2) = 0.9834e^{0.5(4\% - 3\%)} \cong 0.9883$$

euros to a dollar.

**6.6** At time $t$

- borrow and pay (or receive and invest, if negative) the amount $V(t)$ to acquire a short forward contract with forward price $F(0,T)$ and delivery date $T$,
- initiate a new long forward contact with forward price $F(t,T)$ at no cost.

Then at time $T$

- close out both forward contracts receiving (or paying, if negative) the amounts $S(T) - F(0,T)$ and $S(T) - F(t,T)$, respectively;
- collect $V(t)e^{r(T-t)}$ from the risk-free investment, with interest.

The final balance $V(t)e^{r(T-t)} - [F(t,T) - F(0,T)] > 0$ will be your arbitrage profit.

**6.7** By (6.3) the initial forward price is $F(0,1) \cong 45.72$ dollars. This takes into account the dividend paid at time 1/2.

a) If $S(9/12) = 49$ dollars, then $F(9/12, 1) \cong 49.74$ dollars by (6.2). It follows by (6.8) that $V(9/12) \cong 3.96$ dollars.

b) If $S(9/12) = 51$ dollars, then $F(9/12) \cong 51.77$ dollars and $V(9/12) \cong 5.96$ dollars.

**6.8** Let $t = 1/365$, $T = 1/4$. We apply the formula (6.11) to get

$$f(t,T) - f(0,T) = S(t)e^{r(T-t)} + S(0)e^{rT} = 0$$

if $S(t) = S(0)e^{rt}$, that is, if the stock grows at the risk-free rate.

**6.9** Since $f(t,T) = S(t)e^{r(T-t)}$, the random variables $S(t)$ and $f(t,T)$ are perfectly correlated with $\rho_{S(t)f(t,T)} = 1$ and $\sigma_{f(t,T)} = e^{r(T-t)}\sigma_{S(t)}$. It follows that $N = e^{-r(T-t)}$.

**6.10** Observe that Theorem 6.5 on the equality of futures and forward prices applies also in the case of an asset with dividends paid continuously. We can, therefore, use (6.6) to obtain

$$r_{\text{div}} = 8\% - \frac{1}{0.75} \ln \frac{14,100}{13,500} \cong 2.20\%.$$

**6.11** The return on the index will be 3.37%. For $r_F = 1\%$ this gives the futures prices $f(0,3) \cong 916.97$ and $f(1,3) \cong 938.49$. If the beta coefficient for a portfolio is $\beta_V = 1.5$, then the expected return on this portfolio will be $\mu_V \cong 4.56\%$. To construct a portfolio with $\beta_{\widetilde{V}} = 0$ and initial value $V(0) = 100$ dollars, supplement the original portfolio with $N \cong 0.1652$ short futures contracts (observe that $N$ is the same as in Example 6.4).

If the actual return on the original portfolio during the first time step happens to be equal to the expected return, then its value after one step will be $V(1) \cong 104.56$ dollars. Marking to market requires the holder of $N \cong 0.1652$ short forward contracts to pay \$3.56. As a result, after one step the value of the portfolio with forward contracts will be $\widetilde{V}(1) \cong 104.56 - 3.56 = 101.00$ dollars, once again matching the risk-free growth.

## Chapter 7

**7.1** The investment will bring a profit of

$$(36 - S(T))^+ - 4.50\mathrm{e}^{0.12 \times \frac{3}{12}} = 3,$$

where $S(T)$ is the stock price on the exercise date. This gives $S(T) \cong 28.36$ dollars.

**7.2** $E((S(T) - 90)^+ - 8\mathrm{e}^{0.09 \times \frac{6}{12}}) \cong -5.37$ dollars.

**7.3** By put-call parity $2.83 - P^{\mathrm{E}} = 15.60 - 15.00\mathrm{e}^{-\frac{3}{12} \times 0.0672}$, so $P^{\mathrm{E}} \cong 1.98$ dollars.

**7.4** Put-call parity is violated, $5.09 - 7.78 > 20.37 - 24e^{-0.0748 \times \frac{6}{12}}$. Arbitrage can be realised as in the first part of the proof of Theorem 7.1:

- Buy a share for \$20.37;
- Buy a put option for \$7.78;
- Write and sell a call option for \$5.09;
- Borrow \$23.06 at the interest rate of 7.48%.

The balance of these transactions is zero. After six months

- Sell one share for \$24 by exercising the put option or settling the short position in calls, depending on whether the share price turns out to be below or above the strike price;
- Repay the loan with interest, amounting to $23.06e^{\frac{1}{2} \times 0.0748} \cong 23.94$ dollars in total.

The balance of $24 - 23.96 = 0.06$ dollars will be your arbitrage profit.

**7.5** If $C^{\mathrm{E}} - P^{\mathrm{E}} > S(0) - \mathrm{div}_0 - X\mathrm{e}^{-rT}$, then at time 0 buy a share and a put option, write and sell a call option, and invest (or borrow, if negative) the balance on the money market at the interest rate $r$. As soon as you receive the dividend, invest it at the rate $r$. At the exercise time $T$ close the money market investment and sell the share for $X$, either by exercising the put if $S(T) < X$, or by settling the call if $S(T) \geq X$. The final balance $(C^{\mathrm{E}} - P^{\mathrm{E}} - S(0) + \mathrm{div}_0)\mathrm{e}^{rT} + X > 0$ will be your arbitrage profit.

On the other hand, if $C^{\mathrm{E}} - P^{\mathrm{E}} < S(0) - \mathrm{div}_0 - X\mathrm{e}^{-rT}$, then at time 0 sell short a share, write and sell a put, and buy a call option, investing the balance on the money market. When a dividend becomes due on the shorted share, borrow the amount and pay it to the owner of the stock. At time $T$ close the money market position, buy a share for $X$ by exercising the call if $S(T) > X$ or settling the put if $S(T) \leq X$, and close the short position in stock. Your arbitrage profit will be $(-C^{\mathrm{E}} + P^{\mathrm{E}} + S(0) - \mathrm{div}_0)\mathrm{e}^{rT} - X > 0$.

**7.6** If $C^{\mathrm{E}} - P^{\mathrm{E}} < S(0)\mathrm{e}^{-r_{\mathrm{div}}T} - X\mathrm{e}^{-rT}$, then at time 0 sell short $\mathrm{e}^{-r_{\mathrm{div}}T}$ of a share, write and sell a put, and buy a call option, investing the balance at the rate $r$. Between time 0 and $T$ pay dividends to the stock owner, raising cash by shorting the stock. This will lead to one shorted share held at time $T$. If the put option is exercised at time $T$, you will have to buy a share for $X$. Use this share to close the short position in stock. You will be left with a call option and a positive amount $(-C^{\mathrm{E}} + P^{\mathrm{E}} + S(0)\mathrm{e}^{-r_{\mathrm{div}}T} - X\mathrm{e}^{-rT})\mathrm{e}^{rT} > 0$. If the put option is not exercised at all, then you can use the call to buy a share for $X$ at time $T$, closing the short position in stock. You will also be left with a positive final balance $(-C^{\mathrm{E}} + P^{\mathrm{E}} + S(0)\mathrm{e}^{-r_{\mathrm{div}}T} - X\mathrm{e}^{-rT})\mathrm{e}^{rT} > 0$.

On the other hand, if $C^{\mathrm{E}} - P^{\mathrm{E}} > S(0)\mathrm{e}^{-r_{\mathrm{div}}T} - X\mathrm{e}^{-rT}$, then the opposite strategy will also lead to arbitrage.

**7.7** The strike price is equal to the forward price (more precisely, the exchange rate) of 0.9883 euros to a dollar computed in Solution 6.5.

**7.8** If $S(0) - X\mathrm{e}^{-rT} < C^{\mathrm{A}} - P^{\mathrm{A}}$, then write and sell a call, buy a put, and buy a share, investing (or borrowing, if negative) the balance at the rate $r$. Now the same argument as in the first part of the proof of Theorem 7.2 applies, except that the arbitrage profit may also include the dividend if the call is exercised after the dividend becomes due. (Nevertheless, the dividend cannot be included in this inequality because the option may be exercised and the share sold before the dividend is due.)

If $C^{\mathrm{A}} - P^{\mathrm{A}} < S(0) - \mathrm{div}_0 - X$, then at time 0 sell short a share, write and sell a put, and buy a call option, investing the balance at the rate $r$. If the put is exercised at time $t < T$, you will have to buy a share for $X$, borrowing the amount at the rate $r$. As the dividend becomes due, borrow the amount at the rate $r$ and pay it to the owner of the share. At time $T$ return the share to the owner, closing the short sale. You will be left with the call option and a positive amount $(S(0) + P^{\mathrm{A}} - C^{\mathrm{A}} - \mathrm{div}_0)\mathrm{e}^{rT} - X\mathrm{e}^{r(T-t)} > X\mathrm{e}^{rT} - X\mathrm{e}^{r(T-t)} \geq 0$. (If the put is exercised before the dividend becomes due, you can increase your arbitrage profit by closing out the short position in stock immediately, in which case you would not have to pay the dividend.) If the put is not exercised before expiry $T$, then the second part of Solution 7.5 applies.

**7.9** If $S(0) - X\mathrm{e}^{-rT} < C^{\mathrm{A}} - P^{\mathrm{A}}$, then use the same strategy as in the first part of the proof of Theorem 7.2. The resulting arbitrage profit will in fact be increased by the dividends accumulated up to the time when the call option is exercised.

If $C^{\mathrm{A}} - P^{\mathrm{A}} < S(0)\mathrm{e}^{-r_{\mathrm{div}}T} - X$, then at time 0 sell short $\mathrm{e}^{-r_{\mathrm{div}}T}$ of a share, write and sell a put, and buy a call option, investing the balance at the rate $r$. Between time 0 and $T$ pay dividends to the stock owner, raising cash by shorting the stock. This will lead to one shorted share held at time $T$. If the put option is exercised at time $t \leq T$, you will have to buy a share for $X$, borrowing this amount at the rate $r$. At time $T$ use this share to close the short position in stock. You will be left with a call option and a positive amount $(-C^{\mathrm{A}} + P^{\mathrm{A}} + S(0)\mathrm{e}^{-r_{\mathrm{div}}T})\mathrm{e}^{rT} - X\mathrm{e}^{r(T-t)} \geq (-C^{\mathrm{A}} + P^{\mathrm{A}} + S(0)\mathrm{e}^{-r_{\mathrm{div}}T} - X)\mathrm{e}^{rT} > 0$ plus any dividends accumulated since the share was bought at time $t$. If the put option is not exercised at all, then you can use the call to buy a share for $X$ at time $T$, closing the short position in stock. You will also be left with a positive final balance $(-C^{\mathrm{A}} + P^{\mathrm{A}} + S(0)\mathrm{e}^{-r_{\mathrm{div}}T})\mathrm{e}^{rT} - X > (-C^{\mathrm{A}} + P^{\mathrm{A}} + S(0)\mathrm{e}^{-r_{\mathrm{div}}T} - X)\mathrm{e}^{rT} > 0$.

**7.10** If $C^{\mathrm{E}} > C^{\mathrm{A}}$, then write and sell a European call and purchase an American call. The difference $C^{\mathrm{E}} - C^{\mathrm{A}}$ will be your arbitrage income. To keep it, do not exercise the American option until expiry, when either both options will turn out worthless, or the loss from settling the European call will be recovered by exercising the American call. The argument for put options is similar.

**7.11** Suppose that $C^{\mathrm{E}} \geq S(0) - \mathrm{div}_0$. In this case write and sell a call option and buy stock, investing the balance on the money market. As soon as you receive the dividends, also invest them on the money market. On the exercise date you can sell the stock for at least $\min(S(T), X)$, settling the call option. Your final wealth will be positive, $(C^{\mathrm{E}} - S(0) + \mathrm{div}_0)e^{rT} + \min(S(T), X) > 0$. This proves that $C^{\mathrm{E}} < S(0) - \mathrm{div}_0$.

The remaining bounds follow by the put-call parity relation (7.5) for dividend-paying stock: $S(0) - \mathrm{div}_0 - Xe^{-rT} \leq C^{\mathrm{E}}$, since $P^{\mathrm{E}} \geq 0$; $-S(0) + \mathrm{div}_0 + Xe^{-rT} \leq P^{\mathrm{E}}$, since $C^{\mathrm{E}} \geq 0$; and $P^{\mathrm{E}} < Xe^{-rT}$, since $C^{\mathrm{E}} < S(0) - \mathrm{div}_0$.

**7.12** For dividend-paying stock the regions determined by the bounds on call and put prices in Proposition 7.3 are shown as shaded areas in Figure S.9.

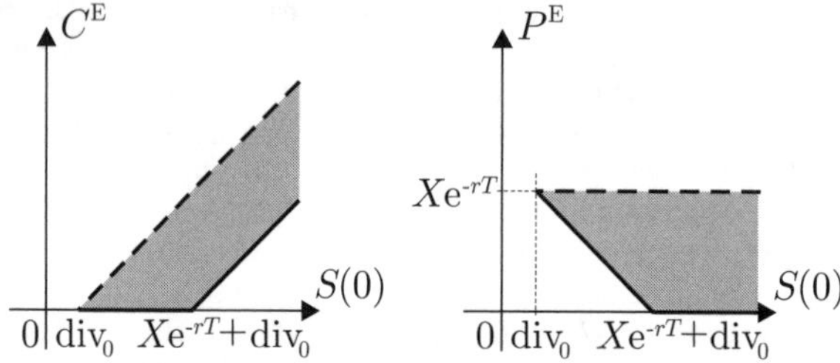


**Figure S.9** Bounds on European call and put prices for dividend-paying stock

**7.13** If $C^{\mathrm{A}} \geq S(0)$, then buy a share, write and sell an American call and invest the balance $C^{\mathrm{A}} - S(0)$ without risk. If the option is exercised before or at expiry, then settle your obligation by selling the share for $X$. If the option is not exercised at all, you will end up with the share worth $S(T)$ at expiry. In either case the final cash value of this strategy will be positive. The final balance will in fact also include the dividend collected, unless the option is exercised before the dividend becomes due.

**7.14** Suppose that $X' < X''$, but $C^{\mathrm{E}}(X') < C^{\mathrm{E}}(X'')$. We can write and sell a call with strike price $X''$ and buy a call with strike price $X'$, investing the difference $C^{\mathrm{E}}(X'') - C^{\mathrm{E}}(X') > 0$ without risk. If the option with strike price $X''$ is exercised at expiry, we will need to pay $(S(T) - X'')^+$. This amount can be raised by exercising the option with strike price $X'$ and cashing the payoff $(S(T) - X')^+$. Since $X' < X''$, and so $(S(T) - X')^+ \geq (S(T) - X'')^+$, an arbitrage profit will be realised.

The inequality for puts follows by a similar arbitrage argument.

**7.15** Consider four cases:

1) If $S(T) \leq X' < X < X''$, then (7.9) reduces to $0 \leq 0$.
2) If $X' < S(T) \leq X < X''$, then (7.9) becomes $0 \leq \alpha(S(T) - X')$, obviously satisfied for $X' < S(T)$.
3) If $X' < X < S(T) \leq X''$, then (7.9) can be written as $S(T) - X \leq \alpha(S(T) - X')$. This holds because $X = \alpha X' + (1-\alpha)X''$ and $S(T) \leq X''$.

4) Finally, if $X' < X < X'' < S(T)$, then (7.9) becomes an equality, $S(T) - X = \alpha(S(T) - X') + (1-\alpha)(S(T) - X'')$ because $X = \alpha X' + (1-\alpha)X''$.

**7.16** Suppose that $P^{\mathrm{E}}(S') < P^{\mathrm{E}}(S'')$ for some $S' < S''$, where $S' = x'S(0)$ and $S'' = x''S(0)$. Write and sell a put option on a portfolio with $x''$ shares and buy a put option on a portfolio with $x'$ shares, investing the balance $P^{\mathrm{E}}(S'') - P^{\mathrm{E}}(S') > 0$ without risk. If the written option is exercised at time $T$, then the liability can be met by exercising the other option. Since $x' < x''$, the payoffs satisfy $(X - x'S(T))^+ \geq (X - x''S(T))^+$. It follows that this is an arbitrage strategy.

**7.17** Suppose that $X' < X''$, but $C^{\mathrm{A}}(X') < C^{\mathrm{A}}(X'')$. We can write and sell the call option with strike price $X''$ and purchase the call option with strike price $X'$, investing the balance $C^{\mathrm{A}}(X'') - C^{\mathrm{A}}(X') > 0$ without risk. If the written option is exercised at time $t \leq T$, we will have to pay $(S(t) - X'')^+$. This liability can be met by exercising the other option immediately, receiving the payoff $(S(t) - X')^+$. Since $(S(t) - X'')^+ \leq (S(t) - X')^+$, this strategy leads to arbitrage.

The inequality for put options can be proved in a similar manner.

**7.18** We shall prove Proposition 7.19 for American put options. The argument for European puts is similar. By Proposition 7.15 $P^{\mathrm{A}}(S)$ is a decreasing function of $S$. When $S \geq X$, the intrinsic value of a put option is zero, and so the time value, being equal to $P^{\mathrm{A}}(S)$, is also a decreasing function of $S$. On the other hand, $P^{\mathrm{A}}(S') - P^{\mathrm{A}}(S'') \leq S'' - S'$ for any $S' < S''$ by Proposition 7.16. This implies that $P^{\mathrm{A}}(S') - (X - S')^+ \leq P^{\mathrm{A}}(S'') - (X - S'')^+$ if $S' < S'' \leq X$, so the time value is an increasing function of $S$ for $S \leq X$. As a result, the time value has a maximum at $S = X$.

## Chapter 8

**8.1** Let us compute the derivative of the price $C^{\mathrm{E}}(0)$ of a call option with respect to $u$. The formula for the price, assuming that $S^{\mathrm{d}} < X < S^{\mathrm{u}}$, is

$$C^{\mathrm{E}}(0) = \frac{1}{1+r}\frac{r-d}{u-d}[S(0)(1+u) - X].$$

The derivative with respect to $u$ is equal to

$$\frac{(r-d)[X - S(0)(1+d)]}{(1+r)(u-d)^2} = \frac{(r-d)[X - S^{\mathrm{d}}]}{(1+r)(u-d)^2}.$$

This is positive in our situation, since $r > d$ and $X > S^{\mathrm{d}}$, so $C^{\mathrm{E}}(0)$ increases as $u$ increases.

The derivative of $C^{\mathrm{E}}(0)$ with respect to $d$ is equal to

$$-\frac{(u-r)[S(0)(1+u) - X]}{(1+r)(u-d)^2} = -\frac{(u-r)[S^{\mathrm{u}} - X]}{(1+r)(u-d)^2},$$

which is negative, since $r < u$ and $X < S^{\mathrm{u}}$. The option price decreases as $d$ increases.

**8.2** If $r = 0$ and $S(0) = X = 1$, then $C^{\mathrm{E}}(0) = \frac{-ud}{u-d}$. For $u = 0.05$ and $d = -0.05$ we have $u - d = 0.1$ and $C^{\mathrm{E}}(0) = 0.025$ dollars. However, if $u = 0.01$ and $d = -0.19$, then $u - d = 0.2$. The variance of the return on stock is equal to $(u-d)^2 p(1-p)$ and is higher in the latter case, but the option price is lower: $C^{\mathrm{E}}(0) = 0.0095$ dollars.

**8.3** To replicate a call option the writer needs to buy stock initially and sell it when the option is exercised. The following system of equations needs to be solved to find the replicating portfolio:

$$\begin{cases} 110(1-c)x + 1.05y = 10, \\ 90(1-c)x + 1.05y = 0. \end{cases}$$

For $c = 2\%$ we obtain $x \cong 0.5102$ and $y \cong -42.8471$, so the initial value of the replicating portfolio will be $100x + y \cong 8.1633$ dollars. If $c = 0$, then the replicating portfolio will be worth 7.1429 dollars. Note that the money market position $y$ is the same for each $c$.

**8.4** The borrowing rate should be used to replicate a call, since the money market position will be negative. This gives $x(1) \cong 0.6667$ and $y(1) \cong -40.1786$, so the replicating portfolio value is 9.8214 dollars. For a put we obtain $x(1) \cong -0.3333$ and $y(1) \cong 27.7778$ using the rate for deposits, so the replicating portfolio will be worth 2.7778 dollars initially.

The results are consistent with the put and call prices obtained from (8.3) with the appropriate risk-neutral probability (computed using the corresponding interest rate), $p_* \cong 0.7333$ for a call and $p_* \cong 0.6$ for a put.

**8.5** The option price at time 0 is 22.92 dollars. In addition to this amount, the option writer should borrow 74.05 dollars and buy 0.8081 of a share. At time 1, if $S(1) = 144$, then the amount of stock held should be increased to 1 share, the purchase being financed by borrowing a further 27.64 dollars, increasing the total amount of money owed to 109.09 dollars. If, on the other hand, $S(1) = 108$ dollars at time 1, then some stock should be sold to reduce the number of shares held to 0.2963, and 55.27 dollars should be repaid, reducing the amount owed to 26.18 dollars. (In either case the amount owed at time 1 includes interest of 7.40 dollars on the amount borrowed at time 0.)

**8.6** At time 1 the stock prices $S^{\mathrm{u}} = 144$ and $S^{\mathrm{d}} = 108$ dollars (the so-called cum-dividend prices) drop by the amount of the dividend to 129 and 93 dollars (the so-called ex-dividend prices). These prices generate the prices at time 2, hence $S^{\mathrm{uu}} = 154.80$, $S^{\mathrm{ud}} = 116.10$, $S^{\mathrm{du}} = 111.60$ and $S^{\mathrm{dd}} = 83.70$ dollars. The option will be exercised with payoff 34.80 dollars if the stock goes up twice. In the remaining scenarios the payoff will be zero. The option value at time 1 will be 21.09 dollars in the up state and zero dollars in the down state. The replicating portfolio constructed at time 1 and based on ex-dividend prices consists of 0.8992 shares and a loan of 94.91 dollars in the up state, and no shares and no money market position in the down state. The option price at time 0 is 12.78 dollars. Replication (based on the cum-dividend prices at time 1, since the dividend is available to the owner of the stock purchased at time 0) involves buying 0.5859 shares and borrowing 57.52 dollars.

**8.7** From the Cox–Ross–Rubinstein formula $C^{\mathrm{E}}(0) \cong 5.93$ dollars, $P^{\mathrm{E}}(0) \cong 7.76$ dollars.

**8.8** The least integer $m$ such that $S(0)(1+u)^m(1+d)^{N-m} > X$ is $m = 35$. From the Cox–Ross–Rubinstein formula we obtain $C^{\mathrm{E}}(0) \cong 3.4661$ dollars and $x(1) = [1 - \Phi(m-1, N, q)] \cong 0.85196$ shares.

**8.9** The delta of a European call becomes equal to 1 at the first step $n$ such that the option will be in the money independently of whether the stock goes up or down at the next step, that is, $S(0)(1+u)^n(1+d) > X$ (in this case $S(0)(1+u)^{n+1} > X$ as well). This gives

$$n > \frac{\ln X - \ln S(0) - \ln(1+d)}{\ln(1+u)}.$$

**8.10** The stock values are

| $n$ | 0 | | 1 | | 2 | | 3 |
|---|---|---|---|---|---|---|---|
| | | | | | | | 79.86 |
| | | | | | 72.60 | < | |
| | | | 66.00 | < | | | 68.97 |
| $S(n)$ | 60.00 | < | | | 62.70 | < | |
| | | | 57.00 | < | | | 59.57 |
| | | | | | 54.15 | < | |
| | | | | | | | 51.44 |

The American put prices are

| $n$ | 0 | | 1 | | 2 | | 3 |
|---|---|---|---|---|---|---|---|
| | | | | | | | 0.00 |
| | | | | | 0.00 | < | |
| | | | 0.50 | < | | | 0.00 |
| $P^{\mathrm{A}}(n)$ | 2.52 | < | | | 1.10 | < | |
| | | | **5.00** | < | | | 2.43 |
| | | | | | **7.85** | < | |
| | | | | | | | 10.56 |

The option will be exercised early in the d node at time 1 or in the dd node at time 2 (bold figures).

**8.11** The values of the European and American calls are the same,

| $n$ | 0 | | 1 | | 2 |
|---|---|---|---|---|---|
| | | | | | 52.80 |
| | | | 34.91 | < | |
| $C^{\mathrm{E}}(n) = C^{\mathrm{A}}(n)$ | 22.92 | < | | | 9.60 |
| | | | 5.82 | < | |
| | | | | | 0.00 |

At time 2 both options have, of course, the same payoff. At time 1 the American call will not be exercised in the up state, as this would bring only 24 dollars, which less than the value of holding the option until expiry. In the down state the American call will be out of the money and will not be exercised either. Similarly, it will not be exercised at time 0. As a result, the American call is equivalent to its European counterpart.

**8.12** The ex-dividend stock prices are

| $n$ | 0 | | 1 | | 2 |
|---|---|---|---|---|---|
| | | | | | 12.32 |
| | | | 11.20 | < | |
| | | / | | | 10.64 |
| $S(n)$ | 12.00 | | | | |
| ex-div | | \ | | | 10.34 |
| | | | 9.40 | < | |
| | | | | | 8.93 |

The corresponding European and American put prices will be

| $n$ | 0 | 1 | | 2 |
|---|---|---|---|---|
| | | | | 1.68<br>1.68 |
| | | 2.53<br>**2.80** | $<$ | |
| | | | | 3.36<br>3.36 |
| $P^{\mathrm{E}}(n)$<br>$P^{\mathrm{A}}(n)$ | 3.42<br>3.69 | | | |
| | | | | 3.66<br>3.66 |
| | | 4.33<br>**4.60** | $<$ | |
| | | | | 5.07<br>5.07 |

At time 1 the payoff of the American put option in both the up and down states will be higher than the value of holding the option to expiry, so the option should be exercised in these states (indicated by bold figures).

**8.13** Take $b$ such that $S(0)\mathrm{e}^{\sigma b+ru-\frac{1}{2}\sigma^2 u}=a$ and put $V(t)=W(t)+\left(m-r+\frac{1}{2}\sigma^2\right)\frac{t}{\sigma}$ for any $t\geq 0$, which is a Wiener process under $P_*$. In particular, $V(u)$ is normally distributed under $P_*$ with mean 0 and variance $u$. The right-hand side of (8.8) is therefore equal to

$$\begin{aligned}
E_*\left(\mathrm{e}^{-ru}S(u)1_{S(u)<a}\right) &= S(0)E_*\left(\mathrm{e}^{\sigma V(u)-\frac{1}{2}\sigma^2 u}1_{V(u)<b}\right)\\
&= S(0)\int_{-\infty}^{b}\mathrm{e}^{\sigma x-\frac{1}{2}\sigma^2 u}\frac{1}{\sqrt{2\pi t}}\mathrm{e}^{-\frac{x^2}{2u}}\,\mathrm{d}x\\
&= S(0)\int_{-\infty}^{b}\frac{1}{\sqrt{2\pi t}}\mathrm{e}^{-\frac{(x-\sigma u)^2}{2u}}\,\mathrm{d}x.
\end{aligned}$$

Now observe that, since $V(t)$ is a Wiener process under $P_*$, the random variables $V(u)$ and $V(t)-V(u)$ are independent and normally distributed with mean 0 and variance $u$ and $t-u$, respectively. As a result, their joint density is $\frac{1}{2\pi t}\mathrm{e}^{-\frac{y^2}{2(t-u)}-\frac{x^2}{2u}}$. This enables us to compute the left-hand side of (8.8),

$$\begin{aligned}
E_*\left(\mathrm{e}^{-rt}S(t)1_{S(u)<a}\right) &= S(0)E_*\left(\mathrm{e}^{\sigma V(t)-\frac{1}{2}\sigma^2 u}1_{V(u)<b}\right)\\
&= S(0)E_*\left(\mathrm{e}^{\sigma(V(t)-V(u))+\sigma V(u)-\frac{1}{2}\sigma^2 u}1_{V(u)<b}\right)\\
&= S(0)\int_{-\infty}^{b}\left(\int_{-\infty}^{\infty}\mathrm{e}^{\sigma y+\sigma x-\frac{1}{2}\sigma^2 t}\frac{1}{2\pi t}\mathrm{e}^{-\frac{y^2}{2(t-u)}-\frac{x^2}{2u}}\,\mathrm{d}y\right)\mathrm{d}x\\
&= S(0)\int_{-\infty}^{b}\left(\int_{-\infty}^{\infty}\frac{1}{2\pi t}\mathrm{e}^{-\frac{(y-\sigma(t-u))^2}{2(t-u)}-\frac{(x-\sigma u)^2}{2u}}\,\mathrm{d}y\right)\mathrm{d}x\\
&= S(0)\int_{-\infty}^{b}\frac{1}{\sqrt{2\pi t}}\mathrm{e}^{-\frac{(x-\sigma u)^2}{2u}}\,\mathrm{d}x
\end{aligned}$$

We can now see that the two sides of (8.8) are equal to one another.

**8.14** Consider the distribution function

$$F(x) = P_* \{W(t) < x\} = P_* \left\{ V(t) < x + \left( m - r + \frac{1}{2}\sigma^2 \right) \frac{t}{\sigma} \right\}$$
$$= \int_{-\infty}^{x + \left(m - r + \frac{1}{2}\sigma^2\right)\frac{t}{\sigma}} \frac{1}{\sqrt{2\pi}} \mathrm{e}^{-\frac{y^2}{2}} \mathrm{d}y,$$

where $V(t) = W(t) + \left(m - r + \frac{1}{2}\sigma^2\right)\frac{t}{\sigma}$ is normally distributed under $P_*$. As a result, the density of $W(t)$ under $P_*$ is

$$\frac{dF(x)}{dx} = \frac{1}{\sqrt{2\pi}} \mathrm{e}^{-\frac{1}{2}\left(x + \left(m - r + \frac{1}{2}\sigma^2\right)\frac{t}{\sigma}\right)^2}.$$

**8.15** By put-call parity, for $t = 0$

$$P^{\mathrm{E}}(0) = C^{\mathrm{E}}(0) - S(0) + X\mathrm{e}^{-rT}$$
$$= S(0)(N(d_1) - 1) - X\mathrm{e}^{-rT}(N(d_2) - 1)$$
$$= -S(0)N(-d_1) + X\mathrm{e}^{-rT}N(-d_2).$$

Now, by substituting $t$ for 0 and $T - t$ for $T$, we obtain the Black–Scholes formula for $P^{\mathrm{E}}(t)$.

## Chapter 9

**9.1** By put-call parity (7.1)

$$\frac{\mathrm{d}}{\mathrm{d}S} P^{\mathrm{E}}(S) = \frac{\mathrm{d}}{\mathrm{d}S} C^{\mathrm{E}}(S) - 1 = N(d_1) - 1 = -(1 - N(d_1)) = -N(-d_1),$$

where $d_1$ is given by (8.9). The delta of a put option is negative, consistently with the fact that the value of a put option decreases as the price of the underlying asset increases.

**9.2** We maximise $581.96 \times S - 30,779.62 - 1,000 \times C^{\mathrm{E}}(S, \frac{1}{365})$, where $S$ stands for the stock price after one day, and $C^{\mathrm{E}}(S, t)$ is the price of a call at time $t$, one day in our case, with 89 days to maturity, and where $\sigma = 30\%$ and $r = 8\%$, as before. Equating the derivative with respect to $S$ to zero, we infer that the delta of the option after one day should be the same as the delta on day zero, $\frac{\mathrm{d}}{\mathrm{d}S} C^{\mathrm{E}}(S, \frac{1}{365}) = 0.58196$. This gives the following condition for the stock price (after inverting the normal distribution function):

$$\frac{\ln \frac{S}{60} + (r + \frac{1}{2}\sigma^2) \times \frac{89}{365}}{\sigma\sqrt{\frac{89}{365}}} = \frac{\ln \frac{60}{60} + (r + \frac{1}{2}\sigma^2) \times \frac{90}{365}}{\sigma\sqrt{\frac{90}{365}}}.$$

The result is $S \cong 60.0104$ dollars.

**9.3** The premium for a single put is 0.031648 dollars (from the Black–Scholes formula), so the bank will receive 1,582.40 dollars by writing and selling 50,000 puts. The delta of a single put is −0.355300, so the delta-hedging portfolio requires shorting 17,765.00 shares, which will raise 32,332.29 dollars. This gives a total of 33,914.69 dollars received to be invested at 5%. The value of the delta neutral portfolio consisting of the shored stock, invested cash and sold options will be $-32,332.29 + 33,914.69 - 1,582.40 = 0.00$ dollars.

One day later the shorted shares will be worth $17,765 \times 1.81 = 32,154.64$ dollars, whereas the cash investment will grow to $33,914.69\mathrm{e}^{0.05/365} \cong 33,919.34$ dollars. The put price will increase to 0.035182 dollars, so the price of 50,000 puts will be 1,759.11 dollars. The value of the delta neutral portfolio will be $-32,154.64 + 33,919.34 - 1,759.11 \cong 5.59$ dollars.

**9.4** The price of a single put after one day will now be 0.038885 dollars, the 50,000 options sold will therefore be worth 1944.26 dollars, the stock and cash deposit positions remaining as in Solution 9.3. The delta neutral portfolio will bring a loss of 179.56 dollars.

**9.5** If the stock price does not change, $S(t) = S(0) = S$, then the value of the portfolio after time $t$ will be given by

$$V(t) = SN(d_1) - X\mathrm{e}^{rt}\mathrm{e}^{-rT}N(d_2) - C^{\mathrm{E}}(S,t),$$

where $C^{\mathrm{E}}(S,t)$ is given by the Black–Scholes formula and $d_1, d_2$ by (8.9). Then

$$\begin{aligned} \frac{\mathrm{d}}{\mathrm{d}t}V(t)\bigg|_{t=0} &= -rX\mathrm{e}^{-rT}N(d_2) - \frac{\mathrm{d}}{\mathrm{d}t}C^{\mathrm{E}}(S,t)\bigg|_{t=0} \\ &= -rX\mathrm{e}^{-rT}N(d_2) - \mathrm{theta}_{C^{\mathrm{E}}} \\ &= \frac{\sigma S}{2\sqrt{2\pi T}}\mathrm{e}^{-d_1^2/2}, \end{aligned}$$

which is positive.

**9.6** Using put-call parity and the Greek parameters for a call, we can find those for a put:

$$\begin{aligned} \mathrm{delta}_{P^{\mathrm{E}}} &= N(d_1) - 1 = \mathrm{delta}_{C^{\mathrm{E}}} - 1 = -N(-d_1), \\ \mathrm{gamma}_{P^{\mathrm{E}}} &= \mathrm{gamma}_{C^{\mathrm{E}}}, \\ \mathrm{theta}_{P^{\mathrm{E}}} &= -\frac{S\sigma}{2\sqrt{2\pi T}}\mathrm{e}^{-\frac{d_1^2}{2}} + rX\mathrm{e}^{-rT}N(-d_2), \\ \mathrm{vega}_{P^{\mathrm{E}}} &= \mathrm{vega}_{C^{\mathrm{E}}}, \\ \mathrm{rho}_{P^{\mathrm{E}}} &= -TX\mathrm{e}^{-rT}N(-d_2). \end{aligned}$$

(The Greek parameters are computed at time $t = 0$.) These equalities can also be verified directly by differentiating the Black–Scholes formula for the put price.

**9.7** The rho of the original option is 7.5878, the delta of the additional option is 0.4104 and the rho is 7.1844. The delta-rho neutral portfolio requires buying approximately 148.48 shares of stock and 1,056.14 additional options, while borrowing $7,693.22. The position after one day is presented in the following table, in which we also recall the results of the delta hedge:

| $S(\frac{1}{365})$ | delta-rho | | | delta |
|---|---|---|---|---|
| | $r = 8\%$ | $r = 9\%$ | $r = 15\%$ | $r = 9\%$ |
| 58.00 | −7.30 | −9.65 | −26.14 | −133.72 |
| 58.50 | −2.71 | −4.63 | −17.95 | −97.22 |
| 59.00 | 0.18 | −1.23 | −10.93 | −72.19 |
| 59.50 | 1.59 | 0.77 | −4.85 | −58.50 |
| 60.00 | 1.76 | 1.60 | 0.52 | −55.96 |
| 60.50 | 0.92 | 1.50 | 5.45 | −64.38 |
| 61.00 | −0.68 | 0.72 | 10.16 | −83.51 |
| 61.50 | −2.78 | −0.47 | 14.90 | −113.07 |
| 62.00 | −5.13 | −1.84 | 19.91 | −152.78 |

**9.8** With 95% probability the logarithmic return on the exchange rate satisfies $k > m + x\sigma \cong -23.68\%$, where $x \cong -1.645$, so that $N(x) \cong 5\%$. The 1,000 dollars converted into euros, invested without risk at the rate $r_{\mathrm{EUR}}$, and converted back into dollars after one year, will give $1,000\mathrm{e}^{r_{\mathrm{EUR}}}\mathrm{e}^{k}$ dollars. With probability 95% this amount will satisfy

$$1,000\mathrm{e}^{r_{\mathrm{EUR}}}\mathrm{e}^{k} > 1,000\mathrm{e}^{r_{\mathrm{EUR}}}\mathrm{e}^{m+x\sigma} \cong 821.40 \text{ dollars.}$$

On the other hand, 1,000 dollars invested at the rate $r_{\mathrm{USD}}$ would have grown to $1,000\mathrm{e}^{r_{\mathrm{USD}}} \cong 1,051.27$ dollars. As a result,

$$\mathrm{VaR} = 1,000\mathrm{e}^{r_{\mathrm{USD}}} - 1,000\mathrm{e}^{r_{\mathrm{EUR}}}\mathrm{e}^{m+x\sigma} \cong 229.88 \text{ dollars.}$$

**9.9** A single call costs \$21.634. We purchase approximately 46.22 options. With probability 5% the stock price will be less than \$49.74. We shall still be able to exercise the options, cashing \$450.18 in the borderline case. The alternative risk-free investment of \$1,000 at 8% would grow to \$1,040.81. Hence VaR $\cong$ 590.63 dollars. If the stock grows at the expected rate, reaching \$63.71, then we shall obtain \$1,095.88 when the options are exercised. With 5% probability the stock price will be above \$81.6 and then our options will be worth at least \$1,922.75.

**9.10** The cost of a single bull spread is \$0.8585, with expected return 29.6523%, standard deviation 99.169%, and VaR equal to \$15,094.74 (at 74.03% confidence level). If 92.9456% of the capital is invested without risk and the remainder in the bull spread, then the expected return will be the same as on stock, with risk of 6.9958% and VaR equal to \$1064.85.

**9.11** A put with strike price \$56 costs \$0.4260. A put with strike price \$58 costs \$0.9282. The expected return on the bear spread is 111.4635%, the risk reaching 174.2334%. The worst case scenario (among those admitted by the analyst) is when the stock price drops to \$58.59. In this scenario, which will happen with conditional probability 0.3901, the investor will lose everything, so VaR = 15,094.74 dollars at 60.99% confidence level (which includes the cost of lost opportunity concerned with risk-free investment).

## Chapter 10

**10.1** The yields are $y(0) \cong 14.08\%$ and $y(3) \cong 13.63\%$. Thus $B(0,3) = \mathrm{e}^{-3\tau y(0)} \cong$ 0.9654 dollars. Arbitrage can be achieved as follows:

- At time 0 buy a 6-month bond for $B(0,6) = 0.9320$ dollars, raising the money by issuing 0.9654 of a 3-month bond, which sells at $B(0,3) \cong 0.9654$ dollars.
- At time 3 (after 3 months) issue 0.9989 of a 3-month bond, which sells at $B(3,6) = 0.9665$ dollars, and use the proceeds of \$0.9654 to settle the fraction of a 3-month bond issued at time 0.
- At time 6 (after half a year) the 6-month bond bought at time 0 will pay \$1, out of which \$0.9989 will settle the fraction of a 3-month bond issued at time 3.

The balance of \$0.0011 will be the arbitrage profit.

**10.2** The implied rates are $y(0) \cong 12.38\%$ and $y(6) \cong 13.06\%$. Investing \$100, we can buy 106.38 bonds now and 113.56 after six months. The logarithmic return over one year is $\ln(113.56/100) \cong 12.72\%$, the arithmetic mean of the semi-annual returns.

**10.3** To achieve a return of 14%, we would have to sell the bond for $0.8700\mathrm{e}^{14\%} \cong 1.0007$ dollars, which is impossible. (A zero-coupon bond can never fetch a price higher than its face value.)

In general, we have to solve the equation $B(0,12)\mathrm{e}^k = \mathrm{e}^{-\tau y(6)}$ to find $y(6)$, where $k$ is the prescribed logarithmic return. The left-hand side must be smaller than 1.

**10.4** During the first six months the rate is $y(n) \cong 8.34\%$, for $n = 0, \ldots, 179$, and during the rest of the year $y(n) \cong 10.34\%$, for $n = 180, \ldots, 360$. The bond should be sold for $0.92\mathrm{e}^{4.88\%} \cong 0.9660$ dollars or more. This cannot be achieved during the first six months, since the highest price before the rate changes is $B(179, 360) \cong 0.9589$ dollars. On the day of the rate change $B(180, 360) \cong 0.9496$ dollars, and we have to wait until day $n = 240$, on which the bond price will exceed the required \$0.9660 for the first time.

**10.5** The rate can be found by using a spreadsheet with goal seek facility to solve the equation

$$10.896 \times \left(10 + 10\mathrm{e}^{-y(1)} + 10\mathrm{e}^{-2y(1)} + 110\mathrm{e}^{-3y(1)}\right) = 1{,}000\mathrm{e}^k.$$

This gives $y(1) \cong 12.00\%$ for $k = 12\%$ in case a), $y(1) \cong 12.81\%$ for $k = 10\%$ in case b) and $y(1) \cong 11.19\%$ for $k = 14\%$ in case c).

**10.6** The numbers were found using an Excel spreadsheet with accuracy higher than the displayed 2 decimal points.

**10.7** Scenario 1: \$1,427.10; Scenario 2: \$1,439.69.

**10.8** Formula (10.2) can be applied directly to find $D \cong 1.6846$.

**10.9** The duration is equal to 4 if the face value is \$73.97. The smallest possible duration, which corresponds to face value $F = \$0$, is about 2.80 years. For very high face values $F$ the duration is close to 5, approaching this number as $F$ goes to infinity.

When $F = 100$, the coupon value $C \cong 13.52$ gives duration of 4 years. If the coupon value is zero, then the duration is 5 years. For very high coupon values $C$ tending to infinity the duration approaches about 2.80 years.

**10.10** Since the second derivative of $P(y)$ is positive,

$$\begin{aligned}\frac{\mathrm{d}^2}{\mathrm{d}y^2}P(y) &= (\tau n_1)^2 C_1 \mathrm{e}^{-\tau n_1 y} + (\tau n_2)^2 C_2 \mathrm{e}^{-\tau n_2 y} + \cdots + (\tau n_N)^2 (C_N + F)\mathrm{e}^{-\tau n_N y} \\ &> 0,\end{aligned}$$

$P$ is a convex function of $y$.

**10.11** Solving the system $6 = 2w_A + 3.4w_B$, $w_A + w_B = 1$, we find $w_A \cong -1.8571$ and $w_B \cong 2.8571$. As a result, we invest \$14,285.71 to buy 14,005.60 bonds $B$, raising the shortfall of \$9,285.71 by issuing 9,475.22 bonds $A$.

**10.12** The yield on the coupon bond $A$ is about 13.37%, so the price of the zero-coupon bond $B$ is \$87.48. The coupon bond has duration 3.29 and we find the weights to be $w_A \cong 0.4366$ and $w_B \cong 0.5634$. This means that we invest \$436.59 to buy 4.2802 bonds $A$ and \$563.41 to buy 6.4403 bonds $B$.

**10.13** Directly from the definition (10.2) of duration we compute the duration $D_t$ at time $t$ (note that the bond price grows by a factor of $\mathrm{e}^{yt}$),

$$\begin{aligned} D_t &= \frac{1}{\mathrm{e}^{yt}P(y)}\left((\tau n_1 - t)C_1\mathrm{e}^{-y(\tau n_1 - t)} + \cdots + (\tau n_N - t)(C_N + F)\mathrm{e}^{-y(\tau n_N - t)}\right) \\ &= \frac{1}{P(y)}\left((\tau n_1 - t)C_1\mathrm{e}^{-\tau n_1 y} + \cdots + (\tau n_N - t)(C_N + F)\mathrm{e}^{-\tau n_N y}\right) \\ &= D_0 - t, \end{aligned}$$

since the weights $C_1\mathrm{e}^{-\tau n_1 y}/P(y), C_2\mathrm{e}^{-\tau n_2 y}/P(y), \ldots, (C_N + F)\mathrm{e}^{-\tau n_N y}/P(y)$ add up to one.

**10.14** Denote the annual payments by $C_1$, $C_2$ and the face value by $F$, so that

$$\begin{aligned} P(y) &= C_1\mathrm{e}^{-y} + (C_2 + F)\mathrm{e}^{-2y}, \\ D(y) &= \frac{C_1\mathrm{e}^{-y} + 2(C_2 + F)\mathrm{e}^{-2y}}{P(y)}. \end{aligned}$$

Compute the derivative of $D(y)$ to see that it is negative:

$$\frac{\mathrm{d}}{\mathrm{d}y}D(y) = \frac{-C_1(C_2 + F)\mathrm{e}^{-3y}}{P(y)^2} < 0.$$

**10.15** We first find the prices and durations of the bonds: $P_A(y) \cong 120.72$, $P_B(y) \cong 434.95$, $D_A(y) \cong 1.8471$, $D_B(y) \cong 1.9894$. The weights $w_A \cong -7.46\%$, $w_B \cong 107.46\%$ give duration 2, which means that we have to buy 49.41 bonds $B$ and issue 12.35 bonds $A$. After one year we shall receive \$247.05 from the coupons of $B$ and will have to pay the same amount for the coupons of $A$. Our final amount will be \$23,470.22, exactly equal to the future value of \$20,000 at 8%, independently of any rate changes.

**10.16** If the term structure is to be flat, then the yield $y(0, 6) = 8.16\%$ applies to any other maturity, which gives $B(0, 3) = 0.9798$ dollars and $B(0, 9) = 0.9406$ dollars.

**10.17** Issue and sell 500 bonds maturing in 6 months with \$100 face value, obtaining \$48,522.28. Use this sum to buy 520.4054 one-year bonds. After 6 months settle the bonds issued by paying \$50,000. After one year cash the face value of the bonds purchased. The resulting rate is 8%.

**10.18** You need to deposit $100,000\mathrm{e}^{-8.41\%/12} \cong 99,301.62$ dollars for one month, which will grow to the desired level of \$100,000, and borrow the same amount for 6 months at 9.54%. Your customer will receive \$100,000 after 1 month and will have to pay $99,301.62\mathrm{e}^{9.54\%/2} \cong 104,153.09$ dollars after 6 months, which implies a forward rate of 9.77%. (The rate can be obtained directly from (10.5).)

The rate for a 4-month loan starting in 2 months is

$$f(0, 2, 6) = \frac{6 \times 9.35\% - 2 \times 8.64\%}{4} \cong 10.09\%,$$

so a deposit at 10.23% would give an arbitrage opportunity.

**10.19** To see that the forward rates $f(n, N)$ may be negative, let us analyse the case with $n = 0$ for simplicity. Then

$$f(0, N) = (N + 1)y(0, N + 1) - Ny(0, N)$$

and $f(0,N) < 0$ requires that $(N+1)y(0,N+1) < Ny(0,N)$. The border case is when $y(0,N+1) = \frac{N}{N+1}y(0,N)$, which enables us to find a numerical example. For instance, for $N = 8$ and $y(0,8) = 9\%$ a negative value $f(0,8)$ will be obtained if $y(0,9) < \frac{8}{9} \times 9\% = 8\%$.

**10.20** Suppose that $f(n,N)$ increases with $N$. We want to show that the same is true for

$$y(n,N) = \frac{f(n,n) + f(n,n+1) + \cdots + f(n,N-1)}{N-n}.$$

This follows from the fact that if a sequence $a_n$ increases, then so does the sequence of averages $S_n = \frac{a_1+\cdots+a_n}{n}$. To see this multiply the target inequality $S_{n+1} > S_n$ by $n(n+1)$ to get (after cancellations) $na_{n+1} > a_1 + \cdots + a_n$. The latter is true, since $a_{n+1} > a_i$ for all $i = 1, \ldots, n$.

**10.21** The values of $B(0,2)$, $B(0,3)$, $B(1,3)$ have no effect on the values of the money market account.

**10.22** a) For an investment of \$100 in zero-coupon bonds, divide the initial cash by the price of the bond $B(0,3)$ to get the number of bonds held, 102.82, which gives final wealth of \$102.82. The logarithmic return is 2.78%. b) For an investment of \$100 in single-period zero-coupon bonds, compute the number of bonds maturing at time 1 as $100/B(0,1) \cong 100.99$. Then, at time 1 find the number of bonds maturing at time 2 in a similar way, $100.99/B(1,2) \cong 101.54$. Finally, we arrive at $101.54/B(2,3) \cong 102.51$ bonds, each giving a dollar at time 3. The logarithmic return is 2.48%. c) An investment of \$100 in the money market account, for which we receive $100A(3) \cong 102.51$ at time 3, produces the same logarithmic return of 2.48% as in b).

## Chapter 11

**11.1** We begin from the right, that is, from the face values of the bonds, first computing the values of $B(2,3)$ in all states. These numbers together with the known returns give $B(1,3;\text{u})$ and $B(1,3;\text{d})$. These, in turn, determine the missing returns $k(2,3;\text{ud}) = 0.20\%$ and $k(2,3;\text{dd}) = 0.16\%$. The same is done for the first step, resulting in $k(1,3;\text{d}) = 0.23\%$. The bond prices are given in Figure S.10.

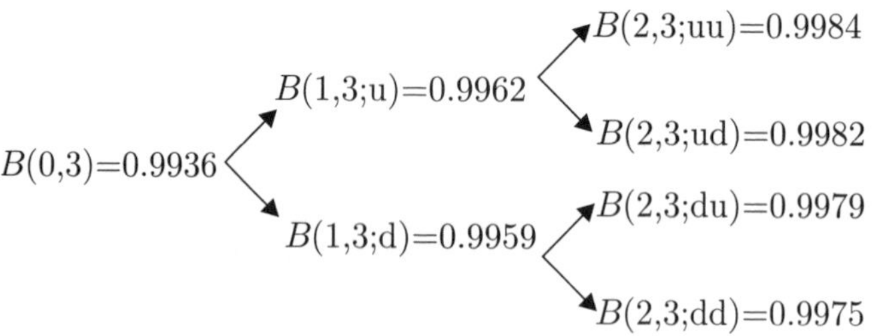


**Figure S.10** Bond prices in Solution 11.1

**11.2** Because of the additivity of the logarithmic returns, $k(1,3;\text{u}) + k(2,3;\text{uu}) + k(3,3;\text{uuu}) = 0.64\%$ gives the return in the period of three weeks. To obtain the yield we have to rescale it to the whole year by multiplying by $52/3$, hence $y(0,3) = 11.09\%$. Note that we must have $k(1,3;\text{u}) + k(2,3;\text{ud}) + k(3,3;\text{udu}) =$

0.64% which allows us to find $k(2,3;\mathrm{ud}) = 0.20\%$. The other missing returns can be computed in a similar manner, first $k(1,3;\mathrm{d})$, then $k(2,3;\mathrm{dd})$.

**11.3** The bond prices are given in Figure S.11.

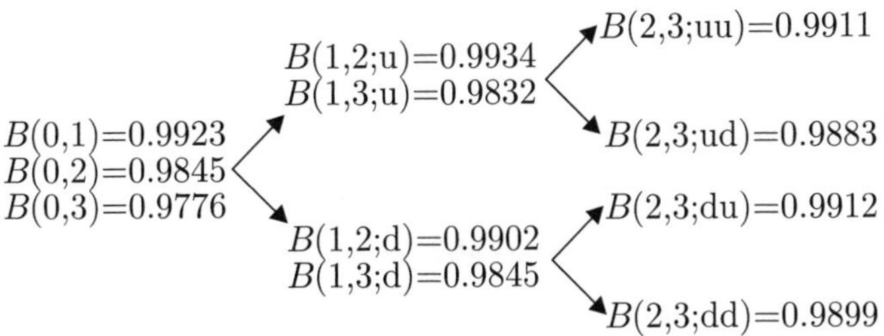


**Figure S.11** Bond prices in Solution 11.3

**11.4** The money market account is given in Figure S.12. Note that the values for the 'up' movements are lower than for the 'down' movements. This is related to the fact that the yield decreases as the bond price increases, and our trees are based on bond price movements.

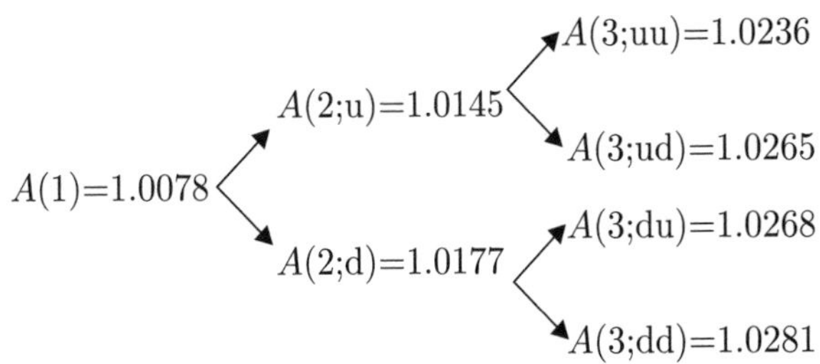


**Figure S.12** Money market account in Solution 11.4

**11.5** The prices $B(1,2;\mathrm{u}) = 0.9980$ and $B(1,2;\mathrm{d}) = 0.9975$ are found by discounting the face value 1 to be received at time 2, using the short rates $r(1;\mathrm{u})$ and $r(1;\mathrm{d})$. The price $B(0,2) = 0.9944$ can be found by the replication procedure.

**11.6** At time 2 the coupons are 0.5227 or 0.8776, depending on whether we are in the up or down state at time 1. At time 1 the coupon is 0.9999.

**11.7** At time 1 we find $18.0647 = (0.8159 \times 20 + 0.1841 \times 10)/1.0052$ in the up state and $1.7951 = (0.1811 \times 10 + 0.8189 \times 0)/1.0088$ in the down state. Next, applying the same formula again, we obtain $7.9188 = (0.3813 \times 18.3928 + 0.6187 \times 1.7951)/1.01$.

**11.8** There is an arbitrage opportunity at time 1 in the up state. The price $B(1,2;\mathrm{u}) = 0.9924$ implies that the growth factor in the money market is 1.00766, whereas the prices of the bond maturing at time 3 imply growth factors 1.01159 and 1.00783. To realise arbitrage, bonds with maturity 3 should be bought, the purchase financed by a loan in the money market.

**11.9** Using formula (11.5) and the short rates given, we find the following structure of bond prices:

$$
\begin{array}{ccccc}
 & & & & B(2,3;\mathrm{uu}) = 0.9931 \\
 & & B(1,3;\mathrm{u}) = 0.9859 & < & \\
 & / & & & B(2,3;\mathrm{ud}) = 0.9926 \\
B(0,3) = 0.9773 & & & & \\
 & \backslash & & & B(2,3;\mathrm{du}) = 0.9924 \\
 & & B(1,3;\mathrm{d}) = 0.9843 & < & \\
 & & & & B(2,3;\mathrm{dd}) = 0.9923
\end{array}
$$

**11.10** It is best to compute the risk-neutral probabilities. The probability at time 1 of the up movement based on the bond maturing at time 3 is 0.76, whereas the probability based on the bond maturing at time 2 is 0.61. The present price of the bond maturing at time 2 computed using the prices of the bond maturing at time 3 and the risk-neutral probabilities computed from these prices is 0.9867. So, shorting at time 0 the bond maturing at time 3 and buying the bond maturing at time 2 will give an arbitrage profit.

**11.11** At time 2 the option is worthless. At time 1 we evaluate the bond prices by adding the coupon to the discounted final payment of 101.00 at the appropriate (monthly) money market rate: 0.521% in the up state and 0.874% in the down state. The results are 101.4748 and 101.1213, respectively. The option can be exercised at that time in the up state, so the cash flow is 0.1748 and 0, respectively. Expectation with respect to the risk-neutral probabilities of the discounted cash flow gives the initial value 0.06598 of the option.

**11.12** The coupons of the bond with the floor provision differ from the par bond at time 2 in the up state: 0.66889 instead of 0.52272. This results in the following bond prices at time 1: 101.14531 in the up state and 100.9999 in the down state. (The latter is the same as for the par bond.) Expectation with respect to the risk-neutral probability gives the initial bond price 100.05489, so the floor is worth 0.05489.

# Bibliography


**Background Reading: Probability and Stochastic Processes**

Ash, R. B. (1970), *Basic Probability Theory*, John Wiley & Sons, New York.

Brzeźniak, Z. and Zastawniak, T. (1999), *Basic Stochastic Processes*, Springer Undergraduate Mathematics Series, Springer-Verlag, London.

Capiński, M. and Kopp, P. E. (1999), *Measure, Integral and Probability*, Springer Undergraduate Mathematics Series, Springer-Verlag, London.

Capiński, M. and Zastawniak, T. (2001), *Probability Through Problems*, Springer-Verlag, New York.

Chung, K. L. (1974), *A Course in Probability Theory*, Academic Press, New York.

Stirzaker, D. (1999), *Probability and Random Variables. A Beginner's Guide*, Cambridge University Press, Cambridge.

**Background Reading: Calculus and Linear Algebra**

Blyth, T. S. and Robertson, E. F. (1998), *Basic Linear Algebra*, Springer Undergraduate Mathematics Series, Springer-Verlag, London.

Jordan, D. W. and Smith, P.(2002), *Mathematical Techniques*, Oxford University Press, Oxford.

Stewart, J. (1999), *Calculus*, Brooks Cole, Pacific Grove, Calif.

**Further Reading: Mathematical Finance**

Baxter, M. W. and Rennie, A. J. O. (1996), *Financial Calculus*, Cambridge University Press, Cambridge.

Benninga, S. and Czaczkes, B. (1997), *Financial Modeling*, MIT Press, Cambridge, Mass.

Bingham, N. H. and Kiesel, R. (1998), *Risk-Neutral Valuation: Pricing and Hedging of Financial Derivatives*, Springer-Verlag, Berlin.

Björk, T. (1998), *Arbitrage Theory in Continuous Time*, Oxford University Press, Oxford.

Chen, L. (1996), *Interest Rate Dynamics, Derivatives Pricing, and Risk Management*, Lecture Notes in Econom. and Math. Systems 435, Springer-Verlag, New York.

Elliott, R. J. and Kopp, P. E. (1998), *Mathematics of Financial Markets*, Springer-Verlag, New York.

Elton, E. J. and Gruber, M. J. (1995), *Modern Portfolio Theory and Investment Analysis*, John Wiley & Sons, New York.

Etheridge, A. (2002), *A Course in Financial Calculus*, Cambridge University Press, Cambridge.

Haugen, R. A. (1993), *Modern Investment Theory*, Prentice Hall, Englewood Cliffs, N.J.

Hull, J. (2000), Options, *Futures and Other Derivatives*, Prentice Hall, Upper Saddle River, N.J.

Jarrow, R. A. (1995), *Modelling Fixed Income Securities and Interest Rate Options*, McGraw-Hill, New York.

Jarrow, R. A. and Turnbull, S. M. (1996), *Derivative Securities*, South-Western College, Cincinnati, Ohio.

Karatzas, I. and Shreve, S. (1998), *Methods of Mathematical Finance*, Springer-Verlag, Berlin.

Korn, R. (1997), *Optimal Portfolios*, World Scientific, Singapore.

Lamberton, D. and Lapeyre, B. (1996), *Introduction to Stochastic Calculus Applied to Finance*, Chapman and Hall, London.

Musiela, M. and Rutkowski, M. (1997), *Martingale Methods in Financial Modelling*, Springer-Verlag, Berlin.

Pliska, S. R. (1997), *Introduction to Mathematical Finance: Discrete Time Models*, Blackwell, Maldon, Mass.

Wilmott, P. (2001), *Paul Wilmott Introduces Quantitative Finance*, John Wiley & Sons, Chichester.

Wilmott, P., Howison, S. and Dewynne, J. (1995), *The Mathematics of Financial Derivatives: A Student Introduction*, Cambridge University Press, Cambridge.

# Glossary of Symbols

| | |
|---|---|
| $A$ | fixed income (risk free) security price; money market account |
| $B$ | bond price |
| $\beta$ | beta factor |
| $c$ | covariance |
| $C$ | call price; coupon value |
| $\boldsymbol{C}$ | covariance matrix |
| $C^{\mathrm{A}}$ | American call price |
| $C^{\mathrm{E}}$ | European call price |
| $\widetilde{C}^{\mathrm{E}}$ | discounted European call price |
| Cov | covariance |
| delta | Greek parameter delta |
| div | dividend |
| $\mathrm{div}_0$ | present value of dividends |
| $D$ | derivative security price; duration |
| $\widetilde{D}$ | discounted derivative security price |
| $D^{\mathrm{A}}$ | price of an American type derivative security |
| $E$ | expectation |
| $E_*$ | risk-neutral expectation |
| $f$ | futures price; payoff of an option; forward rate |
| $F$ | forward price; future value; face value |
| gamma | Greek parameter gamma |
| $\Phi$ | cumulative binomial distribution |
| $k$ | logarithmic return |
| $K$ | return |
| $i$ | coupon rate |
| $m$ | compounding frequency; expected logarithmic return |

| | |
|---|---|
| $M$ | market portfolio |
| $\boldsymbol{m}$ | expected returns as a row matrix |
| $\mu$ | expected return |
| $N$ | cumulative normal distribution |
| $\binom{N}{k}$ | the number of $k$-element combinations out of $N$ elements |
| $\omega$ | scenario |
| $\Omega$ | probability space |
| $p$ | branching probability in a binomial tree |
| $p_*$ | risk-neutral probability |
| $P$ | put price; principal |
| $P^{\mathrm{A}}$ | American put price |
| $P^{\mathrm{E}}$ | European put price |
| $\widetilde{P}^{\mathrm{E}}$ | discounted European put price |
| PA | present value factor of an annuity |
| $r$ | interest rate |
| $r_{\mathrm{div}}$ | dividend yield |
| $r_{\mathrm{e}}$ | effective rate |
| $r_F$ | risk-free return |
| rho | Greek parameter rho |
| $\rho$ | correlation |
| $S$ | risky security (stock) price |
| $\widetilde{S}$ | discounted risky security (stock) price |
| $\sigma$ | standard deviation; risk; volatility |
| $t$ | current time |
| $T$ | maturity time; expiry time; exercise time; delivery time |
| $\tau$ | time step |
| theta | Greek parameter theta |
| $\boldsymbol{u}$ | row matrix with all entries 1 |
| $V$ | portfolio value; forward contract value, futures contract value |
| Var | variance |
| VaR | value at risk |
| vega | Greek parameter vega |
| $w$ | symmetric random walk; weights in a portfolio |
| $\boldsymbol{w}$ | weights in a portfolio as a row matrix |
| $W$ | Wiener process, Brownian motion |
| $x$ | position in a risky security |
| $X$ | strike price |
| $y$ | position in a fixed income (risk free) security; yield of a bond |
| $z$ | position in a derivative security |

# Index

Printed in the United States of America